STUDIES IN
NORTH INDIAN LANGUAGES

STUDIES IN NORTH INDIAN LANGUAGES

by

T. GRAHAME BAILEY, M.A. B.D., D.Litt

Nizam's Reader in Urdu and Reader in Hindi, University of London

(Formerly Missionary of the Church of Scotland, Panjab).

GYAN

Published by

GYAN

Gyan Publishing House
5, Ansari Road
Daryaganj, New Delhi-110002
Phone: 011-47034999, 9811692060
E-mail: books@gyanbooks.com

Distribution Network
gyanbooks.com
India, USA, Canada, UK, Australia, France

ISBN : 978-81-212-2271-6 (PB)
First Published, 1938

2nd Impression 2021

Printed at: Gyan Press, Delhi.

Studies in
North Indian Languages
Author: T. Grahame Bailey

STUDIES IN

NORTH INDIAN LANGUAGES

by

T. GRAHAME BAILEY, M.A., B.D., D.Litt.

Nizam's Reader in Urdū and Reader in Hindī, University of London
(formerly Missionary of the Church of Scotland, Panjab).

1938

WORKS BY THE SAME AUTHOR

Brief Panjābī Grammar, 1904.
Languages of the Northern Himalayas, 1908.
Panjābī Manual (joint), 1913
Kanaurī Vocabulary, 1913.
Panjābī Phonetic Reader, 1914.
English-Panjābī Vocabulary, 1919
Linguistic Studies from the Himalayas, 1920.
Shina Grammar, 1924.
History of Urdū Literature, 1932.
Linguaphone Hindustānī Course, 1934.
Sounds of Kashmīrī, 1937.

PREFACE

This volume contains 54 articles and notes which I have written from time to time and published in *The Journal of the Royal Asiatic Society*, *The Bulletin of the School of Oriental Studies*, *The Journal of the Asiatic Society of Bengal*, *The Journal of the Gypsy Lore Society*, and the *Zeitschrift der Deutschen Morgenländischen Gesellschaft*. I am greatly obliged to the Editors of these journals for permission to reprint them. They give a fair representation of the kind of linguistic work which appeals to me, a study of the pronunciation (phonetics), history, grammar, and poetry of languages, especially those of North India.

The principal languages dealt with are Urdū, Hindī, Panjābī, Shina (Ṣiṇā), Kanaurī, Nepālī, and Rājasthānī. I regret Kashmīrī is not represented except in one note.

When I was in India I spent a large part of many holidays in reducing to writing unknown or little known languages spoken by illiterate people. It is a fascinating occupation, and as one looks back on it there rises to memory an array of delightful and variegated scenes, and the mind dwells on happy experiences of long ago. The only example in this book of that kind of work is the grammar of Kanaurī, a Tibeto-Burman language of considerable interest. Hebrew and Arabic come into an appendix. All but two of the articles have been written in England during the last fifteen years.

A list of the subjects discussed will be found in the table of contents.

T. GRAHAME BAILEY,
June, 1938.

CONTENTS

APPENDIX

URDU: THE NAME AND THE LANGUAGE

PART I

Epitome.—Urdu was born in 1027; its birthplace was Lahore, its parent Old Panjabi; Old Kharī was its step-parent; it had no direct relationship with Braj. The name Urdu first appears 750 years later.

The problem of Urdu has not yet been solved. This note is written with a view to crystallizing thought about the matter, and is of necessity more summary than would be desirable if limitations of space had not to be considered.

Perhaps the most important date in the history of Urdu is 1027, the year in which Maḥmūd Ġaznavī annexed the Panjab. He had already made expeditions into the country, but in that year he formally claimed possession of it and settled troops in the capital, Lahore. To 1027 may be assigned the birth of Urdu. At that time these Persian-speaking soldiers began to live among a people whose language was old Panjabi, to mix with them, to have intercourse with them, and, we cannot doubt, to learn their language. The contrary idea that the people all began to speak Persian may be dismissed. The army must have used this old form of Panjabi, not very different in those days from the early Kharī Bolī of Delhi, but they introduced Persian words and possibly phrases. This means simply that they must have begun to speak early Urdu.

For 160 years Maḥmūd Ġaznavī and his successors held the Panjab; it was wrested from them in 1187. For the second time the country was seized by men who spoke Persian. This time the conqueror was Muḥammad Ġorī whose servant Quṭb ud Dīn Aibak captured Delhi in 1193 and became the first Sulṭān on the death of his master in 1206. It seems clear that his troops made friends with the soldiers whom they defeated in Lahore, and that the two armies went on to Delhi leaving a sufficient force to keep open the lines of communication ; for Aibak cannot have annihilated the fighting men in Lahore and he would not have permitted the menace of a hostile army in his rear. We may conclude that a considerable number of those who entered Delhi with Quṯb ud Dīn Aibak already spoke early Urdu. This language, altered by the influence of the new troops who spoke Persian, and of the city people whose language was old Khaṛī, developed into later Urdu.

This sketch of the origin of Urdu suggests that we should regard Lahore, not Delhi, as its birthplace, and early Panjabi as its parent language. Unfortunately we have no means at present of ascertaining what Panjabi at that time was like ; we feel sure, however, that it had not diverged far from old Khaṛī. We may dismiss Braj from our calculations ; there is no reason to think that it had any direct connection with Urdu. When Urdu was born in 1027 Panjabi was only entering the modern stage. Although we can hardly doubt the general course of events, we do not get on to firm ground till 1326, when Muḥammad Tuglaq invaded the Deccan and founded Daulatābād. We know that his troops spoke Urdu ; and when in 1347 'Alā ud Dīn Bahmanī revolted against him and ascended the throne as the first ruler of the Bahmanī dynasty, his state made Urdu its official language.

If it be objected that there is not complete proof of some of the above statements, we can admit that fact, but point out that the proof is stronger than for the hitherto accepted view that Urdu began in Delhi during the Mugal period.

Indian writers usually consider that the royal camp in Delhi was first called the *urdū* by the Emperor Bābur in his work, *Tuzuk i Bāburī*. It may be so. He was a Turkī who came from Turkistān in 1526 and naturally spoke of his *urdū* ; but the word is found in the *Jahākushā* of Javainī, 1150, e.g. vol. i, p. 162 :—

dar urdū e shāhzādagān dar natavānand āmad, " they cannot enter the camp of the princes " ;

and on p. 148 :—

dar andarūn i urdū āmadand, " they came into the camp."

There seems to be no reason why the army in Lahore or Delhi should not have been called the *urdū* several centuries earlier than Bābur.

When does the word Urdu first occur as the name of a language ? It became common in Lucknow after 1846 and in Delhi after 1857. We must make a sharp distinction between Urdu, used by itself as a proper name, and *zabān i Urdū* ; for we cannot be sure that *zabān i Urdū* is a name ; it may be a mere description, " the language of the army."

Perhaps the earliest example of the word standing alone and bearing the sense of Urdu language is in Muṣḥafī, 1750–1824 :—

Khudā rakkhe zabā̃ ham ne sunī hai Mīr o Mirzā kī
Kahẽ kis mũh se ham ai Muṣḥafī Urdū hamārī hai ?

" I have heard the language of Mīr and Saudā ; how can I dare to assert that Urdū is my language ? "

We are unable to say in what year these words were written. Muṣḥafī may have composed the verse any time after he was grown up. He was a recognized poet in 1776.

J. B. Gilchrist, writing in 1796, mentions the name as well known. His words are : " In the mixed dialect also called Ŏŏrdoo اردو, or the polished language of the Court, and which even at this day pervades the vast provinces of a once powerful Empire " (*A Grammar of the Hindoostanee Language*, p. 261). As we do not know the date of Muṣḥafī's lines we must admit that Gilchrist *may* have been the first person who in literature used Urdu as the name of the language.

Jules Bloch has made a striking suggestion, which he admits is only an intuitive feeling requiring to be substantiated by proof, that the name Urdu is due to Europeans. In this connection it is important to note that Gilchrist in the sentence just quoted mentions Ŏŏrdoo as a name already established. His statement seems to make it clear that Indians used the word. Gilchrist himself always called the language " Hindoostanee ".

W. H. Bayley in an English and " Hindoostanee " thesis, 1802, which may be consulted in the British Museum, says " the language which I have specified by the name of Hindoostanee is also frequently denominated Hindee, Oordoo, Moosulmanee and Rekhtu ".

Sayyid Inshā in *Daryā e Laṭāfat*, 1807 (Lucknow ed., p. 2), writes : *Khush bayānān i ājā muttafiq shuda az zabāhā e muta-'addad alfāẓ i dilcasp judā namūda o dar ba'ẓī 'ibārat bakār burda zabāne tāza sivā e zabāhā e dīgar rasānīdand o ba urdū mausūm sākhtand* : " the good speakers of Delhi united in separating attractive words from several languages and using them in sentences ; in this way they produced a new language, different from other languages, and called it Urdū."

Mīr Amman in the preface to *Bāg o Bahār*, 1802, gives an account of the birth of Urdū, and though he never uses the word alone (he says *Urdū kī zabān*) it is clear from the whole context that he is thinking of a definite name.

We conclude that while Fārsī and Hindī had for long been used as proper names Urdu did not receive similar recognition till near the dawn of the eighteenth century.

The phrase *zabān i urdū e mu'allā* seems to occur for the first time in Mīr's *Nikāt ush Shu'arā*, 1752. On p. 1 of the Badāyū edition he says : *poshīda na mānad ki dar fann i rekhta ki shi'rest bataur i shi'r i Fārsi ba zabān i Urdū e mu'allā e Shāhjahānābād Dihlī kitābe ta ḥāl taṣnīf na shuda* : " we must remember that up to the present no book has been written on the art of *Rekhta*, which is poetry in the style of Persian poetry but in the language of the royal camp of Delhi."

Here *urdū e mu'allā* may possibly mean *faṣīḥ aur mustanad Urdū*, the idiomatic and authoritative Urdu of Delhi.

Two years later Qāim writes in *Makhzan i Nikāt* (Aurangabad ed., 33) :—

akṣare az tarkībāt i Furs ki muāfiq i muḥāvara e urdū e mu'allā mānūs i gosh meyāband minjumla e javāz ul abyān me dānand: "most Persian constructions which strike their ears as familiar from the point of view of the idiom of the royal camp they regard as among the things lawful in poetry."

Here, too, the phrase may mean "correct Urdu idiom", and the author may not be thinking of the army. But as Mīr and Qāim appear always to use Hindī or Rekhta as the name of the language we should perhaps translate "the language, or idiom, of the army".

Mīr's son, 'Arsh, who lived well into the nineteenth century,' says :—

ham haĩ Urdū e mu'allā ke zabā̃dā̃ ai 'Arsh
mustanad hai jo kucch irshād kiyā karte haĩ

"I speak the Urdu e Mu'alla language and what I say is authoritative". The date of the lines is unknown. The author's father died in 1799 at the age of 86 (not in 1810, as usually stated).

Finally, Muḥammad 'Aṭā Ḥusain in *Nau Ṭarz i Muraṣṣa'*, 1798, speaks of *zabān i urdū e mu'allā*.

Mr. G. M. Qādrī has drawn my attention to two MSS. which contain perhaps the earliest instances of the use of *zabān i urdū* without further description. The references are :—

Tazkira e Gulzār i Ibrāhīm, by 'Alī Ibrāhīm Khā̃, 1783 (speaking of Vaṣālat Khā Ṣābit), *tatabbu' i zabān i urdū namūda*, "he followed the Urdu language," or "the language of the *urdū*", i.e. devoted attention to it.

Tazkira e Shu'arā e Hindī, by Muṣḥafī, 1794 (speaking of Muḥammad Amān Niṣār), *adā e zabān i urdū*, "the style of the Urdu language," or "of the language of the *urdū*".

THE PROBLEM OF THE NAME. It is always stated that the language was originally described as the speech of the army or camp, *zabān i urdū*, and that gradually the word *zabān* was dropped, leaving *urdū* to stand alone. This explanation gives rise to a great difficulty. We have seen that Urdu was first used by itself in the poems of Muṣḥafī. We may perhaps guess the date of the couplet in which the word appears as the year 1790, when the author was 40. We are now faced by the fact that the first instance of the use of the word was 763 years after the establishment of the army in Lahore, almost 600 years after the *urdū* was settled in Delhi, and 261 years after Bābur called his camp the *Urdū e Mu'allą*. The Urdu language had been in existence for about 750 years before anyone gave it, in writing at any rate, the name by which it is now always known. Even if we take the earlier date, 1752, when Mīr described it as the language of the royal camp, we deduct only thirty-eight years from our figures. None of the historians of the Mugal period ever used the name. We have to answer three questions :—

(1) Why was there a delay of centuries in giving the name Urdu ?

(2) If a new name had to be given in the eighteenth century, why was this name chosen for the language when it had many, many years previously been given up for the army ?

(3) If the army was not called *urdū* till Babur's time, 1526, the language which had then existed for nearly 500 years must already have had a name. Why was that name given up ?

It is easier to state the problem than to solve it. I see no solution except this : that some name or description such as *zabān i urdū* was in conversational use from the time when the army was first called *urdū*, and that very gradually, hundreds of years later, it crept into books, possibly earlier than we are now aware of, while the use of Urdu alone was still later. I feel the inadequateness of this, but perhaps it will lead to something fuller. We must always remember that in early days Urdu literature was not so accurate a reflection of daily life and speech as it is now, and there may have been much in ordinary talk which found no echo in books.

PART II

In the eighteenth century and earlier Hindi (sometimes Hindavī) was the usual name for the language in general and Rekhta for the literary or poetical form of it.

Ja'far Zaṭallī, 1659–1713, has the lines,

agarci sabhī kūṛa o kurkuṭ ast
ba Hindī o rindī zabā̃ laṭpaṭ ast

" although everything is rubbish and sweepings, the language is lively with Hindi and licentiousness ".

Fazli in the preface to his *Dah Majlis*, 1732, writes :— *aur ab tak tarjuma e Fārsī ba 'ibārat i Hindī nasr nahī̃ huā mustama' :* and so far no one has ever heard of a translation from Persian into Hindi prose.

Asar, in his famous *masnavī Khvāb o Khayāl*, 1740, frequently uses rekhta, as on p. 10 :

rekhta nē yih tab sharaf pāyā,
jab ki Ḥazrat nē usko farmāyā

" Rekhta obtained this eminence only when Ḥazrat (Dard, his brother and teacher) used it ".

On p. 9, talking of the contents of his volume, he calls Urdu " Hindavī " :

Fārsī sau haī Hindavī sau haī,
bāqī ash'ār i masnavī sau haī

" Persian couplets 100, Hindavī 100, and the remaining couplets of the *masnavī* 100."

Afzal Beg in his *tazkira Tuḥfat ush Shu'arā*, 1752, not printed, deals almost entirely with poets who wrote in Persian, but where he refers to Urdu poetry he calls it Hindī. Thus he says of Mīr 'Abd ul Ḥai Viqār : *ash'ār i Fārsī o Hindī ṭab' durust dārad*; " he had good natural ability in Persian and Hindi poetry " (*Camanistān i Shu'arā*, 152).

Shāh Ḥātim, in the preface to his *Dīvānzāda*, 1755, writes : *dar shi'r i Fārsī pairau o Mirzā Ṣāib ast, dar rekhta Valī rā ustād medānad* : " in Persian poetry he (the author) follows

Ṣāib, in Rekhta he regards Valī as his master." See *Āb i Ḥayāt*, ed. 1917, p. 115.

Mīr Ḥasan, d. 1786, uses Hindī or Rekhta and avoids Urdū. In his anthology, 1776, he has the phrase : *tazkira e sukhan āfrīnān i Hindī*, "an anthology of Urdu poets" (p. 40).

Even Shāh 'Abdul Qādir in his well-known Urdu translation of the Qur'ān uses the name Hindī : *is mẽ zabān i rekhta nahī̃ bolī balki Hindī e muta'āraf ki 'avāmm ko be takalluf daryāft ho* ; "I have not used Rekhta in my translation, but well-known Urdu that ordinary people might easily understand it".

Mīr, 1713–99, Saudā, 1713–80, and Qāim (d. about 1790) use the word Rekhta very often. I will content myself with one quotation from Mīr :

mazbūt kaise kaise kahe rekhte vale,
samjhā na koī merī zabā̃ is diyār mẽ.

"What fine Urdū verse I have written, but no one in these parts understands me".

The name Hindi requires no comment. It was the natural word to use in early times. Several explanations have been given of Rekhta, a Persian word which means "poured", and has no literary signification in Persian. The most important are the following :—

(1) Urdu is called Rekhta because Arabic and Persian words were poured into it.

(2) Rekhta means "down and out", and Urdu was at first regarded as something contemptible.

(3) It means verses in two languages, and at first Urdu and Persian were used side by side.

(4) It is a musical term introduced by Amīr Khusrau indicating the application of the music of one language to the words of another.

(5) It means a wall firmly constructed of different materials, as Urdu is of diverse linguistic elements. This is the opposite of (2).

Ṣafīr Bilgrāmī in *Jalva e Khiẓr* says that the name Rekhta has been in use since the time of Shāhjahān. This requires proof.

Other early names may be mentioned.

According to Maḥmūd Shīrānī *zabān i Dihlavī* was used by Amīr Khusrau (d. 1324) and by Abu'l Faẓl (in *Āīn i Akbarī*).

Shāh Ḥātim in the preface to his *Dīvānzāda* quoted above calls Urdu " rozmarra e Ḍihlī " : *rozmarra e Dihlī ki Mirzāiān i Hind dar muḥāvara ārand manẓūr dārad,* " I have accepted the daily speech of Delhi which is the idiom of the Mirzas of India."

Again : *rozmarra rā ki 'ām fahm o khāṣṣ pasand bāshad ikhtiyār namūd,* " I have chosen the daily speech understood by all and liked in select circles." (As has been noted before he refers to himself in the third person.)

To turn to Dakanī writers. Shāh Mīrā̃ Jī, d. 1496, a famous religious writer, who preached and wrote in Urdu, explains that he wrote in " Hindi " in order that people might understand : *yeh bolū̃ Hindī sab, is artõ ke sababb,* " I am saying all this in Urdu for this reason ".

His son, Shāh Burhan ud Dīn, d. 1582, says in his poem *Irshād Nāma* : *'aib na rākhẽ Hindī bol,* " do not blame me for using Urdu." He also calls it Gujrī, which is not unnatural, for his language is marked by many Gujrati features :

je hoe gyān bicārī,
na dekhẽ bhākhā Gujrī (*Ḥujjat ul Baqā*)

" learned people will not look at Gujrī " i.e. Urdu.

yeh sab kīā Gujrī zabā̃ (*Irshād Nāma*)

" I have done all this in Gujrī (Urdu) ".

Vajhī, the famous author of *Quṭb Mushtarī*, 1609, referred to in the India Office Catalogue as nameless and anonymous, wrote in 1634 a prose work *Sab Ras.* After the ascriptions of praise he proceeds : *āgāz i dāstān ba zabān i Hindostān,* " here begins the story in the language of Hindustan," i.e. the Urdu of Delhi as distinguished from Dakanī.

The dialect of the Deccan was often called Daknī or Dakhanī, e.g. Rustamī's *Khāvarnāma*, 1649, *Khāvarnāma e Daknī kītā hū̃ nām* "I have called it the Dakni Khavaranāma" (last line but five).

Shāh Malik's *Sharī'at Nāma*, 1666, *Dakhanī mẽ bolyā hai ṣāf*, "said it plainly in Dakhani." (This author is mistakenly called "Shāh Mulk" in the India Office Cat.)

BĀQIR ĀGĀH AND THE DATE OF THE NAME URDŪ

In *JRAS.*, Apr., 1930, pp. 391–400, under the heading "Urdū : the Name and the Language" I discussed *inter alia* the question of when the word was first used by itself as the name of a language, and said that the first definitely datable instance I could find was in Gilchrist's *Grammar of the Hindoostanee Language*, 1796, p. 261, but that a couplet from one of Muṣḥafī's poems, date unknown, was probably earlier. Another quotation, which also might be earlier, was from Mīr's son 'Arsh. Since then I have not been able to get anything which certainly bears a date before 1796, but the following facts are worth recording as a further contribution to the subject.

Mīr Ḥasan.—The *Tazkira e Ḥasan*, a *tazkira* by the famous poet Mīr Ḥasan, has been published with the title of *Tazkira e Shu'arā e Urdū*. Mīr Ḥasan died in 1786 and the work itself was written about ten years before his death ; it appears, therefore, at first sight, as if here we had an instance twenty years before Gilchrist's Grammar. I do not think, however, that the title of the book is authentic. There is no proof that Mīr Ḥasan ever used the word "Urdū". He refers to his anthology on its first page as a *tazkira e sukhan āfrīnān i Hindī*, an anthology of Hindī poets, meaning Urdū poets.

Bāqir Āgāh.—The word "Urdū" occurs in the introduction to the *Dīwān i Hindī* of Muḥammad Bāqir Āgāh, 1745–1805, a prolific writer in Arabic, Persian, and both dialects of Urdū (the southern dialect spoken in the Deccan, and the northern spoken in Delhi). He was a spiritual disciple of Sayyid Abu'l Ḥasan Qurbā, 1705–68, and belonged to the Deccan, being a native of Ellore. Our chief source of information about him is the *Tazkira Gulzār i A'ẓam*, the compiler and author of which was Muḥ. Gauṣ Khā̃. It is an anthology of Kārnāṭak (Carnatic) poets, begun in 1841 and printed in 1855, the year of the author's death. Other authorities which may be consulted are *Fihrist Urdū Makhṭūṭāt i Kutubkhāna e Kulliya e Jāmi'a e 'Uṣmāniya e Ḥaidarābād Dakan*, pp. 17–21, 127–8; *Urdū*, Apr., 1929, pp. 281–318; and *Urdū ke Asālīb i Bayān*, pp. 30 and 32 (only a few lines).

Āgāh frequently refers to the well-known Delhi poet Saudā, who died in 1780, and indeed sometimes pokes fun at him, as in the following couplet :

Āgāh gar sune namkīn naẓm tirī
Saudā kahe ki shi'r se mere namak gayā

O Āgāh, if Saudā hears this tasty poem of thine, he will say " all the taste has gone out of my verses ".

One of his numerous works was the *Dīvān i Hindī*, a book of *qaṣīdas, gazals, rubā'īs, qiṭ'as* and other poems, almost all in Urdū, the majority in Persian metres, but some in Hindī metres such as the *doha* and the *kabitt*. To this *Dīvān* he wrote a prose *dībāca*, or introduction, of great interest. It was published in *Urdū*, Apr., 1929. From a perusal of it we get valuable information. Amongst other things we learn that he used the name " Hindī " for " Urdū ", whether Delhi Urdū or Daknī, but that when he wished to distinguish the language of Delhi from that of the Deccan he used the terms " Urdū " and " Daknī " (or " Dakhnī "), while verses in either dialect he called *rekhte*.

We have thus the following terms as employed by him :—

Hindī for the Urdū language, whether northern or southern.
Urdū for the language of Delhi.
Daknī for the variety of Urdū spoken in the Deccan.
rekhte for verses in either dialect of Urdū (both Persian and Hindī metres).

The fact that he confines the name " Urdū " to the Delhi dialect and does not include Daknī is very important.

Another interesting Urdū work is *Farāid dar Favāid*. This has not been published, but a MS. exists in the Library of the Osmaniyeh University in Hyderabad.

In the *Dībāca* to the *Dīvān i Hindī* he uses the word Urdū three times. As he was born in 1745 and began writing verse in his fifteenth year, he might have spoken of Urdū any time after 1759. The question to be decided, therefore, is the date of the *Dībāca*, which is nowhere given. We begin our study of it with high hopes that we may be able to put it between 1765 and 1775, and so claim for the use of the term *Urdū* (as the name of a language) a date twenty or thirty years earlier than 1796, when Gilchrist's work appeared.

Alas for such hopes! It soon becomes abundantly clear that the *Dībāca* cannot have been written before 1795 and may have been later. In the second quarter of it he refers to his *Hasht Bihisht*, begun in 1791, in the last quarter he mentions his *Riyāẓ i Jinān*, written in 1792, and to his *Farāid dar bayān i Favāid*, which was not written till 1795. The authority for the date of *Riyāẓ i Jinān* is a quotation from a MS. of the work in the Osmaniyeh University (*Urdū*, Apr., 1929, p. 292), as follows :—

jab the bāra sau aur sāt baras tab banā hai yeh nuskha e aqdas, in the year 1207, was written this holy book. The date of the *Farāid*, given on the same page, is taken from another MS. in the University, but no sentence is quoted.

Just before the reference to *Riyāẓ i Jinān* we read these words : *yeh ḥaqīr i nāras āke tīs battīs baras ke kyā Fārsī aur kyā Hindī mẽ sab aqsām shi'r mẽ naẓm kīā thā*, this unworthy despicable person (the author) thirty or thirty-two years ago wrote poetry in every style of verse, whether Persian or Urdū : (*āke* is, of course, for *āge*). This suggests that he had been writing verse for thirty-two years. If to this we add, say, 14½ years, his age when he began writing, we get 46½, the equivalent of 45 of our years. That brings us to 1790. But it may well be that he dated from a few years after his fifteenth year, and in that case we get back to 1795 or later. We arrive at the reluctant conclusion that Bāqir Āgāh's *Dībāca* to his *Dīvān i Hindī* does not furnish us with a date before 1796 for the use of the word Urdū.

We may now proceed to quotations illustrative of the

terms Urdū, Daknī, Hindī, and rekhtē. We cannot say to what extent, if any, Āgāh pronounced the *iẓāfat*, so I omit it whenever it is not marked in the text.

(*a*) A few lines after the beginning of the *Dībāca* : *makhfī na rahe ki rekhta bajuz muḥāvra Hindī ke sab amūr mẽ Fārsī kā tābi‘ hai*, let us not forget that Urdū verse, apart from its being in the Hindī language (i.e. Urdū), follows Persian in everything.

(*b*) *Farāid dar Favāid*, ii. 5, 6.

Yeh nuskha garci hai Hindī mẽ manẓūm
Yihī haī ijmāl se ẕikr us kā marqūm

Although this book is in Urdū verse and this is in brief an account of it.

(*c*) After discussing different classes of poems in the *Dībāca*, he says *agar shu‘arā e Dakhan alfāẓ maẕkūr ko zer zabar karẽ to candā̃ muẓāiqa nahī̃ rakhtā hai kyā vasṭẽ ki unho taṣfiya muḥāvra mẽ is qadr jadd o kadd nahī̃ kīe bakhilāf ṣāḥibān muḥāvra Urdū ki is bāb mẽ sa‘ī balīg kar kar us rozmarra ko muḥāvra Fārsī kā ham pahlū kar dīe*, if the poets of the Deccan make alterations in the words I have mentioned (Arabic and Persian words), it doesn't matter very much, for they have not made great efforts to purify the language, in contradistinction to those who talk (or write) Delhi Urdū ; they with their enormous efforts in this matter have made that form of speech equal in dignity to Persian.

(*d*) A little over a page further on he writes of his romance, *Gulzār i ‘Ishq, is kā muḥāvra ba‘ainhi muḥāvra Urdū kā hai magar kahī̃ kahī̃ tā ‘alāmat vaṭaniyyat Dakan bāqī rahī*, its language is absolutely Delhi Urdū, but in places there are signs of my belonging to the Deccan.

(*e*) About a page from the end of the *Dībāca* he winds up a long sentence with the words *tā yeh majmū‘a agarci mukhtaṣar hai sab aqsām i sukhan par mushtamil rahe aur ise muḥāvra Urdū se makhṣūṣ kar dīā*, in order that this collection of poems, though short, may include every kind of poetry ; and I have used Delhi Urdū exclusively for it.

(*f*) *ba'ẓ 'ulamā e mutaakhkhirīn khulāṣā 'arabī kitābō kā nikālkar Fārsī mẽ likhe haĩ tā voh log jo 'Arabī nahĩ paṛh sakte haĩ in se fāida pāvẽ, lekin akṣar 'aurtā̃ aur tamām ādmīā̃ Fārsī se bhī āshnā nahĩ haĩ is līe yeh 'āṣī baṭalab unke bahut ikhtiṣār ke sāth lekar Daknī risālō mẽ bolā hai*, some scholars of recent times have made a summary in Persian of their Arabic works in order that those who cannot read Arabic may profit by them, but few women and not all men know even Persian ; so this rebel (the author), at their request has spoken very briefly in Daknī tracts. (Quoted in *Urdū ke asālīb i bayān*, p. 33.)

(*g*) In the *Dībāca*, just before the quotation in (*c*) above, he says *akṣar rekhta koyā̃ alfāẓ mashhūr 'Arabī o Fārsī ko zer o zabar karte haĩ*, generally writers of Urdū verse change well-known Arabic and Persian words.

82.

THE DATE OF OLD URDU COMPOSITION: A CAVEAT

In attempting to assign a date to any given piece of Urdu prose or verse we are in danger of being influenced to a great extent by its likeness or unlikeness to the Urdu of to-day, and assuming that if it does not differ much from modern Urdu it cannot be old. But in this we prejudge a question of prime importance, one which, so far as I know, has never been discussed in books on Urdu literature, viz. whether the author was writing more or less as he was in the habit of speaking, or was aiming at literary style. It is not the case, as one might be inclined to think, that all Urdu writers have striven after literary effect, though it is unfortunately true that affectation and artificiality very soon began to eat the life out of their poetry. Over Persianization was perhaps due in the first place to the fact that Muslim religious terms came to India through a Persian medium, and that the oldest writers were earnest propagandists who had to use many Persian theological words, or Arabic words which had reached them through Persian. Further the only poetry the Urdu writers knew was Persian. It was therefore natural that they should fall at first under the sway of the foreign tongue, which had, in fact, been the native tongue of the ancestors of some of them. It was, on the other hand, quite unnatural afterwards that men who spoke good racy Urdu in their homes, should fill their poetry with exotic phrases and sentiments.

In the early days composition was more natural than in later times, and Dakhani authors were readier to use the Urdu of every day than those who lived in Delhi. The difference between natural and artificial Urdu is almost inconceivably great. A few examples will make this clear.

1. Examples of Urdu striving after literary effect.

(*a*) In 1732 Fazlī wrote a translation of a Persian work, *Dah Majlis*, imagining it to be the first translation from

Persian into "Hindī". It is a striking comment on the ignorance of Dakhani literature among the writers of North India that such an idea should have been possible, or that Āzād should have regarded the preface to that translation as the first work in Urdu prose. Actually prose had been written in Urdu for centuries before this. The subjoined quotation is punctuated as in Āzād's *Āb i Ḥayāt*, 1917, p. 23. Faẓlī says:

phir dil mẽ guzrā ki aise kām ko 'aql cāhiye kāmil aur madad kisū ṭaraf kī hoe shāmil kyũki be tāīd i Ṣamadī aur be madad i janāb i Aḥmadī—yih mushkil ṣūrat pizīr na hove—aur gauhar i murād rishta e maidān mẽ na āve—lihāẕū is ṣan'at kā nahī̃ huā—mukhtari'—aur ab tak tarjuma e Fārsī ba 'ibārat i Hindī naṣr nahī̃ huā—mustama'—pas is andesha e 'amīq mẽ goṭa khāyā—aur bayābān i ta'ammul o tadbīr mẽ sargashta huā—lekin rāh maqṣūd kī na pāī—nāgāh nasīm i 'ināyat i Ilāhī dil i afgār par ihtizāz mẽ a—yih bāt āīna e khāṭir mẽ mũh dikhlāī.

"Then it came into my mind that for such work one needs perfect intelligence and must get help from somewhere; because without Divine strength and the help of Muḥammad this difficulty will not take form (meaning, rather strangely, 'disappear'), and the jewel aimed at will not come into the relation of expectation; so no one has invented this art, and a Persian translation in Hindi prose has not been heard of. I was therefore plunged in deep anxiety and wandered in the desert of hesitation and policy unable to find the way I wanted; suddenly the breath of the grace of God came fluttering on my wounded heart, and this matter showed its face in the mirror of my mind."

Saudā, 1713–80, who is often considered the greatest master of words in Urdu, though not the greatest poet, wrote a prose version of Mīr's *Shu'la e 'Ishq*. The date is not known, but it is some years later than Faẓlī's preface just mentioned. The following is an extract from the preface (say 1755) quoted by Āzād:—

zamīr i munīr par āīnadārān i ma'nī ke mubarhan ho ki maḥẓ 'ināyat Ḥaqq Ta'ālā kī hai jo ṭūṭī e nāṭiqa shīrī̃ sukhan ho—pas yih cand miṣrē' ki az qabīl i rekhta dur i rekhta khāma e do zabān apnī se ṣafḥ e kāgaz par taḥrīr pāe—lāzim hai ki taḥvīl i sukhan[1] *sāmi'a sanjān i rozgār karū̃—tā zabānī in ashkhāṣ kī hamesha maurid i taḥsīn o āfrīn rahū̃—maẓmūn sīna mẽ besh az murg i asīr nahī̃—ki bīc qafs ke—jis vaqt zabān par āyā faryād i bulbul hai vāste gosh i dādras ke—garaẓ jis ahl i sukhan kā dur i munṣif zīnat i lab hai sarrishta e ḥusn ma'ānī kā is kalām ke is se inṣāf ṭalab hai—agar Ḥaqq Ta'ālā ne ṣubḥ kāgaẓ i safed kī mānind i shām syāh karne ko yih khāksār khalq kiyā hai—to har insān ke fānūs i dimāg mẽ cirāg i hosh diyā hai—cāhiye ki dekhkar nukta cīnī kare varna gazand i zahr ālūda se be ajal kāhe ko mare.*

"Let it be demonstrated to the enlightened minds of the mirror holders of semantics that it is only through the gift of Almighty God that the parrot of utterance attains sweet speech; so these few lines of poured out pearls in Rekhta style from my bilingual pen have been written on paper. It is fitting that I should commit them to the hearing of the poets of to-day, so that at the mouth of those men I should be the object of praise and commendation. A theme in one's heart is no better than a captive bird in a cage, but when it gets utterance it is the plaint of the bulbul for the appreciative ear. Therefore this composition in the beauty of its thoughts appeals for justice to those whose lips are adorned by the pearls of impartiality. If God Almighty has created this unworthy one for the purpose of blackening white paper just as evening darkens the day, He has also put intelligence in everyone's brain like the candle under the shade; so people should criticize, for why should one die before one's time from envenomed grief?"

Let us quote from Sayyid Inshā, a passage written about 1780:—

[1] Mistake for *sāmi'a e sukhan.*

ibtidā e sinn i ṣibā tā avāil i rai'ān—aur avāil rai'ān se ila'l ān ishtiyāq i mā lā yuṭāq i taqbīl i 'atba i 'āliya na baḥadde thā—ki silk taḥrīr o taqrīr mẽ muntaẓam ho sake—lihāẓā be vāsṭa o vasīla ḥāẓir huā hū̃.

" From the dawn of childhood to my early youth, and from early youth to now there have been no bounds to the incontrollable desire I have felt to kiss your honoured threshold in order that my writing and speaking might be set in order like a necklace of pearls. Accordingly without cause or intermediary I have presented myself."

2. Examples of natural, unartificial Urdu.

To make the contrast more vivid we take first a couple of sentences from the same writer, Sayyid Inshā. The following words, though ostensibly quoted, are his own. See *Daryā e Laṭāfat*, p. 49. How different they are from the un-Urdu nonsense just quoted :—

ajī āo Mīr ṣāḥib tum to 'Īd ke cānd ho gae. Dillī mẽ āte the do do pahr rāt tak baiṭhte the aur rekhte paṛhte the. Lakhnaū mẽ tumhẽ kyā ho gayā ki kabhī̃ tumhārā asar āsār ma'lūm na huā aisā na kījiyo kahī̃ āṭhõ mẽ bhī na calo, tumhẽ 'Alī kī qasm āṭhõ mẽ muqarrar caliyo.

" Well, my *dear* sir, you've become as hard to find (and as welcome when found) as the new moon before the big feast. There was a time when on your visits to Delhi you used to come and sit in my house till midnight reciting your verses. I don't know what's happened to you in Lucknow, that there's not a trace of you anywhere. Whatever you do don't fail to turn up for the Eighth. I adjure you by ' Alī come without fail for the Eighth."

It is not easy to believe that one man wrote both these extracts, but it is amusing to notice that in the last line of the first quotation he forgets his literary pose and stumbles into sense.

I quote now from Vajhī's *Sab Ras*, one hundred years older than the earliest of the above quotations. Owing to its being in the Dakhanī dialect, it is not quite easy to translate, but it is perfectly straightforward; yet from its date it should be unintelligibly archaic. Mr. G. M. Qādrī, on p. 321 of his *Urdū Shahpāre,* from which the passage is taken. states that the author is Shāh Mīrā̃ Jī. This religious writer died in 1496; as I am not aware that he ever wrote anything called *Sab Ras,* I venture to attribute the words to Vajhī, who wrote *Sab Ras* in 1634.

'āshiq tū use bisar nakū, is kī yād sõ dil kū̃ shād kar aur ăpas kū̃ āpī yād dilātā so ăpas kū̃ dikhlātā hai, ki yū dekho yū merī ṣūrat hai munje dekh kā kū̃ be dil hotā hai maĩ ātā tere nazdīk hū̃ aur tū̃ to mujhe nahī̃ dekhtā.

" O lover of God! do not forget Him; by the remembrance of Him make thy heart glad. He reminds people of Himself and reveals Himself, saying 'Look hither, this is My form, look at Me; why art thou dispirited, I am coming, I am near thee and yet thou seest Me not.' "

In 1668 or a little later Mīrā̃ Ya'qūb translated Khvāja Burhān ud Dīn's *Shamāil ul Atqiā.* A few words may be quoted.

(After some Arabic) *ya'nī ay mominān ṣabr karo hor ustuvār acho tamhīdāt is āyat mẽ tan hor dil hor rūḥ— yū tīno ṣabr karo kar ḥukm huā ya'nī ṣabr karo tan sõ Khudā kī ṭā'at par— ya'nī farmā bardārī raho hor ṣabr karo apne dil sõ Khudā kī balā par hor ustuvār acho apne rūḥ hor sir sõ, Khudā ke dekhne ke shauq hor muḥabbat par.*

(After the Arabic sentence) that means O believers, be patient and firm. The premisses in this verse are body and heart and spirit. To all three comes the command, Be patient; that is be patient in your body in subjection to God, that is be obedient. And be patient from your heart in the afflictions of God; and be firm in your spirit and intellect in your desire and love for a sight of God.

The extracts which have been given enable us to see that simple style and modern phraseology are not a proof of recent date; they are merely the signs of conversational Urdu. I regard the fact as extremely important. It is very significant that the passage from *Sab Ras*, though much simpler than the first quotation from Sayyid Inshā, is at least a century and a half earlier ; indeed, if Mr. Qadri is right in saying that Shāh Mīrā̃ Jī is the author, it is three centuries earlier.

EARLY URDU CONVERSATION

IT is natural that records of the beginnings of Urdu should be almost entirely confined to literature or quasi literature. Yet there are two classes of books which contain references to conversation; firstly, early lives of holy men (especially in the Deccan and Gujrat), whose followers wrote accounts of their sayings and doings, occasionally quoting actual words; secondly, histories such as those by Firishta and Abu'l Fażl, in which we may find Urdu sentences spoken by emperors or kings. Urdu must often have been employed as the language of conversation in exalted circles even though the official language continued to be Persian.

In works by Maḥmūd Shīrānī, Shams Ullāh Qādrī, and the late ʻAbd ul Ḥay Nadvī, a few of these early sayings are given (not always in the same form). Some can be so far verified in printed books, others are taken from MSS. and we cannot be certain of their age. However, in spite of our suspicions they have considerable interest. Exhaustive search would no doubt reveal many more. Regarding the question of date, see my note on the "Date of old Urdu Composition", in *JRAS.*, October, 1930, under "Miscellanea".

Before proceeding to the scraps of talk I give two lines, said to be found in Bābur's Turkī *Dīvān*. It will be seen that a line and a half are Urdu.

mujkā na huā kuj havas mānak o motī
fuqarā ḥālina bas bulgusidur pānī o rutī

"I have no desire for gems or pearls, for (the state of) poor people sufficient are water and bread".

The MS. is in the library of the Navāb of Rāmpūr, and was written in 1529.

c. 1260. She<u>kh</u> Farīd ud Dīn Ganj i Shakar, d. about 1267, used to call a certain friend *bhayyā* "brother" (*Asrār ul Awliyā*, p. 3). On being asked where intelligence dwelt he replied *bīc sir ke* "in the head" (*Malfūẓāt*, p. 40).

c. 1350. Somewhere between 1325 and 1357 <u>Kh</u>vāja Naṣīr ud Dīn Cirāğ, d. 1357, said to his <u>Kh</u>alīfa, comparing him with another holy man, *tum ūpar ve tale* "you are above, he is below" (*Firishta*, ii, 399).

c. 1400. A sentence by the famous Khvāja Banda Navāz is reported in *'Ishq Nāma*, the work of a disciple 'Abd Ullāh bin Raḥmān Cishtī: *bhūkō muve sũ Khudā kach apaṛtā hai Khudā kũ apaṛne kī isti'dād hor hai* " does one reach God by dying of hunger? It is by other means that one reaches God ".

Once a friend said to him: *Khvāja Burhān ud Dīn bālā hai* " Burhān ud Dīn is exalted ". He answered: *pūnō kā cānd bālā hai* " the full moon is exalted ".

c. 1362. According to the *Tārīkh i Fīrozī*, Fīroz Shāh Tuglaq, 1351–88, after his successful attack on Sindh, said: *barkat Shekh theā ik muvā ik nahā* " by the blessing of the Shekh one died one did not ".

The successors of Fīroz Shāh Tuglaq ordered the expulsion of most of the slaves brought by him from other parts of India. Many hid themselves, and when caught claimed to be inhabitants of Delhi. Like the Ephraimites of old who were asked to say *sibolet* and said *ṣibolet*, these men, it is said, were given a test in pronunciation. They were told to say *kharā kharī*, but were not able to say it in the same way as the true city people.

c. 1430. Quṭb 'Ālam, a famous religious leader in Gujrat, who died between 1446 and 1453, had a son called Sirāj ud Dīn. Shāh Bārak Allāh Cishtī gave Sirāj ud Dīn the name of Shāh 'Ālam. On hearing this his father remarked *Cishtīō ne pakāī aur Bukhārīō ne khāī* " the Cishtīs cooked it and the Bukhārīs ate it " (*Tuhfat ul Ikrām*, 47, 8). Quṭb 'Ālam and Shāh 'Ālam were Bukhārīs.

c. 1430. The Mirāt i Sikandarī records six sentences. Two are reported of Quṭb 'Ālam, who has just been mentioned. We may put their date as about 1430. Once on his way to early morning prayer he hurt his foot against a solid substance lying on the ground and exclaimed: *lohe yā lakkaṛ yā patthar yā kyā hai* " iron or wood or stone or what is it? " It turned out to be a bit of a meteorite with the qualities of all three. When his son Shāh 'Ālam's fiancée was taken from him by Muḥammad Shāh, king of Gujrat, and her less well-favoured sister substituted, Shāh 'Ālam complained to his father who replied: *beṭā tussā naṣīb duhū vījh* " son your fate is (bound up) in both ". Another version makes the last two words *dhuā̃ bacca* fancifully translated as " the buffalo and the young one ", or " the buffalo and the calf ". This prophecy was fulfilled, for when the king died his widow went to live with her sister, Shāh 'Ālam's wife. On the death of this sister she married Shāh 'Ālam.

c. 1450. Another sentence is recorded as spoken by Shāh 'Ālam himself. Sulṭān Aḥmad Shāh of Gujrāt sought the life of one of the boy princes, Maḥmūd Shāh, whom Shāh 'Ālam was sheltering in his house. The king arrived unexpectedly at the house, but the saint transformed the boy into a venerable man. As the king entered Shāh 'Ālam said to the boy: *paḍh ḍokre* "recite, old man". Aḥmad Shāh, not finding the boy, went away. This Maḥmūd Shāh was king of Gujrāt from 1459 to 1511. Once on being insulted he said: *nīcī berī har koī jhore* "every one shakes (the fruit off) a low *ber* tree".

c. 1510. To Sikandar Shah, heir apparent, and later king of Gujrāt for two and a half months, is attributed the saying: *pīr muvā murīd jogī huvā* "the saint is dead, the disciple has become a *jogī*".

c. 1535. Finally, when Bahādur Shāh of Gujrāt was betrayed by Rūmī Khā̃ to Humāyū̃ in 1535, his parrot fell into Humāyū̃'s hands. It astonished and no doubt amused him by screaming, upon the announcement of Rūmī Khā̃'s arrival: *phiṭ Rūmī Khā̃ ḥarāmkhor, phiṭ Rūmī Khā̃ ḥarāmkhor* "a curse on Rūmī Khā̃, traitor", a sentiment which he had doubtless many times heard expressed in Bahādur Shāh's palace.

Shekh Vajīh ud Dīn 'Alavī. 1505–90, was another Gujrāt saint. His disciples collected his sayings into a book named *Baḥr ul Ḥaqāiq*. The following are some of them:—

c. 1570. On hearing that Shekh Faẓl Ullāh had given up teaching, he said: *jab taraqqī pakṛẽge tab āpī dars kahẽge* "when he makes more progress he will of his own initiative give lessons".

c. 1570. Another saying was: *is se hor kyā khūb hai is dunyā mẽ ki dil Khudā sū̃ mashgūl hove* "what is better in this world than that the heart should be occupied with God?"

c. 1570. Another was: *'ārif use kahvẽ jo Khudā sū̃ bharyā hove* "we may call him a Knower who is full of God".

c. 1570. Again he said: *agar kisī kū̃ thoṛī bhī ṣafā hove jo ḥarām luqma khāve yā ḥarām fi'l kare to tabīc pāve, dūje bār bhī pāve, tīje bār bhī pāve* "anyone who has even a little purity, if he eats an unlawful morsel or does an unlawful deed, he will immediately find it out, a second time also he will find it out, a third time also he will find it out".

This Vajīh ud Dīn had a nephew Shāh Hāshim 'Alavī, whose sayings were collected in *Maqṣūd ul 'Āshiqīn* by a disciple. I quote three of them. Two are unfortunately in verse, and therefore less conversational.

c. 1600.

dunyā choṛe shekh kahāe *yih ḥijāb tujh bhūle nāe*
dīnī shekhī sū̃ yak maidān *paile jhūṭe dūje shaiṭān*

" If anyone leaves the world he is called a shekh ; this world is a mere covering, do not forget that. Religiousness and shekh-hood make up a great plain, the former are false, the latter devils." These lines are capable of many renderings. After considering a number I have chosen the one which expresses what seems to be the most probable meaning.

c. 1600.

Hāshim jī kī sunīe bāt *jinne rakkhī bāsī bhāt*
uskā jāve hāte hāt

" Listen to what Hāshim says, if anyone keeps stale rice, his wealth will disappear."

bāp ke utnā deve so pūt, bāp nẽ deve so supūt, bāp kā dīā chīne, so kupūt " who gives as much as his father, he is a son ; if the father does not give (and yet he gives) he is a good son ; he who seizes what his father gives, is a bad son ".

In the same book the following is quoted from Shāh Niẓām ud Dīn, a pupil of Vajīh ud Dīn :—

Niẓām bandagī kare to kyā hove *avval jiskā nẽ dil ṣafā*
jāma sūṇḍe mẽ ḍūb rahā *ose khushbū lagāe to kyā nafā*

" when a man worships, then what happens, if his heart is not clean ? If a garment is steeped in perfume, what is the good of putting scent on it ? "

THE WORD HINDŪSTĀN

It has sometimes been said that the only correct spelling of the word is *Hindostān*, and that this is proved by its being made to rhyme with *bostān*. The fact of its so rhyming can prove only that such a form exists in verse. It does not disprove the correctness of other forms. Some confusion arises from our not knowing exactly which spelling is objected to, whether it is *Hindūstān* or *Hindŭstān* or both. There is abundant evidence to show that in Urdū *Hindŭstān* is well known and correct. The following points should be noted.

(1) The spelling without *vāo* is both Turkish and Persian. This is

not important, for we are concerned with Hindī and Urdū, not with foreign languages. Turkish generally omits the *vāo,* indeed the word is usually pronounced *hindistān.* Ahmad Vahid's English-Turkish Dictionary and Redhouse's smaller Turkish Dictionary give only this form. Steingass for Persian gives *hindusān*, *hindŭstān*, and *hindūstān.* Phillott in his English-Persian gives only *hindŭstān. Hindostān* is, of course, impossible in Persian. As I have said, however, all this is irrelevant. Urdū has nothing to do with the forms of other languages.

(2) In speaking Urdū, whether literary or colloquial, people almost always say *-ŭs-*. Occasionally one hears *-o-* in pedantic speech, but *-ŭs-* is practically universal.

Professor 'Abd us Sattār Ṣiddīqī, of Allahabad, writes: *Urdū bolnevāle 'ām ṭaur par is lafẓ kā talaffuẓ maḥẓ pesh ke sāth karte haĩ aur fuṣaḥā kī zabān par bhī hindŭstān aur hindŭstānī hai go ki hindostān aur hindostānī bhī galaṭ nahĩ*; "Urdū speakers usually pronounce this word simply with *pesh* (i.e. *-ŭs-*), and correct speakers, too, say *hindŭstān* and *hindŭstānī*, although *hindostān* and *hindostānī* are not wrong." (*Hindustani*, 1931, p. 453.)

Nūr ul Lugāt, iv, 992, under "*Hind*", uses both forms.

(3) In a matter like this Urdū books have no more claim to be considered than those in Hindī. The latter almost invariably spell the word *hindŭstān* (rarely *hindusthān*); *-o-* sometimes occurs when an author is referring to an Urdū or English work which has that spelling. Even if it were the case that the *-o-* form was the only one in Urdū books and that people trying to speak highflown Urdū always said *-o-*, there would still be no reason for ignoring the Hindī spelling, and writing *-o-* in English to the exclusion of *-ŭ-*.

(4) With the approval and active support of the local Governments, two language academies have recently been formed in north India, one for Hindī and one for Urdū. Both of these bodies have chosen the name "Hindŭstānī Academy", and each of them has a quarterly magazine of considerable interest, one in Hindī, the other in Urdū. The magazines have no connection with one another, the editors, writers, and contents being entirely different; but in both cases the title of the magazine is *Hindŭstānī.* The choice of name for the two academies and two magazines gives quadruple support to my thesis.

(5) In verse the form depends on the metre. The *mutaqārib* metre of the *Būstān*, the *Shāhnāmeh*, and many Urdū *maṣnavīs*,

such as the *Masnavī e Mīr Ḥasan*, does not permit the form *Hindŭstān* ; in place of it we must have *Hindūstān* in Persian and *Hindostān* in Urdū ; but in metres which permit both forms both are found.

(6) Professor Ṣiddīqī has collected a number of instances of the use of *Hindŭstān* in Persian, Urdū, and Arabic literature (*Hindŭstān*, July, Oct., 1931). He quotes the following authors who write in Persian : Mas'ūd Sa'd Salmān, five quotations ; Amīr Khusrau, twelve quotations ; Muḥammad Ibn 'Umr Farqadī, one ; Shekh Farīd ud Dīn 'Aṭṭār. one ; Jalāl ud Dīn Rūmī, four ; 'Abd ur Raḥmān Jāmī, one ; Salīm Tehrānī, three ; Mīr Razā Dānish Mashhadī, one ; 'Abd ur Razzāq Fayyāẓ, one ; Nāṣir 'Alī Sarhindī, one ; Amīn Rāzī, one ; Niẓāmī Ganjavī, four ; Ashraf Mazandarānī, two ; Mīr 'Abd ul Jalīl Bilgrāmī, one ; Gulām 'Alī Āzād Bilgrāmī, one ; Ānand Rām Mukhallaṣ, one ; and the Arabic writer Abu 'Abdullāh Muḥammad Anṣārī (d. A.D. 1327), one.

I take a few quotations at random.

(i) The last-named writer : *balādu Hindŭstān wa ma'nāhu balādu Hind*, "Hindustān, i.e. Hind" (p. 634).

(ii) Jalāl ud Dīn Rūmī : *sālhā mī gasht ā qāṣid az ū gird i Hindŭstān barāe just ū jū* "for years that messenger from him wandered round India for the purpose of investigation" (p. 625).

(iii) Amīr Khusrau: *Turk i Hindŭstānīm man Hindavī gūyam javāb* "I am a Hindustānī Turk, I reply in Hindavī" (p. 627).

(iv) Mas'ūd Sa'd Salmān : *ki man baqil'a a Sū mānam, ū ba Hindŭstān* "(that) I live in the fort of Sū (or fort of unhappiness), he in Hindŭstān" (p. 623).

Professor Ṣiddīqī quotes the *Farhang i Anjuman Ārā i Nāṣirī* of the time of *Nāṣir ud Dīn Shāh* as saying *hamcunī Bagdād az Bāgdād ū paristān az parīstān . . . ū Hindŭstān az Hindūstān* ; "so *Băgdād* is from *Bāgdād*, *paristān* from *parīstān*, and *Hindŭstān* from *Hindūstān*".

He complains that because certain *muftīs* of Urdū preferred to write *Hindostānī* this spelling became fashionable among copyists, sometimes with disastrous results. Thus *Nāsikh* wrote a *tārīkh* on the death of Jur'at :—

hāe Hindŭstān kā shā'ir muā

and one on the death of *Saudā* :—

shā'ir i Hindŭstān rāraila.

But the copyist, like the shopkeeper who put up the sign "Mens and womens conscia recti ", wanted to improve on other people's work. In both lines he wrote *Hindostān,* thus adding six years to the life of each of the two poets.

Finally he points out that while in Part I of Āzād's lectures the copyist has nearly always written Hindōstān, in Part II another copyist has, after the first page or two, always used Hindūstān, which the author himself preferred.

This form Hindūstān, so well supported by the evidence of literature, almost invariably heard in speech, adopted by both Hindūstānī Academies, is surely the form which we should employ in English.

THE MEANING AND USAGE OF CAUSAL VERBS IN URDU AND PANJABI

I. Meaning

THE causal of an intransitive verb means to cause someone or something to perform the action which the intr. verb indicates: *calnā* "function", *calānā* "cause something to function". About this there is no debate. The question of causals of tr. verbs is not so easy. It is important to be entirely practical, and if we cannot get universal rules we must try to make general rules helpful to both students and scholars. To this end we must, as far as possible, use well-known words, and use them in their ordinary sense. New grammatical terms or old ones with new meanings are worse than useless. A student says: "How am I to express 'make him sleep, make him do it'? May I say *usko sulāo, usko karāo*? If not, tell me what to say, and give me a rule for it which I can easily follow." He is entitled to a reply; more than that, he is entitled to a reply which will be of real use to him.

People speaking of trans. verbs mean "vêrbs ordinarily trans.", for most trans. verbs can, at least on rare occasions, be used intransitively ("This mutton eats well"). Again, nearly all of them may dispense with their object, though retaining their trans. sense. For our present purpose this distinction is unimportant. Thus "see" and "hear" are trans. verbs, but are intrans. in "the blind see, the deaf hear". "Kill" is trans., but the object is suppressed in "if a glance could kill".

The causals of verbs which are ordinarily trans. mean "cause a thing to be done", i.e. they are the causals of the passive of the original verb. If we wish to say "he made the blind see and the deaf hear" we cannot say *usne andhõ ko dikhāyā aur bahrõ ko sunāyā*; this sentence, which is perfectly correct Urdu, means he showed something to the blind, and related something to the deaf.

We may put it otherwise. The direct object of one of these causals is not the doer, but the thing done; or again, if the causal of a trans. verb is put in the passive, the nom. is the thing done, not the doer.

ciṭṭhī likhāī gaī "the letter was caused to be written", not *munshī likhāēā gayā* "the clerk was made to write". *baχshnā* "forgive";

but the causal passive means not "he was made to forgive" but "forgiveness was obtained for his sin, his sin was caused to be forgiven". We can say *paise luṭāe gae*, but we may not translate "the boy was made to rob" by *laṛkā luṭāeā gayā*.

We can therefore make a universal rule :—

Universal Rule.—The causal of an ordinarily trans. verb, when it exists, may always mean "cause something to be done"; and it is never wrong to use it with this meaning. To this rule there is no exception.

Further, we can make a second rule :—

Second Rule.—For the causals of ordinarily trans. verbs the meaning "cause to do" is not permissible, whether the original verb is used "absolutely" or not, i.e. whether the object is expressed or not.

This rule may be considered universal, but if it were claimed that *sīkhnā, sīχṇā* "learn" is always trans., it would come in here as an exception, and the rule would then be general, not universal. It is a matter of indifference. It is certainly correct to say *O sχāī ˌoī e* "she has been taught, put up to it".

pilānā means "cause to be drunk". *khilānā* in the best usage means cause to be eaten, not cause to eat. A phrase like *laṛke khilāe gae* is contrary to good idiom, but I have heard it.

The following verbs are indifferently trans. and intrans., but it must not be assumed that the trans. is the causal of the intrans. :—

bhūlnā, (*a*) "forget", (*b*) "err," "pass from memory"; *badalnā* "change", *palaṭnā* "return", *ulaṭnā* "turn upside down", *bharnā* "fill", *ghisnā* "rub", *jhulasnā* "scorch, get hot", *mānnā* "acknowledge, agree", *paṛhnā* "read, study", *samajhnā* "understand", *sīkhnā* "learn". As they are both trans. and intrans. we should expect causals of both kinds. Actually we find that *bhulānā, paṛhānā, sikhānā* are causals of both trans. and intrans. senses; i.e. both cause to err and cause to be forgotten, etc.

badlānā, palṭānā, ulṭānā, ghisānā, jhulsānā are generally causals of the int. sense, i.e. they mean "cause to perform the intrans. action".

badalvānā, palaṭvāna, ulaṭvānā, ghisvānā, jhulasvānā, mean to cause the action to be performed.

bharānā in one sense only is the causal of the intrans. verb, viz. when it is used of a bird feeding its young, "cause to become filled up." Otherwise it is the causal of the trans., "cause a pot to be filled by someone."

manānā in the phrases *deotā manānā*, *χushī manānā*, etc., is not a causal except in form. Apart from this meaning, *manānā*, as also *samjhānā*, prefers the meaning of "cause to be done"; sentences like *merā bāp manāyā gayā* "my father was persuaded", or *'aurat samjhāī gaī* "the woman was consoled", are not to be recommended.

II. Usage

(i) Grammars usually extend the name intrans. to verbs with cognate objects. These might equally be called trans, In U. and P. the causals generally omit the cognate object, as *dauṛānā* "cause to run". Occasionally, but rarely, the object is expressed, and the verb is treated as the causal of a trans. meaning cause a race to be run.

mujh se baṛī lambī dauṛ dauṛāī gaī "I had to run a long run".

(ii) Some verbs have no causals. It is not possible to lay down a final rule on this point, for tastes vary.

(*a*) Verbs, not themselves causals, whose roots end in *-ā* do not make causals., e.g. *pānā* "find", *jānā* "go", *ānā* "come", *lānā* "bring", *le jānā* "take away", *farmānā* "command", *gurrānā* "growl", *sharmānā* "be ashamed", *vargalānā* "lead astray".

Exceptions, *nahānā* "bathe"; *nahlvānā* : *curānā* "steal", *curvānā*.

But causals may make double causals, *banānā* "make"; *banvānā*.

(*b*) Verbs with more than two syllables in the root do not make causals. Verbs with two syllables in the root, the second containing a so-called "long" vowel, make only a *-vā* causal, e.g. *χarīdnā* "buy", *χarīdvānā*; *ghasīṭnā* "drag", *ghasīṭvānā*.

(*c*) A few others have no causals in ordinary use; *khenā* or *kheonā* "row"; *senā* "hatch"; *cāhnā* "wish".

We may add *khonā* "lose"; *socnā* "think"; *lenā* "take"; *honā* "become", for the forms *khuvānā* and *sucvānā* are fanciful; the Hindi *livā lānā* and *livā lejānā* are happily not used in Urdu; besides *livā* has not got the force of a causal; *huvānā* occurs only in the phrase *ho huvāke*, etc., and has no causal meaning.

(iii) The preposition to be used with causals of trans. verbs. We have seen that causals of trans. verbs mean not "cause someone to do something", but "cause something to be done *by* someone". How is this "by" to be expressed? It is translated in two ways according to the closeness of the connexion between the causer and the action performed. When the idea of causation is weak, the tendency is to use *ko*; when it is strong, it is *se*.

The following take *ko*, meaning "to":—*dikhānā* "show"; *samjhānā* "explain", *pilānā* "give something to drink", *khilānā* "give something to eat", *likhānā* "dictate", *luṭānā* "distribute money", *sunānā* "relate", and all causals of verbs meaning "put on", as *pinhānā* "clothe someone with", *uṛhānā* "give a veil or shawl to be put on", *hār bandhānā* "put a garland on someone, give a garland to be put on", *peṭī kasānā* "assist in putting on a belt". (These are free translations.)

maĩ ne usko ciṭṭhī likhāī "I dictated a letter to him"; *maĩ ne us se ciṭṭhī likhāī* (better *likhvāī*) "I got a letter written by him". Compare *kisī ko Fārsī paṛhānā, kām sikhānā, bāt manānā.*

The Four Classes of Urdu Verbs

FROM the point of view of causality, Urdu verbs may be divided theoretically into four classes, according to their form: Intrans., Trans., First Causal, Second Causal. In this note I have kept before myself the difference between the form and the meaning of a verb; but, though fully cognizant of what some grammarians say about "verbs used transitively or intransitively", I find it more convenient in practice to say simply "intr. verb" and "trans. verb". As I am here not writing a treatise on general grammar, but merely making a few remarks on Urdu verbs, I will content myself with defining roughly the terms used: intr. verb, one which does not take a real object; trans. verb, one which can take a real object (so-called cognate objects being ignored).

A trans. verb is trans. whether the object is expressed or not, but a few verbs may be genuinely both trans. and intr. Thus in English: he went to change his clothes (trans.); he went to change (trans., object suppressed); true friends do not change (intrans.).

So in Urdu *palaṭnā* and *badalnā* can be truly intransitive as well as trans. All trans. verbs in Urdu can be used with obj. suppressed, but the suppression of the object leaves them trans.

Intrans. verbs may be further subdivided into ordinary intrans. and purely neuter, as in the phrases: he turned-out of his room for me, and he turned-out a thief.

Some Urdu verbs have no causals in use (I went into this in *Bull. S.O.S.*, v, iii, 521); of a few it may be said that they have three. In practice possibly the most useful method of describing them is that mentioned above, viz. calling the causal of an intr. verb its trans.; or if we start with the trans. verb, we may call the intrans. verb a middle or passive.

Important General Rule.—So far as meaning goes, trans. verbs have no causals. The so-called causals of trans. verbs are causals of their passives.

We may then put verbs in four columns:—

(1) intr. (2) trans. (3) so-called first causal. (4) so-called second causal. Very few verbs appear in all four columns, some appear in only one.

Column 1 contains all truly intrans. verbs.

Column 2 contains trans. verbs (i.e. verbs which can take a true object, expressed or not). When a verb occurs in cols. 1 and 2, the form in col. 2 is usually the trans. of that in col. 1, but generally there is some change of meaning, with the result that two is not a real trans. of one.

Column 2 might be called the causal of col. 1, but the relationship is, perhaps, more conveniently stated as intr. and trans., or middle and active. At this point there are two points to be noted :—

(i) In some verbs the same idea runs through all forms, e.g. *ladnā* ; all the forms contain the idea of loading ; so *bannā*, making or being made. Other verbs, however, do not keep to one idea ; thus *dikhnā* " be visible " goes on to *dekhnā* " look at " or " see " ; *dikhānā* " show "—three distinct ideas.

(ii) When the same idea is retained, cols. 3 and 4 are practically the same in meaning, e.g. *ladānā* and *ladvānā* mean the same, whereas *dikhāna* and *dikhvānā* are quite different. See below.

It is necessary to have a clear idea of the relationship between the four columns.

Col. 1. Let us call the nominative of these verbs " x ". Being intr. they have no obj.

Cols. 2, 3, 4. Let us call the noms. of these verbs A, B, and C respectively.

ladnā " be loaded ".

Col. 1. *asbāb lad rahā hai* " the furniture, x, is being loaded ".

Col. 2. *naukar asbāb lād rahā hai* " the servant, A, is loading the furniture ".

Col. 3 or 4. *mālik asbāb ladvā rahā hai* " the master, B, is getting the furniture loaded ". *ladvānā* does not mean cause to load.

" x " which is the nom. of col. 1 verbs, is the obj., and the only obj. of verbs in cols. 2, 3, 4.

A, which is the nom. or agent of 2, cannot become the obj. of 3 or 4.

B, the nom. or agent of 3, cannot become the obj. of 4.

A, B, C are therefore never found as direct objects.

Col. 3 verbs are usually said to be causals of col. 2 verbs ; e.g. that *banvānā* is the causal of *banānā* and means " cause to make ". Both statements are erroneous. *banvānā* is the causal of *banāeā jānā* and means " cause to be made ". If it meant " cause to make " its obj. would be A, " cause A to make " ; on the contrary its obj. is " x ", and it means " cause x to be made by A ".

Col. 3 verbs fulfil two functions: they are (*a*) causals of col. 1 through the instrumentality of A; (*b*) causals of the passive of col. 2.

So we get *bannā* "become made"; *banānā* "make" (directly, no outside party); *banvānā* "cause to be made through A". It does not mean "cause to make".

The nom. of *bannā* is always the obj. of *banānā* and *banvānā*. The object of *banvānā* is not A, the maker; it is x, the thing made.

Similarly, if we put *banvānā* in the passive, its nom. is x, the nom. of *bannā*, and this same x is the nom. of the passive of *banānā*.

ṣandūq abhī nahī̃ banā "the box has not yet become made".
ṣandūq abhī nahī̃ banāeā geā "the box has not yet been made" (by A, the carpenter).
ṣandūq abhī nahī̃ banvāeā geā "the box has not yet been ordered (by B, the master) to be made" (by A, the carpenter).

But we can never say *us ne baṛhaī ko banvāeā* "he caused the carpenter to make"; or *baṛhaī banvāeā geā* "the carpenter was caused to make".

Preposition of agency. In the *Bull.*, loc. cit., I discussed this point. It may be either *se* or *ko*. Col. 3 verbs mean "cause something to be done by A". This *by* is sometimes *se* and sometimes *ko*. The problem is rather intricate. These col. 3 verbs are causals of the passive of col. 2 verbs. Now, if we study the col. 2 verbs, which are transitive, we note that practically all of them may be compounded with *lenā* or *denā*, some with both. *lenā* suggests a much closer connection than *denā* between the agent and the act.

When we come to col. 3, where we find the causals of the passive of the col. 2 verbs, we see that when the col. 2 verb is a *lenā* verb the corresponding verb in col. 3 has hardly any true causality. The idea is rather that something is done by A with the *help* of B. The agency is consequently expressed by the dative *ko*.

We note, further, that sometimes they are practically new verbs, containing a new thought, e.g. *dikhānā*, from *dekh lenā*, theoretically means "cause to be seen"; in reality it means simply "show"; *sunānā* means "relate or read out or recite (to someone)", not, strictly speaking, "cause to be heard."

B ne A ko kapṛe pinhāe "B helped A on with his clothes, clothed him"; *pahin lenā* "put on".
B ne A ko dāstān sunāī "B told A a story"; *sun lenā* "listen".
B ne A ko sharbat pilāeā "B gave A a sweet drink"; *pī lenā* "drink".

B ne A ko kuch likhvāeā or *likhāeā* "B dictated something to A"; *likh lenā* "write for oneself".

B ne A se kuch likhvāeā "B got something written by A"; *likh denā* "write for someone else".

It is quite natural that the "causal" of a *lenā* verb should not contain any idea of real causality, for a *lenā* verb means doing something for oneself; consequently its "causal", actually the causal of its passive, does not mean "cause it to be done", which is almost meaningless, seeing that the person is doing it for himself; it means "help or enable it to be done", as in the examples above.

Examples

Col. 4 often differs only in form from col. 3, and it is generally preferred when the idea of getting something done by an outside party is prominent. Thus *kām karvānā* is preferable to *kām karānā*, but the meaning is the same. When col. 4 differs from col. 3 we have the following:—

Col. 4 is (*a*) the causal of 1, through agency of A and help of B; (*b*) the causal of passive of 2 through help of B; (*c*) causal of passive of 3. In each case the object is x, never A or B.

Col. 4 is not the causal of the active of 2 or 3.

Col. 4 differs in meaning from col. 3, when col. 3 (which means that B causes something to be done *by* A) uses *ko* to express *by*. See above.

The following examples show how the nominative, x, of class 1 verbs, which are intrans., becomes the object of classes 2, 3, and 4. They show, too, that all so-called causals of trans. verbs are causals of the passive of those verbs, never of the verbs themselves.

Examples

	1	*Nom.*	2	*Nom.*	*Object*
(*a*)	*dikh* .	x	*dekh* . .	A	x
(*b*)			*sun* . .	A	x
(*c*)			*pahin* .	A	x
(*d*)			*pī* . .	A	x
(*e*)	*kat* .	x	*kāt* . .	A	x
(*f*)	*lad* .	x	*lād* . .	A	x
(*g*)	*bandh* .	x	*bā̃dh* . .	A	x
(*h*)	*kaṭ* .	x	*kāṭ* . .	A	x

	3			4	
	Nom.	*Object*		*Nom.*	*Object*
(*a*) *dikhā* .	B	x	*dikhvā* .	B, C	x
(*b*) *sunā* .	B	x	*sunvā* .	C	x
(*c*) *pinhā* .	B	x	*pahinvā* .	C	x
(*d*) *pilā* .	B	x	*pilvā* . .	C	x
(*e*) *katā* .	B	x	*katvā* . .	B	x
(*f*) *ladā* .	B	x	*ladvā* . .	B	x
(*g*) *bandhā* .	B	x	*bandhvā* .	B	x
(*h*) *kaṭā* .	B	x	*kaṭvā* . .	B	x

(*a*) 1, x is visible ; 2, A looks at x ; 3, B shows x to A ; 4, B causes x to be looked at by A, or C causes x to be shown to A by B.

(*b*) 2, A listens to x ; 3, B relates x to A ; 4, C causes x to be related to A by B.

(*c*) 2, A puts on x ; 3, B helps x to be put on by A ; 4, C causes x to be put on by A through B's help.

(*d*) 2, A drinks x ; 3, B gives x to A to be drunk ; 4, C causes x to be given by B to A to be drunk.

(*e*) 1, x is spun ; 2, A spins x ; 3 and 4, B causes x to be spun by A.

(*f*) 1, x is loaded ; 2, A loads x ; 3 and 4, B causes x to be loaded by A.

(*g*) 1, x is tied ; 2, A ties x ; 3 and 4, B causes x to be tied by A (*bandhānā* is hardly ever used in modern Urdu).

(*h*) 1, x is cut ; 2, A cuts x ; 3 and 4, B causes x to be cut by A.

When one studies the details of individual verbs, puzzling and involved problems arise, but the foregoing outline gives the chief points. On the general question of Indo-Aryan causal verbs Beames, *Comp. Gram.*, iii, 75 ff., may be consulted.

REPETITION OF WORDS IN URDU, HINDI AND PANJABI

IT has been stated many times that the principal idea in the repetition of words is that of emphasis or intensity. My observation has led me to conclude that this is incorrect, and that the true sense in almost every case is one of the following :—

distribution (over time, space, or a number of objects),
pleasantness,
no meaning at all.

In order to make the inquiry practical, it is better to confine it to cases of words repeated without alteration. If anyone will in the course of his reading take 1,000 consecutive instances of repetition, he will find that

(i) short words are repeated far oftener than long.

(ii) repetition of adjj. or advv. with a pleasant meaning is much commoner than of those with a nasty meaning, and when the meaning may be either good or bad, the good is intended.

(iii) nearly every instance comes under either *distribution* or *pleasantness*.

(i) It follows that we read of a man's visiting *ghar ghar* or *gāõ gāõ* or *shahr shahr*, but not *dār us salṯanat dār us salṯanat*, and that we may expect to hear of *būṛhe būṛhe ādmī*, *sundar sundar striyā̃*, or *choṭī choṭī laṛkiyā̃*, but hardly of *ẓa'īf ul 'umr ẓa'īf ul 'umr ṣāḥibān*, *χūbṣūrat χūbṣūrat mastūrāt*, or *kam-sinn kam-sinn aṯfāl*.

(ii) See sentences 1, 2, 3, below

(iii) *Distribution*.

adhelī adhelī " eight annas each ".

ṭhīk ṭhīk batāo " explain correctly " (correctness spread over answer).

cappā cappā pānī " four inches of water all along ".

ẓile ke sab baṛe baṛe paṭṭedār " all the important leaseholders of the district ".

ghaṛī ghaṛī " repeatedly " (at each *ghaṛī*).

Repeated verbs come under this heading ; the idea is either continuance or repetition of action :—

dekh dekh kar, Pj. *veχ veχ ke* " looking repeatedly ".

(Pj.) *ṭurdeā̃ ṭurdeā̃* " through continued walking ".

(Pj.) *p̧aχdeā̃ p̧aχdeā̃* " while heating up " (spread over some time).

Pleasantness. This often corresponds to our " nice and ", or the slang " jolly old ", " good old ".

garm garm dūd " nice, hot milk ".

lāl lāl tarbūze " watermelons, nice and red ".

ṭhaṇḍī ṭhaṇḍī havā " refreshing breeze ".

(Pj.) *̧uṇ vag jā chetī chetī* " now off you go, nice and quick ".

Sometimes no real meaning is discernible. People have got into the habit of repeating certain short words, and do so without thinking; the very shortness of the word seems to demand repetition. I knew an Englishman who always said " very very ", never simply " very ".

Before one can claim that the main thought is emphasis it must be shown that other ideas are impossible. Examples must be found in which emphasis is the only possible idea, and is due solely to repetition; many emphatic phrases contain repeated words, but the emphasis would not be less if the word occurred only once. In fact we shall see that often the very reverse of emphasis is in the mind of the speaker. Let us examine a few cases.

(1) *gorī gorī bālikā kī lāl lāl gālhẽ* " the rosy cheeks of the prettily fair girl ".

(2) *ṭhaṇḍī ṭhaṇḍī havā* " a refreshing summer breeze ".

(3) *pio cā garm, garm* " here you are, sir, nice hot tea ".

(4) *voh alag alag baiṭh gae* " they sat down in separate places ".

Now if the idea of emphasis were present, these phrases would mean :—

(1) the hectic cheeks of the deathly pale girl; (2) a piercing winter wind; (3) scalding tea, much too hot to drink before the train goes; (4) they sat absolutely alone.

We have had it impressed upon us that repetition means emphasis, and we shall feel inclined to say offhand that the following expressions are emphatic, but a little study will convince us that they are not.

(5) *kām ke shurū' shurū' mẽ* " in the early days of the work ".

(6) *voh to abhī abhī āyā thā* " he had not long been there "; quite different from *voh to 'ain usī vaqt pahuncā thā* " he had arrived at that very moment ".

(7) *sac sac bolo* " now, my boy, the truth (throughout your answer) ".

(8) *ṭhīk ṭhīk ḥal karo* " work it out correctly ". But note that, if the boy gets the answer " Rs. 23–11–9 ", the teacher, wishing to tell

him that his answer is "absolutely right", will *not* say *tumhārā javāb ṭhīk ṭhīk hai* ; he will say *bi'lkull ṭhīk hai.* Similarly "entirely wrong" will be *bi'lkull galaṯ*, not *galaṯ galat.*

(9) *mahīne ke andar andar* "some time or other within a month".

(10) *somvār se pahle pahle* "some time or other before Monday".

(11) *ham tīn tīn ādmī prastut haĩ* ; when Hariś Candr uses these words, he means "here we are, three of us every time, for every work".

(12) *maĩ ne das das χaṯṯ likhe, tum ne ek bhī javāb na diyā* ; this literally means "on several occasions I sent you ten letters one after another, but you didn't answer any". Actually, no doubt, he wrote a couple of times and got no answer.

THE GENDER OF ARABIC INFINITIVES IN URDU

A Complete Guide to the gender of nearly 1,000 *nouns*

PLATTS'S Urdu Grammar contains rules to help in determining the genders of nouns. As it was published in 1873 and has not been revised since, one would expect that here and there some restatement might be necessary. This short article deals with the Arabic infinitives commonly used in Urdu. Platts gives seven forms (see especially pp. 25–9), pointing out that six are generally masc. and one fem. In every case but one there are exceptions. The student therefore has an uneasy feeling that perhaps the exceptions are nearly as numerous as the examples, and that in any case unless he knows all the exceptions, the rules are of little value. These Arabic infinitives give to Urdu between 900 and 1,000 nouns. It is impossible to say exactly how many, for a hard and fast line cannot be drawn. Some writers, like Abu'l Kalām Āzād, overload their writings with little-known Arabic words, others employ far fewer. I will here state the rules and endeavour to give every exception. *About some words authorities differ.*

One broad rule to cover all others may be stated thus: nouns of the form *taf'īl* are fem., and nouns of the following six forms are masc., *if'āl, tafa''ul, tafā'ul, infi'āl, ifti'āl, istif'āl.* Directly derived from these and closely resembling them are some nouns ending in *-a* (i.e. *-ah* with *h* not pronounced), which are masc., and in *-ăt* which are fem.

Let us take them in detail.

(1) Form II, *taf'īl.* Approximately 230 of this form are found in Urdu literature in addition to forty which end in *-a* or *-ăt*, such as *taṣfiya, taqviyat.* The 230 are all fem. except one, *ta'vīẕ*, amulet, which is masc. Most of them are abstract nouns, but even those which are not, with the exception of *ta'vīẕ*, are fem. Thus *Taṣlīṣ*, the Holy Trinity; *taḥṣīl*, which often means a *taḥṣīldār's* house or court of justice; *taḥvīl*, capital, deposited funds; *tasnīm*, a fountain in Paradise (made masc. by one poet, Shu'ūr), are fem.

About twenty-eight connected nouns end in *-a.* All are masc., but *taḥayya* (for *taḥiyya*), salutation has both genders. The word *takhliya*, letting go, evacuating, is wrongly given fem. by Platts's Dict. It is masc. Approximately twelve end in *-ăt* and are fem.

Quadriliteral words belonging to Form II are all masc. They include words like *tabakhtur*, walking proudly, and fancy words like *takas̲h̲mur*, to act like or become a Kas̲h̲mīrī. There are about nine of them.

taqayyad, fem., urging, insistence, is probably an alteration of *taqīd* < *taqyīd*.

(2) Form IV, *if'āl*. About 131 words; all masc. except eight. This number does not include about twenty-five derivatives in *-ăt* or *-a*; see below.

The eight exceptions are :—

iṣlāḥ, correction.
ilḥāḥ, importunity.
imlāk, property (rare).
īzā, pain.
ifrāṭ, abundance.
imdād, help.
ins̲h̲ā, composition.
irsāl, rent remitted to headquarters.

When *irsāl* means merely " sending ", it is not used as a noun ; it is then part of the verb *irsāl-karnā*, send, or *irsāl-honā*, be sent : *imlā*, dictation, is sometimes fem.

There are about seventeen derived nouns ending in *-ăt*, all fem., e.g. *ijāzat*, permission, and about eight in *-a*, all masc., as *irāda*, m., intention.

The following is a list of words to which Platts has given wrong genders. The genders marked here are the correct ones :—

iḥṣā, m., numbering.
īfā, m., paying.
ijlās, m., session.
irsāl, f., rent sent on.
imdād, f., help.
idbār, m., turning back.
īmā, m., sign, hint.
ifrāṭ, f., abundance.
imlāk, f., giving possession to.

He allows both genders to *iḥṣā* and *ifrāṭ* ; *imdād* is correct in the Gram. but wrong in the Dict. Conversely *idbār* is right in the Dict., but wrong in the Gram. *ikrāh*, m., aversion (rare), and *īrād*, citing, which he gives as fem., have both genders.

(3) Form V, *tafa''ul*. About 173 words plus fourteen ending in *-ī*, 187 in all. The former are all masc. except three, and the latter are all fem. The three exceptions are :—

tavajjuh, f., attention.
tamannā, f., desire.
tavaqqu', f., hope.

Platts has *tavaẓẓū*, f., prayer-ablution, but it is not used in Urdu.

There are a couple of derived nouns in *-a* which are masc. They bring the number up to 188.

(4) Form VI, *tafā'ul*. About eighty-one. Twelve end in *-ī* and are fem. ; three derived nouns end in *-a* and are masc. The remaining sixty-six are all masc., except *tavāẓu'*, politeness, consideration.

(5) Form VII, *infi'āl*. About thirty-five, all masc.

Platts's Dict. gives *imbisāṭ*, gladness, fem. It is found both masc. and fem. The poet Ḥālī makes it masc.

(6) Form VIII, *ifti'āl*. About 130. Masc. with ten exceptions, of which six end in *-ā*. The fem. nouns are :—

iḥtiyāj, need.
iḥtiyāṭ, care.
iṣṭilāḥ, conventional usage.
iṭṭilā', announcement.

And the following in *-ā* :—

ibtidā, beginning.
iṣṭifā, being elect (rare).
ishtihā, longing.
iltijā, petition.
iktifā, sufficiency.
ihtidā, being guided (very rare).
intihā, end.

Platts wrongly gives *i'tirāz* as fem. The following are both masc. and fem. : *iltifāt*, courtesy ; *iltimās*, request ; *imtiyāz*, distinction ; *istinād*, leaning on (rare) ; *ibtilā*, affliction ; *i'tinā*, anxiety, sympathy ; *iqtidā*, imitation.

It will be noticed that of the nouns ending in *-ā* all the common ones are fem., viz. *ibtidā*, *iltijā*, *intihā*, *ishtihā*.

(7) Form X, *istif'āl*. About sixty-eight ; masc. with the following four exceptions :—

isti'dād, capacity.
istid'ā, supplication.
istirẓā, seeking to please (rare).
istimdād, asking help.

The following have both genders : *istisnā*, exception, *istignā*, wealth, independence, *istigfār*, asking forgiveness.

istigfār is generally pronounced *astagfār*.

Pl. Dict. gives m. gender to *istiṣnā*, *istigfār* (so also Gram.), and to *istimdād* (correct in Gram.). *istikrāh*, m., aversion, is correct in the Dict., but wrong in the Gram.

Further, seven derived nouns ending in *-āt* are fem., and five ending in *-a* are masc. Adding them to the sixty-eight already mentioned, we get eighty for this class.

To sum up : I have dealt with about 950 nouns, which may be divided approximately as follows :—

Connected with	Form	II	280
,,	,,	IV	155
,,	,,	V	190
,,	,,	VI	80
,,	,,	VII	35
,,	,,	VIII	130
,,	,,	X	80
	Total		950

Of these 870 are Arabic infinitives and eighty are directly derived nouns ending in *-ăt* or *-a*.

The following simple rules govern them.

Feminine.

All ending in *-ī*	No exceptions.
,, ,, ,, *-ăt*	No exceptions.
The form *taf'īl*	One exception, viz. *tajvīẕ*, amulet.

Masculine all the rest. Some exceptions as below.

Details of Masculine Types.

Quadriliterals of Form II	All masc. ; no exceptions.
Derived nouns in *-a* .	All masc. ; no exceptions.
Form *if'āl* . . .	Eight exceptions given above.
,, *tafa''ul* . .	Three exceptions, *tavajjuh*, *tavaqqu'*, *tamannā*.
,, *tafā'ul* . .	One exception, *tavāẓu'*, f., politeness.
,, *infi'āl*. . .	No exceptions.
,, *ifti'āl* . .	Ten exceptions, given above.
,, *istif'āl* . .	Four exceptions, *istid'ā*, *isti'dād*, *istimdād*, *istirẓā*.

The phrases in Platts's Gram., p. 25, ll. 19, 20, " a few more words that end in *t* or *ā*," etc., and that on p. 26, ll. 17, 18, " a few words ending in *-ā* or *t* " should be omitted. I do not think that in either case there is a purely fem. word ending in *t*, and those which end in *-ā* are about equally divided.

If we omit words of the forms *if'āl* and *ifti'āl* we have 720 nouns with only nine exceptions ; even if we include these two forms with their relatively numerous eighteen exceptions, the total is only 27.

A few words, not Arabic infinitives, may be mentioned in conclusion. Platts gives wrong genders to the fem. nouns *injīl*, Gospel ; *afvāh*, rumour ; *tarāzū*, balance (correct in Grammar). *banafsha*, violet, which he makes fem., is both masc. and fem.

URDU GRAMMATICAL NOTES. I

(a) Masculine Nouns ending in -ī

We are apt to think that all nouns ending in -ī and denoting inanimate things are fem. with the exception of *pānī*, water; *jī*, mind, self; *ghī*, a kind of butter; *motī*, pearl; *dahī*, buttermilk. In this we are wrong. There are many other masc. nouns ending -ī. I submit the following list; perhaps there are others. One or two of them are occasionally heard fem. In the case of some it is possible to explain why they are masc. (e.g. names of months are masc.), but these explanations are often of little value to the student. He wishes simply to know which nouns in *-ī* are masc. The reason for their being masc. is of secondary interest. I have purposely given the Urdu forms of the Arabic words; their Arabic forms do not concern us.

māẓī, past tense.
mut 'addī, trans. verb.
mushtarī, planet Jupiter.
ṭūṭī, parrot (metaph.). *uskā ṭūṭī bol rahā hai*, he is famous.
qālī, carpet (also *qālīn*).
dī, yesterday.
jadī, Pole Star, Aries, Tropic of Capricorn.
jallāmīrī, *jhallāmīrī*, boy's game.
ma'nī, meaning; masc. pl. (commoner *ma'nē*).
janvarī, January.
farvarī, February.
maī, May.
julāī, July.
farvardī, Persian month (also *farvardīn*).
urdī, Persian month (also *urdī bihisht*).
jumādī ul avval (or *ṡānī*, or *ākhir*), Muḥammadan month.

(*b*) THE NOM. PLUR. OF FEM. NOUNS IN *-a*

This is a point not taken up in grammars. The plur. of these nouns is formed not by changing *-a* to *-ē*, but by changing *-a* to *-ā* and adding *-ē*. Thus we get—

fākhtāē, doves: *zaccāē*, women with newly born children: *māda barrāē*, female lambs.

Similarly, if one were to get plurals of Arabic fems. in *-a*, such as *malika*, queen; *vālidā*, mother, they would also end in *-āē*. As a rule these Arabic fems. avoid plurals.

(*c*) PECULIARITIES IN THE USE OF *ne*

To begin with we may state a general rule:—

When the root of one verb is joined to another verb so as to make a single compound verb, if either verb does not take *ne*, the compound verb does not take *ne*; *voh hās dī*, she laughed; *voh leayā*, he brought.

The following verbs, almost all of which are or can be trans., do not take *ne*, whether they have an object or not.

baknā, speak foolishly.
bhūlnā, forget.
cuknā, finish.
jannā, give birth to.
karnā in such phrases as *banāyā karnā*.
lagnā, begin.
lānā, bring (prob. contracted from *le ānā*).
laṛnā, fight (with), bite.
pānā, succeed in, manage to, get permission to.
dikhāī denā, appear.
sunāī denā, be heard.
pakṛāī dena, be caught.
denā used with any other verbal noun of this form.

The following are both trans. and intrans. They take *ne* when they are trans., otherwise they do not.

badalnā, change.
bharnā, fill.
jhulasnā, scorch.
palaṭnā, return.
pukārnā, call out, call to someone for help.
qarār pānā, be decided; obtain rest.
ragaṛnā, rub.
ulaṭnā, turn upside down.

The usage of the following is variable :—

hās denā, laugh (better without *ne*).
paṛhnā, learn, read (better with *ne*).
ro denā, cry (better without).
samajhnā, understand (better without).
sīkhnā, learn (better with).

The following never take *ne* when used without an object. When they have an object they may take it.
bolnā, speak (much better without).
hārnā, lose, be defeated; *jītnā*, win. When these two have an object such as *bāzī*, game, *sharṭ*, bet, they may either take or omit *ne*.

cāhnā omits *ne* when the nom. is *dil*, *jī*, heart, etc. Otherwise it takes it.

It should be mentioned that *bahasnā*, argue; *cillānā*, cry out; do not take *ne*, while *sāth denā*, accompany, does.

The following intrans. verbs take *ne* :—

thūknā, spit. This can be trans. as in *sāre shahr ne us ko thūkā*, the whole city despised him.
hagnā, *mūtna*, perform the offices of nature.
mānnā, agree (sometimes intrans.).

URDU GRAMMATICAL NOTES, II

(*a*) Gender of Nouns Ending in *-ā*.

The rule that nouns in *-ā* are masc., with the exception of some Sanskrit words, all Hindi diminutives in *-iyā*, and certain Arabic abstracts, is only approximately correct. I have made some lists which may be of interest. It might be claimed that one or two of the Hindi nouns are diminutives, but I do not think they can fairly be so described.

Hindi fem. nouns ending in *-ā* :—

aṅgiyā, bodice.
jāṅgiyā, *jāṅghiyā*, drawers.
chāliyā, betel nut.
saṅkhiyā, arsenic.
badhiyā, bullock, gelding.
bhaṭ kaṭayyā, a prickly plant.
gaṛhayyā, large pit.
ṭhiliyā, earthen pot.
muniyā, amadavat.
mainā, starling.
shāmā, magpie robin.
barvā, poor land.

And the proper names :—

Lankā, Ceylon.
Gaṅgā, Ganges.
Jamnā, Jamnā.
Ajodhiyā
Janīvā, Geneva.

The following are worth adding, for they are so common that the fact of their being Sanskrit is forgotten :—

jaṭā, matted hair.
ghaṭā, dark cloud.
mālā, necklace.
sītlā, smallpox.
pūjā, worship.
sabhā, assembly.
dayā, mercy.

To these we might add :—

kirpā, kindness. *bidyā*, knowledge.

The following Persian feminines should be noted :—

shahnā, flute. *āsiyā* corn mill.
qarnā, horn. *sazā*, punishment.
cūn o cirā, excuse. *daġā*, deceit.
sarā, inn. *parvā* caring, etc.
jā, place.

A few Arabic feminines in -*ā* should be recorded as not being abstracts :—

dunyā, world. *qulyā*, name of a sūra in the Qurān.
ṣahbā, wine. *kīmīā*, chemistry (Greek).

(*b*) Are Nouns denoting Males always Masc., an those denoting Females always Fem. ?

It has often been pointed out that *ghar*, house, *qabīla*, family, etc., even when used for "wife", retain (as is natural) their masc. gender. I have never seen any mentioned on the other side, and therefore venture to adduce the following :—

badhiyā f., bullock, gelding.
asāmī f., client, tenant (male or female).
savārī f., passenger (male or female).
sarkār f., the government, also single individual, your honour, his honour.
polis, *pulīs*, *puls*, f., the police.
ra'iyyat f., plur. *ri'āyā* f. subject, landholder, tenant.

(*c*) The Meaning of "Jānā" in Compounds.

jānā, go, when added to the root of another verb to form a kind of compound verb, either contains or does not contain the idea of "going". Can rules be given ? I would suggest the following :—

(i) When added to intr. verbs *jānā* does not contain the idea of "going" :—

baiṭh gayā, sat down. *so gayā*, went to sleep.
ā gayā, came.

The verb *itself* may of course imply motion, as *haṭ gayā*, moved away.

An exception, perhaps, is *uṭh jānā*, which means not to rise up, but to move out of one house into another.

Along with these must be included the occasional use of *jānā* with *karnā*, to form an intr. compound :—

sirāyat kar gayā, penetrated (*mẽ*, into).

jagah pakaṛ gayā, found a place (*mẽ*, in).

As my colleague, Mr. G. E. Leeson, has pointed out, *jānā* often limits the meaning in a peculiar manner. This point deserves a note to itself.

(ii) When added to tr. verbs *jānā* normally contains the idea of " going " :—

rupayā de gayā, he gave a rupee and went off.

khiṛkiyā̃ toṛ gayā, he broke the windows and went away.

Exceptions.—While it is difficult to say with certainty that in any given case the idea of moving away is entirely absent, we do find sentences in which it is so weak that we may disregard it.

(*a*) Verbs meaning " understand ", " take in ", etc. :—

maĩ tāṛ gayā, I saw and went way, or I saw and took in.

maĩ samajh gayā, I took in or have taken in.

maĩ jān gayā, I took in or have taken in.

maĩ dekh gayā, I looked and went, or I looked over (the volume).

(*b*) Verbs meaning " eat " or " drink " :—

sārā khānā ragaṛ gayā, or *haṛap kar gayā*, or *khā gayā*, he ate all the dinner and went off, or he ate it up.

sharbat pī gayā, he drank the sherbet and went off, or he drank up the sherbet.

So *haẓm k.*, *caṭ k.*, *nigalnā*, eat or swallow up.

GRAMMATICAL NOMENCLATURE: UNNECESSARY NAMES

IN the teaching of Indian languages much confusion is caused by the invention of names for ideas which either have well known names already, or do not require any name. This makes otherwise useful grammatical notes very obscure, and causes actual unfairness in examinations because candidates are often unfamiliar with the terms employed. We should avoid attaching labels to the words, constructions, and phrases of the language we are teaching, and when a name is necessary it should be one already known from English or Latin.

I take a few illustrations at random from Platts's *Grammar*. Under verbs we find *acquisitives, potentials, inceptives, permissives, completives, desideratives, continuatives, frequentatives, staticals*, and *reiteratives*. It will hardly be believed that most of these names have been coined to indicate one or, at the most, two words. Thus *acquisitives* means *pānā* alone ; *potential* means *saknā* ; *inceptive, lagnā* ; *permissive, denā* ; *completive, cuknā* ; *desiderative. cāhnā* (and *māgna !*) ; *continuative, jānā* and *rahnā* ; so far we have had seven unnecesary and, for the most part, uncouth names to indicate eight or nine words, nearly one special name per word. *Frequentative* and *statical* refer to two particular idioms, and *reiteratives* to repetition ; none of these need a name. I would strongly advocate making a clean sweep of them all. They are confusing, awkward, and useless. I never myself use any of them.

The teacher can say " to-day we are going to discuss *-saknā* " be able ", or *-lagnā* " begin " ; or " I am going to tell you how to express permission or desire or habit or repetition." The simplest words are best.

Another objectionable word is *postposition*. We have " preposition " well established as a technical term. Why do we need another ? English prepositions often follow their word : " that's the hole he got in by " ; or as the weary nurse said to the intellectual patient after having read aloud to him, " what *did* you choose that book to be read to out of for ? " In my teaching I always say " preposition ", and never has it led to any difficulty or called forth any question.

As a matter of fact, if we wish to be lugubriously accurate, we shall have to say that Urdu and Hindi have prepositions, postpositions, and prepostpositions, for some always precede, some always follow, and some may do both. What is the unfortunate student to say?

The aim we should set before ourselves is this :—

as far as possible (i) avoid coining new terms ; (ii) use well known terms, and use them with their usual meanings.

Thus, if we use transitive and intransitive we must not change their connotation ; we must not equate transitive with " verbs requiring *ne* ", and intrans. with " verbs not requiring *ne* ". Some trans. verbs never need *ne*, and some intrans. verbs always need it with certain tenses.

It is difficult to know what to call the case which in Pj. and U. occurs with all prepositions. " Oblique " and " General Oblique " have been suggested. They are unsatisfactory, for the case is only one out of four oblique cases in Pj. and out of two in U. Perhaps we might call it Prepositional, which, though a new name, carries its meaning on the surface.

The Cases of Nouns and Pronouns in Urdu, Hindi, and Panjabi

In Latin, Greek, and Sanskrit case names are given to definite forms. The syntax of these forms is a different matter. Each case may have ten or twenty uses. If we are to employ the same names in Panjabi Hindi, and Urdu, we must do so in the same way ; we cannot make, say, ablative or dative, equivalent to *se* or *ko*, for either *se* or *ko* may represent a Latin genitive or dative or accusative or ablative. A preposition governs a certain case, but it is no part of the case. *εἰς τὴν οἰκίαν* means *ghar mẽ* ; *οἰκίαν* is accus. Are we to call *ghar* also accus. ? *ghar* is in a certain case, but *ghar-mẽ* is not a case. Again, *μετὰ χαρᾶς* (genitive) is *χushī se* ; the Urdu noun corresponds to a noun in the genitive, why call it ablative ? A Greek dative may *inter alia* stand for a Latin ablative, but we do not, therefore, insist on saddling Greek with an ablative case. The term " case-phrase " has been suggested. But before we speak of a " dative case-phrase ", we shall need to decide whether it is a Latin, Greek, or Sanskrit dative, and also which of the ten or twenty meanings of the dative it bears.

Hindi and Urdu nouns have three cases, nom., voc., and a third, which may be called prepositional. It is used with all prepositions including *ne*. Thus *bahinē, bahino, bahinõ*. Pronouns will need an agent case : *voh* " they " ; *un, unhõ*. I must plead guilty to having in various books given long lists of unnecessary cases, and committed the absurdity of making a preposition part of a case.

It seems to me that in no circumstances should a preposition be included in a case, but when a name is required for a definite *form* there is no objection to choosing the nearest or most suitable of the well-known case names, gen., dat., abl., loc., etc.

Panjabi requires five case names,

masīt " mosque ", *bū'ā* " door."

	Sing.		*Plur.*	
nom.	*masīt,*	*bū'ā*	*masīttā̃*	*bū'e*
prep.	*masīt*	*bū'e*	*masīttā̃*	*bū'eā̃*
loc.	*masīttī*	*bū'e*	*masīttī̃*	*bū'ī̃*
abl.	*masīttõ*	*bū'eõ*	wanting	
voc.	*masītte*	*bū'eā*	*masītto*	*bū'eo*

Pronouns need at least three more : agent, dative, and gen.

	Sing.		*Plur.*	
nom.	*mæ̃,* " I "	*o'* " he "	*asī̃, ahī̃*	*o'*
prep.	*mere*	*os, [o'de]*	*sāḍḍe, asā̃, ahā̃*	*o'nā̃, [o'nā̃ de]*
loc.	*mere, merī*	*[os]*		*o'nī̃*
abl.	*mĕthõ*		*sāthõ*	*[o'nā̃ tõ]*
ag.	*mæ̃*	*os*	*asā̃, ahā̃*	*o'nā̃*
gen.	*merā*	*[o'dā, osdā]*	*sāḍḍā*	*[o'nā̃ dā]*
dat.	*mĕnū̃, minū̃*	*[o'nū̃, osnū̃]*	*sānū̃*	*[o'nā̃ nū̃]*

The loc. forms *merī, o'nī̃* are always adjectival, agreeing with a loc. plur. noun. Other adj. forms have also been included.

Addendum. The First Plural Feminine in Urdu

Some doubt seems to exist as to the proper form of the verb in the 1st plur. fem., and it has been asserted that the masc. form must be used. This is true of only one case.

(i) When a woman speaking of herself alone uses the plur., the verb and adjj. are masc. :—

ham to abhī āte haĩ " I'm coming now ".

This reminds us of Greek usage. Cf. Euripides Alc. 383, where Alcestis is referring to herself.

(ii) If several women speak, the verb is fem. Two cases arise :—

(*a*) when a plur. fem. noun is inserted,

ham tīnõ bahinẽ roṭī khā rahī thī̃ "we three sisters were breakfasting".

(*b*) when there is no noun. A good example occurs in Āzād's *Āb i Ḥayāt*, p. 74 of 1917 ed., where he makes some women say :—

jab tak hamārī bāt na kah degā na pilāẽgī "until you say what we want, we shall not give you water".

Two examples from Prem Cand are :—

ham sab kī sab calẽgī "we shall all go".

āp kā diyā khātī haĩ, to sāth kis ke rahẽgī "what we eat is your gift, then with whom else shall we stay ?"

In this last case (when there is no noun) some speakers are inclined to favour the masc., but among good families the fem. is used.

Early Hindi and Urdu Poets:

The Causes of the Failure of Prayer

By Shāh Malik, 1666

INDIA Office Catalogue of Hindustānī MSS., No. 3, *Sharī'at Nāma*, a Dakhnī poem by Shāh Malik: written on 48 small folios and containing 516 lines. We may describe it as a compendium of Muslim doctrines.

The catalogue, which prints twelve lines of the poem (four taken from the beginning and eight from the end), calls the author Shāh Mulk, but it seems certain that his name was Shāh Malik. This is a natural name, whereas the other is abnormal. One might have hoped to find the name in some line which by its metre would decide the question. It does occur, but unfortunately it is merely spelt out, and the spelling is the same for both forms.

so yū shīn alif he o mīm lām kāf
faraẓ kū so Dakhnī mẽ bolyā hai ṣāf
san i yak hazār hor sattar pau sāt
kiyā hū isī sāl mẽ yū ḥikāt

"So this Shāh Malik (*shīn alif he* and *mīm lām kāf*) has plainly uttered the religious duties in Dakhnī; the year seven over one thousand and seventy, he has finished in this year this story." (A.H. 1077 = A.D. 1666.)

On the outside of the MS. is written *risāla dar fiqh dar zabān i Hindī i Dakkhan; taṣnīf i Shāh Malik tamām*; "a tractate on theology in the Hindī language of the Deccan; the work of Shāh Malik complete." On the next leaf are the same words except that *Dakhnī* is substituted for *Dakkhan*. These words on the outer leaves were no doubt written by some owner of the MS. After most of the lines of the poem are explanatory notes in Dakhnī prose, written in red ink by a later hand, probably seventy years later.

I have chosen these lines for translation partly because they are in themselves interesting, and partly because they are printed in *Urdū Shahpāre* (Ḥaidarabād, 1929), pp. 245–6. For those who may be studying them as printed in that volume, it may not be out of place to point out a number of misprints there.

p. 245, l. 8 from foot :	*us javāb*	should be	*us kā javāb*
4	*paregā*	.. ..	*paregā*
4	*phire*	.. ..	*pare*
1	*mane*	.. ,,	*mene*
p. 246, l. 3 ., top	*ridā*	.. ..	*adā*
5 .. ,.	*kū̃*	., ,.	*koi*
5 ., ..	*hoe*	.. .,	*na hoe*
7 ., ..	*muqtadā*	.. ,,	*muqtadī*

Namāz tuṭne kā beān

From Shāh Malik's *Sharī'at Nāma*, 1666

1. *Namāz ke tuṭne ke haĩ bīst o panj*
Namāzī ne karnā hai yū̃ yād ganj.
2. *Namāz mẽ kare bāt yā khāe tū̃*
Phirāve jo qible te sīnā o mū̃ ;
3. *Bhī karnā salām yā tū̃ us kā javāb*
Dīe tau bī tuṭṭā hai sun ai Shihāb.
4. *Namāz mẽ pukāre o yā āh kahe*
Tuṭegā agar oh hor vāh kae.
5. *Bhī tuṭṭā darad ke rone mane*
Karegā 'amal yak kas̱īrā jine.
6. *Khankāre agar be 'uẕar koī yār*
To jāygā namāz is te sun ai hushyār.
7. *Paregā galaṭ koī Qur'ān kū̃*
Bhī tuṭṭā pare dek Furqān kū̃.
8. *Ṭalab bhī kare yū̃ Khudā te jine*
Jo karte ṭalab jū̃ ki ădmyā̃ mane.
9. *Bhī denā javāb chīk kā dar namāz*
Hãsegā jo qahqih sẽte bā ăvāz.
10. *Tuṭegā faraẕ tark karne mene*
Najis par bī sijda karegā jine.
11. *Imām muqtadī gair bhī leve bol*
Tuṭegā bī us te katā hū̃ so khol.
12. *Bhī bole khaṭā apnī gair az imām*
Nāmāz hoe fāsid bī us kā tamām.
13. *Bhī achnā barābar marad zan agar*
Muāfiq adā taḥrīma yak digar.
14. *Zamīn te ucāve tū sijda mane*
Bhī tuṭṭā agar har do pāvā̃ kane.

15. *Bhī ṣāḥib i tartīb achegā jo koĭ*
Vaqat bī namāz kā use tang na hoĕ.
16. *Tuṭegā namāz is te sun nek rāĕ,*
Namāz mē qaẓā gar use yād āĕ.
17. *Imām te angē muqtadī hoĕ kharā*
Tuṭegā so jāno nhanā tā baṛā.
18. *Khabar nek bad yā 'ajāib jo koĭ*
Agarci baqur'ān ḥadīs̤ sete hoĕ.
19. *Namāz mē jo is kā deve jāb agar*
To jaygā namāz is te sun kān dhar.

1. There are twenty-five causes for prayer's failing,
the praying man must make them his memory treasure.
2. During prayer, if thou (i) speak or (ii) eat
or (iii) turn away from the Qibla thy breast and face
3. And (iv) say Salām, or if thou (v) answer to it (someone's salām),
so also prayer fails ; hear O Shihāb (meteor).
4. In prayer if thou (vi) callest out, or (vii) sayest Ah,
it will fail or if thou sayest Oh and Vāh.
5. It also fails (viii) in crying through pain,
or (ix) if anyone does with one (hand) many things ;
6. Or (x) if any friend clears his throat without reason,
then through that the prayer will go, listen wise one.
7. If any one (xi) shall recite wrongly the Qur'an,
it fails too if (xii) he recite looking at the book,
8. Or if any one (xiii) ask thus of God
as people ask among men.
9. Also (xiv) give an answer to a sneeze during prayer,
or (xv) if one laugh with a guffaw aloud.
10. It fails if one omits a *farẓ* (xvi)
or makes a prostration on anything unclean (xvii).
11. If the Leader and his follower shall say anything wrong (xviii),
It will fail for this, I tell you openly.
12. If anyone tells his fault to other than the Leader, (xix)
his whole prayer also is unlawful.
13. Also if a man and a woman are on a level (xx)
at the opening Takbīr close to one another ;
14. Or from the ground if one lift during a prostration
Both feet, it fails also (xxi) ;

15. Or if there is a master of arrangement
    and the time also for prayer is not short,
16. The prayer shall fail, listen O man of good advice,
    if in prayer he remembers that (a previous prayer) has been
        omitted (xxii).
17. Before the Leader if the follower shall stand (xxiii),
    it shall fail, know this both small and great ;
18. Good news (xxiv) or bad (xxv) or strange, if any one hears,
    even though from the Qur'an or Tradition the answer be,
19. If he give the answer to it,
    then the prayer shall fail for that, listen with attention.

The second part of l. 5 is obscure. The accompanying Dakhnī commentary says " doing three things with one hand, or one thing with two hands ".

l. 7 : Recite the Qur'ān wrongly. Comm. " if in reciting the Qur'ān, i.e. the Al-ḥamd or the sūra, he makes such a mistake as changes the meaning ".

l. 8 : Comm. " asking as from men, O God give me a horse or a wife, or earthly things of this kind ; if he asks for heavenly things the prayer does not fail ".

l. 9 : Comm. " if someone sneezes and says Praise be to God, and the person praying says The mercy of God, the prayer is spoilt ".

l. 10 : Anything unclean, i.e. unclean cloth or place.

l. 11 : Comm. " if the leader forgets something, and an outsider says it, and the leader repeats it after him, the prayer is not valid ". The line may mean " if anyone other than the leader or his follower says anything ".

l. 12 : *taḥrīma* or *takbīr i taḥrīma*, the opening *takbīr* after which all worldly actions are unlawful (*ḥarām*).

l. 15 : *ṣāḥib i tartīb* ; master of arrangement, perhaps the man who sees that the lines of worshippers are even, or the leader.

The meaning is that if during a prayer a man remembers that he omitted his prayers at the previous time of prayer, he must first say those prayers, unless there is actually no time to do so.

ll. 18, 19 : If anyone while praying hears good or bad news, and makes a response, even if he takes the words from the Qur'ān or from the *ḥadīs̤*, his prayer does not count.

In the MS. *kāf* is always used for both *kāf* and *gāf* ; *gāf* does not occur. *ṭ* has four dots over it, *ḍ* and *ṛ* have four dots under them. In the poem we find *paregā* and *pare* for *paṛhegā*, *paṛhe*, but *khaṛā* and *baṛā* are written with *ṛ*. In the commentary *ṛ* is written in *aṛ* hesitate, *ghoṛā* horse, *choṛnā* leave ; *r* in *kapre* cloth, *pareā* read, *kharā* and *kharī* standing.

Special Dakhnī words : *tuṭnā* for *ṭūṭnā* break (in title, etc.), two cerebrals not being allowed in one word ; *achnā* for *honā* be (13, 15) ; *kănā* for *kahnā* say (4, 11) ; the agent *jine* who, for ordinary nominative (5, 8, 10) ; *kū̃* for *ko* to, etc. (7, etc.) ; *bhī* also, at the beginning of a clause (3, 5, 14, 15) ; *admyā̃* for *ādmiyō̃* men (8), and many more.

Shāh Malik's use of the word "Dakhnī" to describe his dialect of Urdu should be noted. It would be interesting to know who was the first to employ the word in this sense. It was quite common among his older contemporaries. The earliest I know of was Gavvāṣī, *c.* 1616.

GLEANINGS FROM EARLY URDU POETS.—

QUṬB MUSHTARĪ, 1609, A DAKNĪ POEM BY MULLĀ VAJHĪ OF GOLKUṆḌA

QUṬB MUSHTARĪ is a MS. poem in the India Office Library. The Catalogue of Hindustani MSS. states (p. 64, No. 122) that the name and author are unknown ; but Mohyeddin Qadri in his recently published *Urdū Shahpāre* gives the name of the poem, points out that twice in the course of it Vajhī is mentioned as the author, and adduces convincing reasons for concluding that this Vajhī and the author of the prose work *Sab Ras*, which was twenty-five years later, are the same person. The date of *Quṭb Mushtarī* is A.H. 1018 = A.D. 1609.

Urdū Shahpāre is a work of great value. It discusses Urdu authors from the earliest times down to the death of Valī and to illustrate their writings gives well-chosen extracts, many of which are taken from MSS.

It has been debated whether Vajhī or the King of Golkuṇḍa, Qulī Quṭb Shāh, was the first literary writer of Urdū poetry. The King reigned from 1580 to 1611. The exact date of his work is not known, but as it is unlikely that he wrote nothing till the last two years of his life, I have no doubt that the greater part of his poetry (which occupies 1,800 MS. pages) was anterior to Vajhī's poem. These two authors are of the highest importance. Before their time verse had been religious and moral, written not as poetry, but as a means of instruction. The chief religious poets before 1600 were Shān Mirā̃ Jī, d. 1496, his son Shāh Burhān, d. 1582, K͟hūb Muḥammad, who wrote in 1578, and the author of *Nūr Nāma* about the same time. Of these Shāh Burhān was a writer of real poetic merit. They all belonged to the Deccan or Gujrāt.

From the ease with which Qulī Quṭb Shāh and Vajhī handle the language it is plain that Urdu poetry was even then not quite in its infancy. There is a surprising modernity about their writing. The bad habit of dependence upon Persian was only beginning.

Quṭb Mushtarī deals with a legendary incident in the life of the King during whose reign it was written. He dreams, while a prince, of a lovely maiden. After a time he sets out in search of her, and at the end of many adventures finds and marries her. Vajhī, who was poet laureate, must have been encouraged by the King to write the romance, for without his sovereign's approval he would not have dared to do so. It will be seen that he is fresher and more direct than most of the poets of the following century, and from the standpoint of poetry his work stands higher than that of many who are far better known. He is in fact little more than a name in prose, and is unknown in poetry.

With a view to making the text accessible to a larger number of scholars and students I have transliterated it into Roman. This has necessitated a decision upon the pronunciation of every syllable. It is perhaps regrettable that a quasi-canonical character has thus been given to ideas about early Dakni pronunciation which are sometimes conjectural, but the advantages outweigh the disadvantages. I have tried to make the spelling fulfil the metrical requirements of the poem, but have omitted the frequently occurring, unwritten extra *-ă*.

"The Dawn of Love," from *Quṭb Mushtarī* by Mullā Vajhī of Golkuṇḍa, 1609

1. *Na bhwī̃ par dise voh na āsmān mẽ*
Rahyā Shăh usī nār ke dhyān mẽ.

2. *Lagyā talmalāne bahūt dhāt sõ*
Kahyā jāe na bāt dū(vū)bāt sõ.

3. *Na yū bāt har ek kū̃ fām hoe*
Vohī jāne jis par jo yū kām hoe.

4. *Kadhī̃ cakh hăse hor kadhī̃ cakh roe*
Kadhī̃ sudh pāve kadhī̃ sudh khoe.

5. *Isī dhāt din rāt rahtā ache*
Apas mẽ ape yū̃ voh kahtā ache.

6. *Bhulāī cācal dhun vū yū̃ Shāh kū̃*
Ki lubdāe jyū̃ kăhrubā kāh kū̃.

7. *Uṭhe hor phir soe Shāh jāe kar*
Ki dū(vū) nār bhī khāb mẽ āe kar.

8. *Jo har bār yū̃ khāb mẽ yār āe*
To 'āshiq kū̃ bin khāb bhī kuc banhāe (nabhāe).

9. *Pareshān ḥairān betāb thā*
Na kuc us kū̃ ārām tā khāb thā.

10. *Lagyā Shāh usāsā̃ bharan āh mār*
Ki nazdīk nẽ hai vū kanvunt (gunvant) nār.

11. *Kadhī̃ be khabar hoe kadhī̃ hoe hushyār*
Kadhī̃ pīv pīv kai kadhī̃ yār yār.
12. *Yū sun muṭribā̃ sab khabardār hue*
Jo mastān the dadan(vū̃) so hushyār hue.
13. *Bahūt dhāt sõ bāt samjhāe kar*
Kahe Shāh kū̃ nazdīk yū̃ āe kar :
14. *Ki ai Shāh tū̃ Jam Shāh khurram ho ac*
Nahī̃ gam tuje kuc tū̃ be gam ho ac.
15. *Jakuc tuj kū̃ honā so ḥāẓir hai sab*
Usāsā̃ jo bhartā so tū̃ kyā sababb
16. *Kahyā Shāh dil mẽc dharnā bhalā*
Kis pās ẓāhir na karnā bhalā.
17. *Kise kaū ki munj 'ishq us kā ahe*
Vohī jāne munj 'ishq jis kā ahe.
18. *Jakoi rāz yū̃ bāp kan khole gā*
Divānā huā kar munje bole gā.
19. *Nahī̃ bāt kahne kī yū khol kar*
Ki samjhāū̃ ab kis kū̃ maĩ bol kar ?
20. *Achū̃ sej par mauj jyū̃ āb mẽ*
Ki caṭkā lagā gaī sakī khāb mẽ.
21. *Jitā muṭribā̃ Shāh kū̃ samjhā kahe*
Tagāful kiye Shāh hor cup rahe.
22. *Kite kai ki mastī ke cāle haĩ yū*
Kite kai pirat ke ulāle haĩ yū.
23. *Kite kai use kucc ochaṭ huā*
Kite kai use 'ishq kā puṭ huā.

Urdū Shahpāre, pp. 189, 190.

"The Wine Feast," from *Quṭb Mushtarī* by Mullā Vajhī, of Golkuṇḍa, 1609

1. *Shahanshāh majālis kiye ek rāt*
Vazīrā̃ ke farzand te sab saṅgāt
2. *Har ek khūbṣūrat har ek khush liqā*
So har ek dilkash har ek dil rubā
3. *Mahābat ke kāmā̃ mẽ jam Jam hai jyū̃*
Shujā'at ke kāmā̃ mẽ Rustam hai jyū̃
4. *Nadīm hor muṭrib sughaṛ fahmdār*
Athe Shāh sū̃ milkar yū sab ek ṭhār.

5. *Ṣurāḥī piyāle le hātā̃ mane*
Nadīmā̃ te mashgūl bātā̃ mane.
6. *Lage mutribā̃ gāne yū̃ sāz sū̃*
Ki dhartī hale mast āvāz sū̃
7. *Jo mutrib dū(vū) ṣaḥrā mē̃ is dhāt gāe*
To phir un kū̃ is shauq te ḥāl āe.
8. *Jo gāvan vū Shāh kū̃ kamāte athe*
So rāgā̃ pa rāgā̃ jamāte athe.
9. *Nadīmā̃ laṭāfat mē̃ jo cakh āe*
To rotyā̃ ko khush kar gharī mē̃ hā̃sā̃e.
10. *Sharāb hor ṣurāḥī nuqal hor jām*
Hue mast majlis ke logā̃ tamām
11. *Jo hwī rāt ādhī bichī do pahar*
Khabardār yārā̃ hue be khabar.
12. *Bisar gai nadīmā̃ ṭaraz bāt kā*
Gāvāe khabar mutribā̃ ẕāt kā.
13. *Na milte na khūbī jhagaṛte kahī̃*
Yakas ke ūpar ek paṛte kahī̃.
14. *Lage mast ho saṭne mastī saṅgāt*
Yakas ke so pāvā̃ ūpar ek hāt.
15. *So yū̃ kuc voh yārā̃ hue be khabar*
Ki pānī pīte the sharāb hai kakar.
16. *Yakas kū̃ bulā ek azmāõ sū̃*
Gale lagte the mast ho chāõ sū̃.
17. *Bajāo jo kaī to uṭhē gāe kar*
Saṭe mutribā̃ hosh khushī pāe kar.
18. *Ṣurāḥī piyāle sū̃ hamdast ho*
Kirā̃ phirte the dū(vū) dono mast ho.
19. *Yitā mast sāqī huā sud gāvāe*
Ki pyālā maṅge to ṣurāḥī kū̃ lyāe.

Urdū Shahpāre, pp. 191–2.

THE DAWN OF LOVE

1. Not on earth she appeared nor in heaven.
The prince recked of naught but the maid ;
2. He was restless in numberless ways.
Nor in words could the matter be told,
3. Nor yet could all understand,
Only he upon whom it had passed.

4. Now a little he smiled, now he wept,
Now lost, now alive, to the world.
5. In this state he remained night and day,
With himself alone had he speech.
6. The charmer absorbed all his thought,
Like amber attracting the grass.
7. He arose, but anon went and slept,
For the maid was seen only in dreams.
8. If the friend comes thus in a dream,
Then the lover wants nothing but sleep.
9. Bewildered, distressed and perturbed—
No peace all the day, save in sleep.
10. The prince breathed out groanings and sighs,
For that virtuous maid was not near.
11. Lost in thought or alert, now he says
" My dear, dear one," and now " my dear friend ".
12. The singers were roused by the news,
E'en the drunken all sober became.
13. They reasoned with him many wise,
They spoke to the prince, coming near,
14. " O prince, like King Jam, be thou glad ;
Thy sorrow is groundless, grieve not :
15. Whatever thou needest is here ;
Then why dost thou utter these sighs " ?
16. Said the prince, " To keep secret is good,
Good also to tell not one soul ;
17. To whom can I say that I love her ?
Let her whom I love alone know.
18. To my Sire be this secret imparted,
He'll surely regard me as mad.
19. Not openly can this be told,
To whom can I trust this my woe ?
20. On my couch I'm a tossing sea surge,
For my dream-friend my thirst has aroused."
21. In vain did the singers console,
He turned a deaf ear and was dumb.
22. Many said " These are follies of youth ",
Or " These are o'erturnings of love ",
23. And " This is love's savour ", said some,
And others " Mere lightheadedness ".

A Wine Feast

1. One night the Emperor an assembly made,
   The sons of ministers sat with him there,
2. And every youth was handsome, fair to see,
   And winsome every one with youthful charm.
3. In war as unafraid as great King Jam,
   In bravery not Rustam's self more bold.
4. Courtiers and singers, elegant and wise
   Sat in one place together with the King.
5. Goblet and pitcher taking in their hand
   The courtiers one and all engaged in talk ;
6. And when the singers rhythmically sang,
   The earth was trembling with the jovial sound.
7. Upon them as they sang in that wild waste
   A frenzy passed through overmuch desire ;
8. And they that served the King in minstrelsy
   Were adding melody to melody.
9. The singers entering into merriment
   Would presently make even mourners gay.
10. With wine and pitcher, salted fruits and cup
    Intoxicated all the guests became.
11. When half the night was come and midnight lowered,
    Bereft of sense were friends with sense before.
12. Courtiers remembered not how to converse,
    And singers their surroundings heeded not.
13. Not meeting as friends meet nor quarrelling,
    But falling every one upon his friend.
14. The drunken courtiers swaying drunkenly
    Placed each his hand upon another's foot.
15. And in this way the friends lost all their sense
    And drinking water, " Sure, 'tis wine " declared,
16. And each to other called by way of test,
    And drunken on the necks of shadows fell.
17. When bidden play the singers sang instead,
    Witless each man through joy and revelry.
18. The pitchers holding goblets by the hand
    Did reel from side to side inebriate.
19. The page became so drunk he lost his wits
    And gave a pitcher when a cup was sought.

Notes

In the transliteration into Roman character the words in brackets are what appear to me to be the correct reading for the word given immediately before, which is that in the printed text.

The chief points of Dakni grammar which emerge are the following: trans. verbs are used in the same way as intrans., even in tenses formed with the past ptcp. The agent prep. *ne* is not found. *-ā̃* is the plur. ending, both nom. and obl., masc. and fem.

It will be noticed that Northern Urdu and Dakni words, forms and constructions are intermixed. A number of the Dakni words have long since disappeared from Urdu. Some are still common in Panjabi.

The spelling frequently reminds us of the actual pronunciation of modern Urdu as distinct from that usually laid down in books.

In these notes " U." stands for Northern Urdu.

The Dawn of Love.

1. *bhwī̃* for *bhuī̃*. *nār*, woman.
2. *dhāt*, manner, kind. *vū*, U. *voh*.
3. *yū*, U. *yeh*. *kū̃*, U. *ko*. *fām*, U. *fahm*.
5. *ache*, is.
6. *lubdāe*, connected with *lubdh*.
7. *hor*, and.
8. *nabhāy*, *na bhāy*, not be pleasing.
11. *kai*, U. *kahe*.
14. *ho ac*, become (either *ac* or *ach*).
15. *jakuc*, U. *jo kucch*.
16. *kis* for *kise*.
17. *kaū̃*, U. *kahū̃*. *ahe*, U. *hai*.
18. *sakī* for *sakhī*.
21. *jitā*, U. *jitnā*.
22. *kite kai*, U. *kitnõ ne kahā*. *pirat*, love, a word still common in the Deccan.
23. *puṭ*, a common word used in North India as well as the Deccan, practically " admixture " or " taint ", but with either good or bad sense. Two hundred years later Sayyid Inshā wrote *Rānī Ketakī kī Kahānī* in pure Hindi ; " *aur na kisī bolī kā mel hai na puṭ*." And 'Alī Ausaṯ Rashk, 1799–1867, said *itnī puṭ īmān kī rakhtā nahī̃*, I have not even so much faith.

The Wine Feast.

1. *sangāt* used prepositionally, with or along with.

3. *jam*, more often *jamjam*, happy, happily ; often like English " with pleasure ", for " certainly ", " by all means ". Here a play on the name of King Jam.

4. *athe*, U. *the*.

6. *hale* ; the vowel in both Pj. and Dak. is *a*, as in eighteenth century U., *halnā*, shake, is not the same as *hilnā*, become accustomed : Pj. *ʿallṇā̆*, *ʿiḷṇā̆*.

7. *ṣaḥrā*, used for the place of meeting, as if a picnic in the desert.

9. *rotyā̆*, U. *rotō*.

14. *saṭne*, also 17 ; *saṭnā*, leave, give up, hence lose ; Pj. *saṭṭṇā̆*, *suṭṭṇā̆*. *mastī saṅgāt*, U. *mastī se*.

15. *kakar*, U. *kahkar*.

19. *yitā*, U. *itnā*.

Some everyday Pj. words occur in the extracts. Such are : *dis*, Pj. *diss* appear : *kadhī̆*, Pj. *kadī̆*, sometimes ; *hor*, Pj. *hor* (*ʿor*) and : *jam*, Pj. *jamjam*, with pleasure : *hal*, Pj. *hall* (*ʿall*), shake : *bisar*, Pj. *vissar*, forget : *gāvā*, Pj. *guā̆*, lose : *saṭ*, Pj. *saṭṭ*, *suṭṭ*, ; in Pj. means throw.

GLEANINGS FROM EARLY URDU POETS

MUḤAMMAD QULĪ QUṬB SHĀH, KING OF GOLKUṆḌA, 1580–1611.

THIS remarkable writer, the founder of Ḥaidarābād, and probably the first literary poet in the language, was the fourth king of the Quṭb Shāhī dynasty which ruled in Golkuṇḍa, one of the five states into which the Deccan was divided after the break up of the Bahmanī kingdom. In the last number of the *Bulletin* I gave reasons for believing that he was an earlier writer than Vajhī, who in 1609 wrote the *maṣnavī* known as *Quṭb Mushtarī*, in which he related a story having this very monarch for hero. Only five years after Qulī Quṭb Shāh's death his works were collected by his nephew and successor. They have never been published, but the beautiful original MS. compiled under the orders of his nephew in 1616 is still in Ḥaidarābād. It consists of 1,800 pages and has perhaps 100,000 lines.

Though he lived so long ago his name is one of the greatest in Urdu. He shows wonderful human interest, for he writes of everyday matters, Hindu and Muḥammadan festivals, the customs of the country, life in his palace, the celebration of his birthday, and of natural objects such as fruit, vegetables, and flowers. The only poets who can be compared with him are Saudā and Naẓir, both of whom he excels in description of nature, while in his sympathetic account of Hindu life he is superior to all other Muḥammadan poets.

I have given here translations of three poems. The first is a charming little lyric, in which he tells of his affection for a nut-brown maid; the second was written on the occasion of his birthday. The third is a love poem rather more general than the first, but not nearly so conventional as most Urdu gazals. There is a directness about it which is very attractive. His Daknī poems were written under the name of Ma'ānī.

The words between brackets in the following text are suggested emendations where the text seems to me to be faulty.

NHANĪ SĀÕLĪ

1. *Nhanī sā̃valī par kiyā hū̃ naẕar*
   Khabar sab gā̃vākar huā be khabar.
2. *Tirā qadd sarv nikle jab chand sõ*
   Dasan [*disan*] *jot munj kū̃ disan jyū̃ qamar.*

3. *Pavan setī hat rākhī hai āp kamar*
   Sūraj cand naman jhamke vū zar kamar.
4. *Maĩ us nūr sõ lubdyā hũ kyā 'ajab*
   Do jag roshnī pāyā kis nē khabar ?
5. *Tū dūrī ḍarāve munje dūr the*
   Vū kyā būjhe mo dil mē hai tū nagar.
6. *Mă'āni ke bātã the jhaṛtā namak*
   Jī cākhe kahe hai namak sõ shakar.

(*Maḥbūb uz Zamān*, 759.)

Baras gãṭh

1. *Nabī kī du'ā the baras gãṭh pāyā*
   Khushyã kī khabar ke damāme bajāyā
2. *Piyā hũ maĩ Ḥaẓrat ke hat āb i kauṣar*
   Tū shāhã ŭpar mujh kalas kar banāyī.
3. *Merā quṭb tārā hai tāryã mē năjl* [*nājıl*]
   Tū mujh bar falak rang kā catr chāyā.
4. *Sūraj candr pī tāl hokar bajē tab*
   Manḍal ho falak ṭamṭamāyã bajāyā.
5. *Kare Mushtarī raqṣ muj bazm mē nıt*
   Baras gãṭh mē Zuhra kalyān gāyā.
6. *Merā gulistã tāza ıs te huā hai*
   Mujh ıs bāg the mevā damdam khılāyā.
7. *Dinde dushmanã kū so yak jā milākar*
   So ispand ke mātarã karnā cāhā.
8. *Khudāyā Ma'ānī kī ummed bar lyā*
   Ki jyũ sãt kī mehũ te jag sab akhāyā [*aghāyā*]
9. *Khudā kī raẓā sõ baras gãṭh āyā*
   Sahī shukr kar tũ baras gãṭh āyā.
10. *Du'ā e ımāmã the mujh rāj qāım*
    Khudā zindagānī kā pānī pilāyā.
11. *Gul i Muṣṭafā sete serā gundāyā*
    Mujh is gul kā serā ḥamail banāyā.

(*Maḥbūb uz Zamān*, p. 752.)

Piyā

1. *Piyā bāj pyālā piyā jāe nā*
   Piyā bāj yaktal jiyā jāe nā.
2. *Kahe the piyā bin ṣubūrī karũ*
   Kahyā jāe ammā kiyā jāe nā.

3. *Nahī̃ 'ishq jis voh baṛā kūr hai*
Kahī̃ us se mil baiseā jāe nā
4. *Quṭăb Shăh na de muj divāne ko pand*
Divāne ko kuc pand diyā jāe nā.

(*Urdu,* ii, 5, 22.)

The Little Dark Girl

From the Dīvān of Muḥammad Qulī Quṭb Shāh,
King of Golkuṇḍa 1580–1611

1. Mine eyes have seen a little girl's dark face
and have become forgetful of all else.
2. Thy cypress form comes out coquettishly
and lights appear to me like moon rays fair.
3. Swift as the wind her hands surround her waist,
that golden waist then shines like sun and moon.
4. No wonder that her radiance conquers me,
the light of earth and heaven : who knows it not ?
5. Thy absence drear affrights me from afar ;
how can she know her home is in my heart ?
6. Look, salt is dropping from Ma'āni's words,
but when one tastes, it is not salt, but sweet.

My Birthday

Muḥammad Qulī Quṭb Shāh, King of Golkuṇḍa

1. Through the prayer of the Prophet I've now reached my birthday
And beaten the drums sounding forth the good news.
2. I have drunk at the hand of Muḥammad sweet nectar ;
God therefore has made me the crown over kings.
3. The Pole star, my name star is nobler than all,
My canopy coloured expands in the sky.
4. The sun and the moon both are clashing like cymbals
With sky for arena and tambourines' sound.
5. There Jupiter dances to honour my birthday,
While Venus is chanting a victory song.
6. My garden is thus overflowing with freshness,
And furnishes fruit every hour of the day.
7. My enemies all in one place God has gathered
And wishes to burn them like incense in fire.

8. Fulfil, O my God, all my hope's expectation,
   As Thou gladdenest the earth with the soft rain of peace.
9. The favour of God has brought me my birthday,
   Give true thanks to Him for thy birthday now reached.
10. Through prayers of the priests my kingdom stands firmly,
   God gives me to drink of the water of life.
11. And weaving a garland of roses from Persia
   Has threaded the garland on me as the cord.

Life in a Love

By Muḥammad Qulī Quṭb Shāh, King of Golkuṇḍa

1. Without the loved one wine cannot be drunk,
   Nor without her one moment life be lived.
2. They said "Show patience absent from your love";
   This can be said, but surely not be done.
3. The man who knows not love is merciless,
   Never with such a one hold speech or sit.
4. I am distracted, give me no advice,
   Never to such as I is counsel given.

Notes

The royal author's fondness for indigenous words should be observed.

Nhanī Sāōlī

1. *nhanī*, U. *nannhī* : *gā̃vākar*, losing.
3. *naman*, like : *vū*, U. *voh* : *quṭb tārā*, a play on his own name.
4. *lubdyā*, connected with *lubdh* ; *nẽ*, U. *nahī̃*.
5. *tū*, U. *terā, terī*.

Barasgā̃ṭh, in later U. *sālgira*

3. *najl*, an obvious mistake. I suggest *nājil*.
7. *ispand* seeds were burnt as incense to drive off evil spirits.
8. *sā̃t* for *shānti*.
9. *sahī*, U. *ṣaḥīḥ*.
11. *gul i Muṣṭafā*, for *gul i Muḥammadī*, the ordinary Persian rose. *sete* for *setī* ; *serā* for *sihrā*.

Piyā. p. 203, line 1, *kūr*, Hindi, not Persian,

Early Hindi and Urdu Poetry

Pen Pictures by Banārsī Dās and Zaṭallī

BANĀRSĪ DĀS of Jaunpūr belonged to the Jain community and was born in 1586. The following charming extracts are taken from his most famous work, *Arddh Kathānak,* an autobiography completed in 1641.

His wonderful power of word painting is exemplified in these passages. The first describes the commotion in Jaunpūr when the news of Akbar's death was received in 1605. We feel the spell of the description, and tremble with the frightened populace. This picture should be compared with Zaṭallī's account of the turmoil after the death of Aurangzeb. (See below.)

The second tells of the Black Death, bubonic plague, in Agra during 1616, the first time the city was visited by that pestilence. Anyone who has been in India during a plague epidemic will realize the force of his words, the rats dying, the spread of the disease among the people, the glandular swellings, the sudden deaths, the mortality among the physicians, the despair and flight of the townsfolk afraid even to partake of food.

The third relates an experience of the author, when he and his friends were caught in torrential rain, the street doors were shut, no one would ask them in, and the caravanserai was full. One woman was prepared to take pity on them, but her husband sternly refused them.

I. The Death of Akbar, 1605

1. *Is hī bīc nagar mẽ sor*
2. *Bhayo udangal cārihu or*
3. *Ghar ghar dar dar diye kapāṭ*
4. *Haṭvānī nahī̃ baiṭhẽ hāṭ*
5. *Bhale bastr aru bhūṣan bhale*
6. *Te sab gāṛe dhartī tale.*
7. *Ghar ghar sabani visāhe sastr*
8. *Logan pahire moṭe bastr.*
9. *Ṭhāṛhau kambal athvā khes*
10. *Nārin pahire moṭe bes.*
11. *Ūc nīc koū na pahicān*

12. *Dhanī daridrī bhaye samān.*
13. *Corī dhārī disai kahū̃ nāhī̃*
14. *Yõhī̃ apabhay log ḍarāhī̃.*

KAVITĀ KAUMUDĪ, 36

II. PLAGUE IN AGRA, 1616

1. *Is hī samay iti bistarī, parī Āgre pahilī marī*
2. *Jahā̃ tahā̃ sab bhāge log pargaṭ bhayā gā̃ṭh kā rog.*
3. *Nikasai gā̃ṭhi marai chin māhī̃, kāhū kī basā̃y kachu nāhī̃ ;*
4. *Cūhe maraī̃ vaidya mari jāhī̃, bhay so lõg ann nahī̃ khāhī̃.*

Id., 35

III. THE RAIN

1. *Phirat phirat phāvā bhaye, baiṭho kahai na koi ;*
2. *Talai kī̃c sõ pag bhare, ūpar barsat toi.*
3. *Andhkār rajnī viṣaī̃ himritu agahan mās*
4. *Nāri ek baiṭhan kahyo, puruṣ uṭhyo lai bā̃s.*

Id., 36

I. THE DEATH OF AKBAR

(*The news of Akbar's death comes to Jaunpūr*)

1. A cry was heard throughout the town :
2. On every side a tumult rose,
3. In every house the doors were locked.
4. No more sat traders in their shops,
5. But garments fine and jewels fine
6. Were buried all beneath the earth.
7. In every house they brought out arms ;
8. Rough were the garments they put on.
9. Men stood in blanket or in shawl ;
10. Women were clad in raiment coarse.
11. Twixt high and low, was difference none.
12. For rich and poor were now the same.
13. Though theft and robbery were not seen,
14. Through causeless fear men were afraid.

II. PLAGUE IN ĀGRA

1. Then spread distress around, plague first on Agra fell.
2. The folk fled forth all ways (the gland-disease had come).
3. The swellings rise, the stricken people helpless die.
4. First rats, then doctors die ; through fear the people fast.

III. The Rain

1. Walking, walking, worn and weary ; none invites to sit ;
2. Feet are clothed with mud beneath, overhead the rain descends :
3. In the murkiest night of winter season's black November ;
4. " Pray be seated " said one woman, but her man rose with a staff.

The word *ṭhāṛhau* in I, 9, means standing. It is used in the Simla hills to-day in the form *ṭhāṛhū* for a kind of servant, a man who brings wood or water for travellers, and does other unskilled menial jobs.

III, 1, *phāvā* is hard to understand. I connect it with Panjabi *phā̃vā̃* " weary ".

The Death of Aurangzeb by Mīr Ja'far Zaṭallī 1659–1713

This poem describing the state of things which prevailed after Aurangzeb's death, should be compared with Banārsī Dās's Braj poem written nearly seventy years earlier, in which he tells of the excitement produced among the people of Agra by the receipt of the news of Akbar's death in 1605.

Zaṭallī was a notorious satirist and jester, sparing no one except the Emperor. Even the princes were not immune. He seems to have had a great respect for Aurangzeb. It is said, but without complete proof, that he was executed by orders of Farrukh Siyar.

The Death of Aurangzeb

1. *Kahā̃ ab pāiye aisā Shahanshāh*
2. *Mukammal akmal va kāmil dil āgāh ?*
3. *Rakat ke ā̃sūõ jag rotā hai*
4. *Na mīṭhī nī̃d koī sotā hai.*
5. *Ṣadā ẽ top o bandūq ast har sū*
6. *Basar asbāb o bandūq ast har sū*
7. *Davādav har ṭaraf bhāg paṛī hai*
8. *Bacca dar god sar khaṭyā dharī hai.*
9. *Kaṭākaṭṭ o laṭālaṭ hast har sū*
10. *Jhaṭā jhaṭṭ o phaṭāphaṭ hast har sū*
11. *Bahar sū mār mār o dhāṛ dhāṛ ast*
12. *Ocalcāl o tabar khanjar kaṭār ast*
13. *Az ā̃ A'ẓam vazī̃ sūe Mu'aẓẓam*
14. *Jhaṛā jhaṛṛ o dhaṛādhaṛ har do pāyam*
15. *Bibīnam tā Khudā az kīst rāẓī*
16. *Bikhrānad khuṭba bar nām kih qāẓī.*

Panjāb mẽ Urdū.

1. Where shall we find so excellent a king,
2. Complete, consummate, perfect, knowing hearts ?
3. The world is weeping tears of blood,
4. And gentle sleep to no one comes.
5. On all sides noise of cannon and of gun
6. Men carrying goods and guns upon their heads.
7. And fleeing here and there on every side,
8. Beds on their heads, and children in their arms.
9. Cutting and smiting on all sides,
10. Wrenching and splitting on all sides,
11. On all sides death and violence.
12. Turmoil, axes, daggers, poniards.
13. That side A'ẕam, this Mu'aẕẕam,
14. Fighting, struggling, both I find,
15. But let me see whom God approves,
16. For whom the priest on Fridays prays.

The last four lines refer to the internecine war between Aurangzeb's sons A'ẕam and Mu'aẕẕam. The author wonders whom God will favour and who as Emperor will be mentioned in the Friday prayers. It was Mu'aẕẕam who was successful and came to the throne. He is known to history as Bahādur Shāh.

l. 15 may have two meanings : (1) whom God makes King, and (2) whom God takes to Himself ; in other words who is defeated and dies. In the first case it is parallel to line 16, in the second case 16 is the reverse of 15, the meaning being " let me see which is defeated, and which becomes Emperor ". l. 16 refers to the fact that the ruling sovereign is prayed for in the Friday prayers.

The author freely uses Persian words ; the second, fifth, sixth, thirteenth, fifteenth, and sixteenth lines are pure Persian.

l. 9, *laṭālaṭ* might be read *luṭāluṭ* " robbery ".

l. 12, *ocalcāl* is probably for *calācal* or *calcalāo.*

In l. 14 the *ṛ* of *jhaṛ* is doubled for metrical reasons. This is specially interesting because it is not possible to pronounce a double *ṛ*, and it looks as if the author was satisfied so long as his eye saw a double *ṛ*, even though his tongue could not say it.

For double *ṛ* compare the following sentence from *Mirā̃ Jī Khudānumā, c.* A.D. 1600, quoted in Urdu, April, 1928, p. 158, *e sab Qur'ān kā chiṛṛācā ḍeke vale maġz nahī̃ cākhe,* these all see the husk of the Qur'ān, but do not taste the marrow.

I. "A VISION OF DEATH." BY AḤMAD

THE following beautiful poem was found in a MS. notebook dated 1748. The date of the poem is unknown, but it must be older than the MS. We may put it provisionally at 1650–1700. The author's name occurs in the last couplet. Nothing is known about him, and there are many poets of the name.

١ چون شب گذشت صبح چرهی تب سمجه پری
٢ جاگن نه هوا ایک گهری تب سمجه پری
٣ جب مرگ کا پیاله پیا آنکهه کهل گیٔ
٤ جب کهاٹ پر چودیه دهری تب سمجه پری
٥ توشک نهالیون سے مجهے فکر نه هوا
٦ جب ایٹ زیر سیس دهری تب سمجه پری
٧ جس وقت یار چهود چلے هم رهے نکو
٨ منکر نکیر پوچهه دهری تب سمجه پری
٩ حساب کا جو وقت هوا آنکهه کهل گیٔ
١٠ چیتهی عمل کی آپ پرهی تب سمجه پری
١١ عمرا تمام گزر گیٔ عمل نه هوا
١٢ جب عمر کی دوپہر دهلی تب سمجه پری
١٣ احمد کون طرف کوی نهین جز خدا رسول
١٤ جب فضل پر امید دهری تب سمجه پری

1. When passed the night and came the day, 'twas then I understood.
2. Ere I had been one hour awake, ah then I understood.
3. When I had drunk the cup of death, my eyes were opened then ;
4. When on the bier my corpse they placed, 'twas then I understood.
5. I nothing recked of covering quilt or cloth,

6. When 'neath my head the stone they placed, 'twas then I understood.
7. What time my friends left me and went, how foolish I remained ;
8. Munkir, Nakīr both questioned me, 'twas then I understood.
9. When came the time of my account, my eyes were opened then ;
10. I read the statement of my works ; 'twas then I understood.
11. My life was spent, the whole of it, no work had I to show ;
12. When passed the noonday of my life 'twas then I understood.
13. Save God and the apostle now on Aḥmad's side was none ;
14. But when I trusted grace divine, 'twas then I understood.

The poem contains no cerebral letters except *ḍ* in *choḍ*, l. 7. This *ḍ* is probably not original. We find *carhī* "ascended", *parī* "fell", *gharī* "hour", *khāt* "bed", *īt* "brick", *cīthī* "letter", *parhī* "read", *dhalī* "descended".

Peculiarities for metrical reasons are *huvvā* for *huā*, l. 2 ; *ḥissāb* for *ḥisāb*, l. 9 ; *'umrā* for *'umr*, l. 11.

In l. 4, *codiya* is doubtful. I read it as *co deh*, though in this case *co* is tautological. The sense appears to require a word for corpse. Or is it *caudīa*, a style of sitting ?

l. 6, stone ; lit. brick.

l. 7, *nakū* is difficult. In Daknī the word would mean "not", which hardly gives sense, and the poem is not Daknī. I am taking it as for نکوی

l. 13, If we retain *ku* we must take *ṭaraf* as "helper", "supporter".

II. Onomatopoetic Lines from Giridhar Dās

The following extract is taken from Narsīh Kathāmrit (Nṛsīh Kathāmṛt), a poem by Gopāl Candr, known as Giridhar Dās, 1833–60. He was the worthy father of a famous son. Hariś Candr, his son, 1850–85, is one of the most famous Hindi poets, certainly the most famous in the last 200 years. The lines convey the impression of deafening noise and blinding light. They are a good test of ability to pronounce *ṛ* smoothly and easily.

1. भयो भयंकर शब्द महान गगड़ गड़ गड़ड़ड़ ।
2. फट्यो खंभ द्वै खंड कराल ककड़ कड़ कड़ड़ड़ ॥
3. बढ़्यो कोटि रवि तेज झमक्कि झझड़ झड़ झड़ड़ड़ ।
4. भगे दनुजगन देखि सरूप सड़ड़ सड़ सड़ड़ड़ ॥
5. भड़ भड़ड़ भड़ड़ परवत गिरहिं हड़ड़ हड़ड़ हाली धरनि ।
6. चहि कमठ कोल करि थरथरे भए तेज तें हत तरनि ॥

1. There came a great and awful sound—*gagaṛa gara gaṛaṛaṛa*.
2. The pillar split in two huge parts—*kakaṛa kaṛa kaṛaṛaṛa*.
3. The glory grew and flashed like suns a hundred thousand—*jhajaṛa jhaṛa jhaṛaṛaṛa*.
4. The demons fled on seeing the sight—*saṛaṛa saṛa saṛaṛaṛa*.
5. *bhaṛa bhaṛaṛa bhaṛaṛa* fall the mountains ; *haṛaṛa haṛaṛa* shakes the earth.
6. Trembled the serpent, tortoise, boar, and elephant ; the sun lost his glory.

It is difficult to convey by sound the ideas of splendour and refulgence, but the word *jhamak* contains those ideas. It occurs in the verb *jhamakki*, l. 3, and the *jh* is repeated four times in the rest of the line. Perhaps one might say that the sounds represented by the letters suggest both noise and dazzling light.

In the line telling of the flight of the demons, we should have expected more sibilants, but evidently Giridhar wished to emphasize the crashing of their departure rather than the swishing and rustling that accompanied it.

A Brief Grammar of the Kanauri Language.

Introduction.

The country of Kanaur is called by its inhabitants *Kănōriṅ*, a man of the country is *kănōrös*, fem. *kănōrē*. The language is *kănōriṅ skad'*, Kanauri speech, or *kănōrĕanŭ skad'*, the speech of the Kanauris. The Kōcī speaking people of lower Bashahr nickname the language *Minchāṇ*. As the words *kănōriṅ skad'* have a somewhat unfamiliar appearance and sound, I have given to the language the more usual name Kanauri, the name which is used by all non-Kanauri people in the state and is more or less familiar all over the Panjab. Kanauris themselves call their language *kanauri* when they are speaking Hĭndī or Kōcī. Kōcī is the generic name given to every Aryan dialect spoken in Bashahr State.

The county of Kanaur lies in Bashahr State, which has an area of 3800 sq. miles and a population of 84 000. The Kanauris themselves number nearly 20 000.

Few languages have their limits defined with such mathematical precision as Kanauri. It begins abruptly at mile 92 on the Hindustan Tibet road just over 20 miles from Rampur, the capital of the state, and continues up the Satlaj River to past mile 192. It is therefore spoken in the Satlaj Valley or sub-valleys for a distance (measured along the road) of one hundred miles.

There are in all four dialects, I. *Kanauri proper*, spoken from mile 92 to mile 162, i. e. from two miles beyond Sărāhăṇ to Jāṅgī. Between mile 92 and Tărăṇḍā, which is at mile 104, it is spoken only on the south side of the river.

II. *Lower Kanauri* spoken between miles 92 and 104 on the north side of the river. This dialect does not greatly differ from Kanauri proper. It uses more Kōcī words, but is in its grammar wholly Tibeto-Himalayan.

III. *Thĕbör skad'*, spoken in the villages of Lĭppā, Āsraṅ, Lābrăṅ, Kāṇăm, S̱hŭnnăm and Shāsō. This dialect I have not had an opportunity of studying. Kanauris living within ten miles of when it begins to be spoken say that they cannot understand more than half of it. Further up the Satlaj than the Thĕbörskad‘ area we come to the Nyamskad‘ dialect of Tibetan.

IV. A dialect spoken in the Baspa valley in two villages called Chhĭtkhŭl or Răkshăm. I have a few notes on this dialect. It certainly is a Kanauri dialect, but differs considerably from Kanauri proper and is not understood at all by ordinary Kanauris.

Roughly speaking we may say that Kanauri proper is spoken between long. 77° 53′ and long. 78° 30′ east of Greenwich and between lat. 30° 23′ and lat. 30° 39′ north.

Into the philological problems connected with Kanauri this Grammar does not attempt to enter. They have been ably treated by Dr. Sten Konow in the Zeitschrift, Vol. 59, p. 117 ff. and more fully in the Linguistic Survey of India Vol. III, part. 1. Dr. Sten Konow shows that Kanauri belongs to the pronominalised group of Tibeto-Himalayan languages, and has many points of affinity with the Muṇḍa languages. All that I have attempted is, working at first hand, to give the Grammar correctly and to explain the pronunciation with the greatest possible care. I trust that these notes will anew draw the attention of philologists to this fascinating speech.

In this Introduction the placenames have been given their more common Kōcī pronunciation.

Pronunciation.

The pronunciation of Kanauri is exceptionally difficult. It is worth while to go into it carefully. There are 23 clearly distinguished vowelsounds, to which there may be added two or three less clearly marked

Vowel sounds. In these notes *a* is used for the following sounds, *ā*, long, like *a* in Italian *trovare*.

a, the same vowel but considerably shorter.

ă, the sound of *a* in America, *u* in *fun*.

e is generally like French *é*, but has various lengths.

ē is long.

e is the same vowel shortened.

ĕ is very short and is a wider vowel than the above, rather like *e* in *pet*.

e followed by *ñ* is extremely narrow, as in *keñ*, give.

There are three sounds represented by *i*, all narrow.

ı long, as in Italian Lina, but longer.

i same vowel, shorter.

ĭ same vowel, very short.

The sounds for which I have used *o* are somewhat complicated.

ō is long narrow Italian *o*.

o the same but shorter. This is sometimes longer and sometimes shorter, and one is tempted to what would probably be an over refinement, the differentiation of two medium *o s*.

ŏ is a diphthongal sound, composed of *o* and very short *ö*, the two pronounced very rapidly as one sound *oö*. Thus *dŏk'ts* = *doök'ts*.

ō above the line, English *aw* in *awe*.

ŏ above the line is the *o* of English *hot*. The length of this is not quite invariable, but it is generally very short.

ö is used for a very short sound of the type of German *ö*, but short and inclining towards the narrower sound of German *ü*:

ȫ is the German *ö*. This sound is somewhat rare.

The *u*'s are

ū long like *oo* in *school*. Rarely this tends to get narrowed slightly towards *ü* as in *shū* a god.

u, same vowel, but shorter.

ŭ a slightly wider vowel, short, like *u* in English *bull*, but not so wide as the English *u*.

ü like German *ü*, very short, but not so narrow, *dumghyür*, kind of temple, *pül(h)* feather, *mül(h)* silver.

Sometimes one hears a *ŭ* which seems almost between *ŭ* and *ü*, as in *zgyŭl* lichen, *pyŭd* woof. Here the *u* resembles a rapid combination of *ŭ* and *ü*, thus *zgyŭül*, the two being very rapidly enunciated. So also *yŭnnig'* go and *yŭnnig'* grind corn. I am not sure that this is really a distinct sound, and as it does not occur in the Grammar no special symbol is needed for it.

ai like *a* in *man*.

au diphthong, slightly different from *ō*. It is in fact a combination of *ŏ* and *ŭ*. *ŏu*.

One feels almost inclined to make an exaggerated generalisation and to say that the normal vowel in Kanauri is half-long, *a*, *e*, *i*, *o*, *u*, and that short and long vowels are exceptional. It is noticeable that in very many loan words the reverse is the case, we have *phŏrk* = *farq*, difference, *băr̄ăbăr*, always. The whole difficulty is greatly enhanced by the fact that the length of the vowels is not always the same.

The greatest difficulty in Kanauri pronunciation is found in connection with the half-uttered *g'* or *k'* as found at the end of a syllable and especially at the end of a word. This letter occurs in all infinitives, *-mig'*, in the first person sing. of all verbal tenses and in a number of ordinary words. I have represented it by *g'*, it might almost equally well be represented by *k'*. When a word like *gŏrmig'* is rapidly enunciated, the final letter sounds like a half uttered *k*, if a very slight emphasis is placed upon it it sounds like *gk'* both letters half uttered, the sound bearing a resemblance to the sound emitted by a German imperfectly acquainted with English, in saying the word *big*. If the syllable be emphasised it becomes *g*. When followed by a sonant it is *g*, when followed by a surd it is *k*, before a vowel it is generally *g*. Thus *reg'*, a kind of tree,

Genitive *regŭ*; *ag‘*, cave, Genitive *agŭ*. Sometimes at the end of a word, preceded by *n*, it becomes *kh*, as *ma lŭnkh, ma ŭnkh,* negative Future of *lŭnmig‘* and *ŭnmig‘*.

I once had a few minutes conversation with a Kanaura man who knew a little Urdu. He stated that in the Infinitive the letter was a *g*, *lŭnmig‘*, but in the Future and Past a *k*, *lŭntok‘*, *lănak‘*. I am not quite convinced, however, that he was not making a difference where none exists.

There is a tendency in Kanauri with other consonants also to leave them half pronounced at the end of syllables, as, e. g. *d* in Imperatives *shĕd‘*, *pŏrĕd‘*.

Verbal roots ending with a sonant generally change it to a surd before another surd; thus

cŏṅmig‘, drip, √ *cŏg*, Past *cŏkshid*.

kammig‘, pierce, √ *kab*, *kapcimig‘* pierce me or you.

Many words ending in a vowel have that vowel closed by a sharp jerk like that which closes words ending in *-g‘*. I have indicated this jerk by the sign ‘. Many examples will be seen in the following grammar, e. g. *tō‘*, *dū‘*, he is, *toke‘*, *dūe‘*, he was, *ka‘*, thou, *niñā‘*, we.

l is generally as in English, but at the end of an accented syllable it tends to become very dental, being pronounced with the tongue against the teeth. This give it almost an aspirated sound. *pül(h)*, feather; *mül(h)*, silver.

n is like English *n*, but at the end of accented syllables a little more dental. Between two vowels *n* tends to become cerebral, but even when cerebralised is less cerebral than the Hindi *ṇ*.

ranmig‘, give, Imve. *raṇiñ*, *raṇic*, Past *raṇŏg‘*.

lănmig, do, Past *laṇŏg‘*.

neg‘, I shall know, *nĭ‘*, it will be, neg. *ma ṇeg‘*, *ma ṇī*.

ñ is the *gn* in Italian *signor*, at the end of an accented syllable very dental, *keñ* give.

ṅ is English *ng* in *singing*. I noticed one or two lightly pronounced *ṅs*, the word for horse is *rŏṅ*, quite distinct from *rŏṅ* mountain.

ch is sometimes more cerebral than in Hindi, e. g. *chū* when *ch* is pronounced rather for back in the mouth.

˜ denotes the nasalisation of a vowel.

A noteworthy tendency is that of prefixing *s* and *z* (occasionally *sh* and *zh*) to words beginning with surds and sonants respectively, especially *p*, *b*, *k*, *g*.

Thus, *zbīọdū‘* for *bīodū‘*, he is going, *skrapshimig‘* for *krapshimig‘*, weep together, mourn. I have indicated this by putting the *s* or *z* in brackets.

Surds at the end of a word are sometimes aspirated; thus,

rŏṭh, native loaf; plural *rŏṭe*.

sŭṭh, bug; plural *sŭṭe*.

All consonants not mentioned above are pronounced as in Hindi.

Dialectic differences. We must always bear in mind the presence of purely dialectic variations, thus Infinitives in *nmig‘* and *nnig‘*, Futures in *-ög‘*, *-ăg‘*, *-ŏg‘*, Pasts in *-ög‘*, *-ag‘*, *-āg‘*; *tocē*, for *toke‘*, *lantŏsh* for *lantish*, *dē‘* for *dūe‘*, represent mere differences of dialect, and all may be regarded as correct.

Noun. Number. The noun has two numbers, singular and plural. There are no special forms for the dual.

Gender. There is no grammatical gender. Sex is indicated by different words and occasionally by different endings.

zāzeā, eater (male), *zāzē*, eater (female).
toṅtseā, striker (male), *toṅtsē*, striker (female).

kyō or *skyō* prefixed to a word denotes a male, *mönth* denotes a female. Thus *kyō pyā*, male bird, *mönth pyā*, female bird.

Case. The cases will be seen from the paradigms. The accusative is generally the same as the nominative, occasionally the same as the dative. Nouns ending in a vowel generally add *-gā* to the nom. plural. The ablative ending seems to be *-kts* (or *kc*), and is generally used simply with inanimate objects, for animate objects it is joined to the preposition *doā‘* and used in the form *dŏk‘ts.*

Agent. There is a certain amount of freedom in the use of the agent case. The common rule seems to be that for Intransitive verbs it is not used: for Transitive verbs.

Nouns which are the subject of Transitive verbs are in the agent case for all tenses.

First and second personal pronouns are in the nominative case. Pronouns of the third person are in the agent case for Past tenses, otherwise they are in the nominative.

This rule is not strictly adhered to, and we find agentive forms for first or second personal pronouns.

ts is often added to a noun to give a diminutive sense as *chaṅ*, son, boy, *chaṅts*, little boy.

Pronouns. The pronouns show a great complexity of form. In the second and third persons there are respectful forms, and all three persons have a dual. In the first personal pronoun there are exclusive and inclusive forms for both the dual and the plural, indicating the exclusion or inclusion of the person spoken to. Thus — we two shall dine at eight, if said to a friend would involve the pronoun *kāshöṅ*, thou and I, but if said to a servant *nishi*, he and I, to avoid the servant's considering himself invited.

Relative. There is no proper relative, but in its place are employed interrogative forms, or forms ending in *-aṅa*, (-ever), as *hūtiaṅa*, whosoever, *thödiaṅa*, whatsoever.

Verb. The verbal forms are very complex, and in some respects very full. Thus every ordinary tense has a polite form for the second and third singular, and dual forms for the first and second persons. The ordinary plural forms are used for the dual of the third person. The first person has exclusive or inclusive forms for the dual and plural.

The verb substantive has two bases *tog'* and *dūg'*. In addition to the forms mentioned below under Conjugation the following should be noted.

There is an indeclinable Present Tense formed by adding *-ts* to the root (roots in *n* frequently dropping the *n*), thus *lŏts*, they say, I say &c. from *lŏnmig'*, *niñā' lŏts*, we say.

māĕts is not, are not, there is not, from the negative *ma* (see below under Negative).

There is a Past in *gyō* or *kyō*, this ending being added to the root. After sonants (including *m*, *n*, *l*) the ending is *gyo*, after surds and vowels it is *kyo*, after *r* both are found. Both transitive or intransitive verbs have this ending.

lăngyō, did, from *lănnig'*, *bĭkyō*, went, from *bĭmig'*,
böngyō, came, from *bŭnnig'*, *cĭkyō*, washed, from *cĭmig'*.

I cannot explain this ending.

A peculiarity about the indeclinable past in *-shid* is worth noting. When it is used with the verb substantive *dūg'*, *dūeg'*, (present and past), the latter is regularly declined both in the present and in the past; thus, *toñshid dūg'*, *dūn*, *dūeg' dūen*, &c. I have, thou hast, I had, thou hadst beaten.

When, however, the verb substantive of the form *tog'*, *tokeg'*, is employed, the nominative is always of the first person, but the verb remains indeclinable in the third person; thus *toñshid to'*, *tokē'*. I have, I had beaten.

The letter *sh*, sometimes with a euphonic *i*, is inserted after the root to express a reflexive or mutual or even passive sense; thus

krammig, (√ *krab*) cry, *krapshimig'* or *skrapshimig'*, cry together (perhaps falling on each other necks).
toñmig', strike, *toñshimig'*, strike oneself or one another.
sarmig', raise, *sarshimig'*, rise (cf. Italian *levarsi*).
zāmig', eat, *zāshimig'*, be eaten.

The letter *c* similarly inserted after the root indicates an object of the first or second person.

tāmig, place, *tācimig'*, place me, us, you &c.
gö shĕcodūg', I am sending you (from *shĕnmig'*, send).
ka' shĕco-dūn, thou art sending me, us.
lañcish tosh, (he, respectful) is waiting for me, us, thee, you.
lancish nītish, will (probably) be waiting for me, us, thee, you.
gö toñcog', *ka' thū toñcon*, I will beat thee, why wilt thou beat me?

The pronouns may also be expressed. There is no form for a third personal object.

Transitive, intransitive. A transitive or intransitive sense is frequently expressed by special verbs, e. g. *shĕnmig'* with verbal noun or conjunctive participle often expresses a transitive or causative sense, as *pö pö shĕnmig‘*, cause to arrive, from *pönnig‘*, arrive, and *hacimig*, become, or some other verb, expresses an intransitive sense.

Often entirely different verbs are used. Not infrequently, however, the only difference is that transitive verbs have an initial surd, while intransitive verbs have the corresponding sonant.

byaṅmig‘, fear, *(s)pyaṅmig‘*, frighten.
dŏnmig‘, go or come out, *tŏnmig‘*, put out.
barmig‘, burst (intr.), *pharmig‘*, burst (tr.).
boṅmig‘, burn (intr.), *poṅmig‘*, burn (tr.).

Of the verbs *kēmig‘* and *ranmig‘*, both meaning ‘give‘, *kēmig‘* is used when the indirect object is of the first or second person, and *ranmig‘* when it is of the third.

gös ranshids, I gave (him &c.).
nŭks kerō‘, he gave (me, you &c.).
aṅ bayās kinŭ ketō‘, my brother will give you.

This rule is not always observed. Thus Ṭīkā Rām has *dŏpŏṅ gö aṇesi khau ketög‘* I will give him food. I have verified this.

Interrogative. The letter *a* is often added to a verb, and sometimes to other parts of speech to indicate a question. Thus with the verb substantive we notice such forms as these, *tona, toña, to‘a, toca, tosha*, and with other verbs *zātona*, wilt thou eat? *toṅaca*, will yout wo strike?

Negative. For the Imperative the negative is *tha*, for all other tenses *ma*. The Future is very often contracted when used along with *ma*. This is occasionally true of other tenses. It should be noticed that this contraction, while a little puzzling, is not nearly so bewildering as in the cognate language Lāhuḷī.

Examples of contraction.

ma toṅg, I will not strike, Fut. *toṅtög‘*.
ma rŏg, I will not cause to graze, Fut. *rŏgtög‘*.
ma pŏrĕăg‘, I will not be obtained, Fut. *pŏrĕătög‘*.
ma dōreg‘, I will not run, Fut. *dōreătög‘*.
ma pög, I will not arrive, Fut. *pötög‘*.

The verb substantive *tog‘*, *tokeg‘* is contracted to *maig‘* (*main, maiñ, mai‘*, regular) and *maī keg‘* (*maī ken, maī keñ, maī kē‘*, &c. regular).

In these words the *a* and *i* are separately pronounced.

As *n* between two vowels tends to become cerebralised, we have forms like

ma ṇeg‘, I do not know, Fut. *nētög‘*.
ma ṇī, there is not, Fut. *nītög‘*.

The **Verbal noun** is formed by adding *-im* or *-am* to a root ending in a consonant, and *-m* to one ending in a vowel. This is the form used in compound verbs, see below.

Sometimes *-mō* or *-mo* is added to the root, especially when the verbal noun is nominative to a verb, as *tŭṅmō zărūr maṇī* it is not necessary to eat, *bīmo om maīkē‘*, going formerly not was, one had not to go formerly; *rēnno tèār tĕsh*, (the sun) is ready to set, *kan* or *kanmo biō‘*, he went to bring.

Loanwords. There are a great many Hindī loanwords. Nouns are often taken over with a mere addition of *öṅ*, as *kāmöṅ*, Hindi *kām*, work, *bātöṅ*, H. *bāt*, matter &c., or *ös*, *cōrös*, H. *cōr*, thief; or *-iṅ* as *pēṭṭiṅ*, H. *pēṭ* stomach.

We find them among adverbs, *bărābăr*, *hămēsh*, and *sᵘda*, all meaning 'always', *bāerăṅ*, outside, *dör*, far, closely resemble H. *bărābăr*, *hămēshă*, *sădā*, *bāhăr*, *dūr*. With *hŭn*, *hŭnā‘* now, and *nēröṅ*, near, compare Panjabi *hŭṇ*, *hŭṇē*, *nēṛē*.

In Verbs they are adapted and then conjugated like regular Kanaurī words. The following will be found conjugated in the lists below.

pŏrĕnnig‘, be obtained, H. *păṛnā*.
pōtshĕnnig‘, arrive, H. *păhŭncnā*.
zītĕnmig‘, win, H. *jītnā*.
hārĕnmig‘, be defeated, H. *hārnā*.
dōrĕnmig‘, run, H. *dauṛnā*.

Compound Verbs. *Wish to, be able to, permit to, learn to* are expressed by means of the verbal noun.

Wish, *gyāmig‘*.

gö bīm mă gyāg‘, I do not wish to go.

kī zām mă gyau dēñ (contracted from *dūyeñ*), you were not wishing to eat.

gö bīm mă gyāgyā tokeg‘, *hŭn bīm gyātög‘*, I had not wished to go, now I wish to go.

tŭṅăm gyāts dūyeg‘, I was wishing to drink.

Be able, *sŏkyĕnnig‘*, loan word from Hindī (*săknā*).

gö cēm ma sŏkĕā‘ (pronounced almost *maskĕā‘*), I cannot write.

gö cēm sŏkĕā‘ tō‘, I can write.

gö pēlĕ cēm mă sŏkĕā‘, *hŭnă sŏkĕā‘ tō‘*, formerly I could not write, now I can.

rī‘ gö bun mă sŏkyĕdā‘, the day before yesterday I could not come.

It is noticeable that the word for *can* or *could* seems invariable. *sŏkĕā‘*, *sŏkĕā‘ tō‘*, *sŏkyĕdā‘*, all have the form of the 3rd sing.

Permit, *shĕnnig‘*, (lit. send).

The verbal noun is used with the required tense of *shĕnnig‘*.

bīm shĕnnig‘, permit to go.

tŭṅam or *zām* or *bun shĕnnig‘*, permit to drink or eat or come.

dŏk‘ts sūra rŏgim shedā‘, he sent him to feed swine, might mean, he allowed him to feed swine.

gasā cīm shedā‘, he sent or allowed to wash clothes.

Learn, *hushimig‘*.

gö cem hushög‘, I shall learn to write.

Necessity is expressed by the Infinitive with the verb substantive, and also by *gyāmig‘*. (See under *advisability*.)

gö bīmig‘ tō‘, I have to go; cf. Hindi *mŭjhē jānā hai.*

dogos ṭhö zāmig‘, what are they to eat?

Advisability or *duty* is rendered by the Infinitive of *gyāmig‘*, wish, with the verbal noun or ordinary infinitive.

bīm gyāmig‘, one should go or will have to go.

kinu zām or *zāmig‘ gyāmig‘*, you should eat.

kinu tŏṅăm or *tŏṅmig gyāmig‘*, you should beat.

aŭ banḍau gyamig‘ tō‘, to me a servant is advisable or necessary, I need a servant.

cōrös mă lăn gyāmig‘, it is not right to do stealing (to steal).

Conditional Clauses. The protasis appears to be always the root of the verb with *ma* affixed. The apodosis varies according to the sense. For the past conditional apodosis the Infinitive with the past of the verb substantive is generally used.

do bönma taṅma paisa pŏrĕnnig duē‘, he come-if, then paisa to-be-obtained was, if he had come, then he would have obtained a pice.

dō zāma ṭŏnmig‘ duē‘, he eat-if, become-ill was; if he had eaten, he would have become ill.

do bönma gö roṭe ranmig‘ dūyeg‘, if he had come I should have given him loaves.

do bönma gö roṭe rantög‘, if he comes I shall give him loaves.

hăth bĭnma, if anyone comes (who come-if).

the batöṅ nīma lī, what matter become-if even, whatever may happen.

ma ṇīma, not become-if, if it be not so, i. e. otherwise (*n* becoming *ṇ* between two vowel).

The Conjugation of the Verb. What may be called the root of the verb is found by dropping the *-mig‘* of the Infinitive.

Infinitive. The Infinitive ends in *-mig‘*. When the root ends in *n* the Infinitive has both *-nig‘* and *-mig‘*, i. e. the *m* may at pleasure be assimilated to the preceding *n*.

Verbal noun see page 667.

Future. The future is formed by adding *-tög‘* to the root. Verbs whose root ends in *-ci* or *-shi*, whether this ending is a pronominal suffix or not, form the Future by changing *ci* or *shi* to *cög* or *shög*. The ending *-ög‘* is sometimes dialectically varied to *-og‘* or *-ag‘*.

Imperative. The Imperative is generally the root. Rootsending in *ī* or *ē* or *ā* are sometimes euphonically changed, as *bīh* or *bīōh* or *bīūh* from *bīmig‘*, go; *ciū* from *cīmig*, wash; *gyau* from *gyāmig‘*, wish.

Three other forms of the Imperative are found; one adds to the root *rā‘*, which is declined. This form seems to be used when immediate compliance with the order is not necessary. What this

-rā‘ is I do not know; can it be connected with *ranmig‘*, give, as in Hindi *chŏrdē*, leave, *banādē*, make, where *de* is from *denā*, give?

Another adds *dā‘* instead of *rā‘*. The special sense of *dā‘* seems obscure. A few verbs have both *rā‘* and *dā‘* forms, as *hacimig‘*, become; *ranmig*, give; *unmig‘*, take; *lanmig*, do; *gyālmig‘*, win, but in most verbs only the *rā‘* form is allowed.

Some Hindi loanwords ending in *-ĕnnig‘* form their Imperatives in *-ed* as *pōtshĕd*, *zītĕd*, from *pōtshĕnnig*, arrive, *zītĕnnig‘*, conquer. So also *sŏmzĕd*, from *sŏmzĕāmig‘*, understand, a verb which forms some of its tenses as if from *sŏmzĕnnig‘*. These Imperatives are regular except for the 2nd sing.

Present and Imperfect Indicative. These tenses are formed by adding the Present or Past of the Verb Substantive to the Present Participle, which in turn is made by adding *-o* to the root. Of the two forms of the verb substantive *dūg* and *dueg‘* are commoner in these tenses than *tog‘* or *tokeg‘*.

The following are irregular: *rŏṅmig‘*, graze, *rŏgodūg‘*; *zŭṅmig*, begin, *zŭgodūg‘*; *tōshimig‘*, sit, remain, *toshidūg‘*; *tŭmmig‘*, drink, *tŭṅădūg‘*; *kēmig‘*, give, *kĕrodūg‘*; *nēmig‘*, know, *nĕŏdūg‘*; *ṅ* is very frequently changed to *g*.

Past. The Past generally formed by adding to the root *-ag‘* or *-shid*, the later being indeclinable. Verbs whose roots end in *n* generally drop the *n*.

toṅmig‘, beat, *toṅag‘*, *toṅshid*; but *dāīōg‘* from *dāīnmig*, run; *rāshid* from *ranmiq*, do; *bŏshid* from *bŭnnig‘*, come.

-ag‘ sometimes becomes *-āg‘* or *-ŏg‘*.

We notice also a past in *-eg‘* specially in verbs with roots in *-shi* or *-ci*, thus *tōshimig‘*, remain, *toshĕg‘*; *hacimig‘*, become, *hacig‘*; *hushimig‘*, learn, *husheg‘*.

Some verbs, usually with roots ending in *-n*, have a past form in *-dag‘*, in addition to one or more other forms, as *shĕnnig‘*, send *shedag‘*; *pŏrĕnnig‘*, be obtained *pŏrĕdag‘*; *dāīnmig‘*, run, *dāīādāg‘*; *ṭŏnmig‘*, become ill, *ṭŏdag‘*; *bŭnnig‘*, come *bŏdag‘*.

Some verbs whose roots end in *-n* or in a vowel drop the *a* of *-ag‘* as, *pŏnnig‘*, arrive, *pŏg‘*; *zāmig‘*, eat, *zāg‘*; *kannig‘*, bring, *kāg‘*; *lŏnnig‘*, say, *lŏg*; *shĕnnig*, send *sheg*; *kēmig‘*, give, has *kerag‘* or *kēshid*.

The Pluperfect. The Pluperfect seems to be made by combining the Conjunctive Participle (see below), with the Past of the Verb substantive; thus *shīshī tokē‘*, having died was, had died; *shō bībī toke‘*, lost having–gone was, had been lost; *gyāgyā tokeg‘*, having wished I was, I had wished. This construction may, however, indicate rather a past state than a pluperfect tense.

The Present Perfect is formed simularly with the Present of the Verb substantive, but we must enter the same caveat. *ṭōṭo to‘*, from *ṭŏnmig‘*, get ill, may be *he has got ill*, but it may also be *he is in a state of having got ill*, i. e. *he is ill*.

Participles. Present. By adding *-o* to the root we get a kind of Present Participle, which seems to be used only in composition with the verb substantive or *nīmig'*, become.

Conjunctive, made by a repetition of the root. *nēnē*, having known, from *nēmig'*; *kākā*, having brought, from *kanmig*; *toṅtoṅ*, having beaten, from *toṅmig'*.

Verbs with more than one syllable before the root repeat only the latter or last syllable, *pŏrĕreā'*, having been obtained from *pŏrĕnnig'*; *dōrĕrea'*, having run, from *dōrenmig'*.

A continuative sense is given to the Conjunctive Participle by adding *-o* to each half: — *bīo bīo*, having continually gone, from *bīmig'*; *tŭṅotŭṅo*, having continually drunk, from *tŭnmig'*, cf. Hindi *jā jā kē*, *pī pī kē*.

Passive Participle. There is a Passive Part. formed by adding *-shĕs* or *shis* to the root, thus *cēshes*, written, *toṅshĕs*, beaten, *ma gyāshĕs*, not desired. In Transitive verbs this participle means in the state of having been beaten &c., in Intransitive verbs it means, in the state of being &c.

Verbs whose roots end in *shi* or *ci* contract *shĕs* to *-ăs* or *-ĭs* or *-ŏs*. thus, *tōshăs*, sitting, from *tōshimig*, *hacas*, having become, from *hacimig'*, *dāshas*, having quarrelled, from *dāshimig*, *chukshas*, having met, from *chukshimig'*.

The Participle expressing *on* doing or *while* doing a thing has two forms made by adding *-ĕröṅ* (or *-eröṅ*) and *ēnĕn* (or *yēnĕn*) to the root. *röṅ* is apparently the preposition meaning *with*. The root undergoes the same changes as in the Present Indicative.

> *kēmig*, give, *kerĕröṅ*, on giving, *kerēnĕn*, while giving.
> *toṅmig'*, beat, *toṅĕröṅ*, on beating, *toṅēnĕn*, while beating.
> *unmig*, take, *unĕröṅ*, on taking, *unyēnĕn*, while taking.
> *bīmig*, go, has *bēnĕn* and *bīeröṅ*.

I am not clear about the exact difference in meaning between these two participles.

Agent. The agentive Participle is formed by adding *-zea* or *-tsea* to the root, *zea* generally being added to a root ending in a consonant, and *tsea* to one ending in a vowel. Verbs whose roots end in *n* frequently drop the *n* and take the latter form. For *tsea* and *zea dea* and *sea* are found. The Feminine is *tsē*, *zē*, *dē*, *sē*.

> *kēmig'*, give, *ketsea*, giver; *unmig'*, take, *unzeā*, taker; *kanmig'*, bring, *katsea*, bringer.

The forms are much interchanged, thus *zāmig'*, has *zāzea*, and *toṅmig'*, beat, has *toṅtsea*.

Roots ending in *shi* or *ci* take *zeā*; *hacimig'*, become, *hacizeā*; *tōshimig*, sit, *toshizeā*.

This ending is commonly used with nouns, chiefly in the form *zea* or *sea* or *tsea*. If there means the 'person or thing connected with', thus *raṅzea*, the man with the horse, the owner or rider or driver.

Central Kanauri.

Nouns.

Masculine.

rŭṅ (*rŭⁿ*), horse.

	Singular.	Plural.
Nom.	*răṅ*, horse	*răṅā*
Gen.	*răṅŭ*	*răṅănŭ*
Dat.	*răṅŭ*, *răṅŭ pöṅ*	*răṅănŭ*, *răṅănŭ pöṅ*
Acc.	*răṅ*, *răṅŭ*, *răṅŭ pöṅ*	*răṅā'*, *răṅănŭ*, *răṅănŭ pöṅ*
Abl.	*răṅŭ dŏk'ts*	*răṅănŭ dŏk'ts*
Agent.	*răṅās*	*răṅās.*

mī, man.

Nom.	*mī*	Plural as Singular.
Gen.	*mīŭ*	
Dat.	*mī pöṅ*	
Abl.	*mī dŏk'ts*	
Agent.	*mīs*	

kim, house.

Nom.	*kim*	*kimā'*
Gen.	*kimū*	*kimanŭ*
Dat.	*kimŭ pöṅ*	*kimanŭ pöṅ*
Abl.	*kimok'ts*	*kimanŭ dŏk'ts*
Locative	*kimau*	*kimanau.*

Nouns ending in a vowel have an alternative form in the plural.

Nom.	*bŏbā*, *bŏwā*, father,	*bŏwā'*, *bŏwagā*
Gen.	*bŏbau*	*bŏwanŭ*, *bŏwagānŭ*
Dat.	*bŏbā pöṅ*	*bŏwanŭ pöṅ*
Abl.	*bŏbā dŏk'ts*	*bŏwanŭ dŏk'ts*
Agent.	*bŏbās*	*bŏwās*, *bŏwāgās.*

Nom.	*atē*, brother.	*atē*
Gen.	*atēō*	*atenŭ*
Dat.	*atē pöṅ*	
Abl.	*atē dŏk'ts*	
Agent.	*atēs*	*atēs*

or *ategā*, Gen. *ateganŭ* &c. regular.

The locative is formed by adding *-ō* or *-au* to the nom., thus, *kimau*, in the house; *rīmō*, in the field; *wŏrkīō*, to far; *mulkīō*, in the county; *kāmöṅō*, in work; *ḍhŏmau*, in the box.

Feminine.

	Singular.	Plural.
Nom.	*cīmĕd*, daughter	*cīmēdā‘*
Gen.	*cīmēdū* or *cīmēdŭ*	*cīmedanŭ*
Dat.	*cīmēdū pöṅ*	*cīmedanŭ pöṅ*
Abl.	*cīmēdū dŏk‘ts*	*cīmedanŭ dŏk‘ts*
Agent.	*cīmēdās*	*cīmēdās*
Nom.	*riṅgz*, *riṅgs*, sister	*riṅgzā‘*
Gen.	*riṅgzū*	*riṅgzanŭ*
Dat.	*riṅgzū* or *riṅgzū pöṅ*	*riṅgzanŭ* or *riṅgzanŭ pöṅ*
Abl.	*riṅgzū dŏk‘ts*	*riṅgzanŭ dŏk‘ts*
Agent.	*riṅgzās*	*riṅgzās*
Nom.	*amā*, mother	*amagā‘*
Gen.	*amau*	*amaganŭ*
Dat.	*amā pöṅ*	*amaganŭ* or *amaganŭ pöṅ*
Abl.	*amā dŏk‘ts*	*amaganŭ dŏk‘ts*
Agent.	*amās*	*amagās*

Pronouns.

First Person.

	Singular.	Dual exclusive.	Dual inclusive.
Nom.	*gö*, I	*nishi*, he and I	*kāshöṅ*, thou and I
Gen.	*aṅ*	*nishū*	*kashöṅŭ*
Dat.	*aṅŭ*	*nishū*	*kashöṅŭ*
Abl.	*aṅ dŏk‘ts*	*nishū dŏk‘ts*	*kashöṅŭ dók‘ts*
Agent.	*gös*	*nishīs*	*kashöṅis*, *kashöṅs*

Plural.

	Exclusive (excluding "you")	Inclusive (including "you")
Nom.	*niṅā‘*	*kishöṅā‘*
Gen.	*niṅanŭ*	*kishöṅānŭ*
Dat.	*niṅanŭ*	*kishöṅānŭ*
Abl.	*niṅanŭ dŏk‘ts*	*kishöṅānŭ dŏk‘ts*
Agent.	*niṅās*	*kishöṅās*

Second Person.

Singular.

	Ordinary, thou.	Polite, you.
Nom.	*ka‘*	*ki*[x]
Gen.	*kan*	*kin*
Dat.	*kanŭ*	*kinŭ*
Abl.	*kan dŏk‘ts*	*kin dŏk‘ts*
Agent.	*kas*	*kis*

Second Person.

	Dual.	Plural.
Nom.	*kishī*	*kinā'*
Gent.	*kishū*	*kinanŭ*
Dat.	*kishū*	*kinanŭ*
Abl.	*kishū dŏk'ts*	*kinanŭ dŏk'ts*
Agent.	*kishis*	*kinās*

Third Person &c.

Nom.	*do*, he, she, that	*nu*, he, she, that	*ju*, this
Gen.	*dō*	*nū*	*jū*
Dat.	*do pöṅ*	*nu pöṅ*	*ju pöṅ*
Abl.	*do dŏk'ts*	*nu dŏk'ts*	*ju dŏk'ts*
Agent.	*dos, doks*	*nus, nŭks*	*jus, jŭks.*

Respectful.

Nom.	*dogo*	*nugo*	*jugo, jogo*
Gen.	*dogonŭ*	*nugonŭ*	*jugonŭ, jogonŭ*
Dat.	*dogonŭ*	*nugonŭ*	*jugonŭ*
Abl.	*dogonŭ dŏk'ts*	*nugonŭ dŏk'ts*	*jugonŭ dŏk'ts*
Agent.	*dogos*	*nugos*	*jugos, jogos.*

Dual.

Nom.	*doksöṅ*	*nŭksöṅ*	*jŭksöṅ*
Gen.	*doksöṅŭ*	*nŭksöṅŭ*	*jŭksöṅŭ*
Dat.	*doksöṅŭ*	*nŭksöṅŭ*	*jŭksöṅŭ*
Abl.	*doksöṅŭ dŏk'ts*	*nŭksöṅŭ dòk'ts*	*jŭksöṅŭ dŏk'ts*
Agent.	*doksöṅös*	*nŭksöṅös*	*jŭksöṅös*

Plural.

Nom.	*dogoa*	*nugoa*	*jugoa*
Gen.	*dogoanŭ*	as *dogoa*	as *dogoa*
Dat.	*dogoanŭ*		
Abl.	*dogoanŭ dŏk'ts*		
Agent.	*dogoas*		

hătt who?

	Singular.	Dual.	Plural.
Nom.	*hătt*	*hătsöṅ*	*hăte*
Gen.	*hătŭ*	*hătsöṅŭ*	*hătenŭ*
Dat.	*hătŭ*	*hătsöṅŭ*	*hătenŭ*
Abl.	*hătŭ dŏk'ts*	*hătsöṅŭ dŏk'ts*	*hătenŭ dŏk'ts*
Agent.	*hătŭs*	*hătsöṅös*	*hătes.*

Other pronouns: *hăti*, someone, anyone, *hăti ma*, no one, e. g. *hăti ma bödā'*, no one came.
ṭhö, *the*, what?, *ṭhötsī*, something, anything.
ṭhötsi ma, nothing, *tsaē*, *tsēi*, all.
-aṅa, -ever, e. g. *hătiaṅa*, whosoever, *ṭhödiaṅa*, whatsoever.
an, self, e. g. *an rokshodū'*, he himself is grazing himself.

Adjectives.

Comparison of adjectives is effected by the use of one ot the words *kā'*, *kē's*, *băskyöṅ*, *nŭ*, than, with the positive form of the adjective. e. g.

dēbāsh or *dăm*, good; *jū kā' dēbāsh*, better than this;
nu băskyöṅ ju dăm tō', than that this is better;
tsēi kē's dēbāsh, better than all, best;
gö băskyöṅ nŭ dăm or *aṅ kā' nŭ dăm*, that is better than I;
nŭ tsēi nŭ dăm or *kā' dăm* or *băskyöṅ dăm*, that is better than all.

Demonstrative (near)	Demonstrative (far) or Correlative	Interrogative
hönē', like this,	*hödē'*, like that	*hatē*, *halā*, like what?
hŏtrā', so much or many,	*hŏtrā'*, so much or many,	*tetrā'*, how much or many?

For the relative *hătiaṅa*, whosoever, and *tetriaṅa*, how much so ever (or the interrogative *tetrā'*) are used.

Adverbs.

Time.

hŭn, *hŭnā'*, now
dŏk, then
tēröṅ, when?
ŏmī, formerly
pēlē, formerly
toro, to-day
nasŭm, to-morrow
romī, day after to-morrow
pāē, on fourth day
ē, *ēī*, on fifth day
cē, *cēī*, on sixth day
kŭroī, on seventh day

mē, yesterday
rī', day before yesterday
rītsomiā', on fourth day back
tēraī, *teröṅ*, ever
tēraī teraī, some times
tēröṅ tēröṅ, some times
hē, again
bărābăr, regularly, always
hămēsh, always
sŏda, always

Place.

jöṅ, *hŏjöṅ*, here
döṅ, *hödöṅ*, there
nöṅ, *hŏnöṅ*, there
hăm, where?
jöṅ töṅ (*stöṅ*), up to this

riṅ, up
shoṅ, down
nēröṅ, near
dör, far
wark, far

Place.

nön töṅ (*stöṅ*), up to there	*oms*, *omts*, in front
döṅ töṅ (*stöṅ*), up to there	*nyums*, behind
jŏk'ts, from here	*kŏmo*, inside
	bāerŭṅ, *bairăṅ*, *bĕrĭṅ*, outside.

Other adverbs: *thū*, why?; *nī*, *ō̃*, yes; *ma*, *tha*, no, not; *lī*, also; *dăm*, well; *hāsŭl*, quickly; *taṅmā*, then (inferential).

The affix *-ī* adds emphasis, as, *hŏnöṅī*, in that very place, so also *hŏdöṅī*, *tĕröṅī*.

Prepositions.

The commonest prepositions have been mentioned in the declension of nouns and pronouns. The same word is sometimes both a preposition and an adverb.

nöṅ, beyond	*dā'*, *doā'*, near, beside
jöṅ, on this side	*röṅ*, with, along with
dĕn, upon	*stöṅ*, (*töṅ*), up to
yuṭhöṅ, beneath	*tĕṅĕs*, for, for sake of

aṅ doā', beside me; *aṅ röṅ*, with me; *jöṅ stöṅ*, up to here, *kan tĕṅĕs*, for thee, for thy sake.

ts or *c* is sometimes affixed to give the idea of from, as, *nöṅts*, from beyond.

Verbs.

Auxiliary.

Present, I am &c. *tog'*, *dūg'*.

	First.		Second.	Third.
Sing.	*tog'*		*ton*; (polite) *toñ*	*to'*; (polite) *tosh*
	dūg'		*dūn*; *dūñ*	*dū'*; *dūsh*
Dual.	*toc* (= he and I),	*to'* (thou and I),	*toc* (you two)	
	dūc	*dū'*	*dūc*	
Plur.	*toñ* (they and I),	*tō'* (you and I)	*toñ*	*tō'*
	dūñ	*dū'*	*dūñ*	*dū'*

Past, I was &c. *tokeg'*, *dūeg'*.

	First.	Second.	Third.
Sing.	*tokeg'*	*token*, *tokeñ*	*toke'*, *tokesh*
	dūeg'	*dūen*, *dūeñ*	*dūe'*, *dūesh*
Dual.	*tokec*, *toke'*	*tokec*	
	dūec, *dūe'*	*duec*	
Plur.	*tokeñ*, *toke'*	*tokeñ*	*toke'*
	dūeñ, *dūe'*	*dūeñ*	*dūe'*

The second forms in the past correspond to the second forms in the present.

gŏrmig‘ fall.

Future, I shall fall &c. *gŏrtŏg‘*.

	First.	Second.	Third.
Sing.	*gŏr-tŏg‘*	*-tŏn*, (polite) *-tiñ*	*-to‘*, (polite) *-tŏsh*, *-tis*
Dual.	*-tic* (he and I),	*-tic*	
	-te‘ (thou and I),		
Plur.	*-tiñ* (they and I),	*-tiñ*	
	-te‘ (you and I),		*-to‘*

Imperative *gŏr* fall.

Sing.	*gŏr*, (polite) *gŏriñ* or	*gŏrdā‘*, *gŏrdiñ*
Dual.	*gŏric*	*gŏrdic*
Plur.	*gŏric*, *gŏriñ*	*gŏrdic*, *gŏrdiñ*

Present Indicative, I am falling.

gŏrodūg‘ or *gŏrotog‘*, like *dūg‘* and *tog‘*, regular.

Imperfect, I was falling.

gŏrodūeg‘ or *gŏrotokeg‘* like *dūeg‘* and *tokeg‘*, regular.

Past, I fell, *gŏrŏg‘*, *gŏrshid*.

	First.	Second.	Third.
Sing.	*gŏr-ŏg‘*	*-ăn*, (polite) *-eñ*	*-ā‘*, (polite) *-esh*
Dual.	*-ec* (he and I):	*-ec*	
	-shē‘ (thou and I):		
Plur.	*-ec* (they and I);	*-eñ*	*-ā‘*
	-shē‘ (you and I);		

gŏrshid is indeclinable for all persons and numbers.

Participles.

gŏrgŏr having fallen, *gŏrogŏro* having kept on falling, repeatedly fallen, *gŏryēnĕn* while falling, *gŏrĕrŏn* on falling, *gortsea* fallen.

toṅmig‘, beat.

Fut. *toṅtŏg‘*. Negative *ma tŏng*, I shall not beat.
Imperat. *toṅ* &c.
also *toṅrā‘* (sing.), *toṅriñ*, *toṅric*.
Pres. Indic. *toṅodūg‘*, *toṅotog‘*,
Imperf. *toṅodūeg*, *toṅotokeg‘*.

Past	*toṅ-ag‘*	*-an*. *-eñ*,	*-ā‘*, *-ash*
	-ec, *-shē‘*	*-ec*	
	-eñ, *-shē‘*	*-eñ*	*-ā‘*

also *toṅshid*

Participles *toṅtoṅ*, *toṅotoṅo*, *toṅyenen*. *toṅerŏn*, *toṅtsea*.

shuṅmig‘, finish, waste.

Fut. *shuṅtög‘*, Negative *ma shuṅg.*
Imperat. *shuṅ* and *shuṅrā‘*
and so on like *toṅmig‘*.

pönmig‘, fill.

like *toṅmig‘*.

gyālmig‘, win.

Imperat. *gyal* &c., *gyalrā‘* &c., *gyaldic* &c.
Past *gyalög*
otherwise like *toṅmig*.

tsŭmmig‘, hold

like *toṅmig*, except.
Negative Future *ma tsŭmkh.*
Past *tsumög‘* as in *gŏrmig‘*.

bammig, be defeated

like *gyalmig‘* except that in the Imperat. the form in *-dic* is not found.

shŭbmig‘, slaughter (animal).

Neg. Future *ma shubg.*
Past *shŭbög‘*
the past like *toṅmig‘*.

rŏṅmig‘, graze (transitive).

ṅ changes to *g* in declension.
Future *rŏgtög.*
Negative (*ma*) *rŏg* *rŏgön*, *rŏgiñ*, *rŏg*,
rŏgic, *rŏgshau* or *rŏgtau* *rŏgic*
rŏgic, *rŏgshau* or *rŏgtau* *rŏgiñ* *rŏg.*
Imperat. *rŏg*, *rŏgiñ* &c. also *rŏgrā‘* &c.
Pres. Ind. *rŏgodūg‘*, *rŏgotog‘*.
Imperf. *rŏgodūeg‘*, *rŏgotokeg‘*.
Past *rŏgög*, *rŏgshid.*

zŭṅmig‘, begin.

Neg. Fut. 1st sing. inclus. dual or plur. *zŭgshē‘* and *zŭgmē‘*.
Past *zŭzag‘*, *zŭgög‘*, *zŭgshid*
otherwise like *rŏṅmig‘*.

Verbs whose root ends in *n*.

Some retain *n*, others change it to *d*. Those changing it to *d* omit it altogether in the Future.

ranmig‘, give.

Fut. *rantög‘*, Neg. *răng.*
Imperat. *ran*, *raṇiñ*, *raṇic*, also *ranrā‘* &c.
Pres. Imperf. *rano-dūg‘-dūeg‘* &c.

Past *raṇög‘*, *ranshid.*
Past *ranran* or *rārā*, *ranēnēn*, *ranzea* &c.

unmig‘, take.

Neg. Fut. *ŭnkh.*
Partic. *ŭnŭn*, *unyēnēn*, *unzeā*, &c.
otherwise like *ranmig‘*, except that *n* does not change to *ṇ*.

lănmig‘, do.

Neg. Fut. *lănkh.*
Imperat. *lăn*, *lanĭñ* &c, *lănrā‘* &c., *lăndic* &c.
Past *laṇög‘*, *lanshid.*
Partic. *lālā.*
otherwise like *unmig‘*.

lŏnmig‘, say, speak.

Future *lōtög‘*, Negative *lŏg.*
Imperat. *lŏn*, *lŏñ*, *lŏc.*
Pres. and Impf. *lŏdo-dūg‘*, *-dūeg‘* &c.
Past *lōg* *lōn*, *lōñ* *lō‘*, *lōsh.*
lōc, *lōshē‘* *lōc*,
lōc, *lōshē‘* *lōñ*, *-lō.*
also *lōshid*, *lōdag.‘* For 1st dual and plur. inclusive, *lōdag‘* has *lōdā‘*.

Participles *lōlō*, *lōdyēnēn*, *lōtseā* &c.

shĕnmig‘, send &c.

Fut. *shētög‘*, Neg. *shĕg‘*.
Imperat. *shen*, *sheñ* &c, *sherā‘* &c.
Pres. *shedo-dūg‘* &c.
Past *sheg*, *shedag‘*, *sheshid.*

Several verbs with roots in *-n* are loanwords from Hindi, e. g. *pŏrĕnmig‘*, be obtained, H. *păṛnā*, *pōtshĕnnig‘*, arrive, H. *pă-hŭncnā*, *zitĕnmig‘*, win, H. *jītnā*, *harĕnmig‘*, be defeated, H. *hārnā*, *dōrĕnmig‘*, run, H. *dauṛnā.*

pŏrĕnmig, be obtained.

Fut. *pŏrĕātög‘*, Neg. *pŏreāg‘*.
Pres. and Impf. *pŏrĕdo-dūg‘*, *-dūeg‘* &c.
Past *pŏrĕdag‘*, *pŏrĕshid.*
Partic. *pŏrĕreā*, &c.

pōtshĕnnig‘, arrive.

Fut. *pōtshĭātög‘*, Neg. *pōtshĕg‘*.
Imperat. *pōtshĕ-d*, *-ñ* &c., also *pōtshĕārā‘* &c.
Pres. and Impf. *pōtshĭādo-dūg‘* &c.
Past *pōtshĕdag‘*, *pōtsheshid*, *pōtshĭāg‘* (which has 1st dual and plur. inclus. *pōtshĭāshē‘*.

zitenmig‘, win.

Fut. *ziteātög‘*, Neg. *zītĕg‘*.
Imperat. *zītĕd*, *zitĕñ* &c. also *zitĕārā‘* &c.
Pres. *zitĕādodūg‘* &c.
Past. *zitĕāg‘*, *zitedag‘*, *ziteshid*.

harĕnmig‘, be defeated.

Fut. *harĕtög‘*, Neg. *hareg‘*.
Pres. and Impf. *harĕdo-dūg‘*, *-dūeg‘* &c.
Past *harĕag‘*, *harĕshid*.
hareshis, defeated.

dōrĕnmig‘, run.

Fut. *dōrĕātög‘*.
Neg. Fut. *dōr-eg‘*, *-en*, *-eñ* *-e‘*.
-ec, *-ĕashē‘* or *-ĕatē‘*, *-ec*.
-ec, *-ĕashē‘* or *-ĕatē‘*, *-eñ* *-ē‘*.
Imperat. *dōrĕd*, *dōrĕñ* &c.
Pres. and Imperf. *dōredo-dug‘*, *-dūeg‘*.
Past *dōrĕāg‘*, *dōrĕdag‘*, *dōrĕshid*.
Partic. *dōrĕreā*, *dōrĕtsea* &c.

dāīnmig‘, run.

Fut. *dāīātög‘*.
Neg. Fut. *dāg‘*, *dān*, *dañ*. *dāshē‘* or *dāshau* or *dātē‘* &c.
Imperat. *dāo*, *dān*, *dāe* &c. also *dārā‘* &c.
Pres. and Imperf. *dāīādo-dūg‘*, *-dūeg‘* &c.
Past *dāīāg‘*, *dāīādag‘*, *dāīāshid*.
Partic. *dāīā*, having run, *dāīdō dāīdō*, *dāīderōn* &c.

ṭōnmig‘, be ill.

Fut. *ṭōtög‘*.
Neg. Fut. *ṭog‘*, *ṭon‘*, *ṭoshē‘* or *ṭotē‘* &c.
Imperat. *ṭōd*, *ṭōn* &c., also *ṭorā‘* &c.
Pres. and Imperf. *ṭōdo-dūg‘*, *-dūeg‘* &c.
Past *ṭōdag‘*, *ṭōshid*.
Partic. *ṭōṭo* &c.

pōnmig‘, arrive.

Fut. *pōtög‘*, Neg. *pög‘*.
Imperat. *pōrā‘* &c.
Pres. and Impf. *pōdo-dūg* &c.
Past *pōdag‘*, *pōshid*, *pög*.
pög has 1st dual and plural inclusive *pöshē‘*.

kanmig‘, bring.

Fut. *kātög‘*, Neg. *kāg‘*.
Imperat. *kan*, *kañ* &c., and *karā‘* &c.
Pres. and Impf. *kado-dūg‘* &c.
Past *kadāg‘*, *kāg*, *kashid*.
Participle *kākā* (accent on second), *kadyĕnĕn*, *katseā*.

Roots ending in a Vowel.

nīmig‘, be, become.

Fut. *nitög‘*, Neg. *nīg*.
Imperat. *nī*, *nītiñ* &c., also *nīrā‘* &c.
Pres. and Impf. *nīo-dūg‘* &c.
Past *nīshid* and *nīg* (*nīn*, *nīñ*, *nī‘*, *nīsh*, *nītē‘* &c.).
Partic. *nīnī*, *nīnĕn*, *nītsea*.

bīmig‘, go.

like *nīmig‘* except the following.
Imperat. 2nd sing. *bīh* or *bĭōh* or *bĭūh*.
Past *bĭog‘* (and *bīshid*).
Partic. retain *ī* of root, except *bĕnĕn*, which has *-ē*.

zāmig‘, eat.

like *nīmig*, substituting *zā* for *nī* except the following *zāū-dūg‘* &c. for *zāodūg‘*.
Past. 1st dual and plural inclusive *zāshē‘* or *zād*.
Partic. *zāenĕn*, *zāzea*, otherwise the same.

phīmig‘, take away.

like *nīmig‘* except the following.
Imperat. *phiū*, *phīñ* &c. (also *phirā‘*).
Past. *phiog‘* (and *phishid*).
Partic. *phīphī* (accent on second), *phīēnĕn*.

shīmig‘, die.

like *phīmig‘*.

tāmig‘, place.

like *nīmig‘* except the following.
Imperat. *tāo*, *tāñ* &c (and *tārā‘*).
Past 1st dual and plural inclusive, *tāshē‘* and *tātē‘*.

cīmig‘, wash (clothes &c.)

like *nīmig‘* except the following.
Imperat. *ciū*, *ciñ* &c. (and *cirā‘*).
Past 1st dual and plural inclusive *cishē‘*.

īmig‘, ask.

like *cīmig‘* except the following.
Past *īāg‘*, (and *ishid*).

gyāmig‘, wish.

like *zāmig‘* except the following.
Imperat. *gyau*, *gyāñ* &c. (and *gyārā‘*).
Past 1st dual and plural inclusive *gyāshē‘* and *gyātē‘*.

sŏmzĕāmig‘, understand.

loanword from Hindi (*sămăjhnā*).
Fut. *sŏmzĕātög‘*, Neg. *sŏmzĕag‘*.

Imperat. *sŏmzĕ-d, -ñ* &c., and *somzerā‘* &c.
Pres. and Impf. *sŏmzĕodūg‘* &c.
Past *sŏmzĕāg‘, sŏmzĕāshid.*

sŏmzāyamig‘, cause to understand.

loanword from Hindi (*sămjhānā*).
like *sŏmzĕāmig‘*.

Verbs with roots ending in *-ci* and *-shi.*

Sometimes *c* denotes an object of the first or second person, me, us, thee, you, and *sh* denotes a reflexive object, oneself, one another, but in a number of verbs whose roots end in *c* and *sh* I have not found any meaning such as that just indicated. The *i* in *-ci* and *-shi* seems to be merely euphonic.

hacimig‘, be, become.

Fut. *hacög,‘* Neg. the same.
Imperat. *hac* &c., *hacrā‘* &c., *hacdic* &c.
Pres. and Impf. *haco-dūg‘* &c.
Past *haceg‘, hacishid.*
Partic. *hachac, hacĕnĕn, hacizea* &c.

tācimig‘, place me, us, thou, you (see *tāmig‘*).

like *hacimig‘* except.
Past *tacög‘*.

sărshimig‘, raise oneself, rise (*sarmig‘*, raise).

like *hacimig‘* except
Imperat. *sarsh, sarshiñ* &c., *sarshrā‘*, but I have not found *sarshdic.*
Partic. *sarshis*, in the state of having risen.

hushimig, learn.

like *hacimig*, except that I have not found *hushdic* in the Imperat.

tōshimig‘, remain, sit.

Fut. *toshög‘*, Neg. the same.
Imperat. *tōsh* &c., *toshrā‘* &c.
Pres. and Impf. *toshi-dūg‘* &c.
Past *toshĕg‘, toshishid.*
Partic. *tŏshtŏsh, toshĕnĕn, toshizea* &c.

The following are slightly irregular.

bŭnnig‘, bŏmig, come.

Fut. *bŏtög‘, būtög‘*, Neg. *bög‘*.
Imperat. Sing. *jĭr, jĭrā‘, jărā‘*, polite *jĭrañ, jāriñ.*
Dual. *jirac, jāric.*
Plur. *jirac, jāric, jĕiñ, jirañ, jāriñ.*
Pres. and Impf. *bödau-dūg‘* &c.
Past *bŏg‘, bödag‘, böshid.*

Partic. *böbö, bödēnen, bötseā, böderön.*

Throughout this verb the sound of *bö* is between *bö* and *bü*, some pronounce it *bū*.

tŭmmig, drink.

Fut. *tũtög*, Neg. *tŭṅg*.
Imperat. *tŭṅ, tŭṅīñ* &c., *tŭṅrā‘* &c.
Pres. and Impf. *tŭṅdūg‘* &c.
Past *tŭög‘, tŭshid*, and *tŭṅög‘, tŭṅshid.*
Partic. *tŭṅtŭṅ, tŭṅyēnĕn, tŭṅzea, tŭṅerön* &c.

kēmig‘. give.

Fut. *ketög‘*, Neg. *kĕg‘*.
Imperat. *kēōh, keñ* &c., and *kerā‘* &c.
Pres. and Impf. *kero-dūg‘* &c.
Past *kerag‘, kēshid.*
Partic. *kēkē, kerēnen, kētsea* &c.

nēmig‘, know.

Fut. *nētög‘*, Neg. *ṇeg‘* (in *mŏ ṇeg‘*).
Imperat. *nēō, neñ* &c., and *nerā* &c.
Pres. and Impf. *neōdūg‘* &c., sometimes *nēōdūg‘* &c.
Past *nēg, neshid.*
Partic. *nēnē, nēnēn, nētsea* &c.

tŏnmig‘, take out, pour out.

Fut. *tōatög‘*, Neg. *tŏg‘*.
Imperat. *tŏd, toñ* &c., and *tōarā‘* &c.
Pres. & Impf. *tō-do-dūg‘* &c.
Past. *tŏāg‘, toshid.*

I have heard *toī‘*, for 2nd sing. Imperat., and *tonodūg‘* for Pres. Ind. but am doubtful of them.

Numerals.

Cardinal.

1 *id‘*
2 *nish*
3 *shŭmm, sŭmm*
4 *pö*
5 *ṅā*
6 *ṭŭg‘*
7 *tissh, stissh*
8 *rai*
9 *zgŭi, gŭi*
10 *sai*
11 *sigid‘*
12 *sōṇish*
13 *sōrŭm*
14 *sapō̄*
15 *soṅā*
16 *sōrŭg‘*
17 *sŏstish*
18 *sŏrai*
19 *sŏzgŭi*
20 *nīzā* (accent on second).
21 *nīzō id‘*
22 *nīzō nish*
29 *nīzō gŭi*
30 *nīzō sai*

31	*nīz*$^{\bar{o}}$ *sigī* or *sigid‘*	300	*sŭmrā*
40	*nish nīzā*	400	*pöra*
41	*nish nīz*$^{\bar{o}}$ *id‘*	500	*ṅārā*
50	*nish nīz*$^{\bar{o}}$ *sai*	600	*ṭŭgrā*
60	*shŭm nīzā*	700	*tishrā*
80	*pö ṇīzā* (not *pȫ*)	800	*rairā*
100	*rā*	900	*guīrā*
101	*rāŭ id‘*	1 000	*hăzār*
200	*nīrā* (accent on second)	100 000	*lākh.*

It will be noticed that enumeration proceeds regularly by twenties. When a number follows *nīzā*, twenty, the *ā* is changed to $^{\bar{o}}$. The accent is always thrown foreward to the last syllable thus *pörā́*, four hundred, *pö ṇīzā́*, eighty, *pö ṇīz*$^{\bar{o}}$ *ṅā́* eighty-five.

Ordinals.

Ordinals are formed by adding -$^{\bar{o}}$ to the cardinal; thus *ṅā*$^{\bar{o}}$, fifth, *pȫ*$^{\bar{o}}$, fourth. *nīzā* and *rai* give *nīz*$^{\bar{o}}$ and *rē*$^{\bar{o}}$.

khāṇöṅ, *ādhöṅ*, half. *Săwā nish*, $2^1/_4$; *sāḍhē pö*, $4^1/_2$.

The Prodigal Son, St. Luke 15.

ī mīŭ nish chaṅ due‘, zigits chaṅēs anō bawā lodā‘,
One man-of two sons were, small son-by own father-to said

babā aṅ hīza (or *hīssa*) *kēō, dōs aṇō bŭṇṭhā rūnā‘; gaṭō*
Father my part give, by him own part gave, few

dīārōc nyums zigits chaṅēs aṇō tsŭc zōma lanā‘ wŏrkīō
days-from after small son-by own all together made far-in

bīō‘, döṅ wāmăṅ kamöṅo aṇō māyā shūṅā: dōs tsōē
went, there foolish work-in own property finished, by him all

khōrts lanī‘ do mūlkīō ăṅkālăṅ bibi mūlī maīts,
spending made, that county-in famine having-gone, quite not-is,

ŏllō pöpö. Do hodō mūlkīō tōshīdŭ (or *tōshizeā*)
straitened having-arrived. He that country-in dweller dweller

dŭā‘ (or *dā‘*) *bīō‘, dōs ănō rīwānō sūrā rogim shedā‘.*
near near went, by-him own fields-ins wine to-make-feed sent.

Dō sūrăs rokshimī khŏlŏp ăn zāmig‘ gyau due‘ hāīsī do
He swine feeding husks self to eat wishing was, by-anyone that

ma rănā‘. Tshĕrĕp yat kadā‘ dog lododū‘ — aṅ
not gave. little remembrance brought he saying-is my

bŏwā doȧ‘ tē mŏzūrī dū‘ pēṭăn pöṅ stöṅ rōṭe
father near how-many labourers are, stomach fill up-to loaves

zāo, gö jön on̤tös shiög‘. Gö an̊ böwā dön̊ bītög‘
eating, I here hungry died I own father there will-go

dopön̊ lōtög‘, böwā Pārmēshūrās kīn pāp lānlān gö kan
him-to will say father God-of your sin having-done I thy

chan̊ hacī lāīk maig‘, an̊u nūkrī tāciñ.
son to-become worthy not-am, me servant make-me-please

Sārshis (or sārshās) anō böwā dön̊ bīō‘. Do chan̊ warkīō
Having-arisen own father there went. That son far-in

dūe‘ an̤o böwās tan̊a‘, kōtsön̊ tsālōdū‘, dāīā (or dōrēreā‘)
was own father-by saw, miserable thinking-is, having-run

an̤ō chan̊ō kākts tsūma‘, papū rūnā‘. Chan̊ās ano bönū
own son-in neck held kiss gave Son-by own father-to

lododū‘. Böwā Pārmēshūrās kīn pāp lanlan gö kan chān
saying-is. Father God-of your sin having-done I thy son

hacī lāīk maig‘. Bönās nūkrēnū lododū‘: — tsūē
to-become worthy not-am. Father-by servants-to saying-is all

nu dām chūgā totöā (or tōtā‘) phögiñ, gudō pratsō
than good coat having-taken-out put-on (please) hand-of finger-in

mundī shen̊, ban̊ō shpōn shēñ yokshid ash
ring send (please), foot-in shoe send (please) fatted calf

kaka shūnmig‘, nin̊ā zātiñ khūsī haciñ (or nītiñ) thū
having-brought to-kill we may-eat happy may-become, why

ān chan̊ shīshī toke‘, hē shöngī hacis, shō bī-
my son having-died was, again alive having-become, lost having-

bī toke‘ hē pōredā‘. Dos khūsi lano due‘. Dō
gone was, again was-obtained. By him happiness making was. His

tēg atē rīmō dūye‘, kimū nērāno böderön̊ (bödyēnōn)
big brother field-in was house-of near on-coming

bazgī bazētsū skad thaso dū‘. I nukrū
musical-instrument sounding-of noise hearing is. One servant-to

kuku dopön̊ īōdū thö hace‘. Nukrös lodo
having-called him-to asking-is what became. Servant-by saying

dū‘ kan dzigits atē bōdā‘ kan böwās yokshid ashu‘ shubā‘:
is thy little brother came thy father-by fatted calf killed:

do taī shūbo dū‘ an̤o chan tsan̊a (or dām) pōrēreā‘,
that for killing is, own son well good having-been-obtained;

dō dūkhön̊ tan̊tan̊ kumo bīm maio dū‘ or ma gyau dū‘,
he angry looked house-in to-go not asking is not wishing is,

dō bōn bāerān bībī anu chan̊u sōmzāēo dū‘.
his father outside having-gone own son-to making-understand is.

Dos lodo dū' gös tē bōshōn kan kāmań lanlan.
Him-by saying is me-by how-many years thy work having-done
kas anū tērānī bōkhārū chań ma keke ań kōṇeā
thee-by me-to ever she-goat's son not having-given my friends
rōń khūsī lantōg', kan chań tēran bōdā' hāīs
with happiness I-shall-make, thy son ever (i. e. when) came whom-by
kan mālā pātārānu ūḍāeā' kas do tańis yōkshid
thy property harlots-to caused-to-fly, thee-by him for fatted
ash shubshub. Bōnös lodo dū' chań ka tū bārābār
calf having-killed. Father-by saying is son thou then always
ań rōń ēkē ton, ṭhödeań ań dōā' to' do kano. Khūsī
me with together art, whatever me near is that thine. Happiness
lanmig', khūsī hacimig' dām tōke' thū kan bāīā shīshī
to-make happy to-become good was, why thy brother having-died
toke' hē shöṅgī hacis shō bībī toke', he
was, again alive having-become, lost having-gone was, again
pōredā'.
was-obtained.

Sentences.

1. *Kan nāmań ṭhö dūn* or *dūī?* Thy name what is?
2. *Nū rań tē bōshań?* That horse how-many years?
3. *Jōṅc Kāshmīrō tē wārkh nītō'?* Here-from Kashmir-to how far will-be?
4. *Kan bāwau kimau tē chańa dū'?* Thy father's house in how-many sons are?
5. *Gö torō dörc yōnyōn bōg'.* I today far-from having-walked came.
6. *Ań dzits bāwau chań nu miu rins rūṇēkāń laṇa'.* My little father's (uncle's) son that man's sister with marriage made.
7. *Kīmo ṭhō rańu zhgā' to'.* In the house white horse's saddle is.
8. *Nu rańu zhgā ran.* That horse to saddle give (saddle that horse).
9. *Gös nu chań gob tońag'.* I (by me) that boy much beat.
10. *Ṭhōlū dēn zē lańa rōgo dū'.* Hill upon goats, cows he causing-to-feed is.
11. *Bōṭańu yūṭhōń rańa den tōshis dū'.* Tree under horse on seated he is.
12. *Do bāīāts anō rins kā tēg dū'.* That little-brother own sister than big is.

13. *Do mōlim nish rūpēa pō pauli dū‘.* Its price two rupees, four two-annas is.

14. *Au bowa zigits kimō tōs͟hid.* My father little house-in has sat (lives).

15. *Nu rūpēa do mī pōn rāndā‘ (or rourā‘).* That rupee that man to give.

16. *Do rūpēa do dŏk‘ts undā‘ (or unrā‘).* That rupee him from take.

17. *Do pŏṅ toṅtoṅ bŏs͟hos tsūrā‘.* Him-to having-beaten rope-with bind.

18. *Khūōc tī toe‘.* Well-from water extract.

19. *Aṅ oms pāi‘.* Me before walk.

20. *Hātū chan kan nyums budo dū‘?* Whose son thee behind coming is?

21. *Ka‘ hātŭ dok‘ts unā‘?* Thou whom from took?

22. *Dēs͟hŏṅu ī bāṇīā dŏk‘ts unay‘.* Town-of one shopkeeper from took—I.

THE DEVELOPMENT OF ENGLISH t, d, IN NORTH INDIAN LANGUAGES

IT is often said that Portuguese dental *t*, *d*, remain dental in India and that English alveolar *t*, *d*, become cerebral. It would follow that words like *kaptān* and *botal* and *haspatāḷ*, usually stated to be from English, must be Portuguese. The question cannot be disposed of so simply; there seem to have been cross influences at work, and sometimes there are different forms of the same word. See S. R. Dalgado's works *passim* for valuable suggestions.

The following lines have in view the area over which Urdū, Panjābī, and Hindī (= UPH.) are spoken, though the facts adduced have a wider application. As this is a matter of pronunciation it is necessary to confine oneself to spoken words and *ignore book words* except where others are not available. Printed forms are often deliberately altered on *à priori* grounds.

We may say without hesitation that a very large majority of English *t*'s and *d*'s do become cerebral when introduced into Indian words. The question is whether any become dental; if so, why? It should be remembered that mere haphazard explanations are of little value. Explanations must follow some definite principle. Thus the facile guess that the ending of P. *ḍāgdār*, doctor, is taken by analogy from the common Persian ending *-dār* is valueless unless we show why "inspector", "director", "master", give us *inspiṭṭar ḍarĕkṭar*, *māsṭar*, and why "canister" yields *kanastar*.

1. Words which probably have a Portuguese origin, though generally said to be English.

	Portuguese.	English.
baptisma	baptismo	baptism
butām (book form)	botão	button
(With this contrast the commoner *baṭan*, Eng. button.)		
gārad	guarda	guard
P. *'aspatāl*, UH. *haspatāl*	hospital	hospital
kaptān	capitão	captain
kārtūs	cartucho	cartridge
mastaul	mastro, masto	mast
pistaul	pistola	pistol

	Portuguese.	English.
salād	salada	salad
sikattar	secretario	secretary
tamākū	tabaco	tabacco
tauliā	toalha	towel

botal (P. botelha, E. bottle) and *patlūn* (P. pantalona, E. pantaloons) may be Portuguese, but it is at least possible that the words were used in N. India before they existed in Portugal.

2. Words which seem to be certainly English, but have a dental *t, d*, corresponding to the English alveolars. When there is a Portuguese word in any way resembling UPH. I have added it.

Landan	London	Port. Londres
U. *Dalhauzī*, P. *Dl‘aujjī*	Dalhousie, the hill station.	
P. *ardaḷī*, UH. *ardalī*	orderly	
P. *ḍāgdār, ḍākdār*	doctor	Port. doutor

ḍākṭăr is the commonest spoken form in UH.
Bookforms : *ḍākṭăr* in Lallū Jī ; *ḍākdăr* modern.

PU. *drāz*, fem. sing., pair of drawers, drawer in cupboard ; plur. *drāzzā, drāzē,* pairs of drawers, drawers in cupboard.

ketlī	kettle	Port. caldeira
kanastar	canister	
tos	piece of toast	
trel	tray	
santrī	sentry	Port. sentinella

The following should probably be added, but they are not so certain :—

darjan	dozen	Port. duzia
hāthīcok (? *hāthī*, elephant ; but why ?)	artichoke	alcachofra
turap	trump card	trunfo
tārpīn	turpentine	terebintina. terebinthia

Bookforms : *turmantīn, tarmantū,* turpentine, suggest Portuguese termentina. Proper names are *Istarling* for Stirling in G̲ālib, and *Gilkrist* for Gilchrist in Lallū Jī's preface. See further below.

The names of the months look more English than Portuguese, and we are perhaps right in including four of them among the words which have changed alveolar *t, d,* to dental. It must not be forgotten that *j* in UPH. represents a sound practically identical with English *j*, but very different from Portuguese *j*.

janvarī	January	Janeiro
farvarī	February	Fevereiro
mārac	March	Março
aprail	April	Abril
maī	May	Maio
jūn	June	Junho
julāī, jaulāī	July	Julho
agast	August	Agosto
sitambar	September	Setembro
aktūbar	October	Outubro
navambar	November	Novembro
dasambar	December	Dezembro

Those which call for attention are *agast*, *sitambar*, *aktūbar*, *dasambar*.

3. Words in which a Portuguese dental *may* have become cerebral: some of these are much disputed and all are doubtful.

Port. balde, pail, bucket ; *bāḷṭī*.

falto, deficient ; PU. *fāltū*, superfluous ; PH. *phāltū* ; Laihndī, *phāḷṭū*, a *kulī* who waits at cross roads for odd jobs ; Nep. *phāḷṭū*, *phāltū*.

foguete, rocket > *paṭākā*, squib, etc. ? Skr. *paṭ* + *ka*.

tope, top of mast, etc. > *ṭopī*, cap, hat.

varanda, balcony > UPH. *barāṇḍā* ; HU. *baraṇḍā* (book form). I take it that *barāmada* is a pseudo-Persian formation manufactured in India and as unknown in Persia as *nom-de-plume* and *double-entendre* are in France. This is a greatly discussed word.

termentina, turpentine : bookform *tarmanṭū*.

The UPH. words *palṭan*, regiment, and *biskuṭ*, biscuit, *jākaṭ*, jacket, are just as likely to be derived from English battalion, biscuit, and jacket as from Portuguese batalhão, biscoito, and jaqueto.

4. I have noted one or two points which go to show that 100 years ago Indians seemed readier to equate Indian dentals with English alveolars than they are now. It would be interesting if further proofs were forthcoming. Asad Ullāh G̲ālib, about 1830 (see *Urdū e Mu'allā*, ed. of 1921, p. 111), writes *Istarling* for Stirling, and twice *sikartar* for Secretary ; Muḥammad Yaḥyā Tanhā, quoting this very passage in *Sair ul Muṣannifīn*, 1924, changes the words to *Isṭarling* and *sikarṭar* ; yet *sikattar* is in general use conversationally to this day. Lallū Lāl in 1803–9 writes *gilkrist* for Gilchrist, whereas the usual

form to-day is *gilkrāisṭ* (so Tanhā, op. cit.). In the same passage Lallū himself freely uses cerebrals to represent English alveolars.

The tip of the tongue when pronouncing an alveolar is between the dental and the cerebral position, almost midway. Taking the hard palate as 1½ inches from front to back we may put cerebral *ṭ*, *ḍ* half an inch from the back edge of the teeth ridge. The centre or lower half of the front teeth (the dental position) is perhaps a quarter to three-eighths of an inch from the front edge of the teeth ridge. But the modern Indian hearing alveolar *t* and *d*, considers them cerebrals. This is not merely a literary device, it is the rule in village talk. Thus we have:—

P. *raṭbī* < *rabṭī* < *rapṭī* < *rapoṭ* + *ī* < report + *ī*; a man who brings in reports of occurrences.

P. *baṭemī* < *beṭemī* < *be* — *ṭem* + *ī* < *be* — time + *ī*. *baṭemī* means lateness, etc.

Inshā Allāh's very clever lines illustrate both tendencies :—

ھے اس آفت کا سبک سیر که راکب اسکا
حاضری کھاے جو کلکته تو لندن مین ٹپن

(He is so fleet footed that if his rider breakfasts in Calcutta he may lunch in London.) I am presuming that *ṭipan* reached U. and P. from England.

I have not touched upon English *th* in "think" or "then". The former is almost always *th* (sometimes *t* when final), as *us ke thrū* < *us ke* through, by means of him: *samit sāhab* (*ṣāḥib*) = Mr. Smith. Against this note *ṭhaḍḍ kalās* for "third class". The latter *th* > *d*: *fādar* < "father," Roman Catholic priest: but *pādrī* < Portuguese "padre," any clergyman.

5. Conclusion.—It appears to be clear that some UPH. words. derived directly from English without possibility of Portuguese influence, have changed alveolar *t*, *d*, to dental *t*, *d*, Is any explanation possible ?

(i) One explanation may be stated to be rejected. It is that the presence of *r* near *t* or *d* affects its pronunciation. Very many native English speakers cerebralize *t*, *d*, *l*, *n*, when *r* immediately precedes, and not a few make *t*, *d*, dental when *r* immediately follows, but there is no reason to think that modern *r* has any such effect in North India. We may satisfy ourselves about this if we listen to Indian schoolboys reading English.

(ii) Some words taken from English have been altered under Portuguese influence, and vice versa.

(iii) When Portuguese must be excluded we are left to random, guesses for individual words, unless we suppose that eighty or a hundred years ago English alveolar *t* and *d* were nearer to dental *t* and *d* than they are now. If this were established it would be all the harder to explain why Lallū used cerebral letters in the transcription of Gilbert, Lord, Minto, Taylor, doctor (*ḍāktăr*), Lieutenant (*lipṭan*), Hunter, and Lockett.

(iv) About any Portuguese *t* and *d*, which may have become cerebral, I say nothing, partly because they are not the real subject of this note, and partly because the very few words which suggest this phenomenon are of dubious origin.

ENGLISH WORDS IN PANJĀBĪ

THE details of philological processes are generally lost in the mists of obscurity, and most recognized linguistic development is difficult to follow because it took place hundreds or thousands of years ago. We must often have wished for the chance of hearing one sound change into another, and the wish is usually vain. But in the case of English words in India it is frequently possible to see them entering the country and watch the changes taking place. We can learn valuable lessons from the detailed study of one Indian language. I have therefore taken Panjābī and given a list of nearly 400 English words which have been incorporated into it. This first article contains the words with their Panjābī equivalents in two dialects. In the second I hope to analyse the words and draw conclusions.

English words in India may be divided into three classes. First there are words which have been wholly assimilated and are known to every villager. At the other extreme we have a large number, an indefinite number, of words used only by educated Indians in conversation or books. They are recognized as foreign words and those who use them try to pronounce them as in English. No object would be served by making a list of them. A man once said to me with much bitterness: "*merā fādarinlā merī vāĩf nū̃ baṛā bæḍlī ṭarīṭ kardā e* (my father-in-law treats my wife very badly)"; or we may hear *mæ̃ baṛā lonlī fīl karnā eā̃* (I feel very lonely). Such Panjābī does not help us.

But there is a third class, viz. technical terms used only in connexion with certain professions or pursuits or amusements. We have military, legal, and scholastic words, or it may be words relating to canals, railways, or games. These words are, it is true, employed by illiterate people, but their sphere is limited. They are difficult to deal with, for one does not know exactly how many of them to include. To take one example, most English military terms are found in the *sipāhī's* vocabulary, but only a few are fully naturalized. I have had to exercise my judgment in the matter.

A word as to the preparation of this list. I first wrote out the words as they are heard in Northern Panjābī, and sent them to Dr. Banārsī Dās Jæn, who belongs to Ludihāṇā and speaks the southern dialect. He very kindly sent me a further list including about sixty words which I had not thought of, and gave his own pronunciation of my words. I in turn added the Northern pronunciation of his new words. Frequently there is no difference between us. To give his forms and mine separately would involve a lot of needless repetition. It is sufficient to indicate the general line of divergence. It is entirely characteristic of the two dialects.

Where the Northern has	The Southern tends towards
<u>*kh*</u>, *g*	*kh*, *g*
f, *v* (faint dento-labials)	*ph*, *b*
ś	*s* or *ch*
ḷ	*l*
ṇ	*n*

Dr. Banārsī Dās has no <u>*kh*</u> or *g*, and uses *ḷ* only when it is assimilated to a following *ṭ* or *ḍ*; his *ṇ*, too, is rarer than mine. The ordinary system of transliteration has been followed except that sounds usually written *au* and *ai* are represented by *aw* and *æ*. This is to prevent the common English distortion of them into the " ow " of " howl " and " y " of " style ". Dr. Banārsī Dās's æ is [ʌe], mine is pure monophthongic [æ].

About a dozen words are taken from a Bengali list prepared by Mr. Sutton Page.

List of English Words in Panjabi

act (legal), *ækaṭ, ikaṭ*.
agency, *aja'nsī*.
agent, *ajanṭ'*.
Africa, *afrī'kā, pharī'kā*.
America, *amrī'kā*.
American, *mārkīn* (a cloth).
allowance, *alawns, laws*.
appeal (legal), *apīl*.
April, *apræl'*.
artichoke, *hāthīcok*.
assistant, *aśtanṭ', asṭanṭ'*.
August, *agast'* (dental *t*).

B.A., *bi'yye*.
ball (for play), *bāl*.
bamboo cart, *ba'mbū kāṭ* (bamboo alone is not used).
? banyan (a vest), *baṇæn', baneān'*.
bank (money), *baṅk* (? Port.).
baptize; *bæpṭāiz 'oṇā*, be baptized.
barracks, *bārak, bārag*.
barrack-master, do. *-māśṭar*, *-māsṭar*; his place of work, do. *-māśṭrī, -māstrī*. A b.-m. is a transport agent.
barrister, *bāliśṭar, balisṭar*; his work, *bāli'śṭarī, bali'sṭarī*.
bat (for play), *bæṭ*.
bearer, *bæ'rā*.
bearing, *baraṅg'* (letter without stamp, person without ticket).
beef, *bīf*.
belt, *bilṭ*.
bench, *banc, binc, brinc*.

Bible, *bæbal*, *bāibal*.
bicycle, *bāiskal'*, *bā'īsikal'*.
? billet, *biḷṭī* (way-bill, etc.).
bioscope, *bāiskop*.
biscuit, *biskuṭ*.
blotting, *blāṭiṅ*, blotting-paper.
board, *boḍ*.
boarding, *boḍiṅ*, *boḍaṅ* (hostel).
boat, see gunboat.
boil, *bæl*; *'āḍbæl*, hard boil; *'āfbæl*, half boil, i.e. boil soft.
bomb, *bamb* (? Port.); see "bum-ball".
boot, *būṭ*.
bottle, *botal*.
box, *bakas*, *baks*.
bowl, *boli-galās* (bowl-glass, i.e. finger-bowl).
braces, *bresaz*; see "gallowses."
brake, *birk*, *brek* (guard's van, etc.)
branch, *brānc*.
brandy, *brāṇḍī*.
breast, see "double".
breeches, *birjas*.
brush, *burs*, *burś*, *burch*.
buggy, *ba'ggī*.
bugle, *bigal*.
bulldog, *bulḍāg*.
bull-terrier, *būlī*, *būlī-kuttā*.
bum-ball, bump-ball (in cricket), *bamb*; see "bomb".
button, *baṭan*.

cake, *kek*.
calendar, *kala'ṇḍar*.
camp, *kampū*, *kamp* (? Port.).
canister, *knastar*, *kana'star* (? Port. *canastra*, basket).
car, see "motor".
card, *kāṭ* (postcard).
castor-oil, *kasṭaræ'l*, *kasṭræ'l*.
catch, *kæc*.
catching house, *kānjī hawd* (pound for stray cattle).
cement, *sī'miḷṭ*, *sī'miṇṭ*, *sir'maṭ*.
centre, *sĕṇṭar awṭ* (run out, stumped).
certificate, *sāṭī'pṭak*, *sā'ṭiphi'ṭak*.
chain, *cæn*.
chalk, *cāk*.
chance, *cāns*, *cānas*; *o'nū cāns miḷeā*, he gave a chance (cricket).
cheque, *cikk*, *cik*.
chief court, *cīpkoṭ*.
chimney, *cimṇī*, *cimnī*.
chocolate, *cakle'ṭ*, *cākoleṭ*.
chop, *cāp*; see "potato".
Christian, *kristān*, *kristān* (? Port.).
cigarette, *sigraṭ*.
civil surgeon, *sival sarjan*.
class, *klās*, *kalās*.
clerk, *klārk*, *kalārak*, *klark*.
cloth, *kalāth*, *kilāth*.
club, *kalaf*; *kalaf k'ar*, club house.
coach, *koc*; coachman, *kocvān*.
coat, *koṭ*.
cocoa, *koko*.
coffee, *kāfī*.
collar, *kālar*.
college, *kālaj*.
colonel, *karnæ'l*.
commander; *kamāniar afsar* (C.O.)
commission, *kamīśan*, *kamīsan*.
commissioner, *kamiśnar*, *kamisnar*.
committee, *kame'ṭī*, *kame'ṭṭī*.
company, *kawmpaṇī*, *kampanī*.

compounder (medical), *kampo'ḍar*, *kampo'ṭar*.
conference, *kānphrœs*.
congress, *kāngras*.
constable, *kā'nsṭebal*, *kansṭe'bal*.
copy, *kāppī*, *kā̃pī* (note-book, copy-book).
cork, *kāk*, *kāg*.
cornflour, *kārnflawr*.
couch, *kawc*.
council, *kāwsal*.
court, *koraṭ* (court of ward), c. fees, *koṭ fīs*, *koṭ phīs* ; see "chief".
cream, *kirm*.
cricket, *kirkaṭ*.
croquette (for eating), *kurkaṭ*.
cuff, *kaff*, *kaph*.
cut piece (tailoring), *kaṭ pī's*.
cutlet, *kaṭlas*.

dead-house (mortuary), *dĕḍ 'aw's*.
December, *dsa'mbar*, *dasa'mbar* (dental *d*).
decree, *ḍi'grī*.
deputy, *ḍipṭī* ; d. commissioner, *ḍipṭī kamiśnar*.
diamond cut, *ḍœmal kaṭ*.
diary, *ḍœrī*.
dictionary, *ḍikśnrī*.
director, *ḍarekṭar*, *ḍarœkṭar*.
dish, *ḍīs*.
dispensary, *ḍispĕnsrī*.
distant signal, *ḍīsī saṅgal*.
doctor, *ḍāgdār*, *ḍāgdar*, *ḍākdar*, *ḍākṭar* ; abstract noun, *ḍāgdārī*, *ḍāgdarī*, *ḍākdarī*, *ḍākṭarī*.
double, *ḍabal* (strong, excellent) ; *ḍabal roṭī*, English bread ; *ḍabal bres*, double breast.

dollar, *ḍāllā*.
down, see "signal".
dozen, *darjan*.
drawer, *drāz*, *drāj*.
drawers, pair of, *drāz*, *drāj*.
dress, *ḍares*, *dres* (*ḍ* and *d*).
dresser, *ḍaresar*.
dressing, *dressī* (levelled ground etc. : dental *d*).
drill, cloth, *ḍaril*.
drill, military, *ḍaril*, *dalel* (dental *d* in latter).
driver, engine-, *ḍaraivar*.

engine, *iñan*, *anjan*.
engineer, *anjī'nyar*, *anjnī'r*, *a'njnīr*, *anjnī'ar*, *a'njniar*.
entrance (exam.), *ĕnṭrœns*, *anṭrœs*.
European, *yūrpīn*, *zūrbīn*.

F.A., *ĕffe*, *œffe*, *œpphe*.
fail, *fel*, *fe'l*, *phel*, *phe'l*.
father (priest), *fādar*.
fashion, *fœśan*, *phœsan*.
February, *farvarī*, *pharbarī*.
fees, *fīs*, *phīs*.
fire, verb, *fœr*, *fœl*.
fireman, *fœrmœn*, *fāirmœn*.
first class, *fasṭklās*, *phasṭklās*, *phaśṭklās*.
flannel, *falālœn*, *phalālœn*.
foot (measure), *fiṭṭ*, *fuṭṭ*, *phuṭṭ* ; foot-rule, *dufuṭṭā*.
football, *fuṭbāl*, *phuṭbāl*.
? forme (printing), *farmā*, *pharmā* (? Port.).
France, *frāns*, *phrā̃s*, *frānsīsī* ; French, *phrā̃sīssī*.
French beans, *frāsbīn*.
frock, *frāk*, *phrāk*.
fry, *fraī*.

fryingpan, *fraīpān*.
furlong, *farlā̃'g*, *pharlāṅ*.

gaiters, *geṭas*, *gæṭas*.
" gallowses " (braces), *gālas*, *gælas*.
gaol, *jel*.
gas, *gæs*.
general (military), *jarnæl'*.
general, adj., *janral*.
gentleman, *jæ'ṇṭalmæn*, *jæṇṭarmæn*.
German, *jarman*.
Germany, *jarmanī*.
gilt, *giḷṭ*, *gi'ḷṭ*.
gingham, *gegam*.
girder, *gāḍar*.
glass, *galās*, *gilās* (usually of metal) ; see " bowl ".
grace (for bills), *glās*, *gilās*.
gravy, *grebbī*.
gross (12 dozen), *guras*.
guard, railway, *gāḍ*.
guard, military, police, *gārad* (prob. Portuguese).
gunboat, *aganboṭ*.

half, see " boil ", " plate ".
hall, *'āl*.
halt, *'ālṭ*.
head (of canal), *'ĕḍ*, *'æḍ*.
headmaster, *'ĕḍ-* or *'æḍ-māsṭar* or *māśṭar*.
headquarters, *'ĕḍkuāṭar*.
high, *'āī*.
high school, *'āī skūl*.
high court, *'āī koṭ*.
hit, *'iṭṭ* (noun).
hockey, *'ākkī*, *'ākī*.
holder, *'awḷdar* (pen).
hot case, *'āṭ'kes*, *'āskeṭ*.
hotel, *'oṭal* (hotel, restaurant).
house, see " catching ", " dead "
hurricane, *'arikæn* (lantern).

inch, *æncī*, *incī*, *inc*.
inspector, *insp-iṭṭar*, *-ĕkṭar*, *-ikṭar*.
intermediate, *iṇṭar*, *iṇṭarmiṇṭam*.
Ireland, *ærland*.
Italy, *iṭḷī*.

jacket, *jākaṭ*.
jam, *jām*.
jam-puff, *jāmpap*.
January, *janvarī*, *janbarī*.
jerk, *yark*.
judge, *jajj*.
July, *julā'ī*, *julā'*, *jawlā'ī*, *jawlā'*.
June, *jūn*.

kettle, *ketlī*.

lamp, *lamp* (? Port. *lampada*).
landau, *læṇḍo*.
lantern, *lāḷṭæn*.
late, *leṭ*.
lecturer, *lĕkcarār*.
lemonade, *lamne'ṭ*, *lamle'ṭ*.
licence, *lasa'ns*.
lieutenant, *lafṭæ'n*, *lafṭa'ṇṭ*.
line, *læṇ*, *læn*.
local, *nokal*, *lokal*.
lord, *lāṭ*.
lower, *loar*.

M.A., *emme*, *æmme*.
ma'am, *mem*.
macaroni, *makrūnī*.
machine, *maśīn*, *masīn*.
magistrate, *maj'isṭreṭ*.
Malta, *māḷṭā* (orange).

manager, ***mænjar***, ***mane'jar***.
March, ***mārac***, ***mārc***.
mark, ***mārkā***, ***mārk*** (trade mark ; ? Port.).
market, ***mārkīṭ***.
marmalade, ***māmleṭ***.
master, ***māsṭar***, ***māśṭar***; see "head".
matches, ***mācis***.
mate, ***meṭ*** (head workman).
May, ***maī***.
meeting, ***mīṭiṅ***, ***mīṭaṅ***.
member, ***mimbar*** ; ***mimbrī***, membership.
mess, ***miskot*** (officers' mess). The Zenana Mission House in Dalhousie is called ***miskoṭ*** because it was once an officers' mess.
middle, ***miḍal***.
mile, ***mīl***, ***mæl*** (? Port. *milhā*).
mill, ***mill***, ***mīl***.
mince, ***mins***.
minute (60 seconds), ***minṭ***, ***minaṭ***.
miss (lady), ***miss***.
mission, ***miśan***.
missionary, ***miśnarī***.
money order, ***manīāḍar***.
monitor, ***manī'ṭar***, ***mnīṭar***.
motor, ***moṭar***.
motor-car, ***moṭokāṭ***, ***moṭarkāṭ***.
municipal, ***myūnispal***.
municipality, ***myūnispælṭī***.

necktie, ***nakṭā'ī***.
note (bank), ***noṭ***, ***loṭ***.
novel (story), ***nāval***.
November, ***navambar***.
number, ***nambaṛ***, ***lambaṛ***, ***nambar***, ***lambar*** ; ***lambaṛdār*** (etc.), village headman.
nurse, ***næs***.

October, ***aktūbar*** (dental *t*).
officer, ***afsar***.
omlet, ***māmleṭ*** ; see " marmalade".
operation (surgical), ***apre'śan***, ***apresan***.
order, ***āḍar*** ; see " money ".
orderly (military), ***ardalī***, ***aṛdalī***.
out, ***awṭ*** (cricket) ; see " centre ".
overcoat, ***uvarkoṭ***.

papa, ***pā'pā***.
parade (ground, or manœuvres), ***pare'ṭ***.
parcel, ***pārsal***.
party, ***pāṭī***, ***pārṭī***, ***pālṭī*** (team).
pass, ***pās***.
passenger, ***psanjar***, ***pasa'njar*** (passenger train).
pencil, ***pilsaṇ***, ***pilsan***.
pension, ***pinśan***, ***pinsan***, ***pilsan***.
peppermint, ***pippalminṭ***.
phaeton, ***fiṭan***, ***phiṭan***.
phenyle, ***fanæl***, ***phanæl***, ***pharnæl***.
photo, ***foṭo***, ***photo***.
pin, ***pīn***.
pipe, ***pæp***.
plague, ***pale'g***, ***pleg***.
plait, ***pale'ṭ***, ***pleṭ***.
plaster, ***plastar*** (dental *t*).
plate, ***pale'ṭ***, ***pleṭ*** ; ***'āf pleṭ*** (half-plate), cheese plate.
plate-layer, ***pleṭī'ar***.
platform, ***pleṭfārm***, ***pleṭphārm***.
platoon ? ***palṭan***.
poach (eggs), ***poc*** ; poached eggs, ***aṇḍā poc***.
police, ***puls***, ***pulas***.
polish, ***pālaś***.
polo, ***pollo***, ***po'llo***.
porter, ***poṭar***.

postcard, *poskāṭ*.
postmaster, *posmāsṭar*, *posmāśṭar*.
pot, *pāṭ*.
potato-chop, *paṭe'ṭar cāp*.
poultice, *pulṭas*.
pound (money), *pāwḍ*.
powder, *poḍar*.
president, *prezīḍanṭ*, *prejiḍanṭ*, *parīzanḍ*.
press (printing), *pres*.
primary (school), *prœmrī*.
pudding, *phuṭī'n*, *puṭī'n*.
pump, *papp*, *pamp*.
putty, *phuṭī'n*, *puṭī'n*, *paṭī'n*.

Quaker Oats, *kuekar oṭ*.
quarantine, *kurāṭīn*.
quarter, *kuāṭar* (for quarter plate, i.e. tea plate); see "head-quarters".
quinine, *kunœ'n*, *kuṛœ'n*.
quorum, *koram*.

rail, *rel*.
ration, *rāsn*.
ream, *rim*, *rīm*.
recruit, *raṅgrūṭ*.
register, *raji'sṭar*; registered, *raji'sṭrī*, *rajistrī*; registrar, *raji'sṭrār*.
report, *ra'paṭ*, *ra'baṭ*, *rapo'ṭ*; *rabṭī*, *rapṭī*, *raṭbī*, reporter (village).
resident, *rezīḍanṭ*.
rifle, *rafal*.
round (police), *rāwd* (dental *d*).
rubber, *rabaṛ*. *rabaṭ*.
ruler, *rūl*, *lūl* (pencil or ruler).
rum, *ram*.
run through, *ran thrū*.

sauce, *sās*.
sauce-boat, *sāsboṭ*.

school, *skūl*; *skūllī*, adj.
Scotch, *sakāc*, *skāc*.
Scotland, *sakāṭlanḍ*, *skāṭlanḍ*.
second (time), *skinṭ*, *saki'nṭ*.
second (class in train), *sĕkan*, *sækan*.
second (course in meal), *sīkan*.
secretary, *skattar*, *saka'ttar* (dental *t*).
semolina, *samlī'nā*.
sentry, *santrī* (dental *t*).
September, *stambar*, *satambar* (dental *t*).
sergeant, *sārjan*, *sārjanṭ*.
servant, *sarvanṭī* (servants' carriage).
session(s), *śiśan*, *sisan*.
signal, *saṅgaḷ*, *suṅgal*, *siṅgal*.
signal, down, do. *ḍāwn*.
slate, *sale'ṭ*, *sleṭ*.
sleeper (railway), *slīpar*, *slīpaṭ*.
slipper, *si'lpaṭ*, *slīpaṭ*.
soda, *soḍḍā*, *so'ḍdā*.
speech, *sapī'c*, *spīc*.
spell, *spĕll* (for noun "spelling").
stamp, *aśṭām*, *asṭām*.
station, *saṭe'śan*, *sṭeśan*, *ṭeśan*, *ṭesan*, *aśṭe'ṭan*.
stew, *iśṭū*.
stool, *ṭūl*.
study, *sṭaḍī*.
stuffing (in duck, etc.), *saṭā'piṅ*, *sṭāpiṅ*.
sub-, *sab*.
superintendent, *sūprinṭĕnḍanṭ*, *suparḍa'nṭ*.

tapioca, *ṭāpiū*.
tar-coal, *ṭārkōl*.
tax, *ṭikas*. *ṭigaṭ*.

team, *ṭīm*.
tennis, *ṭænis*.
thermometer, *tharmāmṭar*, *tha'rmāme'ṭar*.
third class, *ṭhaḍḍ kalās, tharḍ klās* (*ṛ* is a fricative cerebral).
through, *thrū*.
ticket, *ṭikaṭ, ṭikas, ṭigaṭ*; *baṭikṭā*, without a ticket.
tiffin, *ṭipan*.
time, *ṭem, ṭæm*; *baṭemī*, lateness for (*be-ṭem-ī*).
timepiece, *ṭæmfīs, ṭæmpīs*.
time-table, *ṭæmṭebal*.
tin, *ṭīn*.
toast, *tos* (dental *t*).
tomato, *ṭamāṭar*.
tray, *trel* (dental *t*).
train, *ṭaren, ṭren, ṭræn*.
treacle, *ṭrīkal, ṭarīkal*.
trump (in cards), *tu'rap* (dental *t*).
trumpet, *tu'ram* (dental *t*).
trunk (steel), *ṭaraṅk, ṭraṅk*.
tub, *ṭap*.
? tumtum, *ṭamṭam* (pony trap).
tumble, *rambalṭambal* (scrambled eggs).
tunnel, *ṭaṇḍal*.
turpentine, *tārpīn* (dental *t*).
twill, *ṭūl, ṭull*.

upper, *apar*.

vermicelli, *varmselī*.
via, *vīā, vāyā*.
V.P., *vīpī* (value payable).

waistcoat, *vāskaṭ, baskaṭ*.
warrant, *vara'ṇṭ, bara'ṇṭ*.
whiskey, *viskī, biskī, huśkī*.

ADDITIONAL WORDS

custard, *kastar*.
gap, *gæb*.
recess, *rasæ's*.
shed, *shiḍḍ*.

ENGLISH WORDS IN PANJABI

Conclusion

Note.—Northern or Western Panjabi is the dialect spoken to the north and west of Amritsar. It is distinct from Lăhndī, which used to be called Western Panjabi. Southern or Eastern Panjabi is spoken south and east of Amritsar.

† is prefixed to a word to show that it has another form which does not illustrate the rule under consideration.

A GLANCE at the following pages will show apparent confusion in methods of word-formation. We must remember, however, the different influences which have been brought to bear.

(i) Some, especially older words, are fully naturalized; others, probably more recent, are only making their way.

(ii) Some have been taken from newspapers and handed on to illiterate speakers: they remain subject to the influence of those who try to preserve what they believe to be English pronunciation. This accounts for much diversity of treatment.

(iii) *iśṭū*, stew, and *aśṭām*, stamp, show us that some have come through the U.P. to which many servants in the Panjab belong and in which English institutions were established earlier than further north and west.

(iv) Tax and ticket which both become *ṭigaṭ* and *ṭikas*, remind us that borrowed words are often altered to make them resemble other Panjabi words whether former loan words or not.

Pj. *æ*, when it represents Eng. [e] or [ɛ], is shorter than when it has any other origin. Thus *æ* in *hæḍḍ*, head, is shorter than *æ* in *gæb*, gap, *karnæl*, colonel, or *lālṭæn*, lantern; so in *jæṇṭarmæn*, gentleman, the first *æ* is shorter than the second. An exception to the general rule is *lafṭæn* (*æ* long), lieutenant. Other interesting words in this connexion are *'arīkæn*, hurricane; *'acīsæn*, Hutchison; *pāṭīsæn* (also *paṭæsn*), Paterson: these have the longer *æ*. *'acĭsan* and *pāṭĭsan* are also heard.

Stress

The stress is generally on the same syllable as in English, but in the following words a change has been made. The stress mark is placed *after* the stressed vowel.

agency, *aja'nsī.*
agent, *aja'ṇṭ.*
Africa, *afri'kā, pharī'kā.*
America, *amrī'kā.*
April, *aprœ'l.*
assistant, *aśṭa'ṇṭ.*
August, *aga'st.*

B.A., *bī'yye.*
banyan (vest), *baṇœ'n, banyā'n.*
barrister, *bali'śtar.*
bearing, *bara'ṅg.*
bulldog, *bulḍā'g.*

calendar, *kala'ṇḍar.*
canister, *kna'star, kana'star.*
cement, *sī'milṭ, sī'minṭ, si'rmaṭ.*
chocolate, † *caklc'ṭ.*
colonel, *karnœ'l.*
cigarette, *si'graṭ.*
croquette, *ku'rkaṭ.*

dead-house, *ḍĕḍ'aw's.*
decree, *ḍi'grī.*

engineer, *anjī'nyar.*
entrance, *enṭrœ'ns.*

F.A., *ĕ'ffĕ.*
furlong, *farlā'g.*

general, *jarnœ'l.*

hotel, *'o'ṭal.*

lecturer, *lĕkcarā'r.*
licence, *lasa'ns.*

M.A., *ĕ'mmĕ.*
manager, † *mane'jar.*
monitor, *manī'ṭar, mnīṭar.*

necktie, *nakṭā'ī.*

papa, *pā'pā.*
passenger, *psa'njar, pasa'njar.*
platoon, *pa'lṭan.*
police, *puls, pu'las.*
pudding, *phuṭī'n, puṭī'n.*
putty, *phuṭī'n, puṭī'n,* and *paṭī'n.*

register, *raji'sṭar*; so *raji'sṭrī*, registered.
report, † *ra'paṭ*, † *ra'baṭ*; so *ra'pṭī, ra'bṭī, ra'ṭbī*, reporter.

second, *ski'ṇṭ, saki'ṇṭ.*
secretary, *ska'ttar, saka'ttar.*

warrant, *vara'ṇṭ.*

In addition to the above there are words with a double stress. Such are bicycle, *bā'iska'l*; commissioner, *kami'śna'r*; *ḍā'gdā'r*, doctor; quarantine, *ku'rāṭī'n.*

TRANSPOSITION

There are several instances of the transposition of *r* so that a stop + *r* + vowel becomes stop + vowel + *r*.

breeches, *birjas*.
brake, † *birk*.
brush, *burś*.
cream, *kirm*.
cricket, *kirkaṭ*.
croquette, *kurkaṭ*.
February, *farvarī*, *pharbarī*.
gross, *guras*.
trump, *turap*.
trumpet, *turam*.

l is transposed in *palṭan*, platoon ; *falālœn*, flannel ; *ka'laf*, club ; *pilsaṇ*, pencil, is an alteration of *pinsal*, and *raṭbī*, reporter, of *rabṭī*.

STRESSED VOWELS

The symbols between square brackets are phonetic.

English [ɑ] appears twenty-three times as *ā*, in two words it is *ă*, *plastar*, plaster ; *kasṭræl*, castor oil. There is also the alternative form *klărk* for *klārk*, clerk.

[æ] The theoretical pronunciation of this vowel is *ē*, but the examples show that actually this is rare.

ā occurs ten times : *bārăk*, barracks ; † *bālisṭar*, barrister ; *brāṇḍī*, brandy ; *jākaṭ*, jacket ; *jām*, jam ; *lālṭœn*, lantern ; *mācas*, matches ; *rāsn*, ration ; *asṭām*, stamp ; *ṭāpiū*, tapioca.

œ eight times : † *œkṭ*, act ; *bœṭ*, bat ; *kœc*, catch ; *fœśan*, fashion ; *lœṇḍo*, landau ; † *mœnjar*, manager ; *mœn*, man ; *gœb*, gap.

ă five times : *bămbū*, bamboo ; *băṅk*, bank ; *kămpū*, camp ; *lămp*, lamp ; *măkrūnī*, macaroni.

ĭ twice : † *ikaṭ*, act ; *ṭikas*, tax.

e twice : *pleṭfārm*, platform ; *mēm*, ma'am.

[ɒ] twenty-one times becomes *ā*, occasionally it is *ă*, *bămb*, bomb ; *ăfsăr*, officer ; *băkăs*, box. We may add perhaps *ăkṭūbar*, October, † *căkleṭ*, chocolate, and *ăpreśan*, operation, in which the *ă* is unstressed.

[ɑɪ] when initial or medial is *œ* or *āi* ; when final, *āī* or *ăī* : exceptions are *răfăl*, rifle ; † *mīl*, mile ; *jawlā*, July ; *ṭem* (or *ṭœm*), time.

Even [aiə] becomes *œ*, e.g. *fœr*, fire ; *ḍœrī*, diary ; *ḍœmăl*, diamond ; via, is *vīā* or *vāyā* ; bioscope > *bāiskop*.

[ʌ] twenty-four times remains *ă*, but we have *ŭ* three times : *turap*, trump ; *turam*, trumpet ; *burś*, brush ; also *kawmpaṇī*, company ; † *kānsṭebăl*, constable ; *săṭāpiṅ*, stuffing. In *gawrmṇṭ*, government, the vowel is influenced by the *v*.

[ɑʊ] is represented by *aw* seven times, sometimes pronounced [ɒ͡ʊ]; twice by *o*: *kampoḍar*, compounder: and *poḍar*, powder; flour is *flawr*.

English short [e] or [ɛ] appears in various forms. *ĕ* or *ĭ* is the commonest; this *ĕ* is very low, practically [ɛ], and may as a rule be equally well written *æ*: next in frequency is *ĭ*, then ʌ and lastly *ē*.

e, *æ*, sixteen times: *sækan*, second; *sūprinṭĕnḍanṭ*, superintendent; *sĕnṭar*, centre; *darĕkṭar*, director; *ḍĕḍ*, dead; *ĕffĕ*, F.A.; *jænṭalmæn*, gentleman; *hĕḍ*, head; † *inspĕkṭar*, inspector; *lĕkcarār*, lecturer; *spĕl*, spelling; *ṭænis*, tennis; *ĕmmĕ*, M.A.; *rasæ's*, recess; *rezīḍanṭ*, resident; *prezīḍanṭ*, president.

ĭ thirteen times: *bilṭ*, belt; *brinc*, bench; *cik*, cheque; *ḍipṭī*, deputy; † *iñan*, engine; † *inspiṭṭar*, inspector; *miss*, mess; *mimbar*, member; *pilsan*, pencil; *pinśan*, pension; *pippalminṭ*, peppermint; *siśan*, session; *śiḍḍ*, shed.

ă twelve times: *bănc*, bench; *dasambar*, December; *satambar*, September; *navambar*, November; *farvarī*, February; *janral*, general; *lamnēṭ*, lemonade; † *lafṭanṭ*, lieutenant; *samlīnā*, semolina; *santrī*, sentry; † *anjan*, engine; † *anjīnyar*, etc., engineer.

æ: occurs in † *lafṭæ:n*, lieutenant.

ē six times: *brēs*, breast; *darēs*, dress; *darēsar*, dresser; *darēssī*, dressing; *kētlī*, kettle; *prēs*, press.

[ɜ] or [ə] > *ăr*, six times; *jarman*, German (and *jarmanī*, Germany); *yark*, jerk; *sarvanṭī*, adjectival formation from servant; *varmselī*, vermicelli, *karnæl*, colonel.

ăṛ, once: † *thaṛḍ*, third (*ṛ* here is fricative cerebral).

ă, twice: *făsṭ*, first; † *ṭhăḍḍ*, third.

ā, once: *gāḍar*, girder.

ār, once: *tārpīn*, turpentine.

æ, once: *næs*, nurse

[eɪ], twenty times *e*.

ā, twice: *glās*, *gilās*, grace; *vāskaṭ*, *bāskaṭ*, waistcoat.

æ, twice: *gæṭas*, gaiters; *cæn*, chain.

aī, once: *maī*, May.

ĭ, once: *birk*, brake.

[ɛə] occurs in bearer, *bæ'rā*; and in phaeton, *fiṭan*.

[ɪ] *ĭ*, twenty-seven times.

ī, seven times: *kamīśan*, commission; *ḍīsī*, distant; *ḍīs*, dish; *mīl* r *mil*, mill; *pīn*, pin; *ṭīn*, tin; *slīpaṭ*, slipper; *phuṭīn*, *puṭīn*, pudding.

e. three times : *kameṭī*, committee ; *gegam*, gingham ; † *dalel*, drill.

ă, once : *saṅgal*, signal.

æ, once : † *æncī*, inch.

ŭ occurs in *huśkī*, whisky and *tul*, twill, where it stands for "wi" or "whi" (unstressed in *biskuṭ*, biscuit, *kunœn*, *kuṛœn*, quinine).

ū stands for "wi" in *ṭūl*, twill.

[i] appears seven times as *ī*.

Once as *ĭ* : *kĭrm*, cream.

Twice as *œ* : *kunœn*, *kuṛœn*, quinine ; *fanœl*, *phanœl*, *pharnœl*, phenyle. In these words it is based on a pronunciation [-aɪn], [-aɪl].

[oʊ] seventeen times *o*.

Three times *ū* : *makrūnī*, macaroni ; *aktūbar*, October ; *ṭāpɪū* tapioca.

Twice *ŭ* : *uvarkoṭ*, overcoat ; *pulṭas*, poultice.

aw once : '*awlḍar*, holder.

[ɔɪ] becomes *œ* : *bœl*, boil ; *œl*, oil (in castor oil).

[ɔ] ; (i) words without the letter "r", becomes *ā* : *bāl*, ball ; *cāk*, chalk ; '*āḷṭ*, halt ; *kalāth*, *kilāth*, cloth ; '*āl*, hall ; *māḷṭā*, Malta ; *sās*, sauce. Exception, *agast*, August.

(ii) Words with "r" : five times *ā* : *kāk*, *kāg*, cork ; *kānflawr*, cornflour ; *drāz*, drawer, drawers ; *āḍar*, order ; *kuāṭar*, quarter.

ăr twice : *farmā*, *pharmā*, forme : *ardalī*, orderly (note the different treatment in "order" above).

[ʊ], twice *ŭ* : † *fuṭṭ*, *phuṭṭ*, foot ; *bulḍāg*, bulldog.

Once *ū* : *būlī*, bull-terrier.

Once *ĭ* : † *fiṭṭ*, foot.

[u] occurs ten times as *ū*, and once as *ĭ* : *bigal*, bugle.

Unstressed Vowels

Final [ə] unstressed spelt with "r" becomes *-ăr* twenty-eight times.

-ār, twice : *lĕkcarār*, lecturer ; *ḍāgḍār*, doctor.

-ā, twice : *ḍāllā*, dollar ; *bœ'rā*, bearer.

-aṭ, three times : † *rabaṭ*, rubber ; *silpaṭ*, *slīpaṭ*, slipper ; † *slīpaṭ*, sleeper.

-aṛ, once : † *rabaṛ*, rubber.

With these should be connected *-o* in *moṭo kāṭ*, motor-car. Cf. also *gœṭas*, gaiters ; *ardalī*, orderly ; *pippalmiṇṭ*, peppermint ; *anjnīr*, etc., engineer ; *pleṭīar*, plate-layer.

When not spelt with "r" it becomes -*ă*, as *amrīkă*, America; *mălṭă*, Malta.

A closely related question is that of all vowels which in English spelling require the letter "r". There are approximately fifty words in which such vowels are found. Of these thirty have the *r* sound in Panjabi, and twenty have not.

Examples: *rapoṭ*, report; *kăg*, *kăk*, cork; *găḍ*, railway guard; *næs*, nurse; *sărjan*, sergeant; *karnæl*, colonel; *mărc*, March.

Unstressed Vowels nearly always become -*ă* or disappear. [-ɪ] > -*ī*; [-ɪ-] > -*ĭ*- or -*ī*- (-*ŭ*- in *biskuṭ*, biscuit). Occasionally a "spelling" pronunciation is heard, as constable > cons-table < *kansṭebal*.

Consonants

b > *f*, in *kalaf*, club; *p* in *ṭap*, tub; and is inserted in *bamb*, bomb.

ch > *j* in *birjas*, breeches.

Representation of English *d* and *t*. I have dealt with this in a special article in *Bull. S.O.S.*, Vol. IV, Pt. II. The following words were given there in which *t* and *d* have become dental.

t: *ḍăgdăr*, doctor; *agast*, August; *stambar*, September; *aktūbar*, October; *ketlī*, kettle; *kanastar*, canister; *tos*, toast; *trel*, tray; *santrī*, sentry; *hăthīcok*, artichoke; *turap*, trump; *turam*, trumpet; *tărpīn*, turpentine.

d: *dasambar*, December; *ardalī*, orderly; *drăz*, drawer, drawers; *darjan*, dozen. To these should be added *tărkol*, tar coal; *plastar*, plaster; † *băragmăstrī*, barrack-master's office; † *rajistrī*, registered; *răwd*, round; *dalel*, military drill; *dres*, dress; *dressī*, dressing.

d is changed to *ṭ* in *kăṭ*, card; *lăṭ*, lord; *lamneṭ*, *lamleṭ*, lemonade; *mămleṭ*, marmalade; *pareṭ*, parade; *phuṭīn*, *puṭīn*, pudding; *skinṭ sakinṭ*, second (part of minute), and to *l* in *ḍæmal*, diamond; to *nṭ*, in *inṭarminṭam*, intermediate.

d is omitted in *sækan*, second class in train; *sikan*, second course in meal; *kamăniar*, commander.

ḍ is inserted in *ṭanḍal*, tunnel.

f > *p* in *cīpkoṭ*, chief court; † *săṭīpṭak*, certificate; *jămpapp*, jam-puff; *saṭăping*, stuffing; *ṭipan*, tiffin.

f always tends to become *ph* in the Southern dialect.

English *h* occurs (only initially) in about fifteen words. It always gives rise to the low-rising tone. See vocabulary in last article.

j > *j* except in *yark*, jerk (used in cricket).

k usually remains *k*, but > *g* in † *bārag*, barrack ; † *kāg*, cork ; *ḍigrī*, degree ; † *ḍāgdār*, doctor ; *raṅgrūṭ*, recruit ; *ṭigaṭ*, tax or ticket.

kt > *ṭṭ* in † *inspiṭṭar*, inspector.

k is omitted in *ṭāpiū*, tapioca. See " qu ".

l, see also *n*, *r*.

l immediately preceded by a cs. becomes *-ăl*, as *bāibal*, Bible : *rafal*, rifle.

l > *ḷ* in *saṅgaḷ*, signal. It is added in *trel*, tray.

l and *n* are interchanged in *lokal* or *nokal*, local (used of trains) ; *noṭ* or *loṭ*, note (money).

The word " number " is usually *nambar* when standing alone for " number ", but *lambaṛ* when meaning village headman who is called *lambaṛdār* or simply *lambaṛ*.

l is omitted in *pleṭṇar*, plate-layer, and inserted in *pippalmiṇṭ*, peppermint.

l is interchanged with *r* in *ḍaril*, *dalel*, military drill ; *jæṇṭalmæn*, *jæṇṭarmæn*, gentleman ; *rūl*, *lūl*, (wooden) ruler ; *fær*, *fæl*, fire.

l and *n* are transposed in *falālæn*, flannel.

m is omitted in *papp*, pump ; *turap*, trump.

n, see also *l*.

n is omitted in *kampoḍar*, compounder ; *kānphræs*, conference ; † *anṭræs*, entrance ; † *laws*, allowance ; *frāsbīn*, French beans : *kurāṭīn*, quarantine.

ṅ is inserted in *raṅgrūṭ*, recruit ; omitted in *dresī*, dressing ; and changed to *g* in *gegam*, gingham.

n > *ḷ* or *l* in † *sīmiḷṭ*, cement ; *lāḷṭæn*, lantern ; *ḍæmal*, diamond ; † *pilsan*, pension.

n > *ṇī*, in *cimṇī*, chimney ; † *baṇæn*, banyan ; *iñaṇ*, engine : † *læṇ*, line.

n > *ṛ* in † *kuṛæn*, quinine.

p is omitted in *stambar*, September ; *aśṭām*, stamp.

p > *f* in *ṭæmfīs*, timepiece, and *b* in *gæb*, gap, † *rabaṭ*, report.

qu = *kw*, rejects the " w " sound in *kurāṭīn*, quarantine ; *kunæn*, *kuṛæn*, quinine ; *koram*, quorum ; but retains it in *kuekar oṭ*, Quaker Oats ; *kuāṭar*, quarter.

r ; see also *l* and the vowels [ɜ], [ə], and [ɔ], and Unstressed Vowels.

r is inserted in *brinc*, bench ; † *sirmaṭ*, cement ; *ṭamāṭar*, tomato ; *paṭeṭar cāp*, potato chop ; *darjan*, dozen.

r > *l* in *baliśṭar*, etc., barrister ; *gilās*, *glās*, grace (banking).

s is omitted in *ṭūl*, stool ; † *ṭesan*, station.

s > *ś* in *aśṭām*, stamp ; *baliśṭar*, barrister ; *māśṭar*, master ; *iśṭū*, stew ; † *phaśṭklās*, first class ; *huśkī*, whiskey ; † *aśṭanṭ*, assistant.

sh always tends to become *s* in the Southern dialect ; in the Northern this occurs in three words : † *burs*, brush ; *ḍīs*, dish ; *rāsn*, rations.

s + cs. does not present much difficulty ; school, Scotch, Scotland, slate, sleeper, slipper, speech, spell, station, study, stuffing, *can* be pronounced without an extra vowel. When the vowel is introduced it is usually between the *s* and the cs. : *iśṭū*, stew ; *aśṭām*, stamp, come from the UP.

t : see above *t* and *d*.

t is omitted in *sārjan*, sergeant ; *tos*, toast.

It becomes *d* in *ḍāgdār*, doctor, and *s* in *kaṭlas*, cutlet.

The forms *ḍīsī*, distant ; *lafṭæn*, lieutenant, should be noted.

[θ] > *th* : *kalāth*, cloth ; *tharmāmeṭar*, thermometer ; *tharḍ*, third (also *thaḍḍ*) ; *thrū*, through.

[ð] > *d* ; *fādar*, father.

v becomes Pj. *v* : *sival*, civil ; *ḍarævar*, driver ; *uvarkoṭ*, overcoat ; *navambar*, November ; *sarvanṭī*, servant ; *varmselī*, vermicelli ; *vīā*, *vāyā*, via ; *vīpī*, V.P. ; *nāval*, novel.

v > *b* in *grebbī*, gravy. In *gawrmnṭ*, government *avar* > *awr*.

w becomes *b* in S.P. *bāskaṭ*, waistcoat ; *baranṭ*, warrant ; *biskī*, whiskey. For cs. + *w*, see under [ɹ] and *qu*.

Addenda to Last Article

gawrmnṭ, government. *sāgū*, sago. *prāīvēṭ*, private.
jarnælī śarak (not *ṛ*), general road, i.e. Grand Trunk Road.

Corrigenda to Last Article

For *kārnflawr*, cornflour, read *kānflawr* ; for *baskaṭ*, waistcoat, read *bāskaṭ* ; for *pleṭī'ar*, plate-layer, read *ple'ṭīar* ; for *ḍaraivar*, driver, read *ḍarævar* ; for *ærland*, Ireland, read *ærlanḍ*.

z remains in the words for baptise, braces, drawers, president and resident.

z > s in *birjas*, breeches ; *fīs*, fees ; *gæṭas*, gaiters ; *mācis*, matches.

z is omitted in *'ēḍkuāṭar*, headquarters.

In S.Pj. *z* > *j*.

WEST HIMALAYAN *BŎHRI* AND ṢIṆĀ *BODŬ*

Most Indo-Aryan languages have a word for "many" or "much" or "very", and another for "big" or "great", corresponding to Hindi *bahut* and *baṛā* respectively, and each word has generally the same varieties of meaning. Thus the word for "many" also means "much" and "very". In Hindi *baṛā* sometimes stands for *bahut*; Panjabi *baṛā* and *bau't* are the same as *bahut*, and *vaḍḍā* is used for "big" or "great".

So far as I know attention has never been drawn to a remarkable word for *bahut* found in a continuous area which includes the Simla states of Kyũṭhal, Jubbaḷ, and Ba<u>sh</u>ahr (part) as well as the British districts of Simla, Koṭ Gur, and Koṭkhāī. The form under discussion is found in four out of the five Aryan dialects which are spoken in Ba<u>sh</u>ahr and collectively known as Kocī, viz. the dialects of Bāghī, Rohṛū, Surkhuḷī, and Ḍoḍra-Kuār. I have not actually heard it in the remaining Kocī dialect, that of Rāmpur, or across the Satluj in Sirājī, Suketī, or any of the other dialects further down the river, but, as there is much coming and going, the word must be heard outside its proper home.

The following varieties of the word should be noted. Kocī dialects in Ba<u>sh</u>ahr :—

Bāghī	*bŏri, bŏhri*	Surkhuḷī	*bŏri*
Rohṛū	*bŏhri*	Ḍoḍra Kuār	*bŏri*

Jubbaḷ, *bŏˀri* (with glottal stop)
Koṭ Gur *bauhri*
Simla, Kyũṭhal *bhauri*

The final *i* represents a high front vowel often written -ī.

About these words it has to be noted that—

(i) In all of them the *r* is dental, not cerebral.

(ii) All are indeclinable: the ending -*i* occurs with both genders are numbers.

Nearly all the words meaning "much" or "many" have indeclinable forms (this follows from their etymology);

but those meaning "big" are generally declined. Thus words of the type *bau'* (i.e. *bahu, baũ', bau'*) and *bahut* (*bau't, bhaut, bahut*) are not declined. Note, however, that Pj. *bau'tā* "much" is always declined. The words for "big" or great", such as *baṛā, vaḍḍā, bŏṛo, bŏṛau, băṛo, bŏḍḍā, bauṛau, băḍḍā*, etc., have cerebral *ṛ* or *ḍ* and are declinable.

What is the derivation of *bŏhri*. One thinks naturally of *bahutara*. That would explain **bŏhrā*, but does not account for the ending *-i*, which, as we have seen, is not fem. Professor Jules Bloch suggests to me that perhaps *bŏhri* really *is* a fem. and agrees with an unexpressed noun, and Professor R. L. Turner that *-i* is possibly emphatic like the similar ending in Nepali. There are difficulties. The meaning "many" seems incompatible with the idea of an unexpressed word; the emphatic seems to postulate a non-emphatic form, but I do not know of one. Probably all three types, *bŏhri, bahu*, and *bahut* come from forms of the same root, and the words for "big" from forms of another root unconnected with the first.

We proceed now to another type. The Ṣiṇā word for *bahut* is *bodŭ*, very interesting and difficult to explain. Like *bŏhri* and *bahut* it has a dental for its second consonant, but unlike them it is declined. The word for "big" is *bŏṛŭ*, pronounced with cerebral *ṛ*. The suggestion has been made that *bodŭ* and *bŏṛŭ* are merely different spellings or pronunciations of the same word. They differ, however, in both sound and sense. *Bodŭ* has a dental *d*, *bŏṛŭ* a cerebral *ṛ*, and the first vowel is very different. The *ŏ* of *bŏṛŭ* changes to *ă* in the fem. *băṛi*, and plur. *băṛĕ*, going back probably to an original *ă*, while the *o* of *bodŭ*, which never changes, probably comes from original *-o*. One word means "great" or "big", the other "many", "much", or "very".

I add some examples of the use of *bodŭ* :—

bodi băṛi bări, a very big pond.
bodĕ băṛĕ bări, very big loads.
bodĕ agūrĕ bări, very heavy loads.

bodi misṭi pŏn, a very good road.
bodŭ hĭn, much snow.
bodŭ gălīs, very ill.
bodĕ khūnĕ, many murders.
bodŭ valĕ', bring a lot.
bodŭ girān, very difficult.
bodi dūr, very far.
ma bodŭ beṭŭs, I sat much, i.e. I waited a long time.
talāk bodi thēnĕn, they make much divorce, i.e. often divorce their wives.
bodi girόm valĕrĕ', much perspiration cause-to-be-brought, i.e. perspire well.
jăk bodĕ yāgi hanĕ, people are very independent.
tŭs bodŭ chūt thiga, you made much lateness, you were very late.
bodi bĭrgayĕr' bodi shĭkăst khēgĕ, in much warfare much defeat they ate, i.e. they fought much and were severely defeated.

The word *bŏṛŭ* " big " hardly requires further illustration. It will be sufficient to refer to the Parable of the Prodigal Son, which contains both words. We have *bŏṛŭ kōnĕr* " a great famine " and *bŏṛŭ pŭç* " the big son ", i.e. " the elder son " : also *bodi dūr* " very far ". See the first two examples above.

The derivation of *bodŭ* from *vardhakaḥ* does not explain *o*. Professor Turner points out that Mid. I. *a* tends to become *o* in Ṣiṇā under the influence of a following *u*, but that this fact does not appear to have any bearing on the *bodŭ* question.

THE SINDHI IMPLOSIVES[1]

Implosives differ from plosives in being uttered with an intake of breath. It may be taken into the lungs or stopped in the larynx. Theoretically a plosivĕ-implosive is also possible, in which air is expelled from the lungs and simultaneously inhaled, the current in both cases going no further than the larynx. A final decision can only be made in a phonetic laboratory, but without such aid it is possible to give an approximately correct account of these sounds.

The Sindhī implosives are four in number, all unaspirated sonants, a bilabial, a guttural, a retroflex tongue-tip palatal, and palatalized blade-front-dento-alveolar. Three of them correspond to the North Indian sounds usually written *b*, *g*, and *ḍ*. The fourth is supposed to correspond to *j*, but is actually a palatalized *d*. The ordinary *d*-implosive is not found. All four may be initial, medial, or final. Many other sounds may be enunciated in this way, but Sindhi has only four. One must first learn to control one's larynx and to raise or lower it at will. It is not difficult to make a difference of an inch between the high and the low position of the larynx, and with practice this could be increased. The best rule for producing them is perhaps this: try to make an ordinary *b*, *g*, *ḍ*, or palatalized *d*, but at the same time close the glottis and lower the larynx. This will necessitate an intake of breath, and prevent air from going beyond the larynx.

I feel convinced that the amount of air that reaches the lungs is negligible. A simple experiment goes to prove this. If one holds one's breath and repeats the implosive *b* as often as one can without taking a fresh breath (it is easy to do so about 250 times), one will find that at the end one can make a full inhalation. If at each of these 250 repetitions an appreciable amount of air had been taken in, a final inhalation would have been impossible.

---

[1] "Implosive" has sometimes been used in a slightly different sense, e.g. by Professor Jones in *English Phonetics*.

ET DE QUIBUSDAM ALIIS

(1) Hindi, Urdu *bhăī* and *bhāī*, Pj. *văī* or *v̜āī* and *p̜āī* or *pr̜ā*. The words *bhăī* and *văī* differ widely from *bhāī* and *pr̜ā*, but I do not think the difference has ever been pointed out. *bhāī* and *pr̜ā* mean brother or cousin, and include, of course, brother in trade, nation, or religion. *bhăī* and *văī*, on the other hand have nothing to do with brother; they are not even confined to males. The two Pj. words do not resemble each other in sound. *bhăī* and *văī* mean my good fellow, my good woman, my good man. They are constantly used by husband to wife, by master or mistress to servant, by parents to children, by friend to friend. They imply familiarity, and suggest that the person spoken to is inferior, or at least not superior, in rank. A servant would not use it to a master or a wife to a husband.

bhăī and *văī* do not take the stress though they can begin a sentence. Of particular interest is the difference of initial letter in Pj. *p̜āī* or *pr̜ā* and *văī* or *v̜āī*. In Pj. it is generally enclitic, and therefore the initial Sk. *bh* becomes not *p̜* as for *bh-*, but *v̜* or *v*. The change of *v̜* to *v* is due to absence of stress.

(2) Platt's Dictionary gives the word *hilnā* two meanings, "shake" and "become familiar". I would make the suggestion that they should be given as separate words.

hil- " shake " used to be *hal-*. Thus Mīr Asar, writing in 1740, makes *halnā* rhyme with *calnā*. In Dakani Urdu to-day the word is *halnā*, and in Pj. it is *hallṇā̃*, or *ˌallăṇā*. The other word always has *i*, and in Pj. has a cerebral *ḷ*, *ˌiḷṇā̃* " become accustomed " or " familiar."

(3) Pj. *ˌall* and *ˌaḷ*. Unfortunately both the large Pj. dictionaries fail to distinguish *l* from *ḷ*; they thus obscure many interesting differences. Thus *ˌall* " a plough ", plur. *ˌallā̃* (Sk. *halya*), is fem. and has alveolar *l*: *ˌaḷ* " a yoke " (of ploughing oxen) (Sk. *hala-*), is masc. and has cerebral *ḷ*.

dū̃ʻ ˌaḷā̃ dā khūʻ is a well with enough land for two pairs of oxen to plough. The word for ploughman (Sk. *hālika-*) is like this second word. It is *ˌāḷī*, not *ˌālī* or *ˌāllī*. The verb to plough is *ˌaḷ vā̃ʻṇā̃*, not *ˌall vā̃ʻṇā̃*.

(4) Phonetics

(*a*) *The word " Ṣiṇā "*

I have always written the word in this way, feeling that the pronunciation *shĭnāʹ* was the best approximation for a European. It is perhaps advisable, in the interests of accuracy, to indicate the exact pronunciation. The chief thing to avoid is *sheena* (*shīnā*). The *i* is a retracted variety of the *ī* heard in long syllables in Urdu, Pj., and Ṣiṇā. It is almost the Russian [ɨ] in [bɨtʲ] " to be "; more advanced than the normal Russian sound, and is quite short.

ṣ is a retracted *sh*, slightly further back than the *sh* element in English " try ". *ṇ* is an ordinary cerebral *ṇ* with strike point behind the teeth ridge.

(*b*) *The Prefixes* pre- *and* post- *in Phonetics*

These prefixes are common in words like prepalatal, post-dental, postalveolar, and would be useful if there were agreement about their meaning. Unfortunately they are used in two mutually contradictory senses, and every writer assumes that his own meaning is attached to them by others. The question is whether, e.g., prepalatal is a subdivision of palatal or not. I use prepalatal to mean " in front of the palate ", not " on the anterior part of the palate " ; and postalveolar to mean " behind the alveolar position ", not " on the posterior part " of it. This seems to me to correspond with the medical use of pre- and post-, and to be correct. So " prechristian " means not in the early part of the Christian era, but *before* the Christian era. One or two authors, however, employ the prefixes in the contrary sense. My object in writing this note is not to insist on my opinion, but to mention the two meanings and to point out that owing to the confusion, unless we define our terms, we shall not be understood.

(c) *Comparison of Sounds in Different Languages*

In describing an unwritten language we often have to compare its sounds with those of a written one, but we must avoid comparing things which are on different planes. If I compare Urdu or Panjabi words and sounds with those of, say, Lahndī or Ṣiṇā, I must not compare written words with unwritten sounds unless I am quite certain of the pronunciation represented by the former.

The writing of Indian languages, whether in their own character or in Roman letters, is not phonetic. Thus we are told that in Urdu *ă* is pronounced like *u* in " but ". Actually that is one out of seven pronunciations, all perfectly common, viz. approximately the vowel sounds in (1) far, (2) bang, (3) attempt (first vowel), (4) gone, (5) men, (6) but, and (7) complete omission. The same speaker will habitually employ the whole seven. Yet people talk of *the* sound of *ă*.

Again, Urdu speakers will say *vo hātī mere sāt sāt āēā* " that elephant came with me ", but the omission of an aspirate in an unwritten language is treated as something remarkable.

When we say, as I have done myself, that the vowels of certain unwritten languages vary a great deal, we must not suggest that the fact is unusual, or forget how much variation (concealed by fixed spelling) there is in the pronunciation of vowels in the literary languages of India; and if we compare them we must compare actual sounds in both cases. There is a surprising amount of confusion about the sounds of well-known languages, and the pronunciation of many words is very different from what is supposed.

MIDDLE INDIAN -ḍ- > -ṛ- IN VILLAGE KAŚMĪRĪ

When thirty years ago, in the summer of 1898, I began to study Kaśmīrī in a lovely village 20 miles from Srīnagar, my teacher being a city Muḥammadan, I noticed that in certain words he used *r*, while the villagers regularly said *ṛ*, as *gur*, *guṛ* "horse"; *yūr*, *yūṛ* "hither"; while in others both alike said *r*, as *karun* "do"; *vāra vāra* "carefully". There was no variation in this usage; a villager never by accident put *r* into a word with *ṛ*. Subsequent visits to Kaśmīr confirmed not only the fact of diversity between city and village, but also the regularity of it.

In the *Festgabe Hermann Jacobi*, 1925, Professor R. L. Turner, following up some statements of mine in *Bull. S.O.S.*, iii, 2, 382, suggests that MI *-ḍ-* > *-ṛ-* in village Kaśmīrī. In support of this opinion, with which I entirely agree, I submit a list of words taken from the village language. In only two of them do we find an unexpected *r*; both these are connected with cooking, doubtless loanwords from Brahmans: *krāy* "cauldron", Pj. *kaṛā'ī* : *krūtsh* "spoon", Pj. *kaṛchā*.

Noteworthy is *kaṛun* "eject", in which we have a cerebral as we expect, but, contrary to rule, it is *ṛ* instead of *ḍ*.

In *khūr*ᵘ "heel" we expect *r*, for we have it Pj., Lahndī, and Ṣiṇā, but we might easily have got *ṛ* from the other root. In view of the *r* in *harun* "fall", we must either reconsider the tentative equation of *harun* with H. *saṛnā*, or conclude that it is a loanword.

For "myrrh" the *Kaśmīrī Dictionary*, edited by Sir George Grierson, gives (but with a question mark) the strange word *muṛ*—strange because the Paṇḍits cannot say *ṛ*; moreover, villagers say *mūr*. As the word is Hebrew, *r* is natural.

The subjoined list is a good example of the distinction between loanwords and words regularly developed. It is a mere matter of majority. Here we have over forty words in which an anticipated *ṛ* is found, and only two with an unexpected *r*. The necessary conclusion is that the forty represent the rule, and that the two are loanwords.

In order that this list should not depend on my assertion alone I sent most of it to Professor Siddheśvar Varma, asking him to check it with village Muḥammadan Kaśmīrīs. This he has been so kind as to do.

All these words have a special interest; they illustrate well what I said about *ṛ* in this dialect, and incidentally help us with etymologies, as in the case of *harun* "fall".

The four adverbs of place deserve attention. The *-ṛ-* which appears in all of them may not be Sk., but it has several parallels.

	where ?	where	here	there	yonder
Kś	*kōṛ*		*yūṛ*	*tōṛ*	*ōṛ*
Sā̃sī	*kaṛe*	*jaṛe*	*ēṭṭhī*	*ōṭṭhī*	
Bhadravāhī	*kōṛī*	*zaṛī*			
Bhaḷesī	*kŏṛe*	*dzĕṛe*			
Pāḍarī	*kōṛ*	*zāṛ*			
Curāhī	*kōṛe*	*jĕṛe*			
Pj.				*tōṛ* "up to there", "up to the end".	

The *Dictionary* gives some *ḍ* forms, generally as village alternatives. I have put them in brackets with the initial D. Villagers do not use *ḍ* in these words, but Paṇḍits often think they do. It would be useful to make an exhaustive list of village *-ṛ-* words. It is important to realize that they mark a definite dialectic variation, and are perfectly regular.

Village Kaśmīrī	Panjabi
bigaṛun, be spoilt	*vigaṛnā*
bigāṛun, spoil	*vagāṛnā*
bīṛ, crowd	*p.īṛ*
brôṛ^{u}, cat	*billā*
byôṛ^{u}, cat	
chēṛun, annoy	*cheṛnā*
chiṛkāvun, sprinkle	*chiṛakṇā*
chōṛun, leave	H. *choṛnā*
döṛ^{u}, beard	*dāṛ'ī*
doṛ^{u}, firm	
gaṛun, fashion (D. *gaḍun*)	*k̨aṛnā*
gōṛ, sugar	*guṛ*
güṛ, pakkā	
guṛ^{u}, horse	*k̨oṛā*
guṛ^{u}, mare (D. *guḍ*^{u})	*k̨oṛī*
güṛ^{u}, clock	*k̨aṛī*
gūṛ, kaccā	
gagṛā, thunder	
hagoṛ^{u}, cart	*chakṛā*
hāṛ, June-July	*˛āṛ'*
oṛa, pair, etc.	*joṛā*
jūṛ^{i}, do	*joṛī*
kapuṛ, cloth	*kapṛā*
kaṛun, eject	*kaḍḍ'ṇā*
kāṛun, boil	*kāṛ'nā*
kŏkuṛ, cock	*kukkaṛ*
koṛ^{u}, bracelet	*kaṛā*
kōṛ, whither	

Village Kaśmīrī	Panjabi
kūṛ^{u}, girl	*kuṛī*
laṛ, thread	*laṛ*
laṛun, fight	*laṛnā*
laṛöy^{i}, fight (D. *laḍöy*^{i})	*laṛāī*
lāṛun, run	
lāṛun, stain	
lūṛ^{u}, club	*lauṛā*
miṛ^{u}, dovecot	H. *maṭh*
mūṛ, foolish	H. *mūṛh*
moṛ^{u}, body (D. *moḍ*^{u})	
mūṛun, husk	
ōṛ, thither	
paṛun, read	*paṛ'nā*
śuṛ, boy	
thüṛ^{u}, back	
tōṛ, thither	*tōṛ*
tshāṛun, seek (D. *tshāḍun*)	
tsüṛ^{u}, bird	*ciṛī*
yūṛ, hither	

Loanwords

krāy, cauldron	*kaṛā'ī*
krūtsh, ladle	*kaṛchā*

Other words with *r* (not *ṛ*)

khūr^{u}, heel	*khur*
harun, fall	
mūr, myrrh	*mur*

THE OLD TESTAMENT: A NEW TRANSLATION. By JAMES MOFFATT. Vol. I, xi + 571 pp. Vol. II, xi + 483 pp. London: Hodder and Stoughton, 1924. 10*s*. 6*d*. per vol.

In these days of specialized work it is a bold thing for a New Testament scholar to translate the Old Testament, for, although he will naturally mistrust his own opinion in a sphere where he has not expert knowledge, and will follow that of Old Testament scholars, yet he requires a general acquaintance with the whole field in order to be able to pass wise judgments. This is a great work and will be of immense service to all those who really study the Bible, especially to those who do not read the original. It must be judged by its intentions. It aims at giving a popular and accurate translation in good modern English. It cannot supersede the AV. and the RV., but is to be used along with them. We must ask ourselves two questions: is it accurate, and is it couched in good English? The answer to the first question is almost wholly favourable (though I cannot persuade myself that כה יעשה יהוה לי וכה יסיף means "may God kill me and worse"). It is invaluable in throwing new light on obscure or doubtful sentences, it is a wonderful contribution to knowledge. The second question must be answered with much greater reserve.

While there are innumerable passages, especially in the second volume, full of felicitous renderings, some which make one glow with spiritual ardour, there are many others where wrong idioms, even bad grammar, harsh phrases, colloquialisms, almost vulgarisms, impair the pleasure and profit of reading. The faults of idiom, diction and grammar which are observable in the author's New Testament are still present, though happily they are not nearly so prominent. Thus to take his translations of the poetry, one's criticism of the first volume, and to a lesser extent of the second, is that they are a strange mixture. Phrases of rhythmic and poetic beauty jostle colloquial prose; in half a dozen consecutive lines we may find a number of incongruous details—rhyme, metre, and rhythm, along with unrhymed, unmetrical, and unrhythmical lines, or stately prose along with snippets of modern conversation. The following examples from vol. i will illustrate what has been said :—

(*a*) Bad or clumsy English : Who has handed you over your foes, Gen. xiv, 20. In case they *would* kill him, Gen. xxvi, 7. She (Rahab) *stayed* on the wall, Joshua ii, 15. Isaac *stayed* at Gerar, Gen. xxvi, 6. Where you hid *yon* day, 1 Sam. xxvi, 16. All *yon* company that I met, Gen. xxxiii, 8. He and his officers *stiffened themselves*, Ex. ix, 24. Encouraged him from God, 1 Sam. xxiii, 16. Drowsy and asleep, 2 Sam. iv, 6. We *will* never be able, Neh. iv, 10. Destroy all the spots, מקומות, Deut. xii, 2. In 1 Ch. xxvii, 24, " never " occurs twice, apparently for " not ". So Song v, 6, and elsewhere, " check " is used for " find fault with ".

(*b*) Colloquial or undignified English : in the great poem of Deut. xxxii the Almighty is made to refer to His enemies as " fatuous folk " (גוי אבד), v. 28, and to say " I had meant to finish them off " (אפאיהם), v. 26*a*. In the same poem occurs the school phrase " ask your seniors to repeat ". Other examples are : Moses was a most devout creature, Num. xii, 3. Hands off ! Jos. vi, 18. Jacob *started* to mount his sons on camels, Gen. xxxi, 17. This is a bad business, 1 Sam. xxvi, 16. Passing waifs (תושבים), 1 Ch. xxix, 15.

In places there are phrases which convey no clear meaning.

A considerable number of the individual words seem out of place in a Bible translation, for they have a peculiar and narrow meaning. Such words are braves, fetishes, fortalice, sept, sheikhs, midrash, burg and burghers (former not given, latter marked " archaic " in Concise Oxf. Dict.), troglodytes (surely " cave-dwellers " is a far commoner word). מדבר is translated now " desert ", now " country " or " open country " (description, not translation), now " wolds ", now " steppes " (applied to a part of the country where there are no steppes) : David's גבורים are called " knights ", which they were not. Some prophets are termed " dervishes ", others " prophets ", but we are not told what the principle of the distinction is.

The word " clan " is greatly overworked. It does duty for שבט, for גוי, for בני (clan of), for ראשי האבות (chief of the clans), for בית (בית אביך, thy father's clan). "Quivering" is unpleasantly used of human beings for נמוגו, Jos. ii, 9, 24; for ינע, Is. vii, 2; and for ימס, Jos. ii, 11; v, 1; vii, 5; but this last word, נמס, is rendered " melt " in Ps. xxii, 14; Isa. xiii, 7; " tremble " in Ezek. xxi, 7; and " collapse " in 2 Sam. xvii, 10. Hannah's heart " thrills over the Eternal " (עלץ), and in Song i, 4, the bride says " there let us thrill with delight ".

In place of the usual Hebrew or Aramaic text Dr. Moffatt has frequently adopted readings found in the versions, or followed modern conjectures. It would be well if these were indicated in the margin. We should like to know which are conjectures and which come from the versions, and also what degree of credence is to be attached to any particular reading.

Another question is that of order. In many instances the translator departs from the usual arrangement. Sometimes the intention of this is to restore the chronological order, and for this we are grateful, but it is tantalizing to be unable to find a passage which has been removed to a new situation. In other cases, however, where a supposed Hebrew editor has blended two or more narratives into a harmonious whole, Dr. Moffatt undoes his work and gives us the separate documents according to the prevailing view of modern critics—a proceeding which is out of place in a popular translation.

It is greatly to be regretted that Dr. Moffatt has given us a title instead of a name for the Tetragrammaton. The absolutely necessary thing is that whatever word is chosen, it should be a name, not a title. I hope that in the next edition " Jehovah " will be adopted. Why should " Yahweh " be suggested as the only possible name, unless indeed we are also to have Ya'aqobh, Yitschaq, Yarobh'am and Chizqiel ? But if we may and do employ the Anglicized forms of these names, we may also employ " Jehovah ", used in the American RV., long established as an English word, and well suited to a popular translation.

We must note some very happy renderings: deep sea vessels for אניות תרשיש (ships of Tarshish); king's "confidential adviser" for רע המלך (but why David's *friend* for רעה ?); temple attendants, for Nethinim; tutor to the king's sons, עם בני המלך; I am quite ready to die, הנני אמות, 1 Sam. xiv, 43. There are many others, especially in the later books. Perhaps the most successful attempt to translate poetically a poetical passage is in 2 Sam. xxiii, 1–7. It is notable that the translation of poetry in the prose books is not on the whole so good as in the more purely poetical books, the Prophets and Psalms.

The Book of Proverbs lends itself well to his style, and the translation of Pr. xxx, 1, a happy conjecture, adds a pure gem to the book.

Those who desire to know the Bible are under a great debt to Dr. Moffatt for his work; if attention has here been drawn to flaws rather than to merits, it is in order that they may be considered before the next edition comes out.

To sum up, the following are the changes which we should like to see introduced as soon as possible :—

(1) The English improved in very many places.

(2) Indication given of new readings, those found in the great versions being distinguished from modern guesses.

(3) Excision of all reference to different documents or editorial comments; at best they deal only with scholars' subjective conjectures, and they are unsuitable in a popular work.

(4) Order not to be altered except where necessary (never to indicate documents), and all changes to be shown.

(5) " Jehovah " to be used for the Tetragrammaton.

Judge H. T. Colebrooke's Supposed Translation of the Gospels into Hindi, 1806

IN Darlowe and Moule's *Historical Catalogue of the Printed Editions of Holy Scriptures*, 1903 (= DM.), the earliest Hindi translation of the Gospels is entered as follows : " 1806. The Gospels translated by Henry Thomas Colebrooke (1765–1837), president of the bench at Calcutta, and honorary professor in Fort William College, the first great Sanskrit scholar of Europe." This is confirmed by Pearce Carey's book, *William Carey* (= PC.). In the third edition, p. 408, he writes " so far from vaunting how many versions he and his colleagues could add to their credit, they postponed the publication of their translated Hindi Gospels till Colebrooke's was printed in 1806 ". In the eighth edition, 1934, p. 420, " they postponed till 1811 the publication of their translated Hindi Gospels leaving the field to Judge Colebrooke's version for five years."

I suggest that this statement, though found in two important independent works, both involving much research, is entirely incorrect and that to William Carey belongs the great honour of having produced the first translation of any part of the Scriptures in Hindi.

The libraries which might be expected to have a copy of Colebrooke's supposed translation do not possess one. These are the libraries of the Brit. Mus., the India Off., the Brit. and For. Bib. Soc., the Roy. As. Soc., of which Colebrooke's son was president, the Bapt. Miss. Soc., and Serampore Coll. The Catalogue of the As. Soc. of Beng., of which Colebrooke himself was president, does not contain it. Further, *Colebrooke's Life*, by his son, which gives a list of his works, and the *Dict. of Nat. Biog.*, in its " complete list ", do not mention a translation of any part of the Bible.

After a time continued investigation practically convinced me that the idea of a translation by Colebrooke was due to a misunderstanding. But the question remained " What was the source of the categorical statement that Colebrooke published Hindi Gospels in 1806 ? " Among numerous letters to various places I wrote one to Serampore College, and from the Rev. R. A. Barclay I received a reference which gives the probable origin of the story of the translation, though the date (1806) still required explanation. In a letter written by William Carey to Dr. Rylands on 14th December, 1803, which Mr. Barclay most kindly transcribed in full, Carey writes " A few days ago Mr. Buchanan informed me that a military gentleman had translated the Gospels into Hindoostanee and Persian, and had made a present of them to the College, and that the College Council had voted the printing of them. . . . I am glad that Major Colebrooke has done it. We will gladly do what others do not do " (*Periodical Accounts*, vol. ii, 456).

This is perhaps the place to point out the distinction between Hindi and Hindustani. Hindi is largely Sanskritic, many words are pure Sanskrit, while Hindustani, more correctly called Urdu, partially the same language, has Arabic and Persian words instead of Sanskrit. Carey, though using the terms indiscriminately, truly said that two translations were necessary " one into that [language] which draws principally on the Persian and Arabic for its supplies of difficult words, and another into that which has recourse in the same manner to the Sungscrit. Indeed the difference in these kinds is so great, that the Gospels translated into the former kind of Hindee under the auspices of the College of Fort William, is in many places quite unintelligible to Sungscrit pundits born and brought up in Hindoosthan " (*First Memoir*, 1808, p. 9).

Buchanan was Rev. Claudius Buchanan, for some years Vice-Provost of Fort William College, the author of some very interesting books, and a man of earnest Christian piety.

It is evident, as Mr. Barclay has pointed out to me, that Judge Colebrooke has been confused with Major Colebrooke.

The Judge does not seem to have done any Bible translation, though he was a great Oriental scholar and a good friend to the missionaries. He died in 1837—twenty-nine years after Major Colebrooke—and was not a military man. PC. in his earlier editions called him simply "Colebrooke", but in his latest edition added the word "Judge". Major Robert Hyde Colebrooke (1762 or 3–1808), afterwards Lieut.-Colonel, was probably Judge Colebrooke's first cousin. He served in the Indian Army for thirty years, becoming Surveyor-General, and died in Bhagalpur. He was not directly connected with the College.

There has been further misunderstanding. The sole evidence for any translation into Hindustani (Urdu) by Colonel Colebrooke seems to be Carey's letter. But the letter contains merely a second-hand reference to a conversation. Impressions left on one's mind by conversation are notoriously inaccurate; impressions of a verbal report of conversation still more so. Here we have an account of a conversation reporting another which had taken place some time before. According to it Buchanan thought that Colonel Colebrooke had translated the Gospels into Hindustani, but in quarters where we should expect confirmation of this there is none; there is no reason to suppose that Colebrooke ever did so.

We come now to another point. Carey's letter speaks of an Urdu translation of the Gospels, but DM. and PC. refer to Hindi, and there is nothing to show that either of the Colebrookes did anything in Hindi. The evidence to the contrary is strong.

I. The Colebrookes did not Translate the Gospels into Hindi or Hindustani

(*a*) The very Buchanan, who is quoted as having said that Colebrooke translated the Gospels into Urdu, himself published in March, 1805, less than fifteen months after the conversation, a book called *The College of Fort William*,[1] containing the

[1] Published anonymously; but the author's name is given at the end of *Christian Researches* which is by the same writer. See below.

"official papers and literary proceedings of the College" during its first four years. On pp. 219–225 is a list of "Works in Oriental Languages and Literature, printed in the College or published by its learned members", and on pp. 225–231 under the date 20th September, 1804, the list is continued to include those published during the past year or "now in course of publication". Several translations of the N.T. or of the Gospels in different languages are mentioned, but there is no reference to any Hindustani or Hindi translation by either Colebrooke.

(*b*) In 1819 Thomas Roebuck, one of the College staff, published a similar book entitled *The Annals of the College of Fort William from its Foundation on the 4th May, 1800, to the Present Time.* It contains (p. 586) "a general list of all works patronized or encouraged by the College". This does not mention Colonel Colebrooke at all. Two Sanskrit works by Judge Colebrooke are referred to, but nothing by him in Hindi or Urdu. There is, however, the following reference to an Urdu translation of the N.T.: "The New Testament translated into Hindoostanee by [Mirza Mohummud Fitrut and] learned natives of the College of Fort William, revised and compared with the original Greek by Dr. William Hunter, Calcutta, in one volume quarto, 1805." This translation appears in Buchanan's *College of Fort William*, under date September, 1804, as "in the press" (p. 227). The words in brackets, omitted by Roebuck, are on the title-page. Though the language is Urdu, the character is Nagri. Several copies are in existence.

(*c*) Buchanan in 1811 wrote *Christian Researches in Asia*, which went through many editions. I have examined the 1st, 1811; 2nd, 1811; 5th, 1812; and 11th, 1819. On p. 2 we read "the first version of any of the Gospels in the Persian and Hindostanee tongues, which were printed in India, were issued from the press of the College of Fort William. The Persian was superintended by Lieut.-Col. Colebrooke, and the Hindostani by William Hunter, Esq." Here again nothing is said of a Hindi or Hindustani translation by Colebrooke.

A very important passage occurs on p. 223, n. (1st ed., also later edd.). " There are several Orientalists, who have been engaged in translating the Holy Scriptures. We hope hereafter to see the name of Mr. Colebrooke added to their number. Mr. C. is the Father of Shunscrit literature." The translation here hoped for, as the author goes on to say, was a Sanskrit version of the Pentateuch. This quotation shows us that so late as 1811 Judge Colebrooke had not translated any part of the Bible.

On p. 225 of the 1st ed., p. 251 of the 2nd and 5th, omitted in the 19th, we read : " The first Persian translation was made by the late Lieut.-Col. Colebrooke ; and it ' blesses his memory '. Mirza Fitrut furnishes the *Hindostanee.* There is another Hindostanee translation by the Missionaries at Serampore." Fitrut was the principal translator of William Hunter's version ; the other is Carey's first (1811) Hindi version.

We see then that in these contemporary works nothing is said about any Hindi or Hindustani translation published by either Colonel or Judge Colebrooke ; only Fitrat and Hunter's Urdu Gospels (1805) are mentioned. Nor have I come across any reference in the Serampore letters. It is evident that Hunter's translation has been attributed to Colebrooke and changed to Hindi.

II. The Date (1806)

We now ask why was the year 1806 given with such confidence by both DM. and PC. ? The answer is not very difficult. In Carey's letter of 14th December, 1803, we are told that the missionaries had begun the Hindi or Urdu translation in 1802, but were not saying anything about it. On hearing Buchanan's story of the Persian and Urdu translations they stated openly what they were doing. On 24th September, 1804, they write " we are waiting to see the Hindoostanee gospels which are printing at Calcutta for the College. . . . Translations are going on in Persian and Hindoostanee. When we have the advantage of seeing this work we shall probably begin part of the Bible in Hindoostanee ". (*Per. Acc.*, iii, 23, 4. The reference is to Hunter's Urdu N.T., which was in the press in September, 1804.) Further, ibid., iii, 242, 2nd June, 1806, " On the application of brother Carey we have been favoured with four hundred Testaments, from the College." (Reference again to Hunter's N.T., pub. 1805.)

It seems clear that the time at which Carey received Hunter's Urdu N.T. has been assumed to be approximately the time of its publication, and that Colebrooke has erroneously been supposed to have been the translator.

III. Carey did not Deliberately hold up the Printing of his Hindi New Testament in order to leave the Field to another Translation

In Carey's letter we read " About a year and a half ago, some attempts were made to engage Mr. Gilchrist, in the translation of the scriptures into the Hindoostanee language. By something or other it was put by. At this time several considerations prevailed on us to set ourselves silently to work ". We may say that they began the translation in autumn, 1802. (*Per. Accts.*, ii, 456.)

At the very end of 1803 they were verbally given to understand that the Gospels had already been translated into Hindustani (ibid.). But they continued their own work, for in April, 1804, they write that in the previous year they had engaged in the translation of the N.T. into " Hindostannee " and Persian ; the former was nearly finished (a rough draft, doubtless, ibid., ii, 538). In September, 1804, they are waiting to see the other translation. It was published in 1805 (probably the end), and in 1806 they get 400 copies. On 11th and 18th February (? 1806) Carey writes : " The scriptures are translating into eleven languages, of which six are in the press, namely . . . Hindoost'hanee" (iii, 333, 4). At the end of 1807 Carey tells of their having printed "the Hindoostanee (new version) to Mark V". (Marsh, *Hist. of Translations of Sacr. Scripts.*, 1812, quotes this as written on February, 1807.) Apparently the term "new version" is used to distinguish it from Hunter's Urdu version. (*Brief Narr. of the Bapt. Miss. in India*, 1813, p. 66.) Two pages further on "the N.T. in the Hindostanee put to press". In the *First Memoir*, 1808, p. 9, they write: "In the Sungscrit Hindee version nearly the whole of the N.T. waits for revision. We have begun the N.T. in the Deva Nagree character, and the book of Matthew is nearly finished." Ibid., p. 22, "The printing of the whole ten [languages] will probably be completed in about four years; less than half that time will probably complete the N.T. in several of these, as . . . Hindee."

November, 1809. "Circumstances principally of a pecuniary nature" have "affected the printing of the N.T. in the Hindoost'hanee language. We have been enabled, however, to complete the better half of it, and hope soon to be able to finish the whole". (*Per. Accts.*, iv, 53.) (End of 1809) "Hindoost'hanee N.T. above half printed. The printing retarded by the same cause" (want of pecuniary support), ibid. v, vii. Finally we get "March, 1811. In the month of March, 1811, a N.T. in the Hindee and Mahratta languages have been finished at press". (Ibid., iv, 243). "Hindee or Hindoost'hanee. The N.T. translated and printed" (ibid., iv, 244). "20th August, 1811: The versions already printed and now circulating in India comprise five, namely . . . Hindee" (ibid., iv, 370).

The course of events is plain. They began the N.T. in 1802; in December, 1803, they heard of Hunter's Urdu translation; their own first draft was far advanced in 1804; in September, 1804, Hunter's translation was sent to press; it was ready in the end of 1805; they received copies in 1806, and in the same year or in 1807 sent their version to press;

they had printed half by 1809, but money difficulties delayed them, and it was not ready till March, 1811.

V. Confusion between Hindi and Hindustani (Urdu)

This is partly responsible for the mistakes that have been made. Carey's 1st ed. of 1811 and 2nd ed. of 1812 are correctly described by both PC. and DM. as Hindi, and the first Urdu translation of the N.T. (omitting Schultze and Callenberg's which hardly counts), that by Mohummud Fitrut and William Hunter, 1805, is rightly given by DM. under Urdu, not Hindi.

Carey himself did not distinguish between the two terms, but realized the difference between the two dialects, calling one Sanskrit Hindi, and the other Delhi Hindi. (The latter name is not quite certain. Rev. David Brown says, in a letter dated 13th September, 1806, that he had received from Serampore MS. specimens of Shanscrit Hindoostanee and Delhi Hindoostanee.) On the English title-page of the 1811 ed. of his Hindi N.T. he called it Hindoostanee, but on the Hindi title-page of both the 1811 and the 1812 edd. he correctly said Hindi. It is true that it is not pure Hindi, but the Urdu words employed are not impossible in Hindi, whereas a very large number of Hindi words are used which could not occur in Urdu. William Hunter's Urdu is pure Urdu, Carey's Hindi is Urduized, and after the 2nd ed. had been exhausted the pure Hindi translation of another Baptist missionary, John Chamberlain, was printed instead of it.

Conclusions

(1) In 1803 Claudius Buchanan had a conversation in the course of which he learned that the Gospels were being translated into Urdu and Persian. He reported this to Carey and left on his mind the impression that Colonel Colebrooke was the translator. Colonel Colebrooke translated one Gospel into Persian, but nothing into Urdu.

(2) Colonel Colebrooke was confused with Judge Colebrooke who never did Bible translation.

(3) There has been some confusion between Hindi and Urdu (Hindustani), but neither of the Colebrookes translated into either language.

(4) References in Serampore letters to William Hunter's Urdu N.T., 1805, without the mention of his name, have led to further misunderstanding; it was assumed that Colonel Colebrooke had done them, and he was confused with Judge Colebrooke. The fact that the Serampore missionaries received copies in 1806 has led to the belief that Colebrooke published Gospels in that year.

(5) The missionaries proceeded with their translation. Hearing in September, 1804, that Hunter's N.T. had just gone to press they waited for it. They saw it in 1806 and found it was Urdu. They then went on with the printing of their Hindi version, but were delayed by money difficulties.

(6) *Final Conclusion.*—The first translation of any part of the Bible into Hindi was the N.T. done under William Carey's superintendence and published in 1811.

Does Khaṛī Bolī mean nothing more than Rustic Speech ?

(Before proceeding to the discussion of the question I would draw attention to the important quotations from Dr. J. B. Gilchrist on pp. 366, 7 below, which show that at least four times in 1803, and twice in 1804, he used the name Kharī Bolī, and tell us in what sense he used it.)

THIS question arises out of some remarks made by Professor Abdul Haq of the Osmaniya University, Hyderabad, Deccan, who, criticizing views on Khaṛī Bolī (= KB) which I had expressed in my *Hist. of Urdu Lit.*, pp. 5, 8, 9, 13, said :—

hamẽ is se k͟hushī hūī ki ḍākṭar ṣāḥab ne is mugāliṭe ko rafa' kīā hai, lekin aṣl galaṭī mẽ yeh bhī mubtilā haī : khaṛī aur kharī kā farq inhõ ne bahut ṣaḥīḥ bataēā hai, lekin ma'ne taqrīban vohī rakkhe haĩ jo kharī ke haĩ, ya'ne muravvaja, 'ām, mustanad (standard) zabān ; aur dūsrā gaẓab kīā hai ki Khaṛī Bolī ko ek k͟hāṣ zabān qarār dīā hai, aur us kī do shāk͟hẽ batāī haĩ, ek Hindī aur dūsrī Urdū . . . Khaṛī Bolī ke ma'ne Hindostān mẽ 'ām ṭaur par gãvārī bolī ke haĩ jise Hindostān kā bacca bacca jāntā hai ; voh na koī k͟hāṣ zabān hai, aur na zabān kī koī shāk͟h. (*Urdu*, July, 1933, p. 590.)

" We are pleased to note that Dr. Bailey has corrected this mistake (made by some Europeans, of confusing *khaṛī* with *kharī*, T.G.B.), but he too has fallen into what is essentially the same mistake ; for though he has clearly shown the difference between *khaṛī* and *kharī*, he has given *khaṛī* almost the same meaning as *kharī*, i.e. current, common, accepted ; and he has made another amazing statement—that KB. is the name of a particular language ; he has further divided it into two branches, Hindī and Urdū. In Hindustān KB. usually means ' rustic speech ', a fact which every child in Hindustān knows. It is not a particular language or branch of a language."

I must stop here to correct the statement that I have given *khaṛī* and *kharī* " almost the same meaning ". I have never done so. *kharī* means " unadulterated " or " pure ", and while it may be applied as an adjective to a language, it has never been the name of any variety of speech, whether rustic or not. The word *khaṛī* means " standing ", and when first used of a language appears to have signified "current". Only it must not be forgotten that it has never been used of any language except that which we know as KB.

That the word does mean "standing", and has nothing to do with *kharī* "pure", is further evidenced by the corresponding words in other Hindī dialects or languages. I am indebted to you, sir (Sir George Grierson) for a reference (in a private letter) to Kāmtā Prasād Guru's *Hindī Vyākaraṇ*, p. 25. We read there that "in Bundelkhaṇḍ KB. is known as *ṭhāṛh bolī*". This word *ṭhāṛh* of course means "standing". Again, Dr. B. S. Paṇḍit, whose native language is Mārvāṛī, told me that in Mārvāṛī KB. is called "*ṭhaṭh bolī*", where *ṭhaṭh* has the signification of "standing". We thus have three names for this dialect, and in each case it is called "the standing language".

In *Urdu* for January, 1934, p. 158, Paṇḍit Manohar Lāl Zutshī replies to Professor Abdul Haq, and says he is mistaken, for KB undoubtedly *is* the name of a language. The Professor in a note on p. 160, rejoins "in my opinion KB means simply the opposite of polished and literary; it is used in that sense to-day, i.e. rustic speech. Lallū Jī Lāl probably used it with the same meaning. European writers have fallen into error about it, saying it is a particular language. The Hindi authors quoted by Paṇḍit Zutshī have merely followed these Europeans".

It will be noticed that by the phrase "in my opinion" and the word "probably" he has toned down his previous statements, but even so the matter rests simply on his assertion; he gives no references and quotes no authc·ities, nor does he name any of the Europeans who supposedly have misled later generations of Hindi scholars. In matters of *Urdū* his opinion commands respect, for Urdu is his mother tongue, and he has devoted his life to Urdu scholarship; this, however, is a question not of Urdu but of Hindi, and it must be decided from a study of Hindi literature.

In Urdu literature the term has no meaning, for it does not occur; it has practically never been used in an Urdu book, nor is it found in Urdu *tażkiras* (anthologies). Even Urdu dictionaries rarely contain it. The *Farhang i Āṣafiya*, of which Urdu scholars speak with bated breath, does not mention it. The meaning "rustic speech" which we are told every child in Hindustān knows, is not known to the compiler of the voluminous *Nūr ul Luġāt*, for all he says is "*Kharī Bolī* is conversation in the style and pronunciation of men" (*mard*, men, as opposed to women; T. G. B.); nor is it found in 'Abdu'l Majīd's huge Urdu dictionary, *Jāmi' ul Luġāt*, which explains KB simply as *mardõ kī bolī*, "the speech of men." We see then that the compilers of the two large modern Urdu dictionaries, themselves Indians, have never heard that meaning of KB which we are told every child in Hindustān knows. There is nothing about rustic speech in either.

In modern conversational Urdu usage *khaṛī bolī* occasionally does mean, not exactly village speech, but uncouth, boorish speech, though the dictionaries know nothing of this. But again we must remark that Urdu usage does not concern us. We are dealing with a Hindi term, and want to know what it signifies in Hindi. In my *History of Urdu Literature* I gave the term its literary meaning, using it exactly as Hindi writers do to-day.

Three points arise :—

(i) Who are the Europeans who have used the name KB ? And in what way, if any, can it be said that they misled Hindi authors who followed them ?

(ii) What have Hindi writers in the last hundred years meant by the name, what do they mean by it now, and what do they think Sadal Misr and Lallū Lāl meant by it ?

(iii) What did Sadal Misr and Lallū Lāl, who were the first Indians to use the term, mean by it ?

(i) The idea that certain Europeans have led Hindi writers astray by their statements about KB is strange. It would have been helpful if Professor Abdul Haq had told us who they are. The fact is that Europeans have rarely mentioned the name.

I have recently made the very interesting discovery that Dr. John Gilchrist used the term KB at least four times in 1803, the first year in which any Indian is known to have used it, and twice in the year following. He therefore shares with Sadal Misr and Lallū Jī the honour of priority. In fact, as he wrote the name four times in 1803, and they only once, he deserves it perhaps even more than they.

What happened is clear. He was Professor in the College of Fort William for four years, and for nearly the whole of this time Lallū and Sadal Misr worked with him. He learned the name from them, and in his daily intercourse with them had every opportunity of finding out its exact meaning. He often spoke of Hindustani as the colloquial speech of India or the grand popular language of Hindustān. He said on several occasions that it had various styles. The court or high style was Urdu, full of Arabic and Persian. At the other extreme was the " pristine or rustic idiom of that extensive language indefinitely called Bhasha ", while between them came KB. He has told us further that in order to facilitate the transition from Urdu to Bhasha he had caused a KB version of *Sakuntalā* to be prepared.

The state of affairs, as he saw it, was this. In the towns, especially those with a large Muḥammadan population, Urdu was the ordinary spoken language, in the villages some variety of Bhasha, while KB or even simple Hindustani, was the language which appealed to Hindus, particularly those away from Muslim centres. KB, owing to its avoidance of Arabic and Persian words was compelled to use words derived from Sanskrit which were familiar to the rural population. Gilchrist states that the desire to teach these words to his students was one of the reasons for bringing out books in that dialect. To this extent it has, as compared with Urdu, a rural appearance.

There does not, however, seem to be any evidence that in those days the words *khaṛī bolī* in themselves meant village talk. In no books of that or any other period do we find such expressions as " the *khaṛī* talk of Bengal or Madras or the Panjab or of English villages " ; one does not find " so and so has a *khaṛā* pronunciation " or " his conversation is very *khaṛī* ". Now if *khaṛā* (fem. *khaṛī*) meant simply *gāvārī*, rustic, one ought to be able to say all these things. The fact is that Hindi writers always used KB as the name of a dialect, and Urdu writers never used it at all.

The testimony of Gilchrist's *English-Hindustani Dictionary* (1786, 2nd ed., 1810 ; revised 1825) is important. Under " country " he has the entry " the language of the country, opposed to the town *bahur kee bolee* " ; under " colloquial " it has (1810 ed.) *rozmurru moohavuru*. In neither case is *khaṛī bolī* given as a translation, nor do we find it under words like rural, rustic, etc. So far as I know, it does not occur anywhere in the dictionary or in any of the many vocabularies which Gilchrist prepared, though *khaṛā* with the common meaning of " standing " is frequent.

Similarly in the numerous English-Urdū or English-Hindi dictionaries which have been published, one never finds rustic, rural, or country speech translated by *khaṛī bolī*.

As Gilchrist's early references to KB are of great interest, I quote them here :—

(1) *The Hindee Story Teller*, vol. ii, 1803, p. ii : " Many of those (stories) are in the Khufee Bolee or the pure Hinduwee style of the Hindoostanee, while some will be given in the Brij B,hasha."

(2) The *Oriental Fabulist*, 1803, p. v. : "I very much regret that along with the Brij B,hasha, the *Khuree bolee* was omitted since this particular idiom or style of the Hindoostanee would have proved highly useful to the students of that language."

(3) ib. "the real K,huree bolee is distinguished by the general observance of Hindoostanee Grammar and nearly a total exclusion of Arabic & Persian."

(4) ib., p. vii : (The learner) "will find another specimen of the K,huree bolee in the *Story Teller*, p. 24."

(5) The *Hindee-roman Orthoepigraphic Ultimatum*, 1804, p. 19 (foot) : "Another version of Sukoontala in the K,huṛee Bolee, or sterling tongue of India. This differs from the Hindoostanee merely by excluding every Arabic & Persian word."

(6) ib., p. 20 (foot), 21 (top) : "The Prem Sagur, a very entertaining book, rendered with elegance and fidelity from the Bruj B,hasha into the K,huṛee Bolee by Lalloo Jee Lal expressly to effect the grand object of teaching our scholars the Hindoostanee in its most extended sense, and with proper advantages among the grand Hindoo mass of the people at large in British India."

Gilchrist always marked in one way or another the cerebral *ṛ* which occurs in the name Khaṛī Bolī.

In 1814, Lieut. William Price published a "K,huree Bolee and English Vocabulary of all the principal words occurring in the Prem Sāgar" of which the Directors remarked "these (words) are in constant use in other K,huree Bolee and Bhakha compositions". Although the name KB occurs in the Introduction to the *Prem Sāgar*, it is not given in the vocabulary. The only meaning given to *khaṛī* is chalk, a signification, which, so far as I remember, is not to be found in the *Prem Sāgar*.

This vocabulary was reprinted in *Hindoostanee Selections*, 1827, 2nd ed. 1830.

The next whom one should quote is Garcin de Tassy. In his *Hist. de la Litt. Hindouie et Hindoustanie*, 1st ed., vol. i, p. 307, he says that Lallū's Prem Sāgar was "non pas en urdû, mais en khâri-bolî ou thenth, c'est-à-dire en hindoustani pur, en hindoustani hindou de Dehli et Agra, sans mélange de mots arabes ni persans." This is a paraphrase of Lallū's own words, but, mistaking *khaṛī* for *kharī*, he interprets it of Lallū's phrase "omitting Arabic and Persian words", thinking that it means "pure language". G. de T. does not mention *Khaṛī Bolī* at all, but speaks of *kharī*, "pure," i.e. without *mlecch*

" unclean ", words of non-Sanskritic origin. He wrote the words quoted (and almost the same words on p. 1 of the Introduction) in 1839, and repeated them in 1870; as they were French, not English, the confusion between *kharī* and *kharī* passed unnoticed in India.

Eastwick, in his vocabulary, 1851, says that *kharī bolī* means *kharī bolī* " pure language ".

Platts, *Urdu. Dict.*, 1884, under *kharā* has " *kharī bolī*, vulgar *kharī bolī*, pure language ".

The language which Hindi authors call KB English writers prefer to call High Hindi or Classical Hindi, names which correspond to nothing in Hindi itself.

(ii) The name KB is Hindi; the first Indians to use it were, as we shall see below, Lallū Jī Lāl in 1803 and 1818, and Sadal Misr in 1803; it is in constant use now by Hindi writers. We are therefore bound to ascertain what they mean by it. The Urdu meaning, if any, does not matter.

Have any of them given it the sense of rustic speech ? If so, when and where ? For many years after the time of Lallū and Sadal Misr they did not employ it at all. The first I know of to use it since those days was Rājā Śiv Prasād in his Introduction to *Hindi Selections*, 1867.

He regarded it as essentially artificial and literary; in fact, he says that Lallū Jī, though he strove to preserve its literary character, yet failed sometimes to exclude the Braj village words to which he was accustomed in his own speech. His words are: " Whether this new dialect, the Prakrit enriched with Persian and Arabic words, be called Hindí or Hindustání, Bhákhá, or Braj Bhákhá, Rekhta or Khari Bolí, Urdú or Urdú-i-Muaallá, its seeds were sown here by the followers of Mahmúd of Ghuznee " (op. cit., p. vi).

On p. xi he goes on: " When Dr. Gilchrist asked Mír Amman and Lallú jí Lál Kavi, to write some vernacular books in prose, they must have felt themselves very puzzled: it was quite a new thing to them. They wrote, but they both wrote in an artificial language." Six pages further on, p. 17, he says: " Lallúji has not allowed foreign words, Persian or Arabic, a place in his book (*Prem Sāgar*, T. G. B.), but he could not so well keep clear of the patois of his native place Agra." He has the same statement, but in Hindi, on p. 32, of Part I of his *Nayā Guṭkā*, 1900 ed., first published 1867, " he wrote in the kharī bolī of Agra; although he excluded Persian and Arabic words, he was not able to keep out Agra village words."

By Hindi writers the name KB is given to a particular language or dialect, viz. that form of Hindi which is used in every-day Hindi prose (and increasingly in verse), the Hindi which we find in all Hindi magazines, in translations such as the Hindi Bible, scientific works and all school books. This fact is so well known that proof is hardly necessary. In an article (*JRAS.*, Oct., 1926, pp. 717–723) I mentioned and quoted twelve Hindi authors to this effect. This is the ordinary meaning of KB, but the Urdu language itself is sometimes spoken of as a branch of it. KB is contrasted with Braj, Avadhī, and other Hindi dialects.

There is no need to labour this point; I will content myself with one or two further quotations, to illustrate what they mean by KB, and to show that they do not think of it as rustic.

The Miśr Brothers in *Miśr Bandhu Vinod,* vol. i, p. 119, say that "Sītal (A.D. 1723) wrote all his poetry in KB". Sital's language is far removed from rustic speech.

Badrī Nāth Bhaṭṭ in *Hindī*, p. 31, after mentioning that he lives within twenty yards of Lallu's old home in Agra, says that every Hindu household in Agra city speaks the same language as Lallu's in *Prem Sāgar*, the only difference being that which naturally exists between literary language such as Lallu's, and conversational speech, such as is heard in the Hindu homes. He calls Lallu's KB literary, not rustic.

The best known of modern Indian writers on Hindi literature and languages, Shyām Sundar Dās, says in *Hindī Bhāṣā kā Vikās*, p. 54, "between 1250 and 1450 A.D. the older Hindi dialects gradually assumed the form of Braj, Avadhī, and KB," and on p. 55, "KB was used for poetry not only by Musalmāns but by Hindus also."

Ramā Śankar Prasād in *Hindī Sāhitya kā Sankṣipt Itihās*, p. 128, writes "Sadal Miśr and Lallū wrote in KB mixed with Braj bhāṣā". He thus contrasts Braj and KB as two distinct dialects.

There is an important reference in Ramā Kānt Tripāṭhī's *Hindī Gadya Mīmāsā*, p. 33 of Introduction, "the language of the *Prem Sāgar* is adorned to this extent that all through it there is the splendour of Braj bhāṣā. Not only so, but it is characterized by a great pomp of words and by poetical style; it is not the plain idiomatic language of conversation, but poetical prose."

From these quotations and from those in the article referred to (*JRAS.*, Oct., 1926), and indeed from the works of any Hindi author who writes on the literature, it is plain that KB is regarded not as rustic speech, but as a dialect of Hindi, and practically all Hindi writers would deny Śiv Prasād's statement that it was artificial.

(iii) We come now to the important question: What did Sadal Misr and Lallū Jī mean when they said in 1803 that they were translating into KB? Did they mean "into rustic speech"?

Sadal Misr in the Introduction to his *Nāsiketopākhyān* says: "Some people cannot understand the Nāsiketopākhyān because of its being in Sanskrit, so I have translated it into KB."

Let us recall the facts. Lallū belonged to Agra, Sadal Misr to Arrah (Ārā) in Bihār, 450 miles away. To get from the former to the latter we must leave the Braj area where Agra is situated, pass through the country where Bundelī and Kanaujī are spoken, into the Avadhī country, and finally after entering Bihār traverse the Bhojpurī region to a few miles west of Paṭnā, the capital. The only rustic speech Sadal Misr knew was that of his native Arrah and the country round it; it was entirely different from that of Agra; the former was Bihārī, the latter Braj, and the whole country of still another language, Avadhī, lay between. Rām Candr Śukl in his *Hindī Bhāṣā aur Sāhitya* (at the end of the *Śabd Sāgar*, p. 210, also published separately) tells us that KB in those days and previously was the language of educated and polite conversation among Hindus from Delhi to Bihār. It is interesting to note that Sadal Misr, though he lived so far from the real home of KB, wrote it better than Lallū who lived very near it. Lallū's is too much tinged with his native Braj. The style of both men, though simple, was literary, not rustic.

A dozen or so years earlier Sadāsukh Lāl, of Delhi, a man learned in Arabic, Persian, Urdu, and Hindi, wrote KB still better than Sadal Misr and Lallū. He wrote just the straightforward Hindi which he was accustomed to talk to his educated Hindu friends, at least on formal occasions.

We turn now specially to Lallū Jī. In the introduction to his *Prem Sāgar* he stated that avoiding Arabic and Persian words, he had told the story *Dillī Āgre kī KB mẽ*, in the KB of Delhi and Agra. Did he mean "rustic speech"? The rustic speech of the district round the two towns was different. The people round Delhi spoke what we now call KB, those round Agra, 120 miles away, spoke Braj. If he had written in the rustic speech of the former it would not have been the rustic speech of the latter. Secondly, like Sadal Misr, he is literary not rustic. It is true that he sometimes failed to exclude Braj words and forms (perhaps he never tried), but Braj forms are not KB; indeed, we have seen above that KB is contrasted with Braj.

Fifteen years after the *Prem Sāgar* Lallū Jī wrote the *Lāl Candrikā*, a commentary on Bihārī's *Satsaī* ; this was also in KB, and showed less Braj influence. In the Introduction he distinguishes three dialects in which he had written books, viz. Braj, KB, and Rekhte kī Bolī (i.e. Urdu). In his Braj and KB books he usually endeavoured to avoid Persian and Arabic words, but in the Introduction just mentioned he used them rather freely.

Conclusion

We may sum up by saying :—

(i) KB is a Hindi term, and its meaning must be sought in Hindi writings.

(ii) By KB Hindi authors always mean a dialect, often, though not always, a highly polished and literary dialect.

(iii) It is difficult to believe that KB means rustic talk, for if it did it could be used of the village talk of any part of the world, and one never hears this meaning given to it.

(iv) There is no proof that any European writer has misled Hindi authors as to the meaning of KB.

(v) There is a little evidence that in conversational Urdu KB sometimes means boorish and possibly uneducated speech, but this is not supported by Urdu dictionaries whether compiled by Indians or by Europeans.

(vi) The early KB writers, Sadāsukh, Lallū Jī, and Sadal Misr did not write in a rustic style.

THE USE AND MEANING OF THE TERM KHAṚI BOLI

I. The Use of the Term

Khaṛī Bolī is used by Indian literati of to-day to mean (*a*) modern literary Hindī, including, as an admissible but unusual extension of the meaning, the Urdu language, (*b*) speech of the Hindustānī type from the earliest times when Persian and Arabic words were few to the present day when they are numerous, and (*c*) fragments in prose or verse which occur from time to time in writers from Amīr Khusro onwards and show a similar type of speech. The name first appears in 1803; see below.

Confining ourselves to the strictly Hindī area, and omitting the outlying languages Southern Panjābī, Rājputānī, Avadhī, and the Himalayan dialects, we may divide Hindī into two main dialects—Braj and Khaṛī Bolī. Braj is important chiefly on account of its past. For centuries it was the principal medium of poetical composition, but for the last 125 years it has been less and less employed, and since educated Hindus are to an ever-increasing extent speaking Hindustānī in everyday life, varying it with a more Sanskritic kind of Khaṛī Bolī in special *sabhās* and *sammelans*, Braj may for them become nearly as exotic in poetry and unknown in prose as Persian is for the inhabitants of Delhi and Lucknow. Kharī is important as the language of the present and the future. We need not refer to specifically Urdu literature, but Kharī in the form of Hindustānī with dialectic variations in villages and towns has so extended its range that it may be called the national speech of north India and part of south India. In prose it has long ousted Braj and now stands alone, appearing generally as Hindī, but sometimes as Hindustānī, while most Hindī poets express themselves in it to-day, though some of them write in Braj also.

For years there has waged a controversy in India over the respective merits of the two dialects as the vehicles of Hindī poetical thought; the question is frequently discussed in literary gatherings, and comes up constantly in books and periodicals. In this connexion Kharī Bolī and Braj are used as their generic names. Indians usually say *Kharī Bolī*, but one may also find *Kharī Bolcāl*, or simply *Kharī*, or again, *khare rūp mẽ*, where we should say "the language in its Kharī form". A few quotations taken from present-day Hindī writers will be of interest in showing how modern thought regards the matter.

Ayodhyā Sĩh Upādhyāy: खड़ी बोलचाल में मुझ को एक ऐसे ग्रंथ की आवश्यकता देख पड़ी जो महाकाव्य हो . . . आजकल के खड़ीबोली के रसिक व्रजभाषा की कविता से घबराते हैं . . . समय का प्रवाह खड़ी बोली के अनुकूल है (Introduction, *Priyapravās*, pp. 2, 24, 25.)

Paṇḍit Mannan Dvivedī, who does not like Kharī, says: खड़ी बोली की कविता पर हमारे लेखकों का समूह टूट पड़ा है। हमें तो काव्य के गुण इन में बहुत कम जंचते हैं॥ (*Maryyādā*, 1923, p. 99).

Vraj Ratn Dās writes in his Introduction to Khusro: अब कुछ वर्षों से खड़ी बोली का आन्दोलन मचकर हिन्दी गद्य और पद्य की भाषा एक हुई है

Kṛṣṇ Bihārī Miśr, not a brother of the well-known triumvirate, in an article on Nāthū Rām Śaṅkar's poetry, says: वर्तमान समय में खड़ी बोली में जो कविता होती है उसके प्रधान महारथियों में चार सज्जन बहुत प्रसिद्ध हैं ॥ (*Sarasvatī*, January, 1923, p. 128).

Śri Dhar Pāṭhak, the popular poet, in advertising his poems is careful to mention the language in which they are written, thus Braj or Khaṛī Bolī or Sanskrit or misrit, i.e., Khaṛī and Braj.

A young poet, Lakṣmī Dhar Bājpeyī, writes: जब तक खड़ी बोली की कविता में संस्कृत की ललित-वृत्तों की योजना न होगी तब तक भारत के अन्य प्रान्तों के विद्वान उस से सच्चा आनन्द कैसे उठा सकते हैं? (*Meghdūt*, Introduction, 1911, p. 3).

The brothers Gaṇeś and Śyām and Śuk-Dev Bihārī Miśr give as follows the languages chiefly used by the Hindī writers of different periods: 1733–1832, ब्रज, अवधी, खड़ी कुच्छ: 1833–68, ब्रज, खड़ी: 1868 to date, खड़ी, ब्रज कुच्छ ॥ Candr Dhar Gurelī says: मुसलमानों में बहुतों के घर की बोली खड़ी बोली है ॥ He likes punning, for he remarks: पड़ी भाषा को खड़ी बनाकर etc., but, indeed, Śyām Sundar Dās also puns when he denies that उर्दू के आधार पर हिन्दी खड़ी हुई है. This last-named author asserts in another place खड़ी बोली का प्रचार उसी समय से है जब से अवधी या ब्रज भाषा का है ॥. Both quotations are from *Bhāṣā Vigyān*.

In a recent examination set by an Indian for Indians the following question occurred: "What are the outstanding features of modern Khari Boli poetry? Is Khari Boli in any way superior to Vraj Bhasha?"

The foregoing quotations from a dozen Indian authors will suffice. They could be indefinitely multiplied.

II. What is the Age of Khaṛī?

The answer to this will depend on the date we assign to the death of the Apabhrāś dialect which preceded it. If we regard its Apabhrāś progenitor as dead in the twelfth century, we may say that Khaṛī was alive in the eleventh century or earlier. In its narrowest sense it was the language of the tract between Delhi and Meraṭh, as Braj was of the parts round Mathurā and Brindāban, but both extended far beyond these regions. As a spoken language Kharī soon became much more important than Braj, for the headquarters of the Persian speaking court were within its borders, and when the courtiers spoke to the people in the vernacular, they naturally spoke Khaṛī, not Braj. Its importance was increased as the Muhammadans made new conquests and took the newly acquired language with them. And Urdu literature still further added to its importance, for Urdu, especially in its simpler form, is only a variation of it. When finally in the nineteenth century the so-called High Hindī was fully developed there were three forms: the Hindu literary Khaṛī for Hindus, the Muhammadan literary Khaṛī (i.e. Urdu) for Muslims, and the vernacular Khaṛī (i.e. Hindustānī) for both. Its triumph was overwhelming. A threefold cord is not quickly broken.

Literary Khaṛī has existed since the time of Amīr Khusro in the thirteenth century. About 1,000 lines of his Khaṛī verse have survived; some would make the amount much greater, while some supercritics would deny the authenticity of nearly all of it. To disprove is as impossible as to prove, and I am content with the conviction that, though it is difficult to be sure of the genuineness of any particular couplet, such a quantity of verse, so different from anything else handed down to us, must contain not a few lines which remain approximately as Khusro wrote them. The great poet Bhūṣaṇ, born about the time of the death of Shakspere, wrote some Khaṛī in his Śiv Rāj Bhūṣaṇ, of which the subjoined quotation may be taken as a specimen; parts of his Śivā Bāvanī, too, have very much the feel of Khaṛī, for Khaṛī forms occur in lines which are otherwise Braj.

पंज हजारिन बीच खड़ा किया मैं उसका कुछ भेद न पाया।
भूषन यों कहि औरंगजेब उजीरन सों बेहिसाब रिसाया॥
कम्मर की न कटारी दई इसलाम ने गोसलखाना बचाया।
जोर सिवा करता अनरत्थ भली भई हत्थ हथ्यार न आया॥

The earliest known Khaṛī prose is in Gang Bhāṭ's book *Cand Chand Barnan kī Mahimā*, 1570, and in the prose portions of Jatmal's *Gorā Bādal kī Kathā*, 1623.

III. What is the Meaning of Khaṛi ?

The earliest explanation that I know of is Garcin de Tassy's in 1839. He writes: " On nomme thenth ou khârî boli (pur langage) l'hindi, sans mélange de mots persans et arabes " (*Littér. Hind.*, 1st ed., vol. i, p. iv). Here *khaṛī*, standing, is altered to *khārī*, bitter, and explained as *kharī*, pure ; p. 307 has " en kharî boli ou thenth, c'est-à-dire en hindoustani pur, en hindoustani de Dehli et d'Agra, sans mélange de mots arabes ni persans ". 2nd ed., 1870, has *khârî* in both places.

In the anonymous vocabulary of " important words in the Prem Sāgar ", 1831, the word *khaṛī* is not considered important enough to be mentioned. Eastwick, 1851, in his vocabulary, gives the word correctly *khaṛī*, but follows Garcin de Tassy as to its meaning, saying " here it is equal to *kharī* ".

Platts, under *kharā*, gives " *kharī bolī* (vulg. *kharī bolī*). pure language or idiom ". The addition " vulgar " is delightful, condemning as it does every Indian writer who has referred to the subject.

The name *kharī bolī* (as distinct from *khaṛī bolī*), with its explanation " pure language ", seems to be a European invention. I do not think any Indian author has used the term. Indians invariably say " *khaṛī* ", and there appears to be no authority for the statement that " *khaṛā* " ever means " pure ". So far as I know the word has always been printed खड़ी (or खडी in books which do not print the dot). It is so printed in editions of Lallū's *Prem Sāgar*. In the preface to that work he writes (A.D. 1803) :— श्री लल्लूजी लाल ने विसका सार ले यामनी भाषा छोड़ दिल्ली आगरे की खड़ो वाली में कह नाम प्रेम सागर धरा ॥

The word *viskā* refers to Catur Bhuj Dās's translation from the Sanskrit. This preface is dated Saṁvat, 1866, i.e. A.D. 1809, but it was a revised preface. The original preface, which also contained the reference to Khaṛī Bolī, was written *and printed* in Sāvat, 1860 (in some later editions wrongly given as 1830), i.e., A.D. 1803. The incomplete editions of 1803 and 1805 both have the preface with the word printed खड़ी. The complete 1810 edition, which does not use dotted ड़, has खडी. No edition that I have seen has खरी.

The fact that ड़ in some dialects corresponds to र in others, and *vice versâ*, does not here concern us. खड़ी is the only form used by Indians. There is no variation either dialectic or accidental.

Sadal Miśr, in the preface to his *Nāsıketopākhyān*, 1803, says: अब नासिकेतोपाख्यान को देववाणी से कोई कोई समझ नहीं सकता, इस लिये खड़ी बोली में किया

It will be noticed that while Sadal uses the term as a *name* or almost a name, well known and not requiring explanation, Lallū uses it rather as a description, " the *khaṛī* speech of Delhi and Agra," by Agra meaning apparently Agra City of which he was a native, for the district round spoke Braj. The two references taken together suggest that the name Khaṛī Bolī, though established by 1803, had recently come into use. It would be interesting to know whether any earlier instance of the word can be found. The Nāgarī Pracāriṇī Sabhā in a private communication assures me that nothing earlier is known. I have not noticed the name in Inshā Allāh's fascinating writings on Urdū and Hindī.

An Indian scholar suggested to me that *khaṛā* refers to the common *-ā* ending of Khaṛī as contrasted with the *-o* or *-au* of Braj, but I do not feel able to accept this.

My own explanation is that the word means simply " standing ", then " existing ", " current ", " established ", and that at first they *described* the dialect, as Lallū does, loc. cit. It was " the current language of Delhi or Meraṭh " or other large towns, and after a time it became " *the* current language " *par excellence*, as in Sadal Miśr. Lallū probably stretched a point when he mentioned Agra City as Khaṛī speaking, for in those days it probably leaned towards Braj as his own Kharī prose does.

Hindī writers contrast Kharī with Braj and Avadhī more than with Urdu. To them Kharī means naturally the less Persianized form, but they would regard Urdu as a mere variety.

KHAṚĪ BOLĪ

In *JRAS*, October, 1926, p. 721, I mentioned that no Indian writer employed the term *Khaṛī Bolī* for *Kharī Bolī*. It has occurred to me that to avoid possible confusion in any one's mind, it would be well to refer to the late Badrī Nārāyaṇ Caudhrī's remarks on the subject. For him linguistic patriotism was a religion. He believed that the threefold division of creation into gods, men and demons held in other spheres also. The one true religion is Hinduism, the one true language Sanskrit with minor modifications. Language, too, has its threefold division : (1) *Brāhmī*, *Devvāṇī*, or *Vedbhāṣā*, the language of the gods ; (2) slightly modified it is *vaidik apabhrāś*, *mūlbhāṣā* or *narvāṇī*, i.e. Hindī, but he calls it simply *bhāṣā* or *nāgarī* ; further deteriorated it is Marāṭhī, Bengalī, etc. ; (3) leaving India it becomes *āsurī*, *rākṣasī* or *paiśācī* in other languages.

He said *bhāṣā* had two forms, Braj for poetry, and *bol cāl kī bhāṣā* for prose ; but he disliked all names. " Don't say *Hindī*," he cried,[1] " *Hindī* is a foreign word ; don't say *Khaṛī Bolī*, there is only one *bhāṣā* ; you may call it *kharī* if you like, for it alone is pure, for it differs very slightly from the original Devvāṇī " (summarized from his speech).

It will be seen that the Caudhrī's picturesque and patriotic use of the word *kharī* does not conflict with the statement in my article.

HINDI PROSE BEFORE THE NINETEENTH CENTURY

THE early literature of the Hindi group of languages, that is the literature written in Avadhī, Bihārī, Rājputānī, and Hindi proper, was largely poetical, and prose was rare. In the beginning of the nineteenth century Lallū Jī Lāl and Sadal Miśr entered Dr. Gilchrist's service and at his suggestion translated some early works into modern vernaculars. The works selected were chiefly Sanskrit, and they were translated into Braj or *Khaṛī Bolī*. Lallū Jī is the better known of the two, but he was not a pioneer, nor was his example followed. For nearly fifty years after he wrote, nothing of real merit was produced in *Khaṛī*. The practical founder of modern Hindi prose, the man who gave it its impetus and started it on its career of prosperity, was Hariś Chandar. A somewhat exaggerated emphasis has been placed on Lallū's and Sadal Miśr's translations, and this has resulted in a lack of perspective. Lallū has been acclaimed as the " Father of Hindi prose ". The title is inaccurate, and has been made the subject of protest. One Hindi writer, in complaining of his being called the " Creator of *Khaṛī Bolī* ", maintains that such an idea is entirely erroneous, and remarks that before his books were brought out Sadā Sukh Lāl and Inshā Allāh were writing in straightforward Hindi. He adds, in an amusing aside, that they wrote on their own initiative and not at the behest of another. He also criticizes Lallu's style as being too much tainted with Braj idioms and poetical turns of expression. Sadal Miśr he regards as Lallu's superior.

Hindi prose has existed for centuries, some would say for nearly six hundred years, and there are about thirty known writers of prose before Lallū Jī, several of whom wrote in *Khaṛī*. There may have been many more.

Attention should be drawn to another point. It is unfortunate that many authors have written of translations (e.g. Prem Sāgar, Rājnīti, Śakuntalā) as if they ranked with original compositions. This is damaging to the reputation of Hindi literature. A similar mistake has not been made in the case of Urdu. We may be sure that in no language would more than perhaps one translation in a thousand, or even many thousands, be considered worthy of mention in a history of its literature unless that literature were deficient in writers of ability.

The following list, including the dates, has been taken from Hindi sources. Students of Central Indian languages may be glad to have it in a convenient form. It goes without saying that some of the dates are open to reconsideration, but certainty will probably never be attained.

The earliest Hindi prose composition is to be sought in the deeds of gift of early rulers. It is difficult to be sure of their genuineness. The Nāgarī Prachāriṇī Sabhā, in its search for early MSS., found a number of these deeds which, if authentic, take us back to the eleventh century. Confining ourselves to regular composition, we have the following prose writers who preceded Lallū Jī.

1. Gorakh Nāth, the father of Hindi prose. Keay speaks of him as a semi-mythical person living about A.D. 1200, but Śyām Sundar Dās gives his date as 1350. In this he is followed by the Miśr brothers, by Greaves, and by Vraj Ratn Lāl, all of whom favour the middle of the fourteenth century. An extant prose work in the Braj dialect is attributed to him, but it may have been written by his followers. We are much in the dark, and to deny his authorship is as useless as to affirm it. It is noteworthy that Avadhī was not favoured for prose writing. Gorakh Nāth lived far to the east, but this book is in Braj.

The next known extant prose work dates from the sixteenth century, two hundred years later.

2. Viṭṭhal Nāth, 1515–85, son of Vallabhāchārya, wrote in Braj a book entitled *Sriṅgār Ras Maṇḍan.*

3. Gokul Nāth, son of Viṭṭhal Nāth, flor. 1568, wrote the famous "*Chaurāsī* (*Vaiṣṇavō kī*) *Vārtā*" and "*Do sau bāvan Vaiṣṇavō kī Vārtā*". These are devoted chiefly to stories of his grandfather's followers. He probably wrote the *Ban Yātrā*, though the Miśr brothers say it was written by Mahā Prabhu Jī, i.e. Vallabhāchārya. All three are in the Braj dialect.

4. Nand Dās, after the middle of the sixteenth century, was the best known of the four members of the Aṣṭ Chhāp who were attached to Viṭṭhal Nāth. His greatest title to fame is that he was probably Tulsī Dās's brother. He wrote two prose works in Braj, which are not extant.

5. Hari Rāy, a contemporary of Nand Dās, produced three prose works.

6. Gaṅg Bhāṭ, 1570, has the distinction of being the first prose writer who used *khaṛī bolī*. He has left a 16-page book called *Chand Chhand Barnan kī Mahimā.*

7. Before 1614: a Sanskrit treatise on astrology named *Bhuvan Dīpikā*, is accompanied by a commentary in *bhāṣā*. The author is unknown. The MS. bears the date 1614, the composition itself cannot be later, but may be earlier.

8. Jaṭmal, 1623, is the author of *Gorā Bādal kī Kathā*, telling of Ratn Sen, Padmāvatī, Gorā and Bādal. It is poetry with a large admixture of prose in *khaṛī*. Jaṭmal is therefore, so far as our knowledge goes, the second writer of *khaṛī bolī*.

9. Manohar Dās Nirañjanī, about 1650, wrote *Gyān Chūrṇ Vachnikā*, in Braj prose.

10. Jasvant Siṅgh, Mahārājā of Jodhpur, 1625–81, the famous writer on poetic style, was the author of a prose work called *Prabodh Chandroday Nāṭak*.

11. About 1658 Jagjī Chāraṇ produced the *Ratn Maheśdāsot Vachnikā*, in which he extolled the bravery of Ratn Siṅgh Maheśdāsot, Rājā of Ratlām.

12. In the same year, 1658, Dāmodar Dās, the Dādūpanthī, wrote in Rājputānī prose a translation of the Mārkaṇḍeya Purāṇ.

13. In 1663, unknown author: prose translation of the Yogvāsiṣṭh.

14. Seventeenth century, date usually given as 1680; Baikuṇṭhmaṇi Śukl wrote two works, *Vaiśākh Māhātmya* and *Agahan Māhātmya*. These are in Braj poetry, but contain much Khaṛī prose. The Miśr brothers say they are in Braj prose.

15. Bhagvān Dās, 1699, translated the Gītā into prose under the name of *Bhāṣāmrit*. The Miśr brothers refer to this work as "kavitā". This may be an oversight.

16. Surati Miśr flor. probably during the first third of the eighteenth century, though he has been put earlier, translated the *Baitāl Pachīsī* from Sanskrit into Braj prose. This was done at the command of Mahārājā Jai Siṅgh.

17. Ajīt Siṅgh, 1680–1724, son of Mahārājā Jasvant Siṅgh, mentioned above, is known to have written a work named *Guṇsār*, partly in verse and partly in prose. It is an account of Rājā Sumati and Rāṇī Satyarūpā. His language is a mixture of Braj and Rājputānī, the former predominating.

18. Debī Chand, 1720, a translation of *Hitopdeś* in Braj prose.

19. Unknown author, a MS. dated 1720, containing a work in Braj prose called *Kriṣṇ jī kī Līlā*.

20. An unknown author, about 1719; translated into Hindi a Persian translation of the Upaniṣads.

21 and 22. Lalit Kiśorī and Lalit Mohinī, 1743, joint authors of a 46-page book in Braj bearing the title *Śrī Śvāmī Mahārāj jū kī Bachnikā.* The Mahārāj here referred to is the sixteenth century religious leader Hari Dās, to whose sect the authors belonged.

23. Amar Siṅgh Kāyasth, latter half of eighteenth century, wrote *Amar Chandrikā* in verse and prose mixed. This is a commentary on Bihārī's *Sat Saī.*

24 and 25. Agr Nārāyaṇ Dās and Vaiṣṇav Dās, in the end of the eighteenth century, wrote jointly a prose commentary on Nābhā Dās's and Priya Dās's *Bhaktmāl.* The Miśr brothers do not mention the fact of their joint authorship or allude to prose writings. They say that Agr Nārāyaṇ wrote the *Bhaktras Bodhinī Ṭīkā*, explaining that it is a commentary on the *Bhaktmāl.* They give the same name to a work by Vaiṣṇav Dās without the explanatory remark, and they leave the reader to understand that there is no connexion between the two. Vraj Ratn Lāl states that their book exists in two MS. copies, one dated 1772 and called *Bhaktmāl Prasaṅg*, the other dated 1787 and called *Bhakti ras Bodhinī.*

26. Bakhteś, 1765 or 1771, wrote a commentary on the *Rasrāj*, an erotic work by Mati Rām Tripāṭhī, which discusses various kinds of lovers, both men and women, especially women. The Miśr brothers mention only this commentary among the works of Bakhteś, and say that he wrote charming poetry.

27. Śer Siṅgh, killed in 1793, son of Vijay Siṅgh, who was King of Mārvāṛ, wrote a mixture of verse and prose in a work entitled *Rām Kṛiṣṇ kā Jas.* The date was approximately 1789, and the language used Mārvāṛī.

28. Kaibāt Sarbariya, about 1797, was author of *Anant Rāy* (or *Ānand Rām*) *kī Vārtā*, which contains both prose and verse.

29. Sadā Sukh Lāl wrote many articles in Khaṛī. Unfortunately none of his books are extant. He was about a quarter of a century before Lallū Jī.

30. Inshā Allāh Khān, the only Muhammadan in the list, wrote before 1809 *Rānī Ketakī kī Kahānī* in "ṭheṭh Hindī", a somewhat peculiar variety of Khaṛī. This appeared before the Prem Sāgar.

31. Sadal Miśr, 1773–1848 : his chief work was *Chandrāvatī*, 1798, a translation of the Sanskrit *Nāsiketopākhyān.* His other prose works are not extant.

Of the prose writers of the early nineteenth century it has been said that Inshā Allāh was Venus, Sadal Miśr dawn, and Lallū Jī morning.

INTERESTING GENITIVE PREPOSITIONS IN RĀJASTHĀNĪ.

In the fine ballad *Ḍholā Mārū rā Dūhā*, recently published (see review on another page in this number of the *Journal*) occur eight instances of *sandăŭ*, *handăŭ*, and *hundăŭ*, which we may translate "of". Following R. L. Turner we may derive the first and second from *sant*, and the third from *bhavant*, not forgetting, however, his remark that "-nt > -nd" is a development unusual in Rājasthānī.

They are to be connected with Kashmiri *sandŭ* and *handŭ*, which are pronounced *sund* and *hund*, for in Kashmiri an unstressed *a* followed by u-mātra is pronounced *u*.

The following are the lines in which the words occur. The numbers indicate the dohas :—

61 *sajjaṇ sandăĭ kāraṇăĭ hiyăŭ hilūsăĭ nitt.*
because of the loved one, the heart is always eager.

556 *lahrī sāyar sandiyā̃ vūṭhăŭ sandăŭ vāo.*
the waves of the sea, the wind after rain (lit. the wind of rain).

Here one would expect *vūṭhăĭ*, but the ballad is not over anxious about grammar.

656 *bāḷăŭ bābā desṛăŭ pā̃ṇī sandī tāti*
I would burn up, father, a land (which has) difficulty about water.

630 *pīhar sandī ḍū̃mṇī Ūmar handăĭ sathth*
a gipsy woman of her father's house (who was) with Ūmar.

509 *huntā sajjaṇ hīyaṛe sayaṇā̃ handā hatt*
there were on the loved one's heart the lover's hands.

307 *āpaṇ jāe joiyăŭ karhā hundăŭ vagg*
he himself went and searched the camel's stable.

312.

Ḍholā-Mārūrā Dūhā: A Fifteenth-century Ballad from Rājputānā

Is the present conclusion original?

THE story of Ḍholā and Mārū is told in a stirring Rājputānī ballad published in the Bālābakhsh Rājpūt Cāraṇ Pustakmālā series. It is reviewed on another page of this *Bulletin*.

The story of the poem is briefly this. Pingaḷ, the king of Pūgaḷ, had a daughter called Māravaṇī ; Naḷ, the king of Narvar, had a son named Ḍholā. During a famine Pingaḷ sought temporary refuge in Narvar, where the two rajas betrothed their children to each other. Some years after this Naḷ, reflecting that Pingaḷ lived far away, and that the journey to his country was perilous, married his son to Māḷavaṇī, daughter of the Raja of Māḷvā. In due time Pingaḷ sent messengers to call Ḍholā, but the wily Māḷavaṇī had them killed. Ultimately Māravaṇī succeeded in getting a message delivered by singers. Ḍholā was charmed by their description of his early fiancée and set out for her country. After some vicissitudes he reached her. and they were married. On the return journey Māravaṇī died of snake-bite and was restored to life by a jogī. She was nearly seized by a Muhammadan chieftain, but was warned by a Gipsy woman, and through the swiftness of her camel, which, like Māḷavaṇī's parrot, had the gift of speech, she and Ḍholā got to Narvar in safety. There they all lived in mutual affection, an affection clouded once by a domestic disagreement. Each of the wives praised her own country and decried that of the other. Ḍholā supported Māravaṇī, and this, rather inconsequently, restored peace.

This episode which forms the conclusion of the poem, strikes me as unnatural and out of place. The story appears to end properly with dohā 653, which tells us of their settling down in peace, and says that it was God Who had joined them in this happy union.

Now when we think the poem has come to a suitable ending there starts a sudden argument between the two wives about the merits of their respective countries. Ḍholā supports Māravaṇī, whom he obviously prefers to this other wife, and his one-sided attitude appears to satisfy even Māḷavaṇī, whom he had failed to uphold. Once again the poem comes to an end. The final words closely resemble those of dohā 653. The two conclusions are alike ; the sense and several of the actual expressions of the last three lines (dohās 673, 674) are the same as in the previous ending, dohās 651 and 652. Not only so, but three other dohās, Nos. 666–8, are almost letter for letter the same as dohās in an earlier part of the poem. I have drawn attention to them below.

After Ḍholā and Māravaṇī reached Narvar in safety, we read :—

(dohā 651) *Ḍholăŭ Narvar āviyăŭ, mangaḷ gāvăĭ nār*
uchav huvăŭ āyăŭ ghare, harakhyăŭ nagar apār
Sālhkumar bilasăĭ sadā kā̃miṇ suguṇ sugāt.

Ḍholā came to Narvar, the women sing songs of rejoicing. There was a feast ; he came home ; the city rejoiced beyond measure. Sālh Kumār (i.e. Ḍholā) made merry with his wives, virtuous and beautiful.

The next dohā appears to end the story.

653 *Māravaṇī năĭ Māḷavaṇi, Ḍholăŭ tiṇ bhartār*
ekaṇi mandir rang ramăĭ, kī joṛī Kartār.

Māravaṇī and Māḷavaṇī, and Ḍholā their husband lived joyously in one palace ; God had made their union. (This hemistich reminds us of Tennyson's " marriages are made in heaven ".)

654 *tatkhaṇ Māḷavaṇī kahăĭ, " sā̃bhaḷi kant surang*
" sagḷa des suhā̃mṇā, Mārū des virang.

At that time Māḷavaṇī says : " Listen, charming husband ; every country is beautiful, (but) Mārvāṛ is insipid.

655 *" bāḷăŭ, bābā, desṛăŭ, pā̃ṇī jihā̃ kuvā̃h*
ādhīrāt kuhakkaṛā, jyăŭ māṇasā̃ muvā̃h.

" I would burn up, father, a land where the water is in wells, and at midnight there is a shouting as if people had died.

656 *bāḷăŭ, bābā, desṛăŭ, pā̃ṇī sandī tāti*
pāṇī kerăĭ kāraṇăĭ prī chaṇḍăĭ adhrāti (v. l. *sī̃cai*).

I would burn up, father, a land with anxiety about water, where for the sake of water, the husband leaves (the house) at midnight (v. l. draws).

657 *bāḷū̃, Ḍholā, desṛăŭ, jāĭ pā̃ṇī kū̃veṇ*
kū̃kū̃ varaṇā haththṛā nahī̃ sū ghāḍhā jē̃ṇ.

I would burn up, Ḍholā, a land where water is in wells, and where red-coloured hands do not draw it. (*ghāḍhā*, of doubtful meaning ; perhaps connected with H. *kāṛhnā* ; Pj. *kaḍḍhṇā* ; Kś. *kaḍun*.)

658 *bābā, ma deis Māruvā̃, sūdhā evāḷā̃h*
kandhi kuhāṛā̃ŭ, siri ghaṛā̃ŭ, vāsā̃ŭ manjhi Thaḷā̃h.
Father, Thou shalt not give me (in marriage) to Mārvāṛ, to simple shepherds, axe on shoulder, waterpot on head, to live among (the people of) Marusthal (Mārvāṛ).

659 *bābā, ma deis Māruvā̃, var kũāri rahesi*
hā̃thi kacoḷā̃ŭ, siri ghaṛā̃ŭ, sīcantī ya maresi.
Father, thou shalt not give me to Mārvāṛ, I will (rather) remain virgin from a husband ; cup in hand, waterpot on head, I shall die drawing water (or watering) ; (i.e. if I go to Mārvāṛ).

660 *Mārаū, thā̃kā̃ĭ desṛā̃ĭ ek na bhājā̃ĭ riḍḍ*
ūcāḷā̃ŭ ka avarasaṇā̃ŭ, kā̃ĭ phākā̃ŭ, kā̃ĭ tiḍḍ.
O Māravaṇī, in your country, not even one difficulty flees away ; there is either journeying (from the country), or lack of rain, either hunger or locust.

661 *jiṇ bhũi pannag pīyaṇa, kayar kaṇṭārā rũkh*
āke phoge chā̃hrī, hũchā̃ bhā̃jā̃ĭ bhūkh.
A country in which are (blood)-drinking snakes, and the trees are thorns and thorny shrubs ; the shade is only *āk* and leafless shrubs, and hunger flees by (eating) *hũch* (thorny plant, the seeds of which are eaten).

662 *pahiraṇ-oṛhaṇ kambaḷā, sāṭhe purise nīr*
āpaṇ lok ubhā̃kharā, gāḍar chāḷī khīr.
For clothing and putting on (only) blankets ; water sixty puris deep ; the people themselves wanderers ; milk (only) of sheep and goats. (A *puris* is about four feet.)

Māravaṇī replies by running down Māḷvā and praising Mārvāṛ.

663 *vaḷatī Māravaṇī kahā̃ĭ " Mārū des surang*
vījā tā̃ŭ sagḷā bhalā, Māḷav des virang.
In turn (returning) Māravaṇī says " Mārū land is charming : others indeed all are good, (only) Mālvā land is insipid.

664 *bāḷũ, bābā, desṛā̃ŭ, jahā̃ pā̃ṇī sevār*
nā paṇihārī jhūlarā̃ŭ, nā kūvā̃ĭ laikār.
I would burn up, father, a country where the water has *sevār* growing in it ; (*sevār*, Hindi *shaivāl*, a water plant) ; neither companies of water-women, nor melody at the well.

665 *bāḷũ, bābā, desṛā̃ŭ, jahā̃ phīkiriyā log*
ek na dīsā̃ĭ goriyā̃, ghari ghari dīsā̃ĭ sog.

I would burn up, father, a land, where the people are uninteresting ; women are not seen, even one ; in every house is seen sadness.

666 *Mārū des upanniyā, tihā̃kā kā dant suset*
kū̃jh bacī gorangiyā̃, khanjar jehā net.

This dohā has already occurred as No. 457, where for *upanniyā* we have *upanniyā̃*, a better reading. I assume it here.

Girls born in Mārvāṛ, their teeth are beautifully white ; they are fair as young cranes, and their eyes are like those of wagtails (or are like wagtails).

667 *Mārū des upanniyā̃, sar jyā̃ū paddhariyāh*
kaṛvā kade na bolahī, mīṭhā bolaṇiyāh.

This is almost word for word the dohā which we have already had as No. 484. There the ending is *-yā̃h*, which is preferable.

Girls born in Mārvāṛ are straight as an arrow, they never speak bitter words, they are speakers of sweet things.

668 *des nivāṇū̃, sajal jal, mīṭhā bolā loi*
Mārū kā̃miṇi dikhaṇi dhar Hari dīyā̃ū tā̃ū hoi."

This dohā, with one word of difference, occurs as No. 485.

The land is low-lying (therefore fertile), fresh in water, with people speaking sweet words ; Mārvāṛī women (women like them) might be in the land of the south, but only if God gave them.

Now Ḍholā speaks and favours Māravaṇī.

669 *des surangā̃ū, bhuī nijaḷ, na diyā̃ dos Thaḷā̃h*
ghari ghari cand-vadanniyā̃, nīr caṛhā̃ī kamḷā̃h.

The land is charming, (yet) the soil is waterless ; do not attribute fault to Marusthal ; at every door are moon-faced girls, like lotuses which rise to the water (or who ascend to the water like lotuses).

670 *suṇi, sundari, ketā kahā̃ Mārū des vakhā̃ṇ*
Māravaṇī miḷiyā̃ pachā̃ī jāṇyā̃ū janam pravā̃ṇ.

Listen, fair one, how much shall I praise Mārvāṛ ? Since I met Māravaṇī I have regarded my life as fruitful.

This, while a charming compliment to his favourite wife, was depressing to the other. Reading the compliment we think of Browning's:

> The purpose of my being is accomplished
> And I am happy. I, too, Federigo.

671 *jhagṛăŭ bhāgăŭ goriyā̃, Ḍholăĭ pūrī sakhkh*
Mārū ruḷiyāit huī, pā̃mī priya parakhkh.
The quarrel of the fair ones fled away; Ḍholā supported (Māravaṇī); Māravaṇī became happy; she had tested her loved one.

672 *Māḷav des vikhoṛiyā, Mārū kiyā vakhāṇ*
Mārū sohāgiṇ thaī sundari saguṇ sujā̃ṇ.
He decried Māḷvā, and praised Mārvāṛ; Māravaṇī, beautiful, virtuous and wise, became fortunate.

673 *jim madhukar năĭ ketakī, jim koil sahkār*
Māravaṇī man harakhiyăŭ tim Ḍholăĭ bhartār.
As the bee and the *keoṛā*, as the *koel* and the plaintain, so Māravaṇī's soul rejoiced in Ḍholā, her husband.

We are not told how the other wife regarded the situation, and the final couplet which follows is unnatural at this point.

674 *āṇand ati, ūchāh ati, Narvar mā̃he Ḍhol*
sasnehī sayaṇā̃ taṇā̃ kaḷimā̃ rahiyā bol.
Much happiness, much feasting, Ḍholā in Narvar; and the story of those loving lovers continued in this iron age.

The sense of this doha is the same as that of No. 653.

VII.—BROTHERS OF THE ROMANE: A DOWNTRODDEN TRIBE IN NORTH INDIA

THE Čuhras (čū'ṛā) of the Panjab are chiefly scavengers and farm servants. They used to belong to that large, indeterminate body called Criminal Tribes, and known carelessly as Gypsies or nomads. Members of these tribes are found all over India; many of them are now respectable and hardworking. Formerly they had three characteristics: they were nomads, they had a secret language or argot of their own, and they were criminals, that is they were given to theft and sometimes to immorality. The special dialects spoken by them are occasionally Dravidian, but generally Aryan, showing traces of Rājputānī, Hindī, Panjābī, and Marhaṭī (Marāṭhī). Professor Sten Konow[1] concludes on linguistic grounds that they all belong to one race and come from the Dravidian area, but that after leaving their ancestral home and wandering northward, they lived so long in the Vindhya region of central India that they became Aryanised. He suggests further the possibility that the Gypsies of Armenia and Europe belong to the same race, though he admits that linguistic evidence leaves this an open question.

The Čuhras are a lovable race, showing a great power of bettering themselves when given a chance. None of them now are nomads, and few are criminals. On the contrary they live useful lives. Many of them have become Christians, a considerable number have received some education; a few are University graduates, some are clergymen or school teachers. It is the more necessary to make a note of their secret vocabulary while we can; in a few years no one will remember it. They have no real dialect, a few isolated words are all they possess, a remnant of the days when stealing and cattle poisoning were common practices.

[1] *Linguistic Survey of India*, vol. xi. pp. 5-11.

Formerly each company of Čuhras had a poisoner whose duty it was to poison cattle or horses. The tribe had a prescriptive right to all dead animals, and the flesh of a bullock or horse which had apparently sickened and died, but actually been poisoned, would be a valuable addition to their store of food. The payments made to the poisoner seem very inadequate, if one considers the risk of detection and punishment. For a buffalo he got ninepence, for a bullock sevenpence. There were two methods of poisoning—stabbing with a poisoned instrument, and giving medicated food. Horses had to be stabbed, because they detected the poison in food and could not be induced to take it. Two instruments were used, an iron pointed rod, called *čhaggī*, or a much shorter bit of wood tipped with iron and called *lānjī*; it was small enough to be concealed in the hand. When poison was given in food an ounce was mixed with a pailful of fodder for buffaloes, and half an ounce for bullocks. Death ensued in a day.

The tribal fathers are ashamed of the past and inclined to deny knowledge of it, but when one has become sufficiently friendly with them they will tell one what they know. Often it is not much, for they are becoming more and more civilised. The secret words are dropping out of use. Those who know them are unwilling that strangers should learn them, for their value depends on their being unknown. I found that when I had established my position as a friend there were some who laid aside their reserve and spoke freely of their 'Pashto,' taking a pride in recalling half-forgotten words, though some of them preferred to do so behind closed doors. It would hardly be an exaggeration to say that those of the tribe who have become Christians are entirely ignorant of them.

Hindus and Muhammadans do not eat an animal found dead, but unreformed Čuhras do so freely, and have a set of words to describe the flesh and parts of the body. Such an animal is commonly referred to as 'carrion,' but the word is not a good one. The Panjabi equivalent of it applies to all meat not killed according to Hindu or Muslim rites even though it may be fit for food. Christians of Čuhra origin are very particular as to what they eat, and they avoid carrion.

To illustrate the argot I have given a vocabulary of 120 words, a short story, and some poetical texts. The story and texts are in Panjabi mixed with Čuhra words. To disguise an ordinary word they often insert the sound *m*. In the texts secret Čuhra words are indicated by printing the English equivalents in italics. An apostrophe after a vowel indicates that it is pronounced with high pitch, which drops for the vowel after the apostrophe. An inverted comma similarly indicates a low rising tone, low in the syllable after the comma and rising in the succeeding syllable.

TWO BOYS FRUSTRATE TWO THIEVES

ikkī piṇḍ-ič do kūtre ræ'nde sāṇ, ik k̦irbəlā, te ik rāṛkā,
one village-in two *boys* living were, one *Muslim* and one *Hindu*,

āpe -ič baṛe dəmost (dost) sāṇ, rūŋyeā-vallō čokhe
themselves-among great friends were *Čuhras*-towards very

badzan ̦oe sāṇ, rāṛke kūtre-de ku'ḍḍō ṭhelleā
suspicious become were, *Hindu boy*-of *house*-from *ornaments*

te p̦īmṭ̦eā-dī neoḍī ̦oī sī, k̦irbəle-dī ik ardlī lug geī
and *rupees*-of *theft* become was, *Muslim*-of one *buffalo die* gone

sī; k̦irbəle kūtre kəthāeā paī e'nnā rīyyā-dā ətbār koī
was; *Muslim boy*-by *said* that those *Čuhras*-of trust any

neī, e dəmōve (dōve) kamm o'nnā-de p̦ēt-nāḷ ̦oe
not-is, these both works them-of connivance-by become

ne, sāḍḍī ardlī tā χær məreṛī jeī sī, o'-dī eḍḍī lammī
are, our *buffalo* then well feeble like was, it-of so long

gall neī, kamu'ṛe (ku'ṛe) par ik sovā ṭommā khanjəlā ī, o'-rī
matter not, cow-house-in but one *fine fat buffalo* is, it-of

nā kite gæmmī ̦ove; damujje (dujje) kūtre kəthāeā paī
not anywhere *theft* be; second *boy*-by *said* that

mæ̃ ikkī reoṇe te ikki p̦āttū-nā gəmal (gal) kūldeā suṇeā
by me one *Čuhra* and one *Sāsi*-to word *making* heard

sī te č̦aṭebinde sāḍḍe ku'ḍḍ-val čāmde sāṇ, ǂmaj(aj)
was & repeatedly our *house*-towards *looking* were, to-day

jərūr kuj ̦oṇā ī; e'dərō dōve čhurm, rī te
certainly something to-be is; here-from both *thieves*, *Čuhra* &

p̦āttū, teār ̦oke sārā laṭərpaṭər kəmaṭṭhā (kaṭṭhā)
Sāsi, ready having-become all stuff together

kūlke, ṭombū te kāṛkī p̦āttū koḷe, te čhaggī te lānjī
having-*made*, *jemmy* and *stick Sāsi* with, & *stabber* & *stabber*

rūŋge koḷe, paχsat kūndke šūkāšākī nāḷ abre, o' dōve
Čuhre with, *food* having eaten pomp with *came*, those both

kūtre čāmde sāṇ-pæe, jad rī te o'rā litāṛā laγe
boys watching were, when *Čuhra* & him-of *confederate* began

khanjəle koḷ polṇe, tā ikkī kūtre saṭṭeā čhikārā, dujje
buffalo near *to-go*, then one *boy*-by thrown *clod*, second

khəṛkāī ṭ̦āṛkī, eḍḍā rəḷā pāeo ne paī sārā m̦allā jāg
rattled knife, such noise made by-them that all quarter waking

uṭṭheā, k̦irbəle te ṭōmmīā te rāṛke, te rāṛkīā, mudā
arose, *Muslims* & *female do.* & *Hindus* & *female do.*, in-short

kāḷe nepəṛ k̦atte te o'nā nāḷ burī ̦oī.
thieves were-seized and them with evil became.

THE FEAST

1. *Lāl lāl ka'ndī lāeā, čiṭṭe-dā degā čā'ṛīdā,*
Red red on-walls attached, white-of pot is-raised,

2. *k̦ar sāḍḍe thāṇā latthā, vəγyārā ne'ī čhuṭkārī-dā*
house our police-court descended, forced-labour not leisure-of

3. *maddər pīr p̦āṛī ča'ṛeā, khalkət matthā ṭekdī,*
thigh holy-man to-hills ascended, people forehead bow,

4. *suṇḍī māī ākkəṛ-p̦anne, ču'lle de-vič leṭdī,*
chop mother twisting-breaks, fireplace in lies,

5. *giččī māī č̦aṇḍ khəlāre, dandā vallō veχdī,*
knee mother hair raises, teeth towards looks,

6. *jaṭṭ jo puččhdā čū'ṛīe k̦ar kiy e tere?*
farmer when asks 'O-Čurha-woman house-in what is thine?'

7. *čō'drī, nikke-dī ga'ṇḍ e, vaḍḍe-de phere*
farmer, younger-of engagement is, elder-of confirmation-of-
[engagement.

8. *maṭ pəṛ̦āsā čhaḍḍīā, čū'ṛī fire čufere*
pot-by vapours left, the-Čuhri turns on-all-sides.

9. *p̦annī ̦oī sæṇḍkī, čū'ṛī pâṅīā fere*
broken become pot, the-Čuhri marriage-gifts hands-round

10. *pāṭṭī ̦oī ṭæŋguṭ, vaḷ pæṇ čufere*
torn become skirt, turns fall on-all-sides

11. *khā-lɔ mereo kuṛmo, ko'ḷī-de bere.*
eat-take my marriage-relatives, *breast*-of *pieces.*

12. *čhælli de-vič sukkde khuṛdumbe bere*
basket in drying *fat-tailed pieces*

13. *illā č̣urməṭ pā-leā, kā bæ'ṇ bənere.*
kites-by crowd made, crows sit on-roof-edge.

NOTES.—1. Red meat drying on walls, fat boiling in pot. 2. Crowd like police court, but no forced labour. 3. The holy thigh-flesh in pot. 4. Mother chop stretching herself. 5. Flesh of knee rising up. (4 and 5 refer to cooking.) 6. What is there to-day in thy house? 8. Pot steaming, the Čuhri busy. 10. Skirt torn as she bustles round. 11. Feast considered a marriage. 12. Fat-tailed sheep is called *dumbā*.

A JOKE

1. *k̨uṭṭ-k̨aṭṭke ga'ṇḍər ba'ddā, utte thabbā pərāḷī-dā*
pressing bundle tied, on-top load rice-stalks-of

2. *kajje de ̨atth mæ̃ de-ṭoreā, tattā tattā tūrī-dā.*
farmer-of hand-by by-me give-sent, hot hot soup-of.

The Čuhra's wife concealed carrion under rice stalks, and sent it to the village by the hand of a *kajjā*, i.e. any one of superior rank, here probably a Hindu, knowing that he would not have touched it, if he had known what it was. The meat was hot soup-meat.

LIST OF CHURA WORDS

(Contractions: P. = Panjabi, H. = Hindi, Q. = Qasāī, S. = Sāsī, Kś. = Kaśmīri, G. = Gamblers' argot.)

VERBS.

accuse, *nūkərnā.*
arrive, *see* 'come.'
beat, *lothṇā.* *See* 'kill,' 'clod.'
break into house (through wall), *gul lāṇā.*
come, *ābrnā* (cf. Q. *aprnā*, P. *appərnā*, S. *asrnā*), *polṇā.*
die, *luggṇā*: S. *do.*
do, *kūlṇā*: S. *do.*
eat, *tilmṇā, kūndṇā.*
give, *særnā, ṭēlṇā.*
go, *polṇā.*
hide, (tr.) *čhəpelṇā,* (intr.) *ṭhippṇā.*
kill, *lothṇā* (S. *lo'ṇā*, Kś. *lāyun*, P. *lāṇā*), *kermṇā, ga'ṇḍ deṇā.*
look, *čāmṇā.* *See* 'see' and 'watch.'

say, *kəthāṇā* : P. *gallkatth*, Kś. *kath*, word.
see, *čāmṇā*. *See* 'look' and 'watch.'
seize, *nepəṛnā* : P. *nappəṛnā*.
steal, *lāllī lāṇī* : S. *lāllī*, night.
watch, *čāmṇā*.

NOUNS.

(1) Animate beings:

ass, *kortā, khutṛiŋgā*.
boy, *kūtrā*.
buffalo, *ardlī, khanjəlā*.
confidant, *litāṛā*.
cow, *kōsī*.
Čuhra, *rī, reoṇā, rūŋgā*.
European, *kajjā*, (fem.) *kajjī*. (*See* 'gentleman.')
dog, *rēvəl*.
gentleman, any one of good social position, *kajjā*, (fem.) *kajjī* : S. *do*. (*See* 'European.')
girl, *kūtrī*.
goat, kid, *čællī*.
Hindu, *rāṛkā*, (fem.) *rāṛkī*.
horse, *kurmā*.
Muslim, *k̜irbəlā*, (fem.) *ṭommī*. *See* 'fine.'
poisoner, *ruχm*.
Sasi, *p̜āttū*. (S. *p̜attū*.)
thief, *kāḷā, čhuṛm*.

(2) Articles of food:

bread, *paχsat, 'uṇḍək*. *See* 'food.
butter, *see* 'ghī.'
curds, *guls*.
food, *'uṇḍək, paχsat*.
ghī, *nibəl*.
soup, *lās, tārī*.
sugar, *miṭkā, t̜īmmā* : S. *ṭ̜ūllā*.
water, *nirkā* : H. *nīr*.
carrion, *ḍīṭhā, jagəṛ, khānjərā*.

(3) Household and other articles:

cloth, *līpṛā*. *See* 'skin.'
huqqa, *burkṇā* (S. *do*); *kəṛūā*.
jemmy (housebreaker's), *ṭombū*.
knife, *t̜āṛkī*.

match (for lighting), *kəs̨ā*ī.
money, *bəgelā*.
necklace, *ṯhellā*.
pice (farthing), *ərj̨īā*.
poison, *tiārī*, *ṯhīmmā*; ball of, *goḷī*.
rupee, *p̨īmṭā* (G. *do*), *bəgelā*.
shoes, *pæntṛī*.
stabbing instrument, (longer) *čhaggī*, (short) *lānjī*.
stick, *kāṛkī*.
turban, *ṯelnī*.

(4) Parts of the animal found dead:

back, small of, *paṯṯhā*.
brain, *miñ*.
breast, *ko'ḷī*; piece of, *morā*.
entrails, *k̨erā*, *āndrā*.
fat, *minj*, *neorī*; remains of, *batlī*.
heart, *ənjāllā*.
knee, with flesh, *gičlī*.
leg, lower half of lower, *surkaŋg*.
  flesh on front part of this, *khuṛṛā*.
  lower foreleg, upper half, *totīā*.
  upper foreleg, upper half, *ṯikīā*.
    do. lower half, *čūl*.
  lower hind leg, upper half, *jannū*.
  upper hind leg, upper half, *kāṇā*.
    do. lower half, *golū*.
lumbar vertebrae, *paṭrī*, *kaŋgī*.
meat, piece of, *berā*; oblong piece of, *suṇḍī*.
neck, back of, *kənā*.
rump, *pottā*.
shoulder, *muṛkən*, *phar*.
skin, *līpṛū*: Q. *lipṛī*. *See* 'cloth.'
side, *bukkā*, *rukṛā*; upper part of, *kən̨eri*.
spine, flesh near, *bukṛā*.
thigh, *čoṛā*, *maddər*.

(5) Other nouns:

accusation, *nūkər*.
clod, *čhikārā*; strike with clod, throw clod at, *kæŋkər karnā*; throwing of clod as warning to confederate, *neolā*.
direction, *see* 'side.'

house, *kuḍḍ'*.
intrigue, *kokkō*.
sickness (of cows), *almnī*.
side, direction, *palvā*; *palve*, to one side.
theft, *neoḍī*, *gœmmī* (Q. *gœmbī*; *gœmbā*, thief), *lāllī* (only with *lāṇī*, attach).

Adjectives.

bad, worthless, *ṭ̣āṇḍā*; ugly, *pəčhikkā*.
fine, in good condition, fat, *sō'vā*, *ṭommā*. The fem. of the latter is used for 'Muslim woman.'
fat-tailed, *khuṛdumbā*.

Interjection.

heī kūl, hush! *kūl* is imper. of *kūlṇā*, to do.

TWO INDIAN STANDARDS OF THE EIGHTEENTH CENTURY, WITH FACSIMILES AND TRANSLATIONS OF TRACINGS FROM ARABIC INSCRIPTIONS

IN the spring of 1921 Captain Geoffrey Bailey sent me two pairs of tracings made from Indian standards captured in the battle of Seringapatam, 4th May, 1799. The standards are among the treasures of the chapel of the Royal Hospital, Chelsea. On examination they proved to be of considerable interest, and readers of the *Bulletin* will perhaps be glad to have an opportunity of studying them in the facsimiles which, through the kindness of the editor, I am able to present, along with such notes as may be necessary for their elucidation.

The four tracings consist of the obverse and reverse of two standards; in each case the obverse and reverse are identical. The facsimile marked I (flag No. 31 in the Chapel collection) represents Ḥaydar 'Ali's standard, while that marked II (No. 32 in the Chapel collection) shows us Ṭīpū Ṣāḥib's standard(?)It will be observed that this standard is broken in one place; it is, however, possible to supply the lost words from the reverse, which has these words complete, while it lacks the words "Yā Shekh 'Abdu'l Qādir Jīl . . ."

A cursory examination of the Arabic reveals the fact that those who rallied round these flags belonged to the Sunnī faith, for the saints invoked are those specially reverenced by the adherents of that branch of Islam.

While every part of the inscriptions is worthy of study, supreme interest attaches to those words which indicate the date. They appear to read: in the year of Muḥammad, 6121, or (if the figures be read the other way) 1216. This contains two difficulties. Firstly, in no ordinary Muslim writing do we find an era referred to as "the year of Muḥammad". One gentleman, himself an ibn i 'Arab, told me that though he thought he had read pretty widely in his native tongue, he had never come across such a phrase. Secondly, the actual year 6121 or 1216 was inexplicable. I spent some time in fruitlessly studying eras which might account for the larger figure; at the same time the smaller figure, if counted from the Hijra, gave the year 1801, two years subsequent to the capture of the standards, and a mistake in reckoning was inconceivable.

The explanation of both difficulties has been supplied by Mr. C. A. Storey, of the India Office Library, who has been so kind as to send me the following details. In Ṭipū's reign it was customary to use the era of the Mawlūd i Muḥammad, i.e. the spiritual birth or mission of Muḥammad, about twelve years earlier than the Hijra. Dates were written from right to left. In the India Office Library there is a drawing or facsimile extremely like those here given, and there is a MS. entitled " Ḍawābiṭ i Sulṭāni " containing " regulations for the proper shape and form of royal insignia (as the orbs or disks at the top of banners, seals, official signatures, etc.), drawn up under the direction of Tipu Sultan ". Some of the formulæ closely resemble those in the inscriptions before us.

For the sake of those who are not Arabic scholars I have added a translation of the words on both standards. My own Arabic equipment is inadequate, and I have freely sought assistance from colleagues in the School of Oriental Studies, to whom I am much indebted for the help which they have so readily given.

I

[*Top*]

بسم الله الرّحمن الر حيم — يا الله يا حافظ يا حفيظ يا رقيب يا
وكيل يا حى يا قيوّم

[*Between Arms*]

الملك لله الحلم لله

[*Arms*]

يا حضرت عثمان يا حضرت على حيدر صفدر

يا حضرت معروف كرخى يا كا فى المهمات

HAYDAR 'ALĪ'S STANDARD CAPTURED AT SERINGAPATAM 4TH MAY, 1799: FOUR-FIFTHS OF ACTUAL SIZE. (FLAG NO. 81 IN CHAPEL, ROYAL HOSPITAL, CHELSEA.)

[*Circumference, beginning a little to right of top*]

حضرت خواجه عبد الخالق عجدانی حضرت خواجه بایزید

بستانی — حضرت خواجه ابو یوسف همدانی حضرت خواجه بابا

سمأی حضرت خواجه امیرسید کلال حضرت خواجه احمد بغدادی

حضرت خواجه بهاالدّین نقشبندی رضوان اللّه تعالے علیهم اجمعین

[*Centre*]

اذا جآء نصر الله والفتح ورایت الناس یدخلون فی دین اللّه افواجاً

فسبّح بحمد ربك و استغفره انّه کان توّاباً —

[*Foot*]

سنه محمد ۱۲۱۶ — یا حضرت امام حسن —

TRANSLATION I

In the name of God, the compassionate, the merciful! O God, O Preserver, O Protector, O Watcher, O Guardian, O Living One, O Self-subsistent One!

To God belong sovereignty and clemency.

O Ḥaḍrat 'Uthmān! O Ḥaḍrat 'Alī Ḥaydar Ṣafdar! O Ḥaḍrat Ma'rūf Karkhī! O Sufficient for difficulties!

Ḥaḍrat Khawāja 'Abdu'l Khāliq 'Ijdānī, Ḥaḍrat Khawāja Bāyazīd Bustānī, Ḥaḍrat Khawāja Abū Yūsaf Hamadānī, Ḥaḍrat Khawāja Bābā Samāī, Ḥaḍrat Khawāja Amīr Sayyid Kalāl, Ḥaḍrat Khawāja Aḥmad Baghdādī, Ḥaḍrat Khawāja Bahāu'd Dīn Naqshabandī—may the good-pleasure of God exalted be upon them all!

When come the help of God and the victory, and thou seest men entering into the religion of God in multitudes, then laud in the praise of thy Lord, and ask forgiveness of Him, behold He is abundantly pardoning.

In the year of Muḥámmad 1216.

O Ḥaḍrat Imām Hasan!

ṬĪPŪ ṢĀḤIB'S STANDARD CAPTURED AT SERINGAPATAM 4TH MAY, 1799: FOUR-FIFTHS OF ACTUAL SIZE. (FLAG NO. 32 IN CHAPEL, ROYAL HOSPITAL, CHELSEA.)

II

[*Top*]

بسم الله الرحمن الرحيم يسبح الرعد بحمده والملا يكة من خيفته

[*Between Arms*]

يا حي يا قيوم يا محمد

[*Arms*]

يا حضرت ابا بكر صديق يا حضرت عمر يا شيخ عبد القادر جيلا نی

يا حضر[ت امام حسين]

[*Circumference, beginning to right of top*]

اد علياً مظهر العجايب تجده عونا لك فى النوايب كلُّ همٍ و غمٍ

سينجلى بنبوتك يا محمد بولايتك يا على يا على يا على

[*Centre*]

لا اله الّا الله محمّد رسول الله — نصر من الله و فتح قريب و بشّر

المومنين — فالله خيرٌ حافظا وهو ارحم الراحمين

[*Foot*]

سنه محمد ١٢١٦ — يا حضرت امام حسين

TRANSLATION II

In the name of God, the compassionate, the merciful! The thunder lauds in His praise, and the angels from His fear (fear of Him).

O Living One, O Self-subsistent One: O Muḥammad!

O Ḥaḍrat Abu Bakr Ṣiddīq! O Ḥaḍrat ʻUmr! O Shekh ʻAbdu'l Qādir Jīlānī! O Ḥaḍ(rat Imām Ḥusain)!

Call upon ʻAlī, revealer of wonders. Thou wilt find him a help to thee in difficulties. All trouble and sorrow will be removed by thy prophethood, O Muḥammad, by thy vicarship, O ʻAlī, O ʻAlī, O ʻAlī!

There is no god but God, Muḥammad is His apostle. Help from God and victory are near, and announce it to the faithful. For God is the best guardian, and He is the most merciful of the merciful.

In the year of Muḥammad 1216.
O Ḥaḍrat Imām Ḥusain!

NOTES ON PANJABI ASPIRATES AND TONES

(Phonetic Script in square brackets)

NOTE I

The following lines apply to Northern Panjābī, one of the two main dialects into which Panjābī may be divided. It covers roughly all the Panjābī area to the west and north of Amritsar. The problem of aspirates and tones has recently excited much interest, culminating in Professor Jules Bloch's article in *Mélanges Linguistiques* (*Vendrye:s* pp. 57–67.

In order to emphasize the necessary modifications we may say generally that where southern and western languages have an aspirate, Panjābī, in common with many Laihndi dialects, which, however, require separate discussion, shows the following treatment.

(1) In the combinations *kh, ch, ṭh, th, ph,* it has a toneless, voiceless *h.*

(2) Otherwise an aspirate preceding the accented vowel is replaced by a low rising tone, while one following it is replaced by a high falling tone (a word may have both tones).

These two statements need to be modified.

(1) Panjābī's dislike for aspirates is seen in the recent development of some of these aspirated surds. While *ṭh* and *th* remain unchanged, *kh, ch,* and *ph* sometimes lose their aspiration and become fricative. We then have :—

[**-kh, -kh-**], even [**-kkh,** [**-kkh-**] > [**-x**] ; [**-ch**] and [**-ch-**] > [**-ʃ**] ; [**ph**] > [**ꜰ**] (a faint labio-dental *f*, different from English *f*, but *not* a bilabial ; the corresponding sonant is **ʋ**).

[**lɪkhṇɑ**], write, > [**lɪxṇɑ**] ; [**sɪkkhdɑ**], learning, > [**sɪxdɑ**] ; [**rʌkkhnɑ̃**], am placing, [**rʌxnɑ̃**] ; [**ʋɪʃkɑr**], in the middle, from [**ʋɪcc**], with adj. [**ʋɪʃkɑrlɑ**] ; [**pɪʃɑ̃**], backwards, from [**pɪcche**], with adj. [**pɪʃlɑ**]. [**cʌl ꜰɪrɑ̃dɑ**], I shall go, [**phɪrɑ̃dɑ**] ; [**tʌṛəꜰṇɑ**], be agitated, for [**tʌṛəphṇɑ**].

(2) There is also a contrary tendency, for Northern Panjābī now has in certain cases a clearly pronounced *h*, usually sonant, and it is a fact of great interest that it never carries a special tone. This *h* is found :—

(*a*) In one or two isolated words. I can think of the following : *āho* [**ɑɦo**] or *ā̃h* [**ɑ̃ɦh**], yes. *āho* is in some places pronounced *āk͟h͟o* [**ɑxo**]. In *ā̃h* the second half of *h* is devocalized. The [**x**] pronunciation is found in two other words generally written with *h*, an *h* which is not pronounced as an aspirate. They are *ū'oī*, that very one, [**u''oi**] and *ī'yyoī* [**i'jjoi**], this very one, for which one may hear [**uxoi**] and [**exɑi**].

ohho [**ohho**], or *oho* [**oɦo**], Oh (surprise or impatience). This is sometimes [**oxo**].

(*b*) A new development of existing *s*. In rapid speech there is now a tendency towards the following changes except when *s* immediately precedes an accented vowel. I have noticed it, though rarely, with *sh*.

[**-s-**] > [**-ɦ-**]. [**-ss-**] remains unchanged. [**-s**] + cs > [**-ɦ**] + cs.

[**-ss**] + cs. > [**-s**] + cs. > [**-ɦ**] + cs.

In every case the *h* is toneless.

[dʌɦɪ̃ dʌɦɪ̃ pæɦɪ̃ læe ɦɑɦʊ], *dasī̃ dasī̃ paisī̃ lae sāsū̃*, he got them for ten pice each. As **[ɦɑɦʊ]** is an enclitic the consonants in it count as inter-vocalic.

[khʊɦiɑ kɑ‘ de ɟogɑ ‘ʌɦdɑ e peɑ], *Khus̲h̲īā kāh de jogā hassdā e peā*, why is Khushia laughing ?

[ʌɦɑ̃ ɑkhjɑ tʊɦɑ̃], *asā̃ ākheā* ! *tusā̃* ? We said it ! Wasn't it rather you ?

[okkhʊɦiɑ oe:::], *o Khus̲h̲īā oe,* O Khushia (call from a distance).

If we agree to recognize this newly developed aspirate and write it *h,* it will be worth our while to note the difference in pronunciation between certain words, which will then be written alike or nearly alike.

paihe paihe, by road, is **[pæ‘e pæe]** with tone ; but *paihe paihe,* a pice each, is **[pæɦe pæɦe]** without tone.

ḍahā̃, 1st sing. pres. subj. of *ḍahṇā,* is **[ḍɑ̃‘]**, with tone : but *dahā̃,* from *das,* ten, is **[dʌɦɑ̃]** without tone.

ḍahṇā (inf.), *ḍahnnā̃* (pres. ind.) are **[ḍæ‘ṇɑ̃, ḍæ‘nnɑ̃]** with tone, whereas *dassṇā, dassnā̃* > *dahṇā, dahnā̃,* are **[dʌɦṇɑ̃, dʌhnɑ̃]** without tone.

I wish to make it clear that this tendency has not yet become an invariable habit. The *s* is still common especially in slower utterance.

NOTES ON PANJABI ASPIRATES AND TONES

(Northern or Western Dialect)

Note II

Erratum.—In Note I, *JRAS.*, January, 1926, p. 113, l. 6 from foot, " western " should be " eastern ". Southern and eastern languages have an aspirate.

THE PRONUNCIATION OF MEDIAL *gh, jh, ḍh, dh, bh*

Before discussing this, it will be well to give a

Rule applying to all tones.—In the case of all tones, whether dual or triple, i.e. whether low-rising, high-falling, or low-rising-falling, the first part always occurs on the stressed vowel. If that vowel is the last before the next pause, the tone is complete in it, but if another syllable follows before the pause, the rise of the low-rising and the fall of the high-falling tone are completed in that syllable, while in the triple tone the first and second parts are completed in the stressed syllable and the third in the syllable following.

An *h* coming before the stressed vowel always points to the low-rising tone, and one coming after it to the high-falling tone. When an *h* occurs both before and after it, the triple tone is indicated.

When *gh, jh, ḍh, dh, bh* are initial or final little difficulty is experienced. The rules may be briefly stated :

Initial : (i) If no vowel has been elided between the stop and the *h* the stop is devocalized and the *h* is changed to a low-rising tone. (ii) If a vowel has been elided the stop remains sonant. Tone as in (i).

Final : The stops are kept sonant and the *h* is changed to a high-falling tone.

The MEDIAL stops *gh, jh, ḍh, dh, bh* are sonant or surd, as shown below.

Sonant : (*a*) Words with low-rising tone which are derived from words with high-falling tone, have them sonant whether they immediately follow a consonant or a vowel.

ulj̦āṇā, entangle (*u'lajṇā*) : *khuñ̦āṇā*, cause to lose the way (*khu'ññā*) : *kaḍ̦āṇā*, cause to be ejected (*ka'ḍḍṇā*).

(*b*) When these stops immediately follow any vowel which is not the end of a prefix obvious to the village mind, they are sonant. *ḍĕḍ̦aws*, mortuary (Eng. dead-house) : *mad̦āṇī*, churning stick.

Surd : (*c*) Words which appear to Panjabis to be made up of

(i) two words,

(ii) word and prefix,

(iii) word with repetition in same or different form are treated like two words, but only stressed syllables carry the tone.

Examples :—

(i) *p̣a'mbaḷ-p̣ū'se*, inconveniences, etc. *lamṭ̣ī'ṅg*, stork, flamingo, etc. *pad-p̨ai'ṛā*, toadstool : *gaḷ-k̨o'ṭū*, choking : *p̨a'nkaṛ*, money change : *kup-k̨e'r* or *k̨u'p-k̨e'r*, very dark : *p̨e'ḍ-kuṭ*, or *p̣e'ḍ-k̨u'ṭ*, branch of the *Sāsīs* : *kirt-k̨a'ṇ*, ungrateful.

(ii) *at̨a'rm*, irreligion : *kuṭ̨a'bbā*, awkward, ill-shaped.

(iii) *k̨a'ṛī-kaṛī*, repeatedly : *c̨a'v-cav*, quickly.

(i) and (ii) account for words like *paṛp̨ū'njā*, grain-parcher, and for the Panjābī pronunciation of Hindī words like *kaṇ-k̨o'r*, very dark or terrible : *mūr-t̨a'nya*, cerebral. Similarly they explain *prb̨ā'teḷā*, morning : *prd̨ā'n*, chief. These sound like single words, for their prefixes are not recognized.

All cases of intervocalic *gh*, *jh*, *ḍh*, *dh*, *bh*, are covered by the above rules ; there may be a few words in which the rules do not cover instances of these stops occurring in immediate conjunction with consonants, but they must be very few, and I am not at present able to recall any.

TIME TAKEN BY THE STRIKE OF CEREBRAL *ṛ*

In the JOURNAL for July, 1924, p. 436, I stated that the strike of a cerebral *ṛ* lasted not more than one 120th of a second. I was speaking of the commoner cerebrals *ṭ, ḍ, ṇ, ṛ*, especially the last, and was taking exception to the use of the words "firmly pressed" in describing the movement of the tongue in making them. It seemed to me that it was a misuse of terms to say that there was "firm pressure" in an action taking so short a time. There is no more pressure in a cerebral than in a dental.

I do not now remember on what I based my estimate of the time taken by the strike of a cerebral *ṛ*, but no doubt the grounds for it were adequate. Recently, however, a very interesting article in *Zeitschrift für Experimental-Phonetik*, Band 1, Heft 1, Okt. 1930, has furnished evidence that the statement was well on the safe side. In this article there is an analysis of a sentence spoken by Dr. Babu Ram Saksena, who some years ago was a student in the School of Oriental Studies. He repeated the words *ek baṛe rājā rahte haĩ* at a rather slow conversational rate, taking two seconds to the five words. The diagrams accompanying the article enable one to calculate the length of each sound.

There are seven consonants (counting *h* as a vowel), viz. *k, b, ṛ, r, j, r, t,* Of these *k, b,* and *t* take the longest time, one-tenth of a second each ; *j* and the second *r* take seven-hundredths of a second each ; the first *r* takes six-hundredths of a second, while *ṛ*, the only cerebral in the seven, takes two-hundredths of a second. This includes the time taken by the on-glide, the strike, and the off-glide. The strike is probably shorter than either the on-glide or the off-glide, so we may say with confidence that it takes less than one 150th of a second.

The statement in *JRAS.*, loc. cit., was thus comfortably within the mark.

Putting the matter in mathematical language we may say that *k*, *b*, *t* : *j*, 2nd *r* : 1st *r* : *ṛ* = 10 : 7 : 6 : 2. Particularly noteworthy is the proportion *t* : *ṛ* = 5 : 1. The dental *t* in that sentence took five times as long as the cerebral *ṛ*.

R SOUNDS IN KAFIR LANGUAGES

The rather extensive use made of fricative *r′* in Kāfir languages is interesting. The sound itself is very familiar; it occurs in Urdu and Panjabi as a subsidiary member of the *r* phoneme. This is the case also in Waigalī and Ashkun. Dr. Morgenstierne has been good enough to describe and pronounce Kāfir *r′* for me. Katī has it as a separate phoneme. In slight modification of the statement in the Report he says it is made just behind the *r*.

We have here two entirely different classes of sounds (fricative and strike sounds) with little or no phonetic connexion between them. As unfortunately we always use the same symbol *r* for both, it is necessary to make the distinction clear. The fricatives, of which Kāfir *r′* is an example, may occur in any position, front or back, alveolar or cerebral (palatal). A cerebral fricative *r′* is often heard in Urdu, Panjabi, Hindi (and Bengali, so Mr. Sutton Page), where it is a member of the cerebral strike-*ṛ* phoneme. The strike sounds may also be found in any position, front or back; and of course in both classes the number of intermediate positions is limitless.

The fricative *r* sounds are closely related to sibilants (generally sonant) and are often difficult to distinguish from them; some *z* sign would be a more appropriate symbol than *r*. The strike sounds on the other hand belong to the *d* and *t* class. The ordinary *r* and *ṛ* sounds of North India are strike sounds; those which we are for the moment writing *r′* and *ṛ′* are fricatives The important thing to realise is that both the *r′* and the *r* sounds may be either cerebral or alveolar, indeed theoretically may occur in any position on the roof of the mouth which the tip of the tongue can reach.

There remains the question—what is the nature of the cerebral ṛ sounds in village Kaśmīrī and Ṣiṇā? To which class do they belong? Are they fricatives or strike sounds, and where are they produced? I am glad in particular to write a note on the Kaśmīrī ṛ because it has never been described before.

The ṛ in village Kaśmīrī is the same as in Ṣiṇā. It is a pure strike ṛ (not a fricative), essentially the same as the strike ṛ of Waigalī and Ashkun, or for that matter of Pashto, Urdu and Panjabi, quite different from the fricative ṛ′ of Kāfir languages. Its position varies from a little behind the teeth-ridge to a point about a third of the way along the hard palate. This strike ṛ as heard in Panjabi or Ṣiṇā or village Kaśmīrī is usually called cerebral, but there is no objection to calling it post-alveolar, meaning "behind the alveolus or teethridge".

ONE ASPECT OF STRESS IN URDŪ AND HINDĪ

The problem of stress in Urdū and Hindī sometimes seems insoluble. When an Indian, whose native language is Urdū or some dialect of Hindī, speaks English we feel that he stresses the wrong words of a sentence and the wrong syllables of words. He appears to us to say [ʌˈkaḍəmɪk] for [ˈækəˈdɛmɪk]; [ˈbɪgənɪŋ] for [bɪˈgɪnɪŋ]; [ˈæssosjeʃn] for [əˈsousɪˈeɪʃn]. But, apart from the mere shifting of stresses, the nature of the stress and his conception of it appear to be different from ours.

My impression is :—

(i) That stress in the languages mentioned is not wholly unlike that of English, but

(ii) that it is weaker, a stressed syllable closely resembling an unstressed one, and

(iii) that stressed vowels differ very little from unstressed vowels.

The facts in (ii) and (iii) account for the difficulty which English speakers have in hearing the stress. We have all our lives been accustomed to strong stress associated with special forms of vowels. Our dictionaries mark it. Speakers of Urdū and Hindī, on the other hand, are used to weak stress and give little or no thought to it : none of their dictionaries mark it. Consequently they are not in the habit of recognizing it, and I feel sure that when questioned they often make wrong statements about it.

Thus I have sometimes been told by them that words like *măhăknā*, *bhăṛăknā*, *măhăk*, *bhăṛăk*, have the stress on the second syllable, whereas I am convinced that it is on the first. They say, too, sometimes that *băhā*, flowed, and *bănā*, was made, have the same stress as *băhā*, having caused to flow, and *bănā*, having caused to make. I feel that the former are **['baha, 'bʌna]**, and the latter **[bʌ'ha, bʌ'na]**. Is there any proof either way ? (It is necessary to add that Indians differ from one another in their judgment on these stresses ; there is plenty of support for my view.)

The effect of *h* on short vowels in Urdū furnishes, if not a proof, at least a strong argument. I have frequently stated that stressed *ăh* followed by a consonant or *e* or *ɛ* is pronounced **[æh]**, while unstressed *ăh* is **[ʌh]** or **[əh]**.

(1) Let us take *mahaknā* and *mahak*. According to the rule just given, the first vowel will be **[æ]** if the stress is on the first syllable and **[ʌ]** if it is on the second. Similarly *bahalnā*, *ṭahalnā*, will begin with **bæ** and **ṭæ** or **bʌ** and **ṭʌ**, according to whether the stress is on the first or second syllable. Now, in all these words the first vowel is **[æ]** not **[ʌ]** ; it follows therefore that the stress is on the first syllable.

(2) Again, the first vowel of the combination *ăhā* in Urdū is **[a]** when the stress is on the first syllable and **[ʌ]** or even **[ə]** when the second syllable is stressed. Let us take the two words written *băhā* ; we find **[baha]**, flowed, and **[bʌha]**, having caused to flow. By the rule stated the stress of the former is on the first syllable, and of the latter on the second.

(3) Two other words, both written *maḥallõ.* In Psalms xlviii. 3, occurs the phrase *(shahr) ke maḥallõ mẽ,* which means either " in the palaces of the city " or " in the various sections of the city ". To get the first meaning we must pronounce [**mæhlõ**], to get the second [**mʌhʌllõ**] ; this implies that in the former the stress is on the first syllable, in the latter on the second. The singular of the first word is *maḥall,* the correct pronunciation of which is [**mæhl**] or [**'mæhɛl**] ; a few people incorrectly say [**mʌ'hʌl**] or [**mhʌl**].

(4) One more example. *bahar saḥar* is pronounced [**bʌ'hʌr 'sæhɛr**].

We may say to ourselves : " Perhaps stress is not connected with the two pronunciations of *ah.* Is it not possible that *bahar saḥar* is pronounced [**'bʌhʌr sæ'hɛr**], and not [**bʌ'hʌr 'sæhɛr**] ? " It may be possible, but I am sure it is not the case. At any rate no explanation dissociating the two pronunciations from stress has ever been given.

An interesting corroboration is furnished by Panjabi. In that language we get the low rising tone when *h* precedes, and the high falling tone when it follows, a stressed vowel. For *bahar saḥar* a Panjabi would say [**bə''ʌr sæ'r**], showing that he feels the stress as I have stated it. The same holds of the other examples given.

We may perhaps be permitted to conclude that in a matter like this the evidence of trained English ears can be trusted to a very considerable extent.

130.

THE PRONUNCIATION OF URDU AND HINDI

IT is difficult to write correctly about the grammar of a language; it is almost impossible to be accurate about its pronunciation. It follows that the weakest and most unsatisfactory part of books on a language is nearly always that which deals with sounds. The reasons are various. I give some of them here with special reference to Urdu and Hindi.

(1) The tradition is bad. Mistakes were made in the early days of study. One writer after another has copied these mistakes, introducing variations of his own with chaotic results. The statements made by Forbes, who, I believe, was never in India, are still the basis of remarks on Urdu pronunciation.

(2) It is said that every man who has made some progress in the study of a language regards himself as an expert. This may be an exaggeration as regards idiom and syntax, but it is almost literally true of sounds. It is impossible to persuade a man who has made a scholarly study of a spoken tongue in the country where it is spoken that, however much he may know of its grammar and literature, his ear is incapable of hearing its distinctive sounds and that in describing them he is merely guessing (or copying other writers). Yet it is nearly always true. The scholar is perhaps more readily misled than others, for knowing the principal things that he *ought* to hear, he easily persuades himself that he *does* hear them.

(3) It is not possible to write accurately about the sounds of any language without devoting years to the study of phonetics. Most writers have not done this.

(4) This fact leads to another, viz. that Indian speakers are unsafe guides unless they are competent phoneticians. This requires emphasis. Someone will say—surely they know how to pronounce their language. The answer is a simple negative. They may pronounce correctly, but they do not *know* the pronunciation. Englishmen of the richest scholarship in their own tongue will make ludicrous misstatements about its pronunciation if they have not gone far in the study of phonetics. So it is with Indians. This explains the otherwise

remarkable fact that the description of sounds given in grammars written by Indians is often more inaccurate than that of Europeans.

(5) Another source of error to which Indians are liable is the desire to pronounce according to preconceived notions as to how words *ought* to be pronounced. Thus a Mawlavī will import what he thinks are correct (Arabic) sounds into Urdu words. He will discourse on the hamza, on *'ain*, will assure the unfortunate student that words written *ḥukm*, *fikr*, *ṣubḥ*, are monosyllables, that *jadd o jihad* should be pronounced *jidd o jahad*, that *fi'l* is different from *fel*, that the first syllable of *mahdī* is not the same as that of *maḥfil*. Paṇḍits have not the same opportunities in Urdu, for the pronunciation of Sanskrit words in that language has been fixed without consulting them, but in the cognate language Hindi they try to force old forms upon an unwilling people, and teach them to students. It is greatly to be regretted that some Europeans are as guilty as these Paṇḍits, for instead of the correct words used by the people in conversation, they write incorrect forms assimilated to Sanskrit.

The following remarks deal with the pronunciation of educated Delhi men. It is generally known that Delhi and Lucknow, and these places alone, are recognized as *mustanad* or authoritative in all matters of Urdu idiom and pronunciation. When the two cities differ, as they do in a few unimportant points, both are considered correct. I have never met an Indian who questioned their pre-eminence. When one has to choose a form of the language for public purposes it is better to take the Delhi idiom, for it is nearer the centre of the Urdu speaking world. The normal language employed in lectures and speeches before large audiences from Peshawar to Bihar is Urdu, and while Delhi is situated close to the centre of this tract of country, Lucknow is on its eastern border. The revisers of the Urdu New Testament were wisely guided in their decision to make Delhi Urdu their standard. But let me say again that the differences are slight. When I speak of the pronunciation of English I mean English as spoken by an average public school man. (See Professor Jones's *Dictionary*.)

I desire here not to discuss in exhaustive detail the question of Urdu pronunciation, but to go briefly into the various sounds, and give such hints as may be useful to students. When necessary I have added in square brackets the phonetic equivalents.

At the end of the article will be found a special note on Hindi pronunciation.

Common Mistakes

As I write I have no grammars before me, and I have not in mind the words of any writer, European or Indian, but I think that all the following mistakes may be found in books of comparatively recent date.

Hamza.—Directions are often given for enunciating *hamza*, but they are ill-founded, for it is a mere device of writing, disregarded more often than not, even in writing, and wholly ignored in pronunciation. In Urdu *hamza* is never pronounced.

Long Vowels.—So-called long vowels are a frequent source of error. Books speak of "long *a*", "long *i*", "long *u*", and tell us that *e* and *o* are always long. The fact is that long vowels of any kind are infrequent in Urdu. Words like *burāīā*, *sahelīā*, *khushbūā*, are said to contain three long vowels. Actually they contain four short vowels. There is not a long vowel in any of them. Under strong stress vowels are sometimes lengthened, thus we may hear *mulāqāt* meeting, *vajūhāt* reasons, with the last vowel long (but the middle vowel undubitably short); again *dekh* look, standing by itself has a long *e*, but the *e* in *dekho* is always short, and yet this short *e* differs considerably from the *e* in the usual English pronunciation "dekko".

The mistake arises out of the notion that *ī* and *ū* are lengthened forms of *i* and *u*, and that Urdu *e* and *o* are long varieties of the English vowels in "pet" and "hot". The difference is not one of length; in each case the vowels are different. The phrases *mere bete mẽ dekhẽ* and *donõ ghoṛõ ko kholo* contain seven short *e*'s and seven short *o*'s respectively. To determine the length of a vowel we must listen to complete breath groups in conversation, not to isolated words. Any vowel which takes a markedly longer time to utter than its fellows we may consider long.

aw (often written *au*): this is described as the same as or very like the vowel in "how" or "proud", so that the first syllable of *hawlnāk*, terrible, would be practically the English "howl". The sound is, however, quite different. It is often a single half-long vowel, very similar to the *au* in "haul" [ɔ·], but sometimes it is a diphthong of which the first part is the vowel just mentioned and the second a monophthongic *o* [ɔo]. Cf. *Mawlā*, God, generally mɔ·lɑ, occasionally moolɑ; *tawba*, repentance (tɔ·bɑ or tɔobɑ).

ay (or *ai*) is the front vowel corresponding to the back vowel *aw*, not resembling the English *i* in "high", "stile", with which it is compared, but closely approximating to *a* in "hand", "bad".

Like *aw*, it is frequently, perhaps ordinarily, a single vowel. Thus the two words *hai to* (is indeed) sound to the average Englishman's ear not like "high toe", but exactly like "(Bishop) Hatto", and the word *'ayn*, exact, is to him indistinguishable from "Anne". The Urdu vowel is generally half long. Not infrequently it is a diphthong composed of the *a* in "Anne" followed by the *e* in "get". These are the nearest possible English equivalents. Phonetic symbols [hæ to] or [hæe to], and [æ·n] or [æen]. Cf. also *paydā*, born [pæ·da] or [pæeda]; *thailī*, bag [thæli or thæeli].

Cerebral letters: *ṭ, ḍ, ṛ* are often said to be like English *t, d, r,* only more vigorously enunciated, and they are called "hard" *t, d,* and *r*. There is nothing vigorous in their utterance, and it would be just as correct to call them "soft" *t, d,* and *r*. They are neither harder nor softer than the corresponding front letters *t, d, r*. Cerebral or retroflex *ṭ* and *ḍ* are made like English *t* and *d*, but the point of contact is about ⅜ in. from the upper teeth. I am conscious, however, that as no one can measure this distance in his mouth, the direction will not be of practical value. It will be better to say "far back on the hard palate". Note that *ṛ* is very unlike the two American fricative *r*'s. English *t* and *d* do not occur in Urdu. The point of contact for *ṭ* and *ḍ* is considerably further back than for the English letters; for Urdu *t* and *d* the tip of the tongue is further forward than for English *t* and *d*, and the position of the rest of the tongue is of importance. See below under *t* and *d*. To make *ṛ* the tongue is turned back slightly further than for *ṭ* and *ḍ*, and then brought forward with a flap, the under surface of the front of the tongue striking the roof of the mouth further forward than the point of contact for *ṭ* and *ḍ*. It is essential to *begin* far back, otherwise the acoustic effect will be wrong.

ḷ and *ṇ* are common in Urdu, but they are found only before *ṭ* and *ḍ*, and people imagine they are pronouncing ordinary *l* and *n*. If the *ṭ* and *ḍ* are correctly pronounced, the *ḷ* and *ṇ* will automatically come right. The most important point to remember about retroflex letters is that they have no effect whatever upon neighbouring vowels. Englishmen almost invariably allow them to influence the preceding and succeeding vowels. In the case of *ṭ* care is necessary to avoid the aspiration that accompanies English *t*.

v is generally described vaguely as being between English *v* and *w*. Sometimes it is said to be bilabial, i.e. made with both lips. In reality, however, the upper lip is not used in producing it. There is slight contact of the upper teeth with some part, it hardly matters which, of the lower lip. Air may or may not escape at the sides of the point of contact, and there may or may not be audible friction. When the sound is doubled the friction is always audible. One would not be far wrong in saying that *v* is a very faint English *v*, but the acoustic effect is so different that an Urdu *v* in an English word like "very" strikes an Englishman at once as wrong, and Urdu speakers find it almost impossible to distinguish between the three English words "wail", "whale", and "veil". Symbol [ʋ].

f is the corresponding surd.

'ain : few grammars attempt to tell how *'ain* is pronounced. Usually one is told that the pronunciation is very difficult and can only be learnt from an Indian. But a considerable majority of Urdu speakers never pronounce *'ain* at all, and the entire ignoring of it would cause no comment. It is far better to omit it than make an obvious effort to say it. In educated Delhi pronunciation *'ain* is generally omitted; but is pronounced in the following case.

A stressed *a* or *ā* followed or preceded by *'ain* is pronounced with slight, but noticeable, pharyngeal tension ; or putting it in every day words one might say "with slight contraction of throat muscles". It should be noted that the *'ain* is not a consonant at all, it is mere muscular tension which lasts throughout the vowel. Vowels other than *a* and *ā* are not affected in this way.

Accented *a*, *i*, and *u*, followed by an *'ain* which is either (1) final or (2) followed by a consonant, are pronounced *ā*, *e*, and *o* respectively, but the *'ain* itself is not pronounced except as just mentioned. ***ba'd***, after, becomes *bād* [bɑd] ; *mi'da*, stomach, becomes *meda* [medɑ] ; *s̲h̲u'la*, flame, becomes *s̲h̲ola* [ʃolɑ].

Sounds practically the same as in English

Premising that in English voiceless plosives generally receive clearly marked aspiration which must be avoided in unaspirated Urdu plosives, we may say that the following differ only very slightly from the corresponding sounds in English.

p, *b*, *k*, *g*, *m*, *n*, *ṅ*, *s*, *z*, *y* (phonetic symbols *p*, *b*, *k*, *g*, *m*, *n*, ŋ, *s*, *z*, *j*). *l* may be added to the list provided that we understand only English clear *l*, as in "feeling", and not the dark *l* as in "feel". ŋ is always followed by *g* or *k*, but it is not true that *n* followed by *g* or *k* becomes ŋ. The four *z*'s—*z*, *z̲*, *ẓ*, *z̤*—are identical. Similarly the three *s*'s—*s*, *s̤*, and *ṣ*—are the same.

Sounds closely resembling English Sounds

ch, j, sh, zh. All these are pronounced with the tip and blade of the tongue further forward than in English, and *ch* must be as nearly as possible unaspirated. The best phonetic symbols for *ch* and *j* are *c* and ɟ, as it is not open to us to employ the misleading double signs which are found in some books. The symbols will then be (c, ɟ, ʃ, ʒ). These four sounds are produced with unrounded (i.e. not protruded) lips. The English sounds are generally made with rounded or protruded lips.

The Remaining Consonants

t, d are the Italian sounds, uttered with the whole tongue raised so that the surface is against the palate, and the sides against all the upper teeth. Students are often instructed to make these sounds by putting the tip of the tongue against the front teeth. This will result in a noticeably wrong sound unless the surface and sides of the tongue are in the right place. *t* and *ṯ* are the same.

q is a *k* with the point of contact further back than the uvula. Unlike the corresponding Arabic sound it is completely unaspirated; in Arabic there is generally slight aspiration. *q* has no voiced equivalent.

r is made with a single tap of the tip of the tongue against the upper teeth ridge. It is almost the same as the so-called trilled *r* in Scotland, but it should be remembered that many Scotch people do not use it. In some Urdu words it is found double. It is then trilled. Such words are chiefly Arabic, some are Persian, a few are Hindi. The southern English *r* is quite different. Many English speakers who think they can say Urdu *r*, spoil it by the insertion of a neutral vowel. Thus for *tīr, aur, dūr* [ti·r, ɔ·r, du·r] they say [tiər, ɔər, duər].

When *r* is followed by *n* it is sometimes pronounced as an advanced fricative, thus for *varna* (*varna*) we may hear (*vaɹna*). It is dangerous to imitate this.

kh and *gh* are not unlike the German sounds in "ach" and "wagen" (except when this "g" is a simple *g*), but they are further back. The Scotch "ech" heard in "Muchalls", "Buchan", is like *kh*, but is further forward. The Urdu sounds, though far back, are gently enunciated, and are never trilled. In this they differ from Parisian voiced and unvoiced *r*. Symbols [ʁ, ʁ].

h is as in English, both voiced and unvoiced, but the sonant variety is much commoner than in English. An *h* which follows a vowel and closes a syllable is often sonant, and one which comes between two voiced sounds nearly always so, i.e. the vocal chords vibrate while it is being uttered. The difficulty of Urdu *h* lies partly in its strongly vibrant quality (when sonant), and partly in its occurring in positions in which English *h* does not occur. The latter is nearly always found before an accented vowel, whereas in Urdu it is commonly joined to the plosive consonants, including *ch* and *j*, but excluding *q*, also to *r* and *ṛ*; it often ends syllables, and is frequent before unaccented vowels. Unlike English *h* it is never pronounced with the German "ich-laut". The two letters *h* and *ḥ* are identical. Symbols: sonant [ɦ], surd [h].

The question of the influence of *h* or *ḥ* upon preceding vowels is very complicated, but one or two rules may be given here.

When accented *a*, *i*, or *u* is followed by an *h* or *ḥ* which is either (1) final or (2) followed by a consonant, the vowel is pronounced *ai*, *e*, or *o* respectively.

If the *h* or *ḥ* is followed by *a*, *e*, or *i*, the accented *a* which precedes becomes a short *ai*.

Similarly if the letter following *h* or *ḥ* is *ā*, the *a* becomes *ā*, but if the letter following *h* or *ḥ* is *u*, the *a* becomes a short *au*.

If the letter following the *h* is *ī*, *o*, *ū* the preceding *a* is not affected.

ih and *uh* occur seldom except in the circumstances mentioned above, and the words are generally uncommon words with the pronunciation not quite uniform. It would not be worth while attempting to give detailed rules.

The subjoined examples will illustrate the rules: *bahin*, sister [bæɦɪn]; *kahnā*, say [kæɦnɑ]; *kahā*, said [kɑɦɑ]; *kahe* [kæɦe]; *kahī* [kʌɦi]; *bahut*, much [bɔɦut]; *pahunchnā*, arrive [pɔɦuncnɑ]; *bahū*, daughter-in-law [bʌɦu]; *vuh*, that [voh]; *yih*, this [jeh]; *Dihlī*, Delhi [deɦli]; *muḥkam*, firm, etc. [mohkʌm].

Vowels

The vowels in general are formed with the lips more widely spread than in English.

ī, high front, like Italian *i*, higher than English *i* in "marine". [i.]

i, not unlike English *i* in "fin". [ɪ.]

e, pure monophthongic vowel, higher than English *e* in "get", lower than the vowel often heard in Scotch "take", and not so tense, a little lower than cardinal *e* [e]. Whether short, half-long, or long, it is the same vowel.

ay or *ai*, described above; higher than English *a* in "hand" [æ or æe]. See also diphthongs.

a, like *u* in English "bun", lips more spread [ʌ].

ā, not unlike *a* in "calm", but further forward [ɑ].

aw or *au*, described above; [ɔ or ɔo]. See also diphthongs.

o, pure monophthong, not unlike vowel often heard in Scotch "no", but slightly lower; lower also than cardinal *o* [o].

Diphthongs.

aī (ʌi): rarely heard as [əi], e.g. *geī* [gəi], she went.

aw or *au* (sometimes) [ɔo]; see above.

ay or *ai* (sometimes) [æe]; see above.

u resembles the *u* in "pull" [ʊ].

ū is like Italian *u*, French *ou* [u].

Nasal Vowels.—All vowels may be nasalized. This nasalization is often described as "nasal *n*", which suggests that the writers believe there are some *n*'s which are not nasal.

Tones.—There are no tones in Urdu such as we get in Panjabi or Burmese.

Accent.—The only rule of practical value seems to me to be the following. I am speaking, of course, of the natural accent of conversation, not the artificial accent of poetry.

What is generally understood by "inflection" never causes the shifting of an accent from one syllable to another. Therefore :—

(i) If we know upon what vowel the accent in one part of a verb falls, we know how to stress the whole verb. e.g. *pahunchnā*, arrive, has the accent on first syllable. Consequently *pahunch*, *pahunchke*, *pahunchẽge*, *pahunchūgā*, *pahunchnevāla*, *pahunchnevālīā* all have the accent on the first syllable. *pahunchānā*, cause to arrive, has the accent on the third syllable and all other parts of the verb will have it there also.

(ii) The same holds of nouns, adjectives, and pronouns: *roṭī*, loaf; *roṭīā*, *roṭīo* (*roṭiyā̃*, *roṭiyo*); all accent on the first syllable.

Exception: some dissyllabic nouns ending in *-ā*, which have in the first syllable an accented *a*, *i*, or *u*, followed by a single consonant, tend in the plural inflected parts to throw the accent on to the *-ā*: *k͟ha'ṭā*, sin, *k͟haṭā'ē*; *gha'ṭā*, cloud, *ghaṭā'ō*.

HINDI

The word Hindi bears many senses. It may be made to include languages like Avadhī, Rājasthānī, Braj, and Bihārī; it may be confined to "High Hindi" as found in the Hindi Bible and countless modern prose works. If we take it in the latter sense, the only practical one for our purpose, we are at once confronted with the difficulty of deciding how many people (some would add "if any") speak this form of Hindi in their homes, and where they live? If we pass on from that question and try to describe the pronunciation of this Hindi as read aloud from books written in prose, we still have to ask "read by whom? in what part of India?" To give any kind of satisfactory account of the pronunciation we must confine ourselves to the tract extending from Delhi and Saharanpur to Allahabad and Benares.

With this limitation we may say that the description of Urdu sounds given above will be correct for Hindi anywhere near Delhi. (Urdu *kh*, *gh*, *z*, *zh*, *q*, *'ain* are not supposed to be found in *theṭh* or real Hindi. Some of these sounds may occasionally be heard.) As we go further east and south we notice certain changes, but the great majority of sounds remain unaltered.

Consonantal changes: *v* tends towards English *w*, and there is a greater tendency to confuse *b* with *v*, and *j* with *y*.

Vowel changes: tendency to confuse *i* with *ī* and *u* with *ū*. *ai* becomes more like *ăĭ* or even *ăī*, and *au* more like *ăŭ* or *ăū*.

Apart from these few points all that is said of Urdu pronunciation will apply to Hindi.

Of the special Hindi letters it should be noted that no distinction is made between the so-called *ri*-vowel and *ri*, between *ś* and *ṣ*, or between *ṇ* and *n*. This applies to the whole area.

GLOSSARY OF HINDI PHONETIC TERMS

THIS is an attempt, made so far as I know for the first time, to give a Hindi translation of all the more ordinary phonetic terms in use at present. Doubtless the list could have been enlarged by the inclusion of rarer words, but such a course might have lessened its utility. The phonetic words or phrases have been taken for the most part from a work by Professor Jones. They number about 180. A few of the Hindi equivalents will be recognized as common in works on grammar. They do not, however, carry one far. For the rest I have had to put down the words which seemed to me best to express the required idea. Pioneer work of this description is always capable of improvement. It should be undertaken not by an individual but by a learned committee.

The attention of students is drawn to a few points :—

(1) These phonetic terms are intended to apply to any and every language. They do not specially refer to Hindi or Sanskrit. It follows that a term which suits Hindi may have to be discarded because it does not suit English or French or other languages, e.g. *akṣar* for "syllable".

(2) Old words used by Hindi grammarians must be used with a changed connotation and denotation. Thus, it is natural to use *svar* for vowel, but modern phonetic science will not admit that *r̥*, *r̥̄*, *l̥*, *l̥̄* are vowels. Again, *ghoṣ* seems to be the best word for "sonant", and it must therefore apply to sonant vowels, but it may be questioned whether any Hindi grammarian ever contemplated this extension of its meaning.

(3) Spelling : I have aimed at spelling words as they are ordinarily pronounced in conversation by men of moderate education. There are one or two harmless deviations from this ; *ś* and *ṣ* have the same sound to-day in Hindi. Some may criticize the employment of *ṇ*, but in my own pronunciation I always distinguish between *ṇ* and *n*, and some Indians do so. Sanskrit scholars will object to my venturing to alter hoary Sanskrit spellings, but before they hold up their Sanskritic hands in horror or lose any Prakritic hair I would beg them to consider that there is no more reason for giving Hindi words an ancient

dress than there is for using in English such forms as knihte, briddes, constantia, societas, discipula, telegramma, geologia, and others. In English we never dream of spelling *tatsams* or semi-*tatsams* after their Saxon, Latin, or Greek originals ; we feel that we have as much right to alter them to suit our modern requirements as we have to alter any *tadbhav*. Hindi has the same right.

(4) Sanskrit words : I have not wholly avoided Sanskrit words. Some are rooted in grammatical terminology, and are understood by those who are likely to study phonetics. In protesting against every attempt to make Hindi a handmaiden to Sanskrit we must conserve the power it has of taking words from Sanskrit or any other language and assimilating them for its own purposes. Three Indian scholars who wrote in Hindi a large three-volume History of Hindi Literature, have some splendid pages on this subject. I give a translation of one or two sentences :—

" Hindi is the simple language of the people. (If it is rendered difficult by the adoption of Sanskrit forms) the only possible result will be that Hindi, like Sanskrit, will be numbered among dead languages. It is our sacred duty to save it from such a fate." After giving examples of words which may correctly be spelt in several ways, they proceed : " Proud Sanskrit scholars may turn up their noses and raise their eyebrows at these forms, but Hindi fearlessly uses them all and will continue to do so. The truth is that the correct forms of words are those which people of ordinary education use in speech. If anyone writes other forms, we certainly admit them as a concession, but we have no hesitation in calling them improper. We hold that there is no harm in using new forms, and as regards *sandhi* we assert that Hindi is at perfect liberty to disregard it or conform to it at will." These are brave words, and they are wise words. Let it not be forgotten that Sanskrit is dead, Hindi lives.

Vocabulary of Hindi Phonetic Terms

accent, see " stress " ; tonic accent, *ū̃chāī batānevālā bal*, *uchchtā sūchak bal*, m. ; quantitative accent, *parimāṇ sūchak bal*, *mātrā bal*.

affricate (consonant), *sparṣ-saṅgharṣī (vyanjan)*.

alphabet, *varṇmālā*, f.

alveolar, *masūṛe kā*.

artificial palate, see " palate ".

aspirate, aspirated, aspiration, *mahāprāṇ*, m., *h-kār kī dhvani (vālā)*.

back, *pīchhe*, *pīchhe kā*.

back of tongue, *jībh ka pichhlā bhāg*, m.

back vowel, *pīchhe kā svar*, m., *pichhlā svar*.
bilabial, *donõ hõṭhõ kā, dvyoṣṭhya*.
blade of tongue, *jībh kā phal*.
breath, *sā̃s*, f., *śvās*, m.
breathe, *sā̃s lena*; breathe out, *sā̃s chorṇā*.
breathed sounds (so-called), see "voiceless".
broad transcription, *sādhāran lipi* (f.) or *lekhan* (m.).
cacuminal, see "retroflex".
cardinal (vowel), *mukhya svar*, m.; *pradhān svar*.
change, n., *vikār*, m.; v. *badalnā*.
class (of letters, sounds, etc.), *varg*, m.
clear l, *sāf l-kār*, m.
close vowel, *sakṛā svar*.
compound, adj., *sãyukt*.
consonant, *vyañjan*, m.; see "affricate", "plosive".
consonantal vowel, *vyañjan svar*, m.
dark l, *moṭā l-kār*.
dental, *dantya, dāntõ kā*; see "labio-dental", "post-dental", "pre-dental".
devocalization, *aghoṣ karnā* or *honā*.
dialect, *upabhāṣā*, f., *bolī*, f.
diphthong, *do juṛe hue svar, dvisvar*, m., *yaugik svar*, m.
divide, *bā̃ṇṭnā, vibhakt karnā*.
division, *bhāg*, m., *vibhāg*, m.
drum of ear, *kān kā paṭah*, m.
ear, *kān*, m.; see "drum".
epiglottis, *āvarṇ ka ḍhakṇā*, m.
experimental (phonetics), *kal vālā, yantrvālā, yāntrik*.
explosion, *bhak*, f.
food-passage, *ann kī nalī*, f.
form, *ākār*, m.
forward, *āge, āge kā*.
fricative, *ragaṛnevālā, sangharṣī*.
friction, *ragaṛ*, f., *sangharṣ*, m.
front of tongue, *jībh kā aglā bhāg*.
front vowel, *āge kā svar, aglā svar*.
glide, *sankrāmak*, m.; see "off-glide", "on-glide".
glottal, *glauṭis kā*; glottal stop, *hamzā*, m.
glottis, *glauṭis*, f.
gum, *masūṛā*, m.
guttural, *gale kā, kaṇṭh kā, kaṇṭhya*; back guttural, *jihvā mūlīya* (*vyañjan*, m.); gutturo-labial, *kaṇṭh aur hõṭhõ kā, kaṇṭhausṭhya*, gutturo-palatal, *kaṇṭh aur tālu kā, kaṇṭh-tālavya*.
half-close (vowel), *adh sakṛā, adh sankuchit*.
half-open, *adh khulā*.
high vowel, *ū̃chā svar, uchch svar*; this may mean "high voice"; when there is danger of misunderstanding, we may say *ū̃che sthān kā svar*.
intonation, *sur*, m.
inwards, *bhītar*.
inverted sounds, see "retroflex".
labial, *hõṭhõ kā, oṣṭhya*.
labio-dental, *dāntõ aur hõṭhõ kā, dantauṣṭhya*; see "bilabial", "guttural".
language, *bolī*, f., *bhāṣā*, f.
larynx, *śvās yantr*, m.; *sā̃s kā yantr*.
lateral, *ek or ka, or ka*.
lax (vowel), *ḍhīlā* (*svar*).

length, *lambāī*, f.

letter, *achchhar*, m., *akṣar*, m., *varṇ*, m.

lip, *hõṭh*, m. ; lip-rounding *hõṭhõ ko gol karnā*, *hõṭhõ kī golāī*, *hõṭhõ kā baṛhānā*.

long, *lambā*, *dīrgh*.

low (vowel), *nīchā* (*svar*).

lung, *phephṛā*, m.

membrane, *jhillī*, f.

mid (vowel), *bīc kā*, *madhya* (*svar*).

mixed (vowel), *miśrit* (*svar*).

monophthong, *ek svar*, m., *mūl svar*, *śuddh svar*, *maulik svar* ; see " pure ".

mouth, *mũh*, m.

mouth cavity, *mũh kā khol*, *mukh-vivar*, m.

narrow transcription, *byaurevār lekhan* (m.) or *lipi* (f.).

nasal, *sānunāsik*, *anunāsik*.

nasal cavity, *nāk kā khol*, *nāsā vivar*, m., *nāsikā vivar*, m.

nasalization, *sānunāsiktā*, f.

natural, *prākṛitik*, *svābhāvik*.

nature, *prakṛiti*, f., *svabhāo*, m.

neutral (vowel, etc.), *udāsīn*.

nose, *nāk*, f. ; see " nasal ", etc.

off-glide *saṅkrāmak kā dūsrā bhāg*, *paśchāt saṅkrāmak*, m.

on-glide, *saṅkrāmak kā pahlā bhāg*, *pūrv saṅkrāmak*, m.

open (vowel), *khulā* (*svar*).

organs of speech, *bhāṣaṇ ke aṅg* or *avyav*.

outwards, *bāhar*.

palatal, *tālu kā*, *tālavya* ; see " guttural ".

palate, *tālu*, m. ; artificial do., *banāvaṭī tālu*, *kṛitrim tālu* ; hard do., *kaṭhin tālu* ; soft do., *komal tālu*.

phoneme, *dhvani śreṇī*, f. ; no accurate word, "*fonīm*," m., may have to be used.

phonetic, *dhvanyātmak*, *dhvaniśāstrik*, *dhvanitāttvik*.

phonetic sign, *dhvanyātmak saṅket*.

phonetic theory, *dhvaniśāstrik* or *dhvanitāttvik siddhānt*, m.

phonetic transcription, *dhvanyātmak lekhan* (m.) or *lipi* (f.).

phonetics, *dhvaniśāstr*, m., *dhvanitattva*, m.

pitch, *sur*, m., *ũchāī*, f., *ũchāī nīchāī*, f., *uchchtā*, f.

place (of utterance), *sthān*, m., *bhāṣaṇ sthān*, m.

plosive consonant, *sparś vyañjan*.

post-dental, *paśchāt dantya*, *pichhle dāntõ kā*.

pre-dental, *pūrv dantya*, *agle dāntõ kā*.

prefix, *upasarg*, m.

pronunciation, *uchchāran*, m.

pure (vowel), *śuddh* (*svar*, m.), *mūl* (*svar*), *maulik* (*svar*) ; see " monophthong ".

quadrilateral (of vowels), (*svarõ kā*) *caturbhuj*, m.

quantity, see " length ".

resonance chamber, *nād vivar*, m. ; see " sonority ".

retroflex, *mūrdhanya* ; inverted vowel, *mūrdhanya svar*, m.

rolled, see " trilled ".

rounded (vowel), *gol* or *baṛhā huā* (*svar*).

rounding, *golāī*, *gol karnā* ; inner

do., *pīchhe kī golāī* ; outer do., *āge kī golāī*.
semi-vowel, *adh svar*, m., *antasth*.
sentence, *vākya*, m.
short, *chhoṭā, hrasv*.
shortening, *chhoṭā karnā, hrasv karnā*.
sibilant, *ūṣam, ūṣm*.
sign, *saṅket*, m.
significant, *jis se arth mẽ bhed ho, arth-sūchak* ; non-significant, *jis se arth mẽ bhed nahī̃, arth-sūchak nahī̃*.
sonority, *sunāī*, f.
sound, *dhvani*, f.
speech, *bhāṣā*, f., *bhāṣaṇ*, m. ; speech-sound, *bhāṣā dhvani*, f. ; speech-mechanism, *bhāṣan yantr*, m., *vāk-yantr* ; speech-basis, *kisī kī apnī prāntik yā sthānik bolī*.
spreading of lips, *mūh caurā karnā, mūh phailānā*.
standard pronunciation, *prāmāṇik uchchāraṇ*, m.
stop, *ṭhahrāo*, m. ; stop-consonant, see " plosive ".
stress, *bal*, m. ; sentence stress, *vākya bal* ; one must trust to the context to distinguish this meaning from the other possible one, " power of speech" ; syllabic stress, *śabd ke kisī bhāg par bal* ; word stress, *śabd bal* ; to stress, *bal denā (ko) balī karnā (ko)*.
stressed, *balī*.
subsidiary cardinal vowel, *dūsrī śreṇī kā mukhya* (or *pradhān*) *svar*.
suffix, *pratyay*, m.
surd, see " voiceless ".
syllabic, *śabd ke kisī bhāg kā* ; see " syllable ".
syllable, no word, use *bhāg*, m., *śabd kā bhāg* ; *akṣar*, letter, will not meet the case of words taken from English, French, and other non-Sanskritic languages.
teeth-ridge, *masūṛā*, m.
tense, *taṅg*.
throat, *galā*, m.
tip of tongue, *jībh kī nok*, f., *jihvāgra*, m.
tongue, *jībh*, f. ; base or root of tongue, *jībh kī jaṛ, jihvā mūl*, m. ; see " back ", " blade ", " front ", " tip ".
tongue-tip trill, *jībh kī nok kā kampan, jihvāgra kampan*.
tooth, *dānt*, m. ; see " teeth-ridge ".
triangle (of vowels), (*svarõ kā*) *tribhuj*, m.
trill, n., *kampan*, m. ; v. i., *kāmpnā* ; v. t., *kampānā* ; see " uvular trill ", " tongue-tip trill ".
trilled consonant, *kampan vyañjan*, m.
triphthong, *trisvar*, m. ; *tīn juṛe hue svar*.
unaspirated, *alpprāṇ* ; *jis mẽ h-kār nahī̃*.
unrounded, *anbaṛhā, gol nahī̃*.
unstressed, *nirbal, balhīn, durbal* ; see " weak ".
unvoiced, see " voiceless ".
uvula, *ghaṇṭikā*, f.
uvular, *ghaṇṭikā kā, ghaṇṭikāvālā*.

uvular consonant, *ghaṇṭikā vyañjan.*
uvular trill, *ghaṇṭikā kā kampan.*
variety of pronunciation, *uchchāraṇ kī bhinntā.*
velar, *gale kā, kaṇṭh kā, kaṇṭhya.*
vibrate, *kāmpnā* ; v. t., *kampānā.*
vibration, *kampan*, m.
vocal cords (chords), *svar rajju*, m.
voice, *nād*, m. ; voice-indicator, *nād sūchak.*
voiced, *ghoṣ, nād* ; voiced plosive, *ghōṣ* or *nād sparś-vyañjan* ; voiced sound, *ghoṣ dhvani*, f.
voiceless, *aghoṣ.*
vowel, *svar*, m. ; see " back ", " cardinal ", " close ", " consonantal ", " diphthong ", " front ", " half-close ", " half-open ", " high ", " low ", " mid ", " mixed ", " monophthong ", " rounded ", " semi-vowel ", " unrounded ", " subsidiary ".
weak, *durbal* ; and as for " unstressed " ; weak form of small words, *chhoṭe śabdō kā durbal uchchāraṇ.*
whisper, v., *phusphusānā, phusphusāke bolnā* ; n., *phusphusāhaṭ*, f.
windpipe, *sās ki nalī*, f. ; *śvās nalī*, f.
word, *śabd*, m.

Phonetic Notes on Urdu Records Nos. 6825 AK and 6826 AK

THESE records were made in 1920 to the dictation of a well-known professional story-teller, Bāqir 'Alī, who belonged to Delhi.

A phonetic transcript which has been published is of great value for the study of Urdu sounds. I made the original transcript of both records and had two proofs printed. Professor Daniel Jones, Professor of Phonetics in the University of London, who has to take responsibility for the publication of all transcripts in this series, went over my second proof, made some alterations, and prepared the final proof, which was ultimately printed. He is, therefore, responsible for the transcripts in their present form. I have, however, my proofs before me. The differences between his final print and my proofs are slight, and this article gives our joint views. Where there is any necessity for distinguishing them they are marked with the initials J. for his views and B. for mine.

The importance of these transcripts consists in the fact that the records still exist, and may be heard by any one who wishes to test the statements made. It is one thing to claim to have listened to a particular speaker and taken down his sounds. The speaker disappears, and beyond the author's reputation for accurate recording, there is no certainty that the transcription is correct. It is a very different thing when, as in this case, the speaker cannot disappear, and, what is equally important, cannot alter his pronunciation.

The records afford me much pleasure, for they support, in almost every detail, views which I have long held as to Urdu sounds, and taught my students. They were given ten years ago in the *Bulletin*, Vol. II, iii, 539 ff. Practically all that article expresses my views to-day.

CEREBRAL SOUNDS, called also retroflex. The transcriptions do not indicate the exact point on the palate touched by the tip of the tongue, but the introductory remarks make it clear. "*ṭ, ḍ, ṇ, ṛ* : point of contact not far behind the teeth ridge, in a few instances on the teeth ridge." This is what we should expect. Similarly Dr. Mohiuddin Qadri in *Hindustani Phonetics* says of *ṭ* and *ḍ* : "their point of articulation is just behind the teeth ridge" (p. 73), and of *ṛ* : "the tip of the tongue strikes against the teeth ridge" (p. 92).

For the benefit of those who wish to study Urdu cerebrals, I indicate here those which in these records are specially far forward. I make the statement on my own responsibility. I have not consulted anyone else. The Nos. refer to page and line.

ṭ in **ciṭṭha** 2.8, **luṭai** 3.18. *ṛ* in **bʌṛa** 1.1, **lʌṛke** 1.6, **thoṛi** 3.3, **bʌṛe** 7.1. *ḍ* in **khanḍa** 5.15, **ḍub** 6.4, **buḍḍha** 6.24, 7.2, (but not in 7.3).

In **khʌtar** for **kʌṭar** 5,16, and **lʌtʌkne** for **lʌṭʌkne** 6.12 the *t* is dental. These are mere slips.

In the following instances the *ṛ* is rather fricative :—**bʌṛa** 1.1, **thoṛe** 1.5, **doṛa** 3.6, **ləṛke** 3.8, **bʌṛhaẽ** 3.16, **bʌre** 7.1, **pʌkṛa** 7.12.

v is either a faint labio-dental *v* or a *ŭ*. J. printed them all as *v* (except one *wo* 5.4, i.e. *ŭo*). In my proof I marked several as *w*, meaning *ŭ*. It is always safe to advise English speakers to say *v*, and not *w*. An English *w* always sounds wrong.

y between vowels is often *ĕ*. Thus the ending *āyā* occurs 13 times. B. records **aĕa** every time ; J. **aĕa** 12 times, **aja** once. English people greatly exaggerate the *y* quality of the sound. Similarly the ending *-iyā* occurs 8 times. Both B. and J. transcribed **ia** every time.

'AIN. I unhesitatingly teach my students to ignore *'ain*, in accordance with the usual practice of educated Delhi men in ordinary conversation. In the records there are eleven words containing *'ain* when written in Urdu script. J. has recorded it in two out of the eleven. I did not consider it strong enough to be worth recording in any. This means that in the records the *'ain* of the grammars does not exist, and all descriptions of how to pronounce it go for nothing. Even in words like *a'māl*, *mu'āf*, *'arṣe*, *'ayyāshī*, where it would be easy to pronounce *'ain* there is no trace of it. The other day a Delhi man, who is himself a lecturer on Urdu, told me that there was no difference at all between *bād*, wind, and *ba'd*, after.

I will, however, add this. I have heard Urdu speakers, when speaking rather self-consciously, pronounce, with a slight restriction of throat muscles, vowels which immediately precede or follow the letter *'ain*.

Hamza, which is only another name for glottal stop, is not recorded at all. It is important to note this in view of statements sometimes made. *Hamza* exists solely in writing.

ṇ is generally not an independent sound, but occurs before *ṭ* and *ḍ*. The word *sā̃ḍnī* occurs four times, and every time is pronounced **saṇṇi**. *cā̃dnī* is once **canni** and once **cā̃dni**.

h is sonant except in the combinations *kh, ch, ṭh, th,* and *ph.* We may consider it under two main headings : (1) *h* initial or immediately following a vowel ; (2) *h* immediately following a consonant, to which it is more or less closely attached. The chief point which concerns us is to what extent is it omitted. In our records we have the following instances. (The word "unpronounced" must be understood as qualified by the addition "or at least inaudible".)

(1) (*a*) Initial, as *ḥissa, ḥālat, hai,* 56 times pronounced ; 6 unpronounced (in *hai* 4 ; *hũ, hue,* once each ; *hue* appears as *ŭe,* printed *ve*).

(*b*) After vowel before cs. (including the combinations *rah-gae, rah-namūnī, kah-sunāẽā*), e.g. *gunāhgār, bahne, pahlvān* ; pron. 12, unpron. 0.

(*c*) After vowel : pron. only in the word *tarăh* 3 times ; unpron. 17 : viz. *yĕh* je 14 ; *voh* ŭo, *mŭh, jagah* once each. The *h* of *yĕh* is never heard in these records, even though twice it is followed by a vowel. *voh* occurs once and is followed by a vowel, but the *h* is not sounded. The phrase *jagah hai* is pronounced ɟʌga æ.

(*d*) Between vowels : as *kahā, mahallat, sarohī, sahāre,* together with the words *shahr, rahm, qaht,* which like other similar words are invariably dissyllables. *h* pron. 31 ; unpron. 16. All these 16 are in the second record, which is more conversational than the first. They are *kahā* 8, *nahī̃* 5, *suhānā* 2, *yahā̃* 1.

(2) cs. + *h* : (*a*) Initial ; examples : *choṭā, thoṛā, phirnā, jhukāī* ; pron. 57 ; unpron. 0.

(*b*) Between vowels ; either with single cs. as *caṛho, inhõ, ādhī, dekhā* ; or with double cs. as *acchā, bicche, buḍḍhā, samjhā, barchī, khalkhalāhaṭ* ; pron. 26, unpron. 8 (*muje* 4, all in more solemn first record ; *hātī* 4, all in second).

Of the 26, 17 are with single cs. and 9 with double. There is no instance of *h* omitted after double cs.

(*c*) Final ; never pron. ; unpron. 14, viz. *samajh* 3, *mujh* 2, *hāth* 4, *kucch, sīdh* 2, *dekh, bojh, kucch* 1 each. *h* is not pronounced in any of these. In 7 the *h* follows a sonant sound, and in 7 a surd. We should, however, notice that there is no instance of *-ṭh* or *-ph.*

(*d*) Followed by cs. pron. 2, *nikhrī* twice ; unpron. 1, *hathyār.*

VOWELS. The two most interesting vowels are those written in Roman script *-ai* and *-au.* We are almost always told that they are pronounced like *ai* in English *aisle,* and like *-au* in German *Haus* or *auf,* or *ow* in English *how.* Actually they are like *a* in "man" and *au* in " maul ". In both cases they may be either single vowels or diphthongs. When *ai* is a diphthong the second vowel is a variety of *e* (**e** or **ε**), and for *au* the second part is *o*.

The records confirm these statements.

The sound *ai* occurs 52 times and every time both of us have transcribed it **æ** with or without a second **e** or **ε**. Actually J. recorded it 26 times as simple **æ**, and 26 as a diphthong **æe** or **æε**. B. 28 times as **æ** and 24 as **æe, æε**. The important point is that neither of us ever recorded the vowel in " aisle ".

The following are details :—

ai or *aĩ* final, as in *hai, ai, haĩ, maĩ*, 28, of which 22 are **æe** or **æε** and 6 **æ**.

Not final, as in *maidān, naiza, aisā, paidā, saif* 6 times. Here B. had a majority of simple **æ** and J. a majority of **æe**.

ai for -*ă* followed by *h*, as in *shahr, pahlvan, bahnā, rahm, qaht, kah, rah.* This occurred 18 times, and every time B.J. transcribed **æ**. Therefore stressed -*ah*, final, or followed by cs., is always pronounced **æ**.

au occurs in *aur* 21 times ; *daulat* 2 ; and once each in *dauṛā, aulād, faulādī, qaraulī, aubāsh, muhtāj.* (This last word is often prn. *mohtāj*) 29 altogether. The records show almost always the sound of English -*au* in *maul.* J. records 28 out of 29 as **ɔ** or **ɔo** ; in the 21 cases of *aur* he has **ɔr** 20 times and **ər** once. I have marked one *aur* as **or**, and in other words have twice transcribed the vowel as **o** : elsewhere always with **ɔ** or **ɔo**.

In the remaining words J. has **ɔ** 5 times and **ɔo** 3 times. Thus, altogether, out of the 29, J. has a simple vowel **ɔ** 25 times, **ə** once, and the diphthong 3 times. B. had the diphthong only twice.

Conclusion. The normal pron. of the vowel is always either **ɔ** or **ɔo**, and the simple **ɔ** is much the commoner of the two.

The vowel **ʌ**, stressed or unstressed, usually tends towards **ə**.

The influence of h *on preceding short vowels.* I explained this in detail in the article referred to. The records before us confirm the statements there made.

Stressed -*ah*. When -*ah* is either followed by a cs., or final (and stressed), it is not **ʌɦ** but **æɦ**. There are 18 instances here, and in every case the vowel is **æ**. There is not a single case of **ʌ**.

It should also be noted that *rahm, qaht, shahr, ḥukm,* written as monosyllables, of which there are 8 instances, are always disyllables. Students should be made to pronounce them so, and plainly told that to pronounce them as monosyllables is wrong.

'ahā, e.g. *rahā*, *kahā* (so too *yahā̃*, *vahā̃*), i.e. *'ăh* followed by *a*, is always *'āhā* **'aha.**

The preliminary notes say that the first vowel in words like *kahā* (sometimes transcribed **ʌ**) is **a**-like. This may be seen also from the transcription. Of words of this type there are 18. J. has the **a** in 13 cases and **ʌ** in 5 (it being understood that this **ʌ** is **a**-like). B. transcribes it in every case **-a.**

Few examples occur of the other cases mentioned loc. cit., p. 545. *'ih* and *'uh* final or before cs. become *e* and *o*. Here we see it in the word *yih*, which is always **je** and in the one case of *wuh* which is *vo* or *ŭo*. *'ah* followed by *ī*, *o*, *ū* is unchanged, see **kʌhī, kʌhū, nʌhī, nʌī.**

No conclusion can be drawn from the word *nahī̃*, for it is unique, with several common pronunciations. One may hear **nʌhī, nʌī, nī, nehī, neī, nahī, naī.**

h followed by **ʊ** (not **u**) tends towards **ɔ**, e.g. **bɔhʊt, pɔhʊnca** (in the record the **ʊ** has become absorbed in the *h*).

In connection with the English habit of reducing final unstressed **a** and **e** to **ə**, and **i** to **ɪ** it is worthy of note that in these records we have final unstressed *-a* 168 times, all of which are pure **-ɑ**; final unstressed *-e* 110 times, every time correctly uttered **-e**; final unstressed *-i* 98 times, every time correctly uttered **-i**, never **ɪ**. Bāqir 'Alī, when reciting, was apt to heighten final *e* to **ɪ** or **i**, *o* to **ʊ** or **u**. Thus the word *ki* usually pronounced *ke* or *ki*, is sometimes as high as *kī* in the records, and is rarely *ke*.

The *iẓāfat* occurs 8 times, as in *ulfat e padarī*, *nān e shabīna*. It is always **e**, never **i**. This is the more remarkable in view of the speaker's frequent use of high vowels, but it is correct.

Nasal Vowels. Apart from recognized nasal vowels, there is a tendency to nasalize all vowels in contact with nasal consonants. Thus *ne* may become *nẽ*, and *gulāmõ gulā̃mõ*.

In words usually written with a final cs. + *r* there is always a vowel before the final *r*; e.g. *fakhr*, *shahr*, become **fʌxər, ʃæhɛr.**

The negative *na* is often joined to the following word and pronounced **nʌ** or **nə.**

The most important conclusions from the records are :—

(1) *ai*, *au* are pronounced **æ** (sometimes **æɛ**) and **ɔ**; thus *paidā* is **pæda** (or **pæɛda**), and *tauba* is **tɔba.**

(2) The point of contact for the cerebral sounds *ṭ*, *ḍ*, *ṛ* is slightly behind the teeth ridge.

(3) *'ain* may be ignored.

(4) *qāf* is very weak, often not distinguishable from *kāf*.

Appendix

6794 AK. Prodigal Son

Recited by Maulānā Saifī, of Lucknow, May 16, 1920

Transcribed from the record by T. Grahame Bailey

In order to complete these notes, I add a few remarks on a Lucknow record of the " Prodigal Son ". So far as I know, Professor Jones has not heard it. It does not differ much from the two Delhi ones, and for conversation, as distinct from recitation, it is a safer guide. This is specially noticeable in its pronunciation of *au*, *ai*, final *-e*, and final *-o*.

ek ʃʌxs ke do lʌɽke the ; choṭe ne bap se kaha " ʌbba ɟān, mal mʌta mẽ mera hɪssa mʊɟhe de diɟie. ʊs ne ʌpna sʌrmaẽa donõ ko bãṭ dia. thoɽe hi dɪnõ mẽ choṭa beṭa ʌpni cizẽ sʌmeṭ sʌmaṭ ek dur dʌraz maqam pʌr cʌlta hua, ɔr vahã ʌpna mal bʌdcəlni mẽ ʊ'ra dia. ɟʌb vo kʊl dɔlʌt bʌrbad kʌr cuga, to ʊs mʊlk mẽ sʌxt kal pʌra, ɔr vo nan e ʃʌbina ko mohtaɟ ho gea. ʊs vʌqt ek rʌ'is ke dʌrvaze ɟa pʌɽa, ɟɪs ne ʊse ʌpne khetõ pʌr suʌr cʌrane bheɟ dia ; faqa kʌʃi se je nɔbʌt pɔhnci thi kɪ ɟɔo ki bhusi ɟo suʌrõ ko di ɟati æ, ʌgʌr ʊse koi deta, to ʊsi se bʌxuʃi ʌpna peṭ bhʌr leta ; lekɪn koi ɪtna bhi rʌvadar nʌ'tha.

ɟʌb vo ʌpne hoʃ mẽ aẽa to socne lʌga kɪ mere bap ke kɪtne hi mʌzdur bʌfʌragʌt khate pite hæ̃, kʊch ʌndaz bhi kʌrte hæ̃, ɔr mæ̃ bhukõ mʌr raha hũ ; bap sɪ ɟakʌr kjũ nʌ kəhũ kɪ mæ̃ xuda ka ɔr ap ka gunəhgar hũ, ʌb mæ̃ ap ka fʌrzənd kæhe ɟane ke laɪq nehĩ, mʊɟhe ʌpne mʌzdurõ ke zʊmre mẽ rʌkh liɟie. pʌs ʊṭkʌr sidha ʌpne bap ke pas cʌla. ʌbhi fasɪle pʌr tha kɪ bap ne ʊse ate dekha, dɔɽkʌr gʌle lʌga dia ɔr pjar kʌrne lʌga. beṭe ne kaha " ʌbba, mæ̃ xudavʌnd e kʌrim ki ɔr ap ki nʌzʌrõ mẽ mʊɟrɪm hũ, ɔr ʌb ɪs kabɪl nehĩ kɪ ap ka beṭa kæhlaũ ". lekɪn bap ne ʌpne mʊlazɪmõ ko hʊkəm dia " ʌcchi se ʌcchi poʃak, ŋguṭhi, ɟuta ɪse pɪnhao, ɔr ek fʌrbeh bachɽa lakʌr kʌbab lʌgao ki sʌb məze se khaẽ ɔr xuʃiã mʌnaẽ, ɪs lie kɪ mera beṭa mʌrkʌr zɪnda hʊa hæ, khokʌr phɪr mɪla hæ."

vo log ṭæhl pæhl mẽ mʌsruf hue ; bʌɽa beṭa ʊs vʌqt khetõ pʌr tha ; pʌlʌṭkʌr ɟʌb mʌka mʌgan ke kʌrib pɔhnca to rʌks o fʌrod ki avaz kan mẽ ai ; ek mʊlazɪm ko bʊlakʌr dʌrjaft kia kɪ jɪ kja ho raha hæ ? " ʊs ne ʌrz kia " ap ke bhai sab ae hue hæ̃, ɔr ap ke ʌbba jān ne ʊnẽ sʌhi sʌlamʌt pakʌr ek fʌrbeh bʌchɽe ki kurbani kʌrai hæ." je sunkʌr vo naraz hua ɔr ghʌr ke ʌndʌr nʌ gea. ʊs vʌqt bap nɪkla ɔr ʊse mʌnane lʌga. ʌsna e ɟʌvab mẽ bap se ʊs ne kaha " gʌzʌb xuda ka, ɪtni muddʌt se mæ̃ ap ki xɪdmʌt kʌr raha hũ ɔr kɪsi vʌqt

ap ki hukəm ʊduli nehĩ ki, lekɪn kʌbhi ap ne ek bʌkri ka bʌcca bhi muȷhe nʌ dia kɪ mæ̃ ʌpne dostõ ki davʌt kʌrta. mʌgʌr ȷʌb ap ka je lʌṛka aĕa ȷɪs ne ap ki dɔlʌt ʌjjaʃi mẽ ʊṛa ḍali to ap ne ʊs ke lie moṭa taza bʌchṛa zʌba kʌraĕa hæ." ʊs ne kaha "beṭa, tum to hʌmeʃa se mere sat ho, ɔr mere pas ȷo kuc hi hæ vo sʌb tumara hæ, lekɪn ȷʌʃʌn kʌrne ɔr xuʃ hone ka jehi mʌhʌl hæ, kɪ tumhara bhai mʌrkʌr zɪnda hua hæ, khokʌr phir mɪla hæ".

Notes

au and *ai* are single vowels ɔ and æ respectively; thus *daulat* is **dɔlət** and *maĩ* is **mæ̃**.

Final *-e* and *-o* are not so high as in the Delhi records.

ă is almost always ə; when very markedly so, it has been transcribed ə, otherwise ʌ. For this vowel the Delhi records are preferable.

v is nearly always ŭ.

ṭ and *ḍ* have point of contact generally just behind teeth ridge; in a few cases a little further back.

ṛ tends to be fricative; point of contact not far from teeth ridge. In the record it occurs eleven times; of these nine or ten are rather fricative, and only one or two have a real strike. The strike pronunciation is to be recommended.

h is ɦ except in *kh, th, ṭh, ch, ph*.

'ain. Words written with *'ain* occur five times, but the *'ain* is never pronounced.

qāf. There are eleven instances of *qāf*. The pronunciation varies from *q* to a back variety of *k*, on the whole nearer *q* than *k*.

§ 1, l. 5. **cuga** for **cuka**.

§ 3, l. 2. **mʌka mʌgan** is a reciter's slip for **mʌkan**.

NOTE ON COL. LORIMER'S PHONETICS OF GILGIT SHINA (*JRAS*. Jan., pp. 1–42; Apr., pp. 177–212)

[Since the following Note was sent to the printer, I have received a letter from Col. Lorimer in reply to one of mine touching *inter alia* on the definition of cerebrals. He writes: "On this definition of cerebral the results of my inquiries essentially agree with yours. The case seems to be the same with aspirates."]

Colonel Lorimer's article is a moral tonic. It is impossible to be a pessimist while there is a scholar who can write in this way. In spite of his experience and careful ear-training he writes with a modesty, which in a tyro would be becoming, and in a scholar is charming. If we owed him nothing else, we should be heavily in his debt for this one fact here clearly set down, that, even for a well-trained ear, to distinguish between cerebrals and non-cerebrals or between aspirated and unaspirated sounds is a matter of extreme if not insuperable difficulty (except for one who has made the distinction from childhood). The present note deals with this difference. In our *Journal* for July, 1921, I stated that Ṣiṇā contained a series of cerebral sounds *ṭ, ḍ, ṛ, ṇ* (*ḷ* in one dialect), *ṣ, ẓ, ç̣*, and *j̣*, marked off from non-cerebrals, and a series of aspirated surds distinguished from non-aspirates; further that *ṭ, ḍ. ṛ, ṇ, ḷ* and *ṭh, th, kh, ph, ch*, are as distinct from *t, d, r, n, l* and *ṭ, t, k, p, c* respectively as they are in North India. I still hold this.

We must leave on one side inquiries into such points as the following: (*a*) relative frequency; (*b*) exact place of articulation; (*c*) causes; (*d*) etymology; (*e*) division into primary and secondary; (*f*) importance, for this is only a matter of the meaning of the word "important";

they are neither more nor less important than in Urdu, Panjabi, Hindi, or Bengali; and we must confine ourselves to the inquiry—do the two series exist or do they not? A superficial reading of Colonel Lorimer's article may give the impression that he denies their existence, but if one reads it carefully one sees that his investigations confirm my statements at almost every point.

First a matter of definition. What is a cerebral? The author, modestly mistrusting his own observations, has based all his remarks upon a definition taken from a book on phonetics. Unfortunately the definition is wholly incorrect. It gives the point of articulation as "the highest part of the roof of the mouth about the junction of the hard and soft palates", and tells us that "the tip of the tongue must be firmly pressed" against this place. If this is correct, probably no cerebral is ever heard between Cape Comorin and the Pamirs, either in Ṣiṇā or in any other language. As regards the "firm pressing" it is a sufficient answer to say that the contact of ṛ in a word like *ghoṛā* takes less than one-hundredth part of a second; and as regards the place, the proper point of articulation is *anywhere* on the hard palate behind the teeth ridge. When, therefore, Colonel Lorimer says of certain Ṣiṇā sounds that they are not "true cerebrals" or that "they are not rightly described as such", he means merely that they are not cerebrals in the sense of the above definition, and I entirely agree with him. Ṣiṇā certainly contains no such cerebrals, nor does Urdu or Panjabi.

Now two questions emerge: (1) Do Colonel Lorimer's observations support the view of the existence of cerebrals and non-cerebrals, and of aspirated and unaspirated sounds? (2) When he sets himself to make these distinctions is he generally correct? The answer in both cases is an unhesitating affirmative. Let us take them in order. The quotations and page-numbers are from his article.

(1) pp. 17, 18, he gives a list of words with forward *t*, and another with back *ṭ* (i.e. dental and cerebral *t*).

p. 18, "*t* slightly further back than normal . . . the difference is recognized by Shina speakers."

p. 20, "a *d* produced slightly further back than normal," "a decided cerebral *ḍ* exists."

p. 25, "it is possible that *n* is sometimes post-alveolar" (i.e. cerebral).

p. 30, "a sound which on first hearing I mistake for *r*, on examination found to be cerebral *ḍ*." This "mistake" is very creditable to Colonel Lorimer's ear, for it is not a mistake at all. The sound in question is cerebral *ṛ*.

p. 38, "there is a distinct cerebral *ḍ*": (in certain circumstances) "*t, d, r* are cerebralized and *n* is similarly influenced": (in certain other cases) "*t, d, r* are post-alveolar or pre-cerebral." As we have seen, these terms are other names for "cerebral".

On p. 188 is a list of words containing cerebral *ṇ*, and on pp. 186, 187 a list of words with cerebral *ḍ*.

The author quotes a competent Ṣīṇ whom he calls S.R. Thus, on p. 210, "S.R.'s *ḍ* sounds to me like English *r*." It is, in fact, *r*, cerebral *r*. Again, "S.R. agrees about (post-alveolar or pre-cerebral) *t, r, n*": i.e. recognizes cerebral *t, r, n*. We must again remind ourselves that when Colonel Lorimer says that *t, d, r*, etc., are post-alveolar or pre-cerebral, he means what we call cerebral. The cerebrals in modern Indian vernaculars are also post-alveolar or pre-cerebral. They are not cerebral in the sense of the definition.

(2) Now we come to aspirates.

p. 196, "the difference between aspirates and non-aspirates is recognized by intelligent Shina speakers, and the difference may constitute the sole difference between similar words."

On pp. 198, 199, is a list of words containing aspirated and unaspirated plosives respectively.

p. 207, "factors important in distinguishing words (otherwise) identical are . . . aspiration."

p. 211, "S.R. is pretty clear in his own mind as to what are and what are not aspirates."

Let us now examine the author's lists of words containing cerebrals, non-cerebrals, aspirates, and non-aspirates. On pp. 17, 18, words with dental or cerebral *ṭ*. The distinction has been made with absolute correctness.

p. 20, a list of post-alveolar (i.e. cerebral) *ḍ*'s—perfectly correct, except that perhaps by a clerical slip, the two words **dʌm** and **ḍʌm** are interchanged. As printed the words are **ḍʌm bɛ**, all together, and **du dʌm**, twice. The first should be **dʌm**, and the second **ḍʌm**.

pp. 186, 187, a list of words with cerebral *ḍ*, said to be "much more akin to *r*". As stated above it *is* cerebral *ṛ*. In this Colonel Lorimer's ear guided him aright. All the words in the list do actually contain either *ṛ* or (in two or three cases) *ḍ*.

p. 188, a list of words with cerebral *ṇ*—correct.

pp. 198, 199, long lists of aspirates and non-aspirates. I agree with all but two or three.

We may conclude that in the author's opinion—

(i) Ṣiṇā (besides *d*, *t*, *n*, *r*) contains cerebral *ḍ*, *ṭ*, *ṇ* (what he calls post-alveolar or pre-cerebral), and in addition another cerebral *ḍ*, "much more akin to *r*," i.e. cerebral *ṛ*.

(ii) The distinction between aspirates and non-aspirates is recognized by S.R. and other Ṣiṇā speakers;

and further that—

(iii) when Colonel Lorimer prepares special lists of words to indicate the distinctions nearly all his words are correctly chosen. I think I could hardly have asked for a fuller endorsement of my judgment in the matter.

On p. 191 the author suggests that on "so simple a phonetic matter" as cerebrals I would claim that I was "not likely to be mistaken". This is an important point of principle. I should reply: No, on the contrary I should like every language scholar to keep before him on his desk the following words printed in large and clear letters: "Sounds to which you have not been accustomed all your life you will probably never be able to recognize clearly or produce correctly. If there is an exception it will only be the result of prolonged phonetic study and almost superhuman effort." Now it is quite true that I have no difficulty in recognizing these cerebrals and in distinguishing aspirates, but it is not because they are *per se* "easy phonetic matters": the reason is that I was born among them and have used them all my life. I cannot recall a time when they were not perfectly familiar to me.

ARE THE FOUR SERIES (FRONT *t*, *d*, *r*, *n*; BACK *ṭ*, *ḍ*, *ṛ*, *ṇ*; ASPIRATES, AND NON-ASPIRATES) FOUND IN SINA?

The article of my old friend, Sir George Grierson (Misc., *JRAS.*, Oct., 1924), raises some interesting points. The greater part of it is devoted to a protest against the common use of *mūrdhanya* and "cerebral". I pass over the former, as I did not use the word, and go on to two points connected with "cerebral". It is advisable to touch on these two very minor details in order to clear the way for the discussion of the real question.

Minor point (i): the meaning usually assigned to "cerebral".

In many of the Indian vernaculars there are pairs of sounds generally represented by *t*, *ṭ* : *d*, *ḍ* : *r*, *ṛ* : *n*, *ṇ* (and others with which we are not now dealing). In each case the point of articulation is further forward for the first-named than for the second. "Dental" and "cerebral" are conventional terms applied by Orientalists and philologists to the forward set and back set respectively. They *may* be unsuitable terms, but they hold the field at present, for they are employed in this sense by countless Orientalists, including Sir George Grierson himself. To take the latest instance, Professor Turner tells me that in his article on Sindhi Cerebralization (*JRAS.*, Oct., 1924) he has used them in this purely conventional sense without regard to the actual place of articulation. Similarly, Professor Jules Bloch, referring to his monumental work on Marathi, writes : " Il va de soi que je n'ai pas voulu employer le mot cérébrale dans un autre sens que le sens conventionnel."

Phoneticians, however, dislike the word " cerebral ", and prefer " retroflex consonant ", which Professor Jones defines as " made with the tip of the tongue against any part of the hard palate, i.e. between the back of the teeth-ridge and the junction of the hard and soft palates ". The Orientalist's " cerebral " is a relative term, the phonetician's " retroflex " is a precise definition. When I write for Orientalists I use " cerebral ", but when a year ago, writing as a phonetician, I attempted to translate into Hindi all the more usual phonetic terms, it did not even occur to me to include " cerebral ".

The question of nomenclature is relatively unimportant ; what concerns us more is the nature of the sounds indicated.

Before proceeding we must remind ourselves of the enormous advance made by the science of speech sounds in the last few years. Indian sounds are now being scientifically studied by Europeans and many of them are known with accuracy : the descriptions of them in standard Grammars are out of date and cannot be appealed to. This science has revealed *inter alia* three facts : (1) a man usually pronounces his native language well according to his own particular dialect, but is apt to go wrong and give wrong information when being questioned ; (ii) the description of a speech sound is an extraordinarily difficult matter, and anyone who wishes to attempt it requires a long course of phonetics. This shows us the reason for the unreliability of most descriptions written by Indians ; (iii) a man may have a scholarly knowledge of a language without an accurate knowledge of its sounds.

Minor point (ii) : Where are these " cerebrals " articulated ?

Professor Daniel Jones is probably the most eminent living exponent of speech sounds, and very few Oriental scholars have spent as much time as he in the study of Indian sounds.

He states his opinion that in the Indian languages whose sounds he has studied the furthest back "cerebrals" are found in the Dravidian languages, but that even in their case the place of contact is no further back than half-way along the hard palate. In one of his books there is a diagram of a typical retroflex consonant. Articulation takes place at a point between two-ninths and three-ninths of the distance from the back boundary of the teeth-ridge to the junction of the hard and the soft palate. In another book he tells us that the Singhalese "retroflex *ṭ* and *ḍ*" are articulated "a little further back than English *t* and *d*".

Mr. Lloyd James, Phonetic Lecturer in University College, a very able phonetician who has given great attention to the study of African and Indian sounds, mentions as the place of articulation for Indian "cerebrals" "anywhere from the alveolar position to half-way between the teeth-ridge and the end of the hard palate".

The greatest authorities on Bengali sounds are Mr. Sutton Page and Dr. S. K. Chatterji. Mr. Page says that the place of articulation for Bengali "cerebrals" varies from an alveolar position to about a third of the way between the teeth-ridge and the junction of the hard and soft palates. Dr. Chatterji, speaking of his own pronunciation, says for *ṭ* and *ḍ* "just behind the teeth-ridge", and for *ṛ*, beginning in the same place but striking against the teeth-ridge with the under surface of the tongue.

I myself have made a first-hand study of languages from Darjiling in the east to beyond Kashmir (to the Ṣiṇā country and Hazara in the north-west), and in that area extending for more than 1,500 miles I have not come across a "cerebral" further back than half-way along the hard palate.

It will thus be seen that, so far as is at present known to science, *no Indian language possesses a "cerebral" sound which has a point of articulation further back than the middle of the hard palate.*

In the same way "dental" is a conventional term. In

point of fact a majority of the sounds which Orientalists call "dental" are alveolar. Usually *t* and *d* are dental, and *r, n, l* alveolar, but they are all conventionally called "dental".

The main question: Are the four series found in Ṣiṇā?

Let me emphasize the fact that this is the sole real issue. The inquiries as to the meaning of "cerebral" and the exact place of articulation are so subordinate as to be almost irrelevant.

Having cleared the ground, we proceed to the main problem, which is twofold. (i) Has Ṣiṇā got any of these pairs, and if so which? Col. Lorimer and I assert that it has four pairs, viz. *t, ṭ : d, ḍ : r, ṛ : n, ṇ*. (ii) Does it distinguish aspirated from non-aspirated sounds? We say that it does. In both cases the two sets are as plainly distinguished as in other modern Indian vernaculars. The agreement of his views with mine is a fact of great interest, for we approach the study from different standpoints. Col. Lorimer, whose humility and honesty impart an abiding fragrance to all his writings, has stated over and over again that he does not trust his ear in the differentiation of these sounds. He therefore endeavours to obtain information by direct interrogation. After long experience, he knows better than most the difficulties of the task. I have used the sounds all my life and can trust my ear. His results are derived from inquiry, mine from observation. The striking thing is that they agree. His views must be sought in his latest writings, not in the *ad interim* reports of his investigations printed in the *JRAS.*, January and April, 1924. His mature conclusions are given in his article on Ṣiṇā Transitive Verbs (*Bull. Sch. Or. Stud.*, vol. iii, pt. iii, 1924). Knowing that he had written this article, I asked him to indicate by his method of transcription all his latest decisions. It will be seen that throughout he distinguishes "cerebrals" from non-"cerebrals", and aspirated sounds from unaspirated.

Let us examine it to see whether it agrees with my conclusions. There are 385 instances of *t, d, r, n,* each of which might have been printed either "cerebral" or non-"cerebral", and 500 sounds which he might have written either aspirated or unaspirated—885 sounds in all. I am acquainted with the words used by Col. Lorimer in this article, and in every single case I agree with his transcription of them. Greater unanimity than this would be inconceivable. Be it remembered that we were not writing words whose stereotyped spelling could be looked up in a dictionary; we were putting down new words in a virgin language. It will be noticed that he always writes *thoiki,* to distinguish it from *toiki* which is incorrect; *tʰoiki* is a mere variant of *thoiki.*

Another line of investigation is Khān Ṣāḥib 'Abdu'l Hakīm Khān's testimony. Sir George Grierson says that the Khān Ṣāḥib's views differ from mine. This can be tested. In *Ling. Surv. Ind.*, vol. viii, pt. ii, pp. 171–2, a text prepared by him may be found. In it are 380 sounds which might have been printed either aspirated or unaspirated. He has marked them one way or the other, according to the evidence of his ear. In these 380 instances there is one sole case in which I differ from him—one out of 380, perhaps a mere slip. We come to "cerebrals" and non-"cerebrals". There are 174 possible cases. In one there is an obvious oversight, for an ending several times given correctly is once given wrong. I omit this. There is one other word, *uth,* which in Urdu and Panjabi is *uṭh, uṭṭh.* This has twice been wrongly printed with *ṭ.* It may be a printer's error. There is no other word in which I differ from him. If even we count these two we get 172 points of agreement to two of disagreement. As a matter of convenience, not of mathematical accuracy, let us add the two results. We then get 3 points of difference in 554 instances—approximately a half of one per cent. A degree of agreement so amazing bewilders one. Remembering the possibility of author's clerical errors, copyist's blunders, printer's mistakes, I should have been prepared for 10 per cent of difference, and should still have considered that we were entirely in accord. But here we have two men, the Khān Ṣāḥib and myself, one an Indian, one a European, working in different years, in different places, with different people, on an unknown tongue not reduced to writing, and yet producing results with 99½ per cent of agreement. Such a measure of agreement—100 per cent with Col. Lorimer and 99½ per cent with 'Abdu'l Hakīm K͟hān—is unbelievable, it is uncanny, yet it is fact. The whole range of the Linguistic Survey will probably not furnish anything approaching to a parallel, nor, I should think, will any other linguistic work.

This makes it clear that these distinctions between "cerebrals" and "dentals", and between aspirates and non-aspirates, are not accidental or imaginary, that they do not depend upon individual speakers, but are real and permanent.

Minor point (iii): There remains only the question of the place of articulation of Ṣiṇā "cerebrals" and "dentals". Sir George proposes that we should call nearly all Ṣiṇā *t*-sounds, and presumably *d*-sounds, alveolar, never dental or cerebral, and remarks that much of what he has said applies also to *n* and *r*. I do not mind what terms are used so long as they convey the facts, but I should be a little afraid that Sir George, in carrying so far his protest against the usual use of the terms, might create misapprehension. However, I will here set down the place where the sounds are articulated, and he can then choose those terms which will best indicate to scholars the nature of the sounds and, in particular, the fact that the two series are rigidly separated from one another. The same terms will have to be used for Bengali, Marathi, Urdu, Panjabi, and other Indian vernaculars, for to use one set of terms for Ṣiṇā and another for the same sounds in other languages would tend to confusion.

Ṣiṇā "dentals": (i) pure dental, made right on the teeth: *t*, *d*, final *l*, and in certain circumstances *n*. (ii) alveolar, made on the teeth-ridge: *r*, non-final *l*, and *n* (except as above).

Ṣiṇā "cerebrals": *ṭ*, *ḍ*, *ṛ*, *ṇ* against the hard palate, point of articulation varying according to definite rules, from a little behind the teeth-ridge, but not on it, to about a third of the distance along the hard palate; the exact position depends on accompanying vowels.

Note.—An alveolar *n* in a few words attracts a following *t* or *d* to an alveolar position.

I have taken Col. Lorimer's views, correctly I believe, from his letters and latest article. In his last communication, dated 20th November, 1924, the following statements are made: "two *t*'s and two *d*'s are consistently distinguished by intelligent Ṣiṇā speakers. The distinction is significant." They speak also of a third *ḍ*, which his chief informant is "prepared to write as *ṛ*", and he himself is "inclined to think" may be *ṛ*. (To describe it as *ṛ* is correct. I hope to deal with it in a systematic exposé of Ṣiṇā sounds.—T. G. B.) Ṣiṇā speakers, he adds, also consistently distinguish *t*, *ṭ*, *k*, *p*, *c*, *ç*, from *th*, *ṭh*, *kh*, *ph*, *ch*, *çh*. "There is," he says, "no question but that aspiration in Ṣiṇā is significant."

Sir George asks how I can be so positive about the "cerebral" *ṛ*. I answer—because I have used it since babyhood. Like Alexander Pope

I lisp'd in cer'brals for the cer'brals came.

Having known them all my life I cannot now confuse them with other sounds.

May I strongly urge that in future writing on this subject attention should be directed solely to the question of the existence of the four series in Ṣiṇā—as in other Indo-Aryan languages, and that until all are agreed on this point, inquiries into the three minor points mentioned above should be deferred?

Prof. Bloch's admirable words about the "dental" and "cerebral" series cannot be bettered:—"C'est là l'essentiel: les faits peuvent varier dans le détail, l'écartement entre les deux points d'articulation peut être ± grand, la rétroversion de la langue peut être ± forte dans le cas de la 2e série, ce qui importe, c'est l'existence de deux séries."

DENTALS AND CEREBRALS IN SINA

Sir George Grierson's kind words about the debt he thinks he owes me have greatly touched me; I am proud to acknowledge my far deeper debt to him; a friendly discussion, the best way of reaching the truth, gives me special pleasure; he is criticizing not me, but most living Orientalists. He admits (*JRAS.*, April, 1925, p. 313) that "cerebral" includes two classes of sounds, (*a*) cerebral sounds (edge of soft palate), and (*b*) sounds "written locally with cerebral letters". The first are not known to exist: so far as we know, India has none (ib. Jan. 1925, p. 89): the second, called "cerebral" by most scholars, are found all over India. The same sounds in languages which are rarely (as Ṣiṇā) or never (many Hindi and Laihndi dialects) locally written, are rightly attached to this class and called "cerebral" by Professor Turner and other philologists. Otherwise the claim of a language to cerebrals would be admitted only if and when some local patriot wrote in it.

I know well the difference between "letter" and "sound", but wish to avoid pedantry. Strictly speaking "cerebral letter", "cerebral *t*", "retroflex sound", and the very word "cerebral", are pure nonsense, yet one uses these terms. I try to be scrupulously fair in evidence, and as it would be most unfair to quote in phonetic matters the opinions of men whose competence lies in literature, grammar, or philology, I deprive myself of such support.

Sir George refers (with approbation, alas!) to two old mistakes of mine made long ago, when, though knowing the sounds and able to distinguish them from others, just as well as now, they being my native sounds, I had insufficient phonetic knowledge, and like other writers in similar case made mistakes in description. It shows once more that without thorough phonetic training it is impossible to describe sounds correctly. In my books written years ago (including Ṣiṇā Grammar, written 1917), the popular descriptions of sounds, their nature, and difference from other sounds, may be taken as correct, but phonetic details must be treated with reserve. Northern Panjabi cerebral *ṭ*, *ḍ*, *ṇ*, *ḷ*, are articulated about a third of the way along the hard palate, (Laihndi just behind, Southern Panjabi in front; tongue-tip contact for *ṛ* further forward than for *ṭ*, *ḍ*, *ṇ*, *ḷ*).

But my chief interest in Ṣiṇā sounds for the past seventeen years has been to establish beyond question the fact that there are two series *t*, *d*, *n*, *r*, and *ṭ*, *ḍ*, *ṇ*, *ṛ*, and that they are approximately the sounds denoted by these symbols in the Panjab and U.P. A few people have written on Ṣiṇā, but only Colonel Lorimer and I have studied and described the sounds. I may refer to my article, *Bull. Sch. Or. Stud.*, vol. iii, pt. iv, 1925, on "The Sounds of Ṣiṇā", written in collaboration with Colonel Lorimer and Miss Armstrong. Aspirates are also dealt with. For dentals and cerebrals see, too, *JRAS.*, Jan. 1925, p. 92, and for the striking confirmation by 'Abdu'l Ḥakīm's text, ib. p. 91.

CHART OF ṢIṆĀ CONSONANTAL PHONEMES

	Bi-labial	Labio-dental	Dental	Alveo-lar	Palato-Alveolar	Retracted		Palatal	V
Plosive	p, b, ph		t, d, th			ṭ, ḍ, ṭh			k g
Affricate			ʦ, ʦh		c, ɟ, ch		c̣ j̣ c̣h		
Nasal	m		(n)	n	ɲ	ṇ		(ŋ)	[illegible]
Lateral			(l)	l		(ḷ)			
Tapped				r		ṛ			
Fricative		f, v		s z	ʃ ʒ		ṣ ẓ		χ
Vowel glide								j	
Aspirate	h, ɦ in any vowel position.								

ɲ is strictly speaking dento-alveolo-palatal.

Symbols in brackets indicate subsidiary members of other phonemes.

In my *Shina Grammar* just published there is a popular description of the sounds written eight years ago in India, when it was impossible for me to consult anyone. Now I should like to alter some of it. In phonetics advance is so rapid that one's descriptions are out of date almost as soon as they are written. Happily it is all advance. There is no retrogression.

In order to indicate graphically the sounds of a language one must (i) decide what sounds are found in it, (ii) group them in phonemes, assigning one symbol to each phoneme (not to each speech sound), (iii) show their tongue position or place of articulation by correctly placing them on a sound chart. A phoneme may be *popularly* defined as a distinct, essential, and significant sound of a language, minor variations being disregarded.

CHART OF ṢINĀ VOWEL PHONEMES

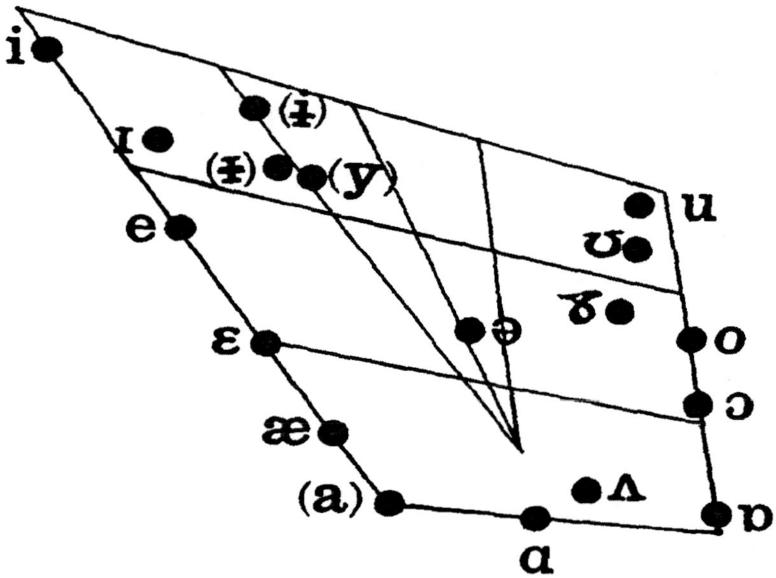

Most of the above vowels are found nasal as well as non-nasal. I do not remember nasal ə, ɒ, ɔ, ɤ.

Section I gives Col. Lorimer's and my joint views, with such qualifications on his part as are inserted within square brackets followed by the initial " L ". Section II contains a number of minuter details for which I alone am responsible. The sound charts have been prepared by Miss Armstrong and myself. Col. Lorimer is in general agreement with them, but does not wish to commit himself to all the details [" regarding which I do not feel competent to form definite opinions " : L.]. No two people speak a language alike ; in India, especially in hilly regions, there are differences from village to village. Col. Lorimer and I worked with different men in different years. There are therefore naturally a few minor variations in our estimates of sounds. This holds in particular of vowels.

SECTION I

There are approximately 64 to 68 phonemes in Ṣiṇā, of which 40, including aspirated sounds, are consonantal. [Add " w " : L.] This number may be slightly increased or decreased after further investigation ; thus ʐ, ʒ may be varieties of j, ȷ. [I think they are : L.] But for the present it may be accepted as practically correct. Of these phonemes, sixteen consist of pairs of advanced and retracted consonantal sounds, as follows. (The difference is significant.)

Advanced :—t, d, c, ɟ, n, r, ʃ, ʒ ; retracted :—ṭ, ḍ, ç, j̣, ṇ, ṛ, ṣ, ẓ. [The retraction of ç, j̣ (ẓ), ṣ, ṛ is often so considerable as to be obvious to a European ear : L.] There are seven sounds which are found both aspirated and unaspirated, the difference being significant : **p, t, ts, c, ṭ, ç, k**; aspirated, **ph, th, tsh, ch, ṭh, çh, kh** [**ph** being interchangeable with **ᵖf** or **f** : L.] Sonants are not aspirated.

The dental fricatives **θ** and **ð** (English *th* in *think* and *then*) are not heard in Ṣiṇā. The velar fricatives *χ* and *γ* (sometimes interchangeable with **kh** and **g**) are generally found in loan words such as **khuda** or **χuda**, God : **jaγɪstan**, Yāgistān. They are faintly pronounced.

There are approximately 24–28 vowel phonemes, 14 non-nasal vowels, 10 or more of these also nasal. [**a** doubtful : L.] **i** and **ɪ** are retracted to **ɨ** and **ɪ̶** when one of the sounds **ç, j̣, ṣ, ẓ** immediately follows or precedes. **u** is advanced towards **y** in a few words. Doubtless some law, not yet discovered, governs this fact. In the meantime, we may enter **y** as belonging to the **u** phoneme. [I know the change only as occurring optionally in a few words, when there is an i vowel in the next syllable : L.]

Some of the vowels appear in certain cases to be interchanged. Such are **ɑ, ʌ, ə, æ : i, ɪ : o, ɤ, ə, u : e, ɛ.**

c, ɟ, ʃ, ʒ are not unlike English *ch, j, sh, zh,* but are unrounded and more advanced : **c** is unaspirated. **ç, j̣, ṣ, ẓ** are the corresponding retracted sounds : lips unrounded.

b, m, g, n, s, z do not differ appreciably from the corresponding English sounds ; **p** and **k** differ from English *p* and *k* in lacking aspiration.

f and **v** are not unlike English *f* and *v*, but are fainter. The friction is less and the acoustic effect is different. **v** is sometimes weakened to **u** [? L.]

r is a single tap *r* as sometimes heard in Scotland or in English *thrill.*

ŋ is as in English, but when accompanying **-i** is very far forward.

j is less consonantal, i.e. is more like **e** than in English. [T. G. B.'s medial **j** is often omitted by me, or rendered by **i** : L.]

Section II

ɲ is not unlike the Italian and French sound [I agree : L.], but is further forward. It is made with the blade of the tongue against the alveolar ridge behind the upper teeth.

t, d are dental : **ṭ, ḍ** are the corresponding retracted sounds.

Their position is normally the same as in Panjabi, and Urdu, but when accompanying high front vowels, they are more advanced.

ṇ is never initial: when medial it is the same as in Panjabi, but is further forward when final or with a high front vowel.

ṛ is as in Urdu and Panjabi. It is never initial, and rarely [if ever, L.] final.

h following a vowel tends to become sonant, but otherwise is as in English.

b, g, d, ḍ are sometimes, and **l, r** always, partly or wholly devocalized when final. [With more phonetic knowledge I should probably agree. I frequently have final **p, k, t,** corresponding to medial **b, g, d**: also sometimes final **s, c, ṣ,** corresponding to medial **z, ɉ, ẓ(ɉ̣)**: L.]

The numbers in the following paragraphs refer to positions between the cardinal vowels. The nature of the vowels is shown by their position on the chart.

e has a position of about $1\frac{1}{3}$.

ɛ in the diphthong **ɛi** has a range of approximately 3 to $3\frac{1}{2}$.

a is probably a member of the **ɑ** phoneme. "**i**" in a following syllable advances **ɑ** from $4\frac{1}{2}$ to about 4, i.e. to **a**: **ɑ·lɤ** "he came"; **a·li**, "she came."

ɔ is heard chiefly in loan-words: **mɔ·lɑ·**, "Sunni priest," **gɔgɑ·**, "noise."

o is about $6\frac{2}{3}$: an unrounded and advanced variety of it, **ɤ**, is always short. **ɤ**, when final and unstressed, has a range of about $6\frac{2}{3}$ to $7\frac{1}{3}$. In Roman letters therefore one writes it sometimes -o and sometimes -ŭ.

ʌ is very low, not much above **ɑ**: **ʃʌṣ**, "mother-in-law."

Tone.—There is a low rising tone heard in a certain number of words. Its first part occurs always in a stressed syllable; the second part is about a tone higher than the first. The rule for its incidence is not known except to this extent that all abstract nouns ending in **-ɑr** and all conjunctive participles have it. Thus **bʌṛɪɑr**, "greatness"; **ʃɤ̃ʒi·**, "swollen"; **thɛ·**, "having done."

Words illustrating cerebrals and aspirates: **ɉi·nɛ**, "living"; **ɉi·ṇɛ**, "rows": **tʌm**, "swimming"; **ṭʌm**, "falling," "shutting"; **ṭhʌm**, "cleaning," "sweeping": **cʌk**, "pitchfork"; **chʌk**, "day": **bʌṭ**, "stone"; **bʌt**, "rice": **bʌri bʌri**, "a big pond": **kheṇ**, "time"; **keṇ**, "rock": **pʌr**, "last year"; **phʌr**, "turn": **ɛk dʌm**, "altogether, etc."; **ɛk ḍʌm**, "once": **khɤṇ**, "shawl"; **kɤn**, "ear."

[Continued from foot of p. 252.

wehlā, *adj.*, at leisure.
whalā, *adv.*, then, in that case.
widdh, *f.*, boil in vagina.
wiḍḍī, *f.*, troublesome profitless work.
wiḍḍṇā, arrange (marriage), prepare (huqqa), spread out to dry (saṇ).
will, *f.*, moisture.
willṇā, *v.*, get moist.
wircṇā, *v.*, be quiet (of child).

Y

yabb, *f.* (*gen. pl.*), silly talk (mārnā).
yaddhṇā, *v.*, copulate with (abuse), *i.q.* jaddhṇā.
yōrōyōrī, *adv.*, by force.
yūsaf khūh, what the dove says (*lit.* 'Joseph in the well,' referring to doves having told where Joseph's brethren had put him).

Supplement to the Panjabi Dictionary.

A

ā, pronominal suffix, to thee, for thee.
abbal haftā, *m.*, Saturday.
aḍḍokhoṛe, *m. pl.*, unevennesses, ruts in road.
adhlāmū̃, half and half.
adhlhūṭhā, *adj.*, appetite half satisfied.
adhmāhṇū, *m.*, abortion of 4 or 5 months.
adhraṅgī, *f.*, palsy.
aḍrā., *adj.*, separate.
agath, *m.*, star rising in January about midnight, Canopus.
āggal, *m.*, word in *khaḍḍī* or well.
aggõwālī, *f.*, meeting a person.
ainj, *adv.*, thus, bravo!
air, *m.*, tracks, lines on ground.
ajokā, *adj.*, belonging to to-day or this day next week.
akāṇā, *v. tr.*, weary, bore.
akhe, he said, they said, one says (for *ōs ākhẽā*).
alhar, *adj.*, beardless.
alū̃, *adj.*, beardless.
aṇchāttā, *adj.*, not passed through sieve.
anchōp, *adv.*, quietly.
āndā, *pa. part.*, brought (rest of verb not used).
andāṛhīā, *adj.*, beardless.
aṇḍī, *f.*, iron band round *ṭhippā* in *khrās* (corn-mill).
āṇke, having come (from *auṇā*, come).
anrhātā, *m.*, night-blindness.
aṇwāṇā, *v.*, cause to bring.
ar, *m.*, one of cross pieces in cart-wheel.
ār, ārpār, *m.*, consideration, thought, attention.
aṛāṇā, *v.*, low (of cattle, buffaloes).
areṛ, *m.*, the biggest of the *arēṛīā̃*, also *reṛ*: see next.
areṛṇā, fix *areṛīā̃*, on *māhl*, also *reṛṇā*.
ariṅgṇā, *v.*, low (especially of buffaloes).
artānā, *m.*, night-blindness.
aṭhāīā̃, aṭhāīwā̃, *adj.*, twenty-eighth.
aṭhīwā̃, *adj.*, twenty-eighth, especially twenty-eighth day of Ramẓān.
āthri, *m.*, full-time servant of farmers.
atte, *adv.*, altogether, with negative, not at all.
atthar, *f.*, tear.

atthrū, *m.*, half choking in drinking.
augghī, *f.*, bunch of thread in loom.
auhr, *f.*, straitness, difficulty (illness, &c.).
auhṛ, *f.*, rainlessness.
auj, *m.*, trouble.
aukaṛ *f.*, difficulty, straitness.
aukhat, *f.*, difficulty.
aukṛā, *adj.*, inimical, tyrannical.
auḷā, *m.*, niche in wall for warming milk.
auḷū, *m.*, hollow into which water falls from *nisār*.
awāghatt, *adv.*, suddenly.
awāzār, awājār, straitened, in difficulties.

B

bā, *f.*, sense, intelligence.
babbar, *m.*, large bit of earthenware.
babbrī, *f.*, small bit of earthenware.
baccā, *m.*, broad iron hoop inserted in well to preserve it.
baddhā ruddhā, *adj.*, bound, unwillingly.
badobadī, *adj.*, by force, under compulsion.
bāggaṛ, *f.*, paring of lower end of *narī* and *ḍaṭṭā* in huqqa (*kaḍḍhṇā*).
bagalgan, *f.*, offensive smell from mouth, etc.
bahāḷṇā, *v.*, seat.
baiṛ, *m.*, string joining two wheels of *khambaṛ* in *carkhā*.
bājjū, *m.*, cross pieces of wood in *dharakkaṛ*.
bākrā, *adj.*, pertaining to sheep, goats, hence collective = sheep and goats.
bak͟hāhndī *m.*, quarreller, from *bak͟hāhn̈d m.*, quarrel, noise.
balellaṛ, *adj.*, senseless, foolish.
banjar, *adj.* or *n. m.*, poor, almost barren land.
bannh, *f.*, hump of bull.
banne, *adv.*, outside.
bannī *f.*, little *bannā*, or bank between fields.
baraṛ, *m.*, rope round *baiṛ*, to prevent breakage.
bāṛī, *f.*, preparation of green parched *jaū* for eating.
barkī, *f.*, mouthful.
bāṭī, *f.*, iron or brass vessel.
bāuḷā, *adj.*, mad.
beraṛa, *m.*, add, 'wheat and *jaū* (barley).'
bhā, *m.*, opinion, view, *mere bhā dā*, according to my opinion.
bhagāṇā, *v.*, squint (of eyes).
bhaggī, *f.*, accusation, slander.
bhambīrī, *f.*, circular piece of wood in spinning-wheel between *khambaṛ* and *munnā*.
bhān, *f.*, bits of cotton fallen from pod = bhann.
bhaṅgāṇā, *v.*, squint (of eye).
bhankaṛ, *m.*, change for money.
bhantṛik, *m.*, plan, arrangement.
bhārū, *m.*, ram, big lamb.
bheṭṇā, *v.*, defile (ceremonially).
bhiṛāī, *f.*, fighting, gen. laṛāī bhiṛāī.
bhitt, *m.*, half of double door, window.
bhiṭṭaṛ, *adj.*, old, useless (of earthen vessel).
bhōg. *m.*, account, mention, (pāṇā).
bhōhrā, *m.*, women's and girls' spinning bee
bhrā, *m.*, brother.
bhurhaṛĕāṇ, bhuṛhĕāṇ, *f.*, smell of burnt cloth, leather, &c.
bhussā, *adj.*, pale through illness, heat, &c.

bibta, *f.*, trouble, affliction = biptā.
billā, *m.*, non-folding Quran stand with legs, wooden catch for door.
biltī *f.*, receipt (especially railway), article consigned.
bīṛā, *m.*, roll of tobacco composed of three laṛīā.
bīṛī, *f.*, thread round *taraklā* of *carkha*.
bohjā, *m.*, pocket.
boṛmā, *m.*, *ghī* and sugar (*khanḍ*).
brũ, *f.*, gen. plur. brũā, threshold of door.
bucc, *m.*, small tuft of shrub. &c.
bujhārat, *f.*, riddle.
bujjī, stopper made of feather in shuttle (in loom).
būlī, *m.*, kind of bull-dog.
bulle, *m.*, *pl.*, (lutṇe) amuse oneself, have good time.
būṇḍā, *m.*, tail of bird.
būṇḍā, *m.*, rope attaching *gādhī* to *tīr*.
būrā, *m.*, sawdust. fine wood shavings.
burkṇā, make noise like camel.
buttṇā, vomit.

C

cābbī, *f.* (1) key, (2) iron peg in iron sugarcane-press.
cākhrī, *f.* stick connecting fork of *gādhī*.
cakkā, *m.*, heap of wooden sleepers.
cakkal, *m.*, vertical cogged wheel of well.
cakkīrāh, *m.*, wood pecker.
cakkṇā, *v.*, lift, = cukkṇā.
cambṛī., *f.*, one of 4 iron nails in cart.
cāmcṛikk, *f.*, bat (animal).
camṛī, *f.*, bit of leather in *guddī* of *carkhā*.
cāṇā, *v.*, lift.
candra. *m.*, hail.
canḍī, *f.*, corn on foot, &c.
cappṇā, *m.*, earthen lid of vessel.
car, *f.*, oblong hole in ground over which large quantities of food are cooked.
cāṛāpāṛā. *m.*, compensatory days inserted in Hindu month.
carakli, *f.*, vertical cogged wheel of well.
caṛepṛī, *f.*, bit of caked earth, *e.g.* in pond.
caṭākā. *m.*. slap.
cāṭī, *f.*. *ghaṛā* with wide mouth.
caukhar. *m.*. cattle.
chābṛī. *f.*. shallow basket, especially for sweetmeats.
chacch, *f.*, long hair (animal).
chaheṛū, *m.*, scum of boiled *ghī*.
chajj, *m.*, basket.
chaillī, *f.*, deep basket made of reeds.
chaiṇī, *f.*, small iron, pointed wedge.
challī, *f.*, ear of maize, roll of thread on *taraklā* in *carkhā*, calf of leg.
chān, *m.*, what is left in sieve after *āṭā* has passed through it.
chattā, *m.*, man's lock of hair.
chātta, *adj.*, what has passed through sieve.
chappar, *m.*, instep, eyelid.
chaṛ, *m.*, long crook for bringing down branches.
chaṛāchānḍ, *adj.*, alone, unmarried.
chattrī, *f.*, pigeon-roost.
chekṛe, *adv.*, finally.
chenjā, *m.*, large basket made of twigs.
chenjī, *f.*, small basket made of twigs.

cheṛū, *m.*, herdsman.
cheti, *adv.*, quickly.
chetnī, shoemaker's iron-pointed tool.
chīhṛā, *m.*, hard *guṛ*.
chikkā, *m.*, rope muzzle for cattle.
chill, *f.*, rupee.
cho, *f.*, ceremonial defilement.
chohḷī, *f.*, haste.
chōī, *f.*, dry leaves of sugarcane.
chōṇā, *v.*, defile ceremonially.
chūṇā, *m.*, earthen cover for vessel.
cilittar, *m.*, deceit.
cilittrī, *adj.*, deceitful.
cinjh, *f.*, point, nib of pen.
cippī, *f.*, broad, short-handed wooden spoon for hot *guṛ*.
cirkā, *adj.*, late.
citt, *m.*, mind, heart.
cittar, *m.*, little round ornament.
copā, *m.*, iron pointed digging instrument.
corīchappī, *adv.*, by stealth.
cūcā, *m.*, chicken.
cugarn, *m.*, eclipse of moon, sun.
cuhā, *m.*, quarter of *paṛōpī*.
cuhāī, *f.*, quarter, especially of land.
cukaī, *f.*, pulley in loom.
cūḷī, *f.*, Hindū word for *krūḷi*, rinsing mouth.
cumba, *m.*, round hole over which food and *rahu* are cooked.
cūṇḍwī, *f.*, plaited lock over women's temple.
cuṅg cor, *m.*, thief with whom stolen property is left.
cupkītā, *adj.*, quiet, silent.

D

ḍāḍ, *f.*, one of 4 pieces of wood between upper and lower parts of cart.
ḍag, *m.*, kind of common dog.
ḍākarnā, *v.*, vomit.
darāṇak, *f.*, wood passing through *tur* in loom = gadrāṇak.
daṛopā, *m.*, measure containing two *ṭopas*.
ḍaṭṭā, *m.*, upright stem of huqqa.
dalhūṭhā, *adj.*, with appetite half satisfied.
ḍall, *f.*, old, unused well.
daḷṇā, *v.*, chop firewood, break grain.
dambūsā, *m.*, tool for flattening down road.
ḍāṇḍ, *f.*, swelling from blow (caṛhṇī).
dāttar, *m.*, large toothless sickle, crook for bringing down branches.
ḍaurēā hoēā, mad, foolish.
dawākhā, *m.*, recess in wall for lamp.
dhaddhar, *m.*, ringworm.
ḍhakḷā, *m.*, large lump of cowdung.
dhāṇā, *v.*, be of effect, have effect.
ḍhāṅgar, *m.*, tall leafy plant (about 10 feet high).
dhaṛā, *m.*, dry *āṭā* added to *chapātī*.
dharakkaṛ, *m.*, two cross beams in *ḍhol* and 1 in *carakḷī*.
dharkonnā, *m.*, berry of *dhrek* tree, man of sour disposition.
dhauṛ, *m.*, wood next *taleāṭh*, under *parāṇā* (well).
dhauṛī, *f.*, bag-shaped leather, ready for colouring by *kikkar* bark.
ḍhenḍhḷa, *m.*, big cake of cowdung.
dhikkṇa, *v.*, shove, drive.
dhīṅgrī, expletive with *fulāṇī*.
ḍhoḍḍar-kā, *m.*, raven = ḍoḍḍar-kā.

ḍhol, *m.*, horizontal wheel of well.
dhranjhṇā *v.*, cough violently.
dhrappaṛ, *m.*, large rash, flea-bites, marks of scratching.
dhrauṇā, *v.*, sink down, *e.g.*, centre of roof, ground.
dhrehmā, *m.*, gentle rain.
dhrūṇā, *v.*, drag.
dhuccṇā, *v.*, be washed (clothes, &c.)
dhumāṇa, *v.*, noise abroad.
dhumṇā, *v.*, get noised abroad.
dhupṇā, *v.*, be washed (*e.g.* clothes).
dhūr, *m.*, *rahu* while being cooked.
ḍicc, *adj.*, warned, annoyed.
dihū̃, *m.*, sun.
ḍikkdārī, *f.*, trouble, annoyance.
dīūṛī, *f.*, wooden lamp-stand.
ḍoggar tāra, *m.*, name of a planet.
ḍokkaḷ, *adj.*, having large udder and giving little milk (camel, cow, buffalo).
ḍolṇā, *v.*, pour out.
dudhārnī, *f.*, vessel for boiling milk.
duhājjū, *m.*, duhājjaṇ, *f.*, twice married.
dukh, waḍḍā dukh, leprosy.
dullaṛ, *m.*, rope of two strands.
dusāṅgā, *m.*, piece of wood at end of warp.

G

gabbhē, *adv.*, under armpit.
gabbhī, *f.*, part between fingers and toes.
gadrāṇak, *f.*, wood passing through *tur* in loom (=darāṇak).
gāhd, long horizontal pole of iron sugar-cane press.
gaib, *f.*, dip in road, especially in pakka road.
gail, *f.*, track of cart.
gainṭhī, *f.*, pick-axe.
gāhk *m.*, purchaser.
gāḷā, *m.*, cross wood above millstone in *khrās*.
gandalṇā, *v.*, become muddy (water).
gandhṛī., *f.*, bundle.
gaṅgāḷṇā, *v.*, foul (water).
gaṅgḷēā, *adj.*, muddied (water).
gann, *m.*, piece of wood in circular part of cart-wheel.
gannh, *f.*, bad smell
gannī, *f.*, edge of eyelid (upper or lower).
gannī, *f.*, one of pieces of wood composing *ḍhoḷ* and *carakṛī*.
garle, *m*, *pl.*, gargling.
garmī, *f.*, indigestion.
gaṛowā, *m.*, man who makes *guṛ*.
ghāhgā, *m.*, broken off neck of *ghaṛa* or *ṭinḍ*.
ghair, *f.*, sound of something which one attentively listens for.
ghair, *m.*, dull haze.
ghaṇ., *m.*, bees ?
ghasmailṛā, *adj.*, dust coloured, brown.
ghassā, *m.*, delay, loss, (laggṇā).
ghasunnā, ghasunn, *m.*, blow from fist.
ghaswaṭṭī, *f.*, touchstone.
ghattṇā, *v.*, used in composition with passive sense, *e.g.*, wāh ghatteā, was ploughed.
ghawš, *m.*, stick for stirring *rahu*.
ghirlī, *f.*, piece of wood, near *muṭhiya* in ox yoke.
ghīsī, *adj.*, sliding along ground.
ghommā, *m.*, absence of wind.
ghoṛi, *f.*, piece of wood supporting *maṛēār* in *jhallaṇ*.
ghukkā, *m.*, (i) cowry, (ii) hole in *āḍ* or *ghaṛā* (paiṇā).

ghumaiḷ, *f.*, underground dovecot.
ghurākī, *f.*, angry appearance of eyes (laiṇī, watṇī).
ghutkaḷ, *f.*, slander, backbiting.
gīcī, *f.*, part of back of neck.
giḷṭ., *m.*, swelling (glandular).
giḷṭī, small glandular swelling.
gir, *f.*, girī, *f.*, meat in fruit stone, edible part of mango.
girārī, *f.*, iron cogged wheel in iron sugar-cane press.
gīṭā, *m.*, stone.
gõggā., *m.*, child's word for bread.
gõmmā, *m.*, absence of wind.
gõt, *adj.*, wet (hojāṇā).
gubb, *f.*, blow with fist.
guḍḍī, *f.*, one of three upright pieces of wood in *carkhā*.
guggaḷ karnā, *v.*, spoil (an affair).
guggaḷṇā, *v.*, be spoiled (an affair).
gujāḷī, *f.*, wheat mixed with barley, better than *gojjī*.
gujjhṇā, *v.*, be hidden.
gulī, *f.*, pure *kaīh*, bellmetal.
gum, *m.*, absence of wind.
guṅgaḷṇā, *v.*, became muddy (water).
guṭkā, *m.*, piece of iron in iron sugar-cane press.
guṭṭh, *f.*, direction between any two of four cardinal points of compass.
gutthī, *f.*, purse.

H

hãẽ mãẽ, *adv.*, without difficulty, easily.
haḷ, *m.*, oxen and plough, contrasted with *hall*, f., plough.
hālī, *adv.*, at present, now.
hambṇa, *v.*, grow faint (wind, person).
hanāī, *adj.*, brown (paper).
hanakk, *adv.*, unjustly, without reason = nahakk.
haṇḍhāṇā, *v.*, wear out (tr).
haṇḍhṇā, *v.*, wear, wear out (intr.)
hanekṇā, spoil, gen. in passive of well, cart, *welna*, person (*e.g.* through cold).
haṅgīrā, *m.*, kind of large ground lizard.
hanorā, *m.*, pride, boasting = māṇ.
haṛbācī, *f.*, right or left side of jaw.
haṭṭ, *m.*, well.
haṭṭī, *m.*, man who sits on *gādhī* and drives the oxen.
hauḷṭā = haulā, light (not heavy), small.
hekh! hekkhā̃, *interjection* (disbelief and astonishment).
hī̃, *f.*, side piece of bed or side door post.
hīyyā, *m.*, rainbow.
hohā, *m.*, slight puff of wind.
hūā! *interj.*, used to incite dog.
hubārā, *m.*, one of radiating pieces of wood in *baiṛ*.
hūī hā hā hā, *interj.*, to incite dog.
huliyā, *m.*, description.
humbḷī, *f.*, capering, jumping about (mārnī).
huṅghārā *m.*, agreement, saying 'yes' (bharnā).
huṅglaṇā, *v.*, nod sleepily.
hū̃jṇā, *v.*, sweep.
hūṇṭe, *m.*, *pl.*, riding on, (laiṇe).
hussaṛṇā, *v.*, be irritated, worried, be distressed through heat.
huṭṭar, *m.*, excuse, pretence.

I

ī, pronominal suffix, to thee, for thee.

ijjaṛ, *m.*, flock of goats, sheep.
ikārā, *adj.*, single (cloth &c.).
iṭṭī, *f.*, name of small piece of wood to which (1) warp is tied, (2) *kaḷā̃* are tied.

J

jabdē, *adv.*, quickly, recently.
jāc, *f.*, experience, skill.
jāg, *f.*, lymph, fermentation.
jāgō miṭī, *adj.*, half asleep.
jam jam ! *interj.*, by all means, certainly, welcome.
jāmnū̃, *m.*, Eugenia jambolana and its fruit.
jāmnū̃, *m.*, iron or brass binder binding *naṛī* to *daṭṭā*.
jandrī *f.*, vessel for preparing *sewīā̃*.
japphaḷ, *adj.*, one variety of the game *kauḍḍī*.
jātak, *m.*, boy.
jātkṛī, *f.*, girl.
jatt, *f.*, longish hair (animal).
jawātrā, *m.*, son-in-law.
jē, pronominal suffix, for you, to you.
jhaberā, *m.*, quarrel, noise.
jhāgṇā, *v.*, endure.
jhaī, *f.*, angry appearance (laiṇī)
jhā̃kī, *f.*, window.
jharapṇā, *v.*, catch.
jhaṭe binḍe, *adv.* repeatedly.
jhau, jhaw, *adv.* quickly, recently.
jhiggā, *m.*, shirt.
jhiggī, *f.*, boy's shirt.
jhissṇā, *v.*, lose heart = jhissī khāṇī.
jhōḷ, *m.*, mixture of *ghi* and sugar and milk.
jhōpṇā, *v.*, catch (ball, &c).
jhulānnī, *f.*, little room where Muhammadans cook food.
jhusmusṛā, *m.*, morning twilight.
jī āẽā̃ nū̃ ! welcome.
jī saddke, welcome.
jīndar, *f.*, mud and dirt at bottom of well.
jist, *m.*, lead.
jōtrā, *m.*, string attaching parts of loom.
juman, *m.*, power, strength.

K

kābula, *m.*, iron bolt.
kāgānī, *m.*, goat with very long hair.
kāhḍ, *f.*, one of the pieces of wood in lower part of *carkhā*.
kahḷ, *f.*, haste, hurry.
kaĩh, *f.*, bell metal.
kaiṛ *f.*, sound, sign which one intently watches for (laiṇī).
kākōrauḷā', *m.*, noise (pāṇā).
kaḷ, *f.*, string attaching warp to ceiling.
kalaṇ, *f.*, praise (by mirāsī).
kalernā, *m.*, kunernā, *m.*, rope attaching *panjaḷī* to *tīr*.
kaḷiṅgā, *adj.*, blackish.
kalpā, *m.*, long hook for pulling down branches.
kammī, *m.*, one who performs regular menial services.
kāṇ, *m.* = karū = 5 feet.
kaṇ., *m.*, grain borrowed and payable with interest.
kaṇ, *m.*, excellence or sweetness in *guṛ*.
kaṇ maṇ, *f.*, slight rain (hoṇī).
kandūrī, *f.*, small cloth for bread.
kandḷā, *m.*, rounded iron rod.
kaṅgī, *f.*, part of weaving machine for tightening warp.
kaṅgī, *f.*, part of chest (body).
kaṇī, *f.*, half-formed butter in milk (ājāṇī).
kaṇī muṇī, *f.*, slight rain.
kann, *m.*, roughness on neck of cattle (due to yoke).

kānnā, *m.*, reed in weaver's warp.
kānnī, *f.*, reed in warp (different from *kānnā*).
kāṇõ, *f.*, warping unnevenness in framework of bed (paīṇī).
kāppā, *m.* = kalpā.
kaṛāh, *m.*, big iron vessel with handles.
kaṛāhī, *f.*, smaller *kaṛāh.*
karnaiḷ, *f.*, side piece of *kaṛgī* (loom).
karū, *m.*, measure of length = [5½ feet.
kauḍḍī *f.*, breast bone.
kauḍḍī, *f.*, a game = *kabaḍḍī.*
kerī, *f.*, very small pieces of charcoal.
kesarnā, be angry, displeased.
khabbaṛ, *m.*, khabbṛī., *f.*, rope of stalks of *bajra*, &c.
khabīrā, wooden instrument of shoemaker.
khachõpaṛ, *m.*, turtle.
khāḍḍā, *m.*, irregular ditch.
khāḍḍī, *f.*, hole in ground beside potter's oven.
khaggā, *m.*, wasp's nest.
khaiḷ, *f.*, row, line, *e.g.* of cabbages.
khākh, *f.*, corner of mouth.
khakkhar, *f.*, lump of *guṛ* and popcorn.
khaḷ, *f.*, remains after extracting oil.
khalārnā, *v.*, cause to stand.
khalihārnā, *m.*, wood attached to ceiling (loom).
khambaṛ, *m.*, main wheel of *carkhā.*
khāṇḍ, *f.*, mine, hole for digging *kankar.*
khann, *m.*, fragment of *ḍhenḍhḷā* (karnā).
khāõpiyyā, *m.*, time of evening meal.
khappā, *m.*, space.
khārā, *adj.*, salt, bitter.
kharak, *f.*, cross piece of wood supporting warp.
khaṛkannā, *adj.*, big-eared, attentive.
kharkaṇā, *m.*, broom of twigs.
khaṛkillī, *f.*, peg holding up *kharak* (loom).
kharwā, *adj.*, rough.
khasrā, *m.*, measles.
khaṭak, *f.*, treating as important, valuable.
khicc, *f.*, rope attached to foot piece in loom. [&c.
khīṅgar, *m.*, piece of *kankar*,
khittiā, *f.*, *pl.* Pleiades.
khobṇā, *v.*, cause to sink or pierce.
khocḷā, *adj.*, large, loose.
khokh, *m.*, hollow.
khoḷā, *m.*, old dismantled, broken-down house.
khṛappē, *m.*, *pl.*, unevennesses in road.
khṛoc, *m.*, unevenness in road.
khunnā, *m.*, part of face above eye.
khuṇḍ, *m.*, large-hooked stick, side of welṇa.
khuṇḍī, *f.*, small-hooked stick.
khurnā, *v.*, crumble.
khushkā, *m.*, dry *āṭā* added to *rōṭī*, = *palethaṇ.*
khuṭṭar, *m.*, deceit (karnā).
kīkaṇā, kīkarā, *adv.*, how.
kiṛnā, be angry with.
kirtghaṇ, *adj.*, ungrateful, unthankful.
kirtghaṇī, *n.*, ingratitude, unthankfulness.
kojhā, *adj.*, ugly, ill-suited, defective (in member).
kōkkā, *m.*, cowry.
kōkkā, *m.*, mouthful of sugar-cane.
kraihd, kraiht, *f.*, loathing.
kuāṛī, *m.*, man who sells old furniture.
kubbā, *m.*, cross piece of wood in *ḍhoḷ.*
kucajj, foolishness.

kuḍḍhaṇ, *m.*, wooden poker.
kuḍhō, *m.*, hindrance (laggṇā).
kuhāṭrā, *m.*, half kos.
kuhmuk, *f.*, crowd.
kūkkā, *f.*, whispering, plotting.
kukkaṛ uḍārī, *f.* (cock-flight), very short distance.
kukkrē, *m. pl.*, granulation of eyelids (paiṇe).
kuṇḍaḷ, *f.*, coil of snake (marnī).
kuṛh, *f.*, cow house.
kuṛkuṛ, *f.*, chattering.
kurmāṇā, *v.*, wither.
kus͟hāla, *m.*, attention, effort.
kutarnā, *v.*, cut up small.
kuweḷ, *f.*, lateness.
kuwelā, *adj.*, late.

L

labhat, *f.*, profit.
lāg, *m.*, expense.
lāgā dāgā, *m.*, connection, business.
lāhmbe, *adv.*, to one side.
lāī, *f.*, one day's harvesting.
lalāran, *f.*, joy.
lālli, *f.*, maina (bird).
lamerā, *adj.*, longish.
lamittaṇ, *f.*, length.
lamkṇā, *v.*, desire, covet.
lā̃, *f.*, pulley-rope in loom.
laŋāṇā *v.*, walk lame.
laṭṭh, *f.*, axle of khambaṛ in carkhā.
lāṭū, *m.*, handle of door.
lauṇ, *m.*, meat.
laus, laũs, *f.*, weal from blow.
lī, *f.*, line, track.
lickṇā, *v.*, bend, (*intr.*)
lik͟hat, *f.*, bill of divorce.
lillā̃, *f. pl.* (luṭṭṇiā̃), amuse oneself.
limbh, *f.*, lock of hair.
liṭ, *f.*, lock of hair.
liṭṭ, *f.*, faqir's lock of hair.
lohṛā, *m.*, half of rope *baraṛ*.
lūmbā, *m.*, chimney.
luṇḍā, *adj.*, tailless, with hairless tail.
lūṛā. ?
lūsṇā, *v.*, burn with anger.

M

mackāṇa, *m.*, incite.
madāsā, *m.*, cloth tied round head to keep off cold.
madé, *m.*, one who will not give.
mahḷ, *m.*, brickwork round inside of well.
māhngā, *m.*, clapping of hands (mārnā).
mājhā, *adj.*, pertaining to buffalo.
mak͟he, *v.*, I said, contrd. from *maĩ ākheā*.
mākhyõ, *f.*, honey, honey-comb.
makkū, *m.*, (1) cloth binding *naṛī* to *ḍattā*, iron point of *nāhḷ*; *makkū ṭhappṇā*, fig. sit upon some body. (2) steel point to weaver's shuttle.
makṛā, *m.*, forked wood in *kānjaṇ* holding *tīr*.
makṛī, *f.*, locust, spider.
mal, *m.*, word of address to a man or boy, voc. *malā*.
maḷ, *f.*, earth deposit from river.
maḷēā hoćā, *adj.*, ill.
maḷēā jāṇā, become ill.
maḷhī, *f.*, dirt in well or on ox-walk.
maḷōmaḷī, maḷḷō maḷī, *adv.*, by force.
malṇā, *v.*, escape, get away.
māḷṭā, *m.*, Malta orange.
maṇ, *f.*, raised brickwork round well.
mandhāṛnā, *v.*, crush.
maṇḍhila, *m.*, piece of wood in *bharwannī*.
mandhrā, *adj.*, short in stature.

māngat, *m.*, beggar.
maṇkā, *m.*, circular bit of bone in *taraklā* of *carkhā*.
masātar, *f.*, height from ground to tips of fingers of hand held above head.
massī, *f.*, sock, especially leather sock.
matē, *conj.*, lest.
maṭṭaṇ, *f.*, large earthen jar, = maṭṭ.
matthā, *m.*, forehead.
maurī, *f.*, back over scapula.
māyā, *f.*, starch.
mec, *m.*, table.
mentar, *f.*, measuring.
mindhṇā, *v.*, crush.
moghā, *m.*, small canal, channel.
mohṛā, *m.*, long dry branch with twigs.
mohrak, *f.*, rope on head and mouth of cattle.
mohrī, *f.*, small dry branch with twigs.
mohrlā, *adj.*, in front.
muhāl, *f.*, small piece of wood in cart-wheel.
muhānjḷā, *m.*, morning twilight.
muhāṭh, *f.*, side post of door.
muhattaḷ, period of time, appointed period.
mūhrā, *m.*, piece of wood between two long side pieces of cart.
mukāḷā, *m.*, bad name, evil report.
mūḷī kaṇḍā, *m.*, iron grater for radishes, carrots, &c.
muŋgararā, *m.*, mixture of grain, *muŋgī* and *māh* or *cholle*.
munnā, *adj.*, three quarters.
munnā, *m.*, upright stick in cart to keep in load.
muṛ, *adv.*, again.

N

nadī, *f.*, Nūh nadī, Noachian flood.
nāhb, *f.*, ellipsoidal wood round *dhurā* of cart.
nainhdar, *f.*, wood on which *laṭṭh* of well rests.
nakhākhrā, *adj.*, pure, unmixed, good.
namīnā, *adj.*, blind.
nāŋan, *adj.*, naked.
nanierā, *m.*, huqqa with cocoanut base.
napṇa, *v.*, seize.
napaṛna, *v.*, seize.
naṭṭi, *f.*, centre of game with cowries; naṭṭī bahāṇā, keep waiting.
ne, *v.*, they are.
ne, ṇe, pronominal suffix: to, for or by them.
nehṇā, *v.*, cause to stand on ground *e.g. maṭṭ, ghaṛā*.
neṛe, *interj.*, said to right ox to make him turn to left.
nhernī, *f.*, vertigo.
nhorā, *m.*, = hanorā.
nī., ṇī., pronominal suffix, are to or for thee.
nikheṛnā, *v.*, separate.
nikkaṛ, *m.*, piece of anything, = *pikkā*.
nikkhaṛnā, *v.*, be separated.
ninghā, *adj.*, warm.

P

pabbī, *f.*, hill.
paḍāṇā, paḍhāṇā, *m.*, oxwalk at well.
paihṛā, *m.*, way.
pāhrēā, *m.*, cry of distress (pāṇā).
paṛōppī, *f.*, vertical cylinder in millstone of *khrās*.
pashū, *m.*, buffalo.
pāssā, *m.*, pure gold (pāsse dā seonā).

pāttū, *m.*, one handful of cattle excrement.
paī, *conj.*, that.
pailā, *adj.*, further, beyond.
paintṛā, *m.*, dry place for placing feet in wet ground.
pair pair! said to right ox to make him turn to left.
pasār, *m.*, piece of wood below *racch* in weaving.
pasār, *m.*, front-room.
pasār, *m.*, piece of wood under warp in loom.
paṭā, *m.*, document, lease.
paṭṭhā, *m.*, pupil of wrestler.
pattha, *m.*, wood into which *cūthī* of *laṭṭh* in well comes.
paṭṭhe, *m. pl.*, green chopped food for cattle.
paṭṭṇā, *v.*, spend, waste (money).
paund paṭṭ = paund saṭṭe.
paund saṭṭe, *adv.*, at first go off, at once.
pauṛī, *f.*, foot piece in loom.
pauṛī, *f.*, long side beam in cart.
peṭhā, *m.*, kind of vegetable-marrow.
phaīh, *adv.*, violently (of beating or throwing down).
phalṛī, *f.*, wood on which potter sits.
phalṛi, *f.*, wooden tool of shoemaker.
phaṇḍ, *f.*, beating, gust of rain.
phaṇḍākā, *m.*, shaking dust out of cloth (mārnā).
phāṅgā, *m.*, trouble, loss (laggṇā).
phaṛhī, *f.*, regular mass of sleepers, bricks, *kankar*.
phaṭṭ, *f.*, lower piece of wood in *panjālī*.
phēṇā, *v.*, squeeze, burst.
phiḍḍā, *m.*, little hollow, hole, depression.
phōs, *m.*, collection of cattle ordure after one evacuation.
phūk, *f.*, air, blowing with mouth or inflator.
phull, *m.*, popcorn, black spot in *capātī*.
phuṭṭṇā, *v.*, have offspring (woman).
phutūhī*f.*, waistcoat.
piākal, *m.*, great smoker or drinker.
pichāṛī, *f.*, rope attached to *pauṛi* of loom.
pīcṇā, *v.*, absorb water, be watered (especially land).
pīṅgh, *f*, guḍḍī gudde dī p., rainbow.
piīī, *f.*, spoked wheel, little wheel at end of *gāhd* in iron *welṇā*.
pinnī, *f.*, leg between thigh and ankle.
pipṇī, *f.*, eyelash, upper or lower.
pīṛhī, *f.*, generation.
pittā, *m.*, pure *kaīh* (bell metal).
pōt, crop of bird.
pukkarnā, *v.*, give.
pūr, *m.*, *rahu* while being cooked.
pūshal, *f.*, tail.

R

rach, *m.*, part of weaving machine where bobbin passes.
rahl, *f.*, unploughed land surrounded by ploughed.
rahtaṛ, *f.*, condition of living.
rail, *f.*, appearance of something visible to eyes.
ralakṇā, *v.*, go or walk slowly.
rambṇā, *v.* make arrangements for (*e.g.*, marriage).
rappharṛ, *m.*, noise, quarrel.
raṛā, *adj.*, of uncultivated, level ground.

raṛī, *f.*, uncultivated level ground.
rashm, *f.*, ray of sun or cloth.
raṭṭā, *m.*, noise.
rauṇā, *m.*, buttermilk.
rehl, *f.*, Qurān stand (folding).
reṛ, *m.*, reṛi, *f.*, = areṛ, areṛī.
rhaṇḍā, *m.*, widower.
rōṛ, *m.*, *kankar*, or piece of *kankar*.
rōṛā, *m.*, long continued time without rain.

S

—s, pronominal suffix, by, for or to him = sū.
sāh, *f.*, ashes.
sajhāṇ, *f.*, power of recognition.
sajhāṇṇā, *v.*, recognise.
sak, sakṛa, *m.*, little bits or shavings of wood.
saḷāī, *f.*, needle in shuttle.
salūkā, *m.*, waistcoat.
samaddhar, *adj.*, short in size.
samāwār, *m.*, metal teapot and heating apparatus combined.
samūlṛā, *adj.*, all, the whole of, with everything.
sāṇak, *f.*, *i.q. kunāḷī*, earthen dish.
saṇḍh, *f.*, grown buffalo which has not had young.
sandhōā, *m.*, house-breaking instrument.
saṅgā, *m.*, collection of 4—10 strings on sides of bed or pīṛhi.
saṅgaṛnā, *v.*, became contracted (as leather).
sānjhā, *adj.*, in common, joint.
sanjhāṇ, *f.*, recognition.
sanjhāṇṇā, *v.*, recognise.
sāṇkī, *f.*, earthen dish, *i.q. kunāḷī*.
sānnhā, *m.*, kind of lizard.
sansār, *m.*, crocodile.
sarājīt, *adj.* well, alive, (after illness).
sarīā, *m.*, iron rod.
satāīā̃, satāīwā̃, *adj.*, twenty-seventh.
satīwā̃, *adj.*, twenty-seventh, especially of day in Ramzān.
satrāṇā, *adj.*, strong.
sawakẖtā, *m.*, early time.
sawakẖtē, *adv.*, in good time.
sawikk, *m.*, evil deed
sehd, *f.*, direction.
sejjal, *f.*, moisture.
sepī, *m.*, master receiving or servant doing menial service on contract pay.
shām, *f.*, iron or brass band round wood.
sharlāṭā, *m.*, gust of rain or wind.
shokẖ, *adj.*, bright (of light or colour); quick (of hearing).
shokẖā, *adj.*, cheeky, smart.
shū̃ shā̃, *f.*, display, grandeur.
shūkā shākī, *f.*, display, grandeur.
shūmpuṇā, *m.*, miserliness.
sīdh, sīdhā̃, *prep. with fem.*, up to.
sidharnā, *v.*, become good, improve.
sihāṇ, *f.*, recognition.
sihāṇṇā, *v.*, recognise.
sijjhṇā, *v.*, pay out, take revenge on.
sillṇā, *v.*, get wet.
sir matthe te, (on head and forehead), by all means, welcome!
sīrī, *m.*, partner.
sitthā, *m.*, wax in honeycomb.
siwāī, *f.*, sewing, price of sewing.
sōhḍā, *adj.*, pinkish red.
sōkkā, *m.*, collection of 4—10 strings along sides of bed or *pīṛhī*.
sū, pronominal suffix, to, for or by him = -s.
suāhrā, *adj.*, straight on.

sucajjā, *adj.*, intelligent.
sudharnā, *v.*, become good, improve.
sudhārnā, *v.*, make good, improve.
sukhall, sukhallā, *adj.*, easy.
sumbā, *m.*, rounded, pointed instrument for making holes.
sūṇā, *v.*, have offspring (animals).
suṇhippaṇ, , beauty.
sun mun, *adj.*, quiet.
suraŋ, *f.* tunnel.
suṛaŋ, *f.*, tibia.
sūṭ, *m.*, puff (of huqqa) (lāṇā).
sūtlar, *m.*, piece of wood in well to keep *māhl* in position.

T

tabākhṛī, *f.*, metal plate, *i.q.* thāḷī.
ṭakāṇā, *m.*, cross piece in floor of cart.
ṭakāṇī, *f.*, =ṭakāṇā.
takbīr wagāṇā, *v.*, kill for food.
takmā, *m.*, medal.
ṭākrā, *m.*, meeting.
taléāṭh, tarēāṭh, *m.*, wood at top of well beside *parāṇā*.
tāḷū, oblong pieces shaved on top of head, palate.
talwaṭṭh, ,, part of *kuŋgī* in loom.
tandūḷi, *f.*, one of strands in *laṛ*.
ṭaŋgṇā, *m.*, hanging frame for clothes.
ṭap, *m.*, dry thorn-branch.
ṭapḷā, *m.*, confusion, mistake, (laggṇā).
ṭappā, *m.*, hole in ground made by blow from spade.
tāṛ, *f.*, haste, anxiety.
tar, *f.*, ray of sun.
taraŋgaṛ, *m.*, Orion's Belt.
taraŋgaṛnā, *v.*, do in a rough and ready way.
tarauṇā, *m.*, little reedstand for sweetmeat seller's basket.
tarcauḷī, *f.*, rice and sugar (*shakkar*) and *tiḷ*.
tarnā, *v.*, be paid (of money).
tārnā, *v.* pay (money).
ṭas, *f.*, adornment (kaḍḍhṇā).
tasbī, *f.*, Muhammadan rosary.
tatatat, *interj.*, to make left bullock turn to right.
ṭaṭauḷī, *f.*, kind of bird, lapwing
taullī, *f.*, earthen cooking pot = tauṛī.
tāzī, *adj.*, tāzī kuttā, greyhound, tāzīghoṛā, racehorse.
ṭekṇā, *v.*, bow.
ṭhāh, *m.*, *f.*, sharp noise = paṭākā.
thakkā, *m.*, cold wind.
thaṇ, *m.*, woman's breast.
thapṇā, *v.*, fold.
ṭhār, *m.*, cold.
ṭhār, *f.*, acquaintance, resting place.
thaṛā, *m.*, raised brickwork before house or on well.
thaṭṭh, *f.*, wave.
ṭhēr, *f.*, cowry with piece out of back, = citt.
ṭhet, *m.*, sense, intelligence.
thuḷṇā, *v.*, make known.
thumṇā, *v.*, lean against.
ṭibbā, *m.*, hillock.
ṭikkī, *f.*, ball of sun just before setting or after rising: hard lumpy bit in *capātī*.
til, *m.*, force.
tilakṇā, *v.*, slip.
tillaṛ, *m.*, rope of three strands.
ṭiṇḍ, *f.*, camel's stomach brought into mouth, bald head, shaved head.
tīr, *m.*, vertical beam, axle of *ḍhoḷ*.
tissā, trissā, *m.*, three kinds of grain mixed.
ṭōḍḍā, *m.*, young of camel.
ṭōhṇā, *v.*, feel (to).

ṭōppā, *m.*, circular piece of wood joining two parts of *khambaṛ*.
ṭōṭṭā, *m.*, piece, fragment.
traihṇā, *v.*, be startled.
trāhṇā, *v.*, startle.
trappaṛ, *m.*, sackcloth.
trappṛī, *f.*, small piece of sackcloth.
trauh, *m.*, alarm.
threhrā, *adj.*, threefold.
treḷīōtreḷī, *adj.*, covered with perspiration.
treõṛ, *m.*, milk and ghi and sugar mixed.
trikkh, *f.*, swiftness.
trōppā, *m.*, stitch.
tukk, *f.*, guess.
tuḷ, *f.*, lever, lāṇī = apply lever.
tuö, *interj.*, calling to dog.

U

ū̃, pronominal suffix, for thee, to thee, thee.
uccā, *m.*, tongs.
ucecā, *adj.*, especially.
uḍāī̃, *f. pl.* winnowing.
udhāḷā, *m.*, elopement.
uggharnā, *v.*, raise (stick).
ukkā, *adj.*, altogether.
ulār. **ulārā**, *m.*, tilting over or back.
ulārnā, *v.*, raise (stick).
ulhārā, *m.*, bending trees in wind (khāṇā).
ukhkhaṇṇā, *v.*, with mātā (*f.*) vaccinate.
ukhkhaṇwāṇā, *v.*, with mātā (*f.*) get vaccinated.
ullarnā, *v.*. get tilted to one side.
uṇ̃, *adv.*, in this way, any how, &c.
ureb, *m.*, bending, slanting.
utāṇā, *adj.*, lying on back.

W

wā, *m.*, association, connection.
wā warōlā, *m.*, **wā warōḷī**, *f.*, whirlwind with dust.
wacherā, *m.*, foal.
wāḍhīā̃, *f. pl.*, cutting harvest.
wagghī, *f.*, part between fingers and between toes.
wahṇā, *adj.*, smart, clever, intelligent.
wāhṇā, *adj.*, barefoot, pairā̃ tõ wāhṇā.
wahṇī, *f.*, small drain.
wahṛ tārā, *m.*, Venus, Morning Star.
wāhṛī, *f.*, earthen vessel like teapot.
waihtar, *m.*, ass, mule, &c.
waiṇ, *m.*, mourning (gen. plural).
wajjṇā, *v.*, be struck or sounded, be shut (door).
wal, *prep.*, with *masc.* towards, with *fem.*, towards one's wife.
waḷ (nikaḷṇā), muscle get out of place, causing pain.
waḷā, *m.*, turn, twist.
walaŋgḷā, **walā̃ŋglā**, *m.*, turn, twist.
walaŋglī, **walā̃ŋglī**, *f.*, turn, twist.
walh, *f.*, rope attaching *panjāḷī* to *gāhḍī*).
walū̃ndarnā, *v.*, spoil.
wānd, *f.*, fine weather.
wāndhā, *adj.*, free, disengaged.
waŋ, *f.*, one of pieces of wood composing *baiṛ*.
warā̃ŋgḷā, *m.*, turn, twist.
wasāṛ, *m.*, spice, *e.g.*, haldī.
wāskaṭ, *m.*, waistcoat.
wasṇā, *v.*, rain.
waṭṭā, *m.*, lobe of ear.
waṭṭā, *m.*, stone pestle.
waṭṭṇā, *m.*, stick for twisting rope.
waṭṭī, *f.*, weight of two sers.
waule. *adv.*, in the open air.
wehl, *f.* and *m.*, leisure.

A Guide to the Metres of Urdū Verse

FROM the point of view of Europeans there is no book that deals satisfactorily with Urdū metres, and as the metres are numerous, it is difficult for a student to recognize any except the three or four commonest. They have all been taken over unaltered from Persian, and Persian took them almost unaltered from Arabic. To Europeans the rules of Urdū prosody seem arbitrary, because metres must conform to certain rules for which there seems to be no adequate reason.

For example the commonest Urdū metre is scanned as follows: *maf'ūlu fā'ilātu mafā'īlu fā'ilun.* It might just as well be scanned *mustaf'ilun mafā'ilu mustaf'ilun fa'al* or in other ways, but we should be arbitrarily told that there are no such metres and that in fact they would be impossible.

Urdū writers have no conception of long or short syllables. They have names for fragments of two and three letters, and they have names for metrical feet, but they do not call syllables long or short. I am, however, writing for Europeans who are accustomed to prosodical length in Latin and Greek verse, and the idea is almost necessary for them if they are to make any progress.

The question I have set myself to answer here is this. When a student comes across a poem or a quotation how is he to decide what its metre is ? He will, if he knows the language, be able to say that certain syllables are short or long, but he will still be ignorant of the metre. How is he to discover it ?

To enable him to do so I have prepared two lists. The first is divided into sections according to the number of syllables in each line or hemistich, and in each section the metres are given—not in alphabetical order indeed, for that would not be possible, but—in order of short syllables. In other words a short syllable is given precedence over a long. Thus a line beginning — ⏑ — — ⏑ ⏑ would precede one which begins — ⏑ — — ⏑ —, because, while the first five syllables are the same in the two lines, the sixth syllable in the first is short, and in the second long. The second list is devoted to *rubā'ī* metres. In it, too, the metres are in order of short syllables.

Method of Ascertaining Metres

To discover the metre of a line, first count the number of syllables. This number shows the section of List 1 in which the metre is given. Next determine the sequence of short and long syllables, and finally look up the metre, according to that sequence, in its proper place in the section. There the name of the metre and the feet which compose it will be found. This last stage can be shortened by first looking for the metre in the short list below. It will almost certainly be there.

The two lists contain between them 176 metres, counting each variety separately. The first has 152; the second is devoted to the 24 *rubā‘ī* metres. The latter are entered by themselves for the reasons mentioned at the head of the list. The 176 metres may be reduced to about eighty or ninety if small differences are ignored.

For the purpose of this article I have examined 450 poems or quotations (330 poems and 120 quotations), in addition to *rubā‘īs*. If we count as single metres two groups of eight, one of five, two of four, three of three, and thirteen pairs, we find that there are only twenty-five distinct metres. This is perhaps an over-simplification, but even if every variety is reckoned separately, there are only sixty-eight.

It will be interesting to mention here all the metres of the 450 poems. Probably the six or eight which occur more frequently than the others would be common in any longish collection of different kinds of Urdū verse. The number after each metre indicates how often it occurred.

The Metres of the 450 Poems Examined: *rubā‘īs* excluded

(1) 14.16, 17 *muẓāri‘* — — ⏑ | — ⏑ — ⏑ | ⏑ — — ⏑ | — ⏑ — | 80

(2) 15.11, 12 *raml* — ⏑ — — | — ⏑ — — | — ⏑ — — | — ⏑ — | 66

(3) 16.9, 10 *hazaj* ⏑ — — — | four times 53

(4) 14.1*a*, *b*, 11, 12; 15.1*a*, *b*, 9, 10 } *raml* — ⏑ — — | ⏑ ⏑ — — | ⏑ ⏑ — — | — — | etc. 49

(5) 10.1, 2, 10, 11; 11.1, 2, 15, 16 } *khafīf* — ⏑ — — | ⏑ — ⏑ — | — — | etc. 31

(6) 14.2*a*, *b*; 15.2*a*, *b*; 13.1 *mujtaṣṣ*
⏑ — ⏑ — | ⏑ ⏑ — — | ⏑ — ⏑ — | — — | etc. 29

(7) 24.3 and 12.6 *mutaqārib* ⏑ — — | four or eight times 21

(8) 14.13, 14 *hazaj* — — ⏑ | ⏑ — — ⏑ | ⏑ — — ⏑ | ⏑ — — | 20

(9) 11.5, 6 and 22.1 *mutaqārib* ⏑ — — | ⏑ — — | ⏑ — — | ⏑ — | 17

(10) 10.12, 13 and 9.6, 7 *hazaj* — — ⏑ | ⏑ — ⏑ — | ⏑ — — etc. 15

3

(11)	11.7, 8 and 22.2 *hazaj* ⏑ — — — | ⏑ — — — | ⏑ — — |	13
(12)	14.18, 19 *muẓāri‘* — — ⏑ | — ⏑ — — | — — ⏑ | — ⏑ — — |	11
(13)	20.2 and 10.3 *mutaqārib* ⏑ — | ⏑ — — | four times	8
(14)	16.11 *rajaz* — ⏑ ⏑ — | ⏑ — ⏑ — | — ⏑ ⏑ — | ⏑ — ⏑ — |	7
(15)	24.2 ; 12.1 ; 8.4, etc. *mutadārik* ⏑ ⏑ — | ⏑ ⏑ — | ⏑ ⏑ — | ⏑ ⏑ — | etc. and | — — | — — | — — | — — | etc.	5
(16)	14.5, 6 *munsariḥ* — ⏑ ⏑ — | — ⏑ — | — ⏑ ⏑ — | — ⏑ —	4
(17)	20.1 *kāmil* | ⏑ ⏑ — ⏑ — | four times	4
(18)	11.18, 19 *raml* — ⏑ — — | — ⏑ — — | — ⏑ — |	4
(19)	10.8, 9 (11.13, 14) *raml* — ⏑ — — | ⏑ ⏑ — — | — — |	3
(20)	16.6, 7 *hazaj* | ⏑ — ⏑ — | four times	3
(21)	14.7 or 8, i.e. *muqtaẓab* | — ⏑ — ⏑ | — — — | — ⏑ — ⏑ | — — — | or *hazaj* | — ⏑ — | ⏑ — — — | — ⏑ — | ⏑ — — — |	2
(22)	16.19, 20 *rajaz* | — — ⏑ — | four times	2
(23)	16.17, 18 *raml* | — ⏑ — — | four times	1
(24)	10.11*a* *mutadārik* — ⏑ — | — ⏑ — | — ⏑ — | —	1
(25)	14.15 *hazaj* — — ⏑ | ⏑ — — — | — — ⏑ | ⏑ — — — |	1
		450

The first four metres account for over half the poems, and the first seven for three-quarters. Eighty-four are not represented at all.

In Urdū some metres are almost confined to certain types of verse, and conversely certain types of verse are usually in two or three fixed metres.

Maṣnavī Metres.—The commonest are perhaps *hazaj* 10.12, 13 (and 9.6, 7) and *khafīf* 10.1, 2 and the rest of that group. Others are *mutaqārib* 11.5, 6 ; *hazaj* 11.7, 8 ; *rajaz* 16.11 ; *sarī‘* 11.9, 10 ; and *raml* 11.13, 14 and 11.18, 19.

Qaṣīda Metres.—The commonest metre is 14.1*a*, *b* and the rest of that group (*raml*), and next comes the *mujtaṣṣ* group 14.2*a*, *b*, etc. Others are rare.

Marṣiya Metres.—Much the commonest is *muẓāri‘* 14.16, 17 ; next is the *mujtaṣṣ* group 14.2*a*, *b*, etc. Others not so common are *hazaj* 14.13, 14 ; the *raml* group 14.1*a*, *b*, etc. ; *hazaj* 16.9, and *mutaqārib* 20.2.

The Two Lists of Metres

The number after the name of a metre in the first list shows how often that metre occurred in the 450 poems examined. From these numbers we can get a fair idea of the relative frequency of the different Urdū metres. The word "group" after a number means that the metre is one of a group of metres which may be used interchangeably in one and the same poem. The same number is given for every member of the group.

Each section is numbered separately, and metres are referred to by the number of the section followed by the number of the metre. Thus 10.8 would mean the 8th metre in Section 10, viz. the section containing ten syllabled lines; 14.18, 19 would be the 18th and 19th metres in Section 14.

Metres which are identical except for a very slight difference in the first or last syllable are bracketed. They can be used interchangeably.

For convenience sake I have sometimes drawn attention to similarity between two metres, but it must not be assumed that they too are interchangeable unless that is expressly stated. I do not profess to have given every metre ever used in Urdū, but students will only on rare occasions come across one not mentioned in these lists.

Two consecutive short syllables are frequently combined into one long syllable. In this way new varieties are formed. Many examples of this will be found noted in both lists. Apart from the cases actually referred to it is possible to make a general rule that in the metre *mujtaṣṣ*, — ⏑ ⏑ —, mufta'ilun, may become — — —, maf'ūlun; in *sarī'*, the second foot ⏑ ⏑ — —, fă'ĭlātun, may become — — —, maf'ūlun; in *raml*, — ⏑ — —, fā'ilātun, or ⏑ ⏑ — —, fă'ĭlātun, may become — — —, maf'ūlun.

A last syllable can always be regarded as long. It may be —· | or — |. These signs differ simply in this that — means either a consonant plus a long vowel, or two consonants with a short vowel between them; —· means two consonants with a long vowel between them. The sign —· has not been used before. I have adopted it merely to make this small distinction. In Urdū — has two letters; —· has three.

First List

(Metres not used in *rubā'īs*)

Twenty-four Syllables

1. ⏑ ⏑ — ⏑ ⏑ — | ⏑ ⏑ — ⏑ ⏑ — | ⏑ ⏑ — ⏑ ⏑ — | ⏑ ⏑ — ⏑ ⏑ — |
mutafā'ilatun four times. Kāmil.

2. ⏑ ⏑ — | ⏑ ⏑ — | ⏑ ⏑ — | ⏑ ⏑ — | ⏑ ⏑ — | ⏑ ⏑ — | ⏑ ⏑ — | ⏑ ⏑ — |
fă'ilun eight times. Mutadārik. 5 group

Nos. 1 and 2 are really identical. No. 2 is 12.1 doubled. Any or every foot in 24.2 may be — — | fa'lun. The line may therefore, theoretically at any rate, have from 16 to 24 syllables. See 8.4.

3. ⏑ — — | ⏑ — — | ⏑ — — | ⏑ — — | ⏑ — — | ⏑ — — | ⏑ — — | ⏑ — — |
fa'ūlun eight times. Mutaqārib. 21
(6 of this and 15 of 12.6)

Twenty-two Syllables

1. ⏑ — — | ⏑ — — | ⏑ — — | ⏑ — | ⏑ — — | ⏑ — — | ⏑ — — | ⏑ — |
fa'ūlun fa'ūlun fa'ūlan fa'al fa'ūlun fa'ūlun fa'ūlun fa'al.
This is 11.5 doubled. Mutaqārib. 17
(3 of this and 14 of 11.5, 6)

2. ⏑ — — — | ⏑ — — — | ⏑ — — | ⏑ — — — | ⏑ — — — | ⏑ — — |
mafā'īlun mafā'īlun fa'ūlun mafā'īlun mafā'īlun fa'ūlun.
This is 11.7 doubled. Hazaj. 13
(2 of this and 11 of 11.7, 8)

Twenty Syllables

1. ⏑ ⏑ — ⏑ — | ⏑ ⏑ — ⏑ — | ⏑ ⏑ — ⏑ — | ⏑ ⏑ — ⏑ — |
mutafā'ilun four times. Kāmil. 4

2. ⏑ — | ⏑ — — | ⏑ — | ⏑ — — | ⏑ — | ⏑ — — | ⏑ — | ⏑ — — |
fa'al fa'ūlun four times.
This is 10.3 doubled. Mutaqārib. 8

Sixteen Syllables

1. ⏑ ⏑ — ⏑ | — ⏑ — — | ⏑ ⏑ — ⏑ | — ⏑ — — |
fă'ilātu fā'ilātun fă'ilātu fā'ilātun. Raml.

2. ⏑ ⏑ — ⏑ | — ⏑ — — | ⏑ ⏑ — ⏑ | — ⏑ — — . |
fă'ilātu fā'ilātun fă'ilātu fā'ilīyān. Raml.

3. ⏑ ⏑ — — | ⏑ ⏑ — — | ⏑ ⏑ — — | ⏑ ⏑ — — |
fă'ilātun four times.
This is 16.15 with first syllable short. Raml.

4. ⏑ — ⏑ — | ⏑ ⏑ — — | ⏑ — ⏑ — | ⏑ ⏑ — — |
mafā‘īlun fă‘ilātun mafā‘īlun fă‘ilātun. Mujtas̤s̤.

5. ⏑ — ⏑ — | ⏑ ⏑ — — | ⏑ — ⏑ — | ⏑ ⏑ — — . |
mafā‘īlun fă‘ilātun mafā‘īlun fă‘ilīyān. Mujtas̤s̤.
This is the same as 15.2*a*, *b* ; 14.2*a*, *b* and 13.1 except for the last foot.

6. ⏑ — ⏑ — | ⏑ — ⏑ — | ⏑ — ⏑ — | ⏑ — ⏑ — |
mafā‘īlun mafā‘īlun mafā‘īlun mafā‘īlun. Hazaj. 3

7. ⏑ — ⏑ — | ⏑ — ⏑ — | ⏑ — ⏑ — | ⏑ — ⏑ — . |
mafā‘īlun mafā‘īlun mafā‘īlun mafā‘īlān. Hazaj.

8. ⏑ — ⏑ — | — ⏑ ⏑ — | ⏑ — ⏑ — | — ⏑ ⏑ — |
mafā‘īlun muftă‘īlun mafā‘īlun muftă‘īlun. Rajaz.

9. ⏑ — — — | ⏑ — — — | ⏑ — — — | ⏑ — — — |
mafā‘īlun four times. Hazaj. 53

10. ⏑ — — — | ⏑ — — — | ⏑ — — — | ⏑ — — — . |
mafā‘īlun mafā‘īlun mafā‘īlun mafā‘īlān. Hazaj.

11. — ⏑ ⏑ — | ⏑ — ⏑ — | — ⏑ ⏑ — | ⏑ — ⏑ — |
mufta‘ilun mafā‘īlun mufta‘ilun mafā‘īlun. Rajaz. 7

12. — ⏑ ⏑ — | — ⏑ ⏑ — | — ⏑ ⏑ — | — ⏑ ⏑ — |
mufta‘ilun four times. Rajaz.

13. — ⏑ ⏑ — | — ⏑ ⏑ — | — ⏑ ⏑ — | — ⏑ ⏑ — · |
mufta‘ilun mufta‘ilun mufta‘ilun mufta‘ilān. Rajaz.

14. — ⏑ — ⏑ | — ⏑ ⏑ — | — ⏑ — ⏑ | — ⏑ ⏑ — |
fā‘ilātu mufta‘ilun fā‘ilātu mufta‘ilun. Muqtaẓab.

15. — ⏑ — — | ⏑ ⏑ — — | ⏑ ⏑ — — | ⏑ ⏑ — — |
fā‘ilātun fă‘īlātun fă‘īlātun fă‘īlātun.
This is 16.3 with first syllable long. Raml.

16. — ⏑ — — | ⏑ ⏑ — — | ⏑ ⏑ — — | ⏑ ⏑ — — · |
fā‘ilātun fă‘īlātun fă‘īlātun fă‘īlīyān. Raml.

17. — ⏑ — — | — ⏑ — — | — ⏑ — — | — ⏑ — — |
fā‘ilātun four times. Raml. 1

18. — ⏑ — — | — ⏑ — — | — ⏑ — — | — ⏑ — — · |
fā‘ilātun fā‘ilātun fā‘ilātun fā‘ilīyān. Raml.

19. — — ⏑ — | — — ⏑ — | — — ⏑ — | — — ⏑ — |
mustaf‘ilun four times. Rajaz. 2

20. — — ⏑ — | — — ⏑ — | — — ⏑ — | — — ⏑ — · |
mustaf‘ilun mustaf‘ilun mustaf‘ilun mustaf‘ilān. Rajaz.

Fifteen Syllables

1*a*. ⏑ ⏑ — — | ⏑ ⏑ — — | ⏑ ⏑ — — | ⏑ ⏑ — |
fă‘īlātun fă‘īlātun fă‘īlātun fă‘īlun. Raml. 49 group

1*b*. ⏑ ⏑ — — | ⏑ ⏑ — — | ⏑ ⏑ — — | ⏑ ⏑ — · |
fă‘īlātun fă‘īlātun fă‘īlātun fă‘īlān. Raml.

1*a*, *b*, are the same as 15.9, 10, except for the first syllable. See also 14.1*a*, *b*, and 14.11, 12.

2*a*. ⏑ — ⏑ — | ⏑ ⏑ — — | ⏑ — ⏑ — | ⏑ ⏑ — |
mafā'īlun fă'īlātun mafā'īlun fă'īlun. Mujtaṣṣ. 29 group

2*b*. ⏑ — ⏑ — | ⏑ ⏑ — — | ⏑ — ⏑ — | ⏑ ⏑ — · |
mafā'īlun fă'īlātun mafā'īlun fă'īlān. Mujtaṣṣ.

Except for the last foot Nos. 2*a* and *b* are the same as 14.2*a*, *b* and 13.1. Cf. also 16.4, 5.

3. ⏑ — — ⏑ | ⏑ — — ⏑ | ⏑ — — ⏑ | ⏑ — — |
mafā'īlu mafā'īlu mafā'īlu fa'ūlun. Hazaj.

4. ⏑ — — ⏑ | ⏑ — — ⏑ | ⏑ — — ⏑ | ⏑ — — · |
mafā'īlu mafā'īlu mafā'īlu mafā'īl. Hazaj.

5. ⏑ — — ⏑ | ⏑ — — ⏑ | ⏑ — — ⏑ | — — — |
mafā'īlu mafā'īlu mafā'īlu maf'ūlun. Hazaj.

6. ⏑ — — ⏑ | — ⏑ — ⏑ | ⏑ — — ⏑ | — ⏑ — |
mafā'īlu fā'ilātu mafā'īlu fā'ilun. Muẓāri'.

7. ⏑ — — ⏑ | — ⏑ — ⏑ | ⏑ — — ⏑ | — ⏑ — · |
mafā'īlu fā'ilātu mafā'īlu fā'ilān. Muẓāri'.

15.6, 7 may be interchanged with 14.3, 4. They are same the as 14.16, 17 except for the first foot.

8. — ⏑ ⏑ — | — ⏑ — ⏑ | — ⏑ ⏑ — | — ⏑ — · |
mufta'ilun fā'ilātu mufta'ilun fā'ilān.

This is really the same as 14.6. Munsariḥ.

9. — ⏑ — — | ⏑ ⏑ — — | ⏑ ⏑ — — | ⏑ ⏑ — |
fā'ilātun fă'īlātun fă'īlātun fă'īlun. Raml. 49 group

10. — ⏑ — — | ⏑ ⏑ — — | ⏑ ⏑ — — | ⏑ ⏑ — · |
fā'ilātun fă'īlātun fă'īlātun fă'īlān. Raml.

See 15.1*a*, *b*; 14.11, 12; 14.1*a*, *b*. If from 15.9, 10 we omit the 3rd foot we get 11.13, 14.

11. — ⏑ — — | — ⏑ — — | — ⏑ — — | — ⏑ — |
fā'ilātun fā'ilātun fā'ilātun fā'ilun. Raml. 66

12. — ⏑ — — | — ⏑ — — | — ⏑ — — | — ⏑ — · |
fā'ilātun fā'ilātun fā'ilātūn fā'ilāt. Raml.

13. — — ⏑ | ⏑ — — ⏑ | ⏑ — — ⏑ | ⏑ — — ⏑ |
maf'ūlu mafā'īlu mafā'īlu mafā'īlu. Hazaj.

14. — — ⏑ | — ⏑ — ⏑ | ⏑ — — ⏑ | — ⏑ — — |
maf'ūlu fā'ilātu mafā'īlu fā'ilātun. Muẓāri'.

This is the same as 14.16 with an extra syllable. If we change the short seventh and eighth syllables into one long syllable we get 14.18.

Fourteen Syllables

Nos. 1*a* and 1*b* are the same as 11 and 12 except for the first syllable. Students will find that the eight metres 14.1*a*, 1*b*; 14.11, 12; 15.1*a*, 1*b*, and 15.9, 10 may all be interchanged in the same poem.

1a. ⏑ ⏑ – – | ⏑ ⏑ – – | ⏑ ⏑ – – | – – |
fă'ĭlātun fă'ĭlātun fă'ĭlātun fa'lun. Raml. 49 group
1b. ⏑ ⏑ – – | ⏑ ⏑ – – | ⏑ ⏑ – – | – – · |
fă'ĭlātun fă'ĭlātun fă'ĭlātun fa'lān.

2a. ⏑ – ⏑ – | ⏑ ⏑ – – | ⏑ – ⏑ – | – – |
mafā'ĭlun fă'ĭlātun mafā'ĭlun fa'lun. Mujtaṣṣ. 29 group
2b. ⏑ – ⏑ – | ⏑ ⏑ – – | ⏑ – ⏑ – | – – · |
mafā'ĭlun fă'ĭlātun mafā'ĭlun fa'lān. Mujtaṣṣ.

Nos. 2*a* and 2*b* are the same as 15.2*a*, 2*b* and 13.1 except for the first foot and may be interchanged. Cf. also 16.4, 5.

3. ⏑ – – ⏑ | – ⏑ – | ⏑ – – ⏑ | – ⏑ – |
mafā'ĭlu fā'ilun mafā'ĭlu fā'ilun. Muẓāri'.
4. ⏑ – – ⏑ | – ⏑ – | ⏑ – – ⏑ | – ⏑ – · |
mafā'ĭlu fā'ilun mafā'ĭlu fā'ilān. Muẓāri'.

5. – ⏑ ⏑ – | – ⏑ – | – ⏑ ⏑ – | – ⏑ – |
mufta'ilun fā'ilun mufta'ilun fā'ilun. Munsariḥ. 4
5a. – ⏑ ⏑ – | – ⏑ – | – ⏑ ⏑ – | – ⏑ – · |
mufta'ilun fā'ilun mufta'ilun fā'ilāt. Munsariḥ.
6, 6a. – ⏑ ⏑ – | – ⏑ – · | – ⏑ ⏑ – | – ⏑ – | or | – ⏑ – · |
mufta'ilun fā'ilāt mufta'ilun fā'ilun or fā'ilāt. Munsariḥ.

14.6 is really the same as 15.8. 14.5, 5*a*, 6, 6*a* resemble 13.2, 3 ; see also 12.16, 17.

7. – ⏑ – ⏑ | – – – | – ⏑ – ⏑ | – – – |
fā'ilātu maf'ūlun fā'ilātu maf'ūlun. Muqtaẓab. } 2
8. – ⏑ – | ⏑ – – – | – ⏑ – | ⏑ – – – |
fā'ilun mafā'ĭlun fā'ilun mafā'ĭlun. Hazaj. } 2

Note that 7 and 8 are the same metre under different names. Nos. 9 and 10 are mere varieties of 8.

9. – ⏑ – | ⏑ – – – · | – ⏑ – | ⏑ – – – |
fā'ilun mafā'ĭlān fā'ilun mafā'ĭlun. Hazaj.
10. – ⏑ – | ⏑ – – – | – ⏑ – | ⏑ – – – · |
fā'ilun mafā'ĭlun fā'ilun mafā'ĭlān.

See No. 8. Hazaj.

11. – ⏑ – – | ⏑ ⏑ – – | ⏑ ⏑ – – | – – |
fā'ilātun fă'ilātun fă'ilātun fa'lun. Raml. 49 group
12. – ⏑ – – | ⏑ ⏑ – – | ⏑ ⏑ – – | – – · |
fā'ilātun fă'ilātun fă'ilātun fa'lān. Raml.

15.9, 10 are varieties of this.

13. – – ⏑ | ⏑ – – ⏑ | ⏑ – – ⏑ | ⏑ – – |
maf'ūlu mafā'ĭlu mafā'ĭlu fa'ūlun. Hazaj. 20
14. – – ⏑ | ⏑ – – ⏑ | ⏑ – – ⏑ | ⏑ – – · |
maf'ūlu mafā'ĭlu mafā'ĭlu mafā'ĭl. Hazaj.

13.4, 5, 8, 9 are varieties of 14.13, 14 ; formed by running together into one long syllable either the third and fourth syllables, which gives us 13.8, 9, or the seventh and eighth, which results in 13.4, 5.

15. — — ⏑ | ⏑ — — — | — — ⏑ | ⏑ — — — |
maf‘ūlu mafā‘īlun maf‘ūlu mafā‘īlun. **Hazaj. 1**

16. — — ⏑ | — ⏑ — ⏑ | ⏑ — — ⏑ | — ⏑ — |
maf‘ūlu fā‘ilātu mafā‘īlu fā‘ilun. **Muẓāri‘. 80**

17. — — ⏑ | — ⏑ — ⏑ | ⏑ — — ⏑ | — ⏑ — · |
maf‘ūlu fā‘ilātu mafā‘īlu fā‘ilāt.
See 13.6, 7. Cf. 15.14. **Muẓāri‘.**

18. — — ⏑ | — ⏑ — — | — — ⏑ | — ⏑ — — |
maf‘ūlu fā‘ilātun maf‘ūlu fā‘ilātun. **Muẓāri‘. 11**

19. — — ⏑ | — ⏑ — — | — — ⏑ | — ⏑ — — · |
maf‘ūlu fā‘ilātun maf‘ūlu fā‘ilīyān.
See 15.14. **Muẓāri‘.**

Thirteen Syllables

1. ⏑ — ⏑ — | ⏑ ⏑ — — | ⏑ — ⏑ — | — |
mafā‘īlun fā‘ilātun mafā‘īlun fā‘.
Cf. 14.2*a*, *b* ; 15.2*a*, *b* ; 16.4, 5. **Mujtas̤s̤. 29 group**

2. — ⏑ ⏑ — | — ⏑ — ⏑ | — ⏑ ⏑ — | — |
mufta‘ilun fā‘ilātu mufta‘ilun fā‘. **Munsariḥ.**

3. — ⏑ ⏑ — | — ⏑ — ⏑ | — ⏑ ⏑ — | — · |
mufta‘ilun fā‘ilātu mufta‘ilun fā‘.
See 14.5, 6 and 15.8. **Munsariḥ.**
Nos. 4, 5, 8, 9 are varieties of 14.13, 14 ; all are used in Masnavīs.

4. — — ⏑ | ⏑ — — — | — — ⏑ | ⏑ — — |
maf‘ūlu mafā‘īlun maf‘ūlu fa‘ūlun. **Hazaj.**

5. — — ⏑ | ⏑ — — — | — — ⏑ | ⏑ — — · |
maf‘ūlu mafā‘īlun maf‘ūlu mafā‘īl. **Hazaj.**

6. — — ⏑ | — ⏑ — — | — — ⏑ | — ⏑ — |
maf‘ūlu fā‘ilātun maf‘ūlu fā‘ilun. **Muẓāri‘.**

7. — — ⏑ | — ⏑ — — | — — ⏑ | — ⏑ — · |
maf‘ūlu fā‘ilātun maf‘ūlu fā‘ilān. **Muẓāri‘.**
This is formed from 14.16, 17 by joining the short 7th and 8th syllables into one long syllable.

8. — — — | — — ⏑ | ⏑ — — ⏑ | ⏑ — — |
maf‘ūlun maf‘ūlu mafā‘īlu fa‘ūlun. **Hazaj.**

9. — — — | — — ⏑ | ⏑ — — ⏑ | ⏑ — — · |
maf‘ūlun maf‘ūlu mafā‘īlu mafā‘īl. **Hazaj.**

Twelve Syllables

1. ⏑ ⏑ — | ⏑ ⏑ — | ⏑ ⏑ — | ⏑ ⏑ — |
fă'ilun fă'ilun fă'ilun fă'ilun. Mutadārik.
This metre is found double. See 24.2. Any or all of these feet may be | — — | *fa'lun* ; see 8, 4.

2. ⏑ ⏑ — — | ⏑ ⏑ — — | ⏑ — ⏑ — |
fă'ilātun fă'ilātun mafā'īlun. Jadīd.

3. ⏑ ⏑ — — | — — | ⏑ ⏑ — — | — — |
fă'ilātun fa'lun fă'ilātun fa'lun. Raml.

4. ⏑ — ⏑ — | ⏑ — ⏑ — | ⏑ — ⏑ — |
mafā'īlun mafā'īlun mafā'īlun. Rajaz.

5. ⏑ — — ⏑ | ⏑ — — ⏑ | — ⏑ — — |
mafā'īlu mafā'īlu fā'ilātun. Qarīb.

6. ⏑ — — | ⏑ — — | ⏑ — — | ⏑ — — |
fa'ūlun fa'ūlun fa'ūlun fa'ūlun. Mutaqārib. 21
See 24.3 for double form. (15 of this and 6 of 24.3)

7. Omitted.

8. ⏑ — — — | ⏑ — — — | ⏑ — — — |
mafā'īlun mafā'īlun mafā'īlun. Hazaj.

9. — ⏑ ⏑ — | — ⏑ ⏑ — | — ⏑ ⏑ — |
mufta'ilun mufta'ilun mufta'ilun. Rajaz.

10. — ⏑ ⏑ — | — ⏑ — ⏑ | — ⏑ ⏑ — |
mufta'ilun fā'ilātu mufta'ilun. Munsariḥ.
By running the 10th and 11th syllables into one long syllable we get 11.11 which is interchangeable with it.

11. — ⏑ — — | ⏑ — ⏑ — | ⏑ ⏑ — — |
fā'ilātun mafā'īlun fă'ilātun.
See 11.15, 16, 17, and 10.10, 11. Khafīf.

12. — ⏑ — | — ⏑ — | — ⏑ — | — ⏑ — |
fā'ilun fā'ilun fā'ilun fā'ilun. Mutadārik.

13. — ⏑ — — | — ⏑ — — | — ⏑ — — |
fā'ilātun fā'ilātun fā'ilātun. Raml.

14. — — ⏑ — | — ⏑ — — | — ⏑ — — |
mustaf'ilun fā'ilātun fā'ilātun. Mujtass.

15. — — ⏑ — | — — ⏑ — | — — ⏑ — |
mustaf'ilun mustaf'ilun mustaf'ilun. Rajaz.

16. — — — | — ⏑ — | — — — | — ⏑ — |
maf'ūlun fā'ilun maf'ūlun fā'ilun. Munsariḥ.

17. — — — | — ⏑ — · | — — — | — ⏑ — · |
maf'ūlun fā'ilāt maf'ūlun fā'ilāt. Munsariḥ.

12.16, 17 are obtained from 14.5,6 by substituting a long syllable for the short syllables which come second and third, and one for the ninth and tenth syllables.

12.17 might be called a thirteen-syllabled line, for the -lāt at the end of the second foot would generally be read -lātu.

Eleven Syllables

1. ⏑ ⏑ — — | ⏑ — ⏑ — | ⏑ ⏑ — |
fă'ilātun mafā'īlun fă'ilun. **Khafīf.**

2. ⏑ ⏑ — — | ⏑ — ⏑ — | ⏑ ⏑ — · |
fă'ilātun mafā'īlun fă'ilāt. **Khafīf. 31 group**

Nos. 1, 2 are the same as 11.15, 16 except for the first syllable, and the same as 10.1, 2 except for the last syllable.

3. ⏑ — — ⏑ | ⏑ — — ⏑ | ⏑ — — |
mafa'īlu mafā'īlu fa'ūlun. **Hazaj.**

4. ⏑ — — ⏑ | ⏑ — — ⏑ | ⏑ — — · |
mafā'īlu mafā'īlu mafā'īl. **Hazaj.**

5. ⏑ — — | ⏑ — — | ⏑ — — | ⏑ — |
fa'ūlun fa'ūlun fa'ūlun fa'al. **Mutaqārib. 17**
See 22.1 for double form. **(14 of this and 3 of 22.1)**

6. ⏑ — — | ⏑ — — | ⏑ — — | ⏑ — · |
fa'ūlun fa'ūlun fa'ūlun fa'ūl. **Mutaqārib.**

7. ⏑ — — — | ⏑ — — — | ⏑ — — |
mafā'īlun mafā'īlun fa'ūlun. **Hazaj. 13**
See 22.2. for double form. **(11 of this and 2 of 22.2)**

8. ⏑ — — — | ⏑ — — — | ⏑ — — · |
mafā'īlun mafā'īlun mafā'īl. **Hazaj.**

9. — ⏑ ⏑ — | — ⏑ ⏑ — | — ⏑ — |
mufta'ilun mufta'ilun fā'ilun. **Sarī'.**

10. — ⏑ ⏑ — | — ⏑ ⏑ — | — ⏑ — · |
mufta'ilun mufta'ilun fā'ilān. **Sarī'.**

By running together the short syllables in the second foot we get 10.6*a*, *b* ; if we do so in both the first and the second foot we get 9.8, 9. They are interchangeable.

11. — ⏑ ⏑ — | — ⏑ — ⏑ | — — — |
mufta'ilun fā'ilātu maf'ūlun. **Munsariḥ.**
See 12.10.

12. — ⏑ — ⏑ | ⏑ — — ⏑ | ⏑ — — · |
fā'ilātu mafā'īlu mafā'īl. **Mushākil.**

13. — ⏑ — — | ⏑ ⏑ — — | ⏑ ⏑ — |
fā'ilātun fă'ilātun fă'ilun. **Raml.**

14. — ⏑ — — | ⏑ ⏑ — — | ⏑ ⏑ — · |
fā'ilātun fă'ilātun fă'ilāt. **Raml.**

See 10.8, 9. If we double the middle foot of 11.13, 14, we get 15.9, 10.

14*a*. — ⏑ — — | — ⏑ — — | — ⏑ — |
fā'ilātun fā'ilātun fā'ilun. Raml.

14*b*. — ⏑ — — | — ⏑ — — | — ⏑ — · |
fā'ilātun fā'ilātun fā'ilāt. Raml.

15. — ⏑ — — | ⏑ — ⏑ — | ⏑ ⏑ — |
fā'ilātun mafā'īlun fă'īlun. Khafīf. 31 group

16. — ⏑ — — | ⏑ — ⏑ — | ⏑ ⏑ — · |
fā'ilātun mafā'īlun fă'īlāt. Khafīf.

11.15, 16 are the same as 12.11 and 10.10, 11, except for the last foot, and as 11.1, 2 except for the first syllable. See also 11.17.

17. — ⏑ — — | ⏑ — ⏑ — | — — — |
fā'ilātun mafā'īlun maf'ūlun. Khafīf.

This is derived from 12.11 by changing into one long syllable the two short ones found in the last foot. See also 11.15, 16.

18. — ⏑ — — | — ⏑ — — | — ⏑ — |
fā'ilātun fā'ilātun fā'ilun. Raml. 4

19. — ⏑ — — | — ⏑ — — | — ⏑ — · |
fā'ilātun fā'ilātun fā'ilāt. Raml.

20. — — ⏑ | ⏑ — ⏑ — | ⏑ — — — |
maf'ūlu mafā'īlun mafā'īlun. Hazaj.

21. — — ⏑ | ⏑ — ⏑ — | ⏑ — — — · |
maf'ūlu mafā'īlun mafā'īlān. Hazaj.

22. — — ⏑ | ⏑ — — ⏑ | — ⏑ — — |
maf'ūlu mafā'īlu fā'ilātun. Qarīb.

23. — — ⏑ | ⏑ — — ⏑ | ⏑ — — — |
maf'ūlu mafā'īlu mafā'īlun. Hazaj.

24. — — ⏑ | — ⏑ — ⏑ | ⏑ — — |
maf'ūlu fā'ilātu mafā'īlun. Muẓāri'.

25. — — ⏑ — | — — ⏑ — | — — — |
mustaf'ilun mustaf'ilun maf'ūlun. Rajaz.

Ten Syllables

1. ⏑ ⏑ — — | ⏑ — ⏑ — | — — |
fă'ilātun mafā'īlun fa'lun. Khafīf. 31 group

2. ⏑ ⏑ — — | ⏑ — ⏑ — | — — · |
fă'ilātun mafā'īlun fa'lān. Khafīf.

Except for the first syllable 10.1, 2 are the same as 10.10, 11 below, and except for the last foot the same as 11.1, 2.

3. ⏑ — | ⏑ — — | ⏑ — | ⏑ — — |
fa'al fa'ūlun fa'al fa'ūlun.

This metre is found double ; see 20.2. Mutaqārib. 8

4. ᴗ — ᴗ | — — | ᴗ — ᴗ | — — |
fa'ūlu fa'lun fa'ūlu fa'lun. Mutaqārib.

5. ᴗ — ᴗ | — — | ᴗ — ᴗ | — — · |
fa'ūlu fa'lun fa'ūlu fa'lān. Mutaqārib.

6a. — ᴗ ᴗ — | — — — | — ᴗ — |
mufta'ilun maf'ūlun fā'ilun. Sarī'.

6b. — ᴗ ᴗ — | — — — | — ᴗ — · |
mufta'ilun maf'ūlun fā'ilāt. Sarī'.

6a, b, are derived from 11.9, 10, q.v.

7. — ᴗ — | ᴗ — | — ᴗ — | ᴗ — |
fā'ilun fa'al fā'ilun fa'al. Mutadārik.

8. — ᴗ — — | ᴗ ᴗ — — | — — |
fā'ilātun fā'ilātun fa'lun. Raml. 2

9. — ᴗ — — | ᴗ ᴗ — — | — — · |
fā'ilātun fā'ilātun fa'lān. Raml.

See 11.13, 14, which are the same except in the last foot.

10. — ᴗ — — | ᴗ — ᴗ — | — — |
fā'ilātun mafā'īlun fa'lun. Khafīf. 31 group

11. — ᴗ — — | ᴗ — ᴗ — | — — · |
fā'ilātun mafā'īlun fa'lān. Khafīf.

See 10.1, 2; 12.11; 11.15, 16, 17.

11a. — ᴗ — | — ᴗ — | — ᴗ — | — |
fā'ilun fā'ilun fā'ilun fa'. Mutadārik. 1

12. — — ᴗ | ᴗ — ᴗ — | ᴗ — — |
maf'ūlu mafā'īlun fa'ūlun. Hazaj. 13 group

13. — — ᴗ | ᴗ — ᴗ — | ᴗ — — · |
maf'ūlu mafā'īlun fa'ūlān (mafā'īl). Hazaj.

By combining the third and fourth syllables into one long syllable we get 9.6, 7. All four are interchangeable.

14. — — ᴗ | ᴗ — — ᴗ | — ᴗ — |
maf'ūlu mafā'īlu fā'ilun. Muẓāri'.

15. — — ᴗ | — ᴗ — ᴗ | ᴗ — — |
maf'ūlu fā'ilātu fa'ūlun. Muẓāri'.

16. — — | ᴗ — — | — — | ᴗ — — |
fa'lun fa'ūlun fa'lun fa'ūlun. Mutaqārib.

17. — — | ᴗ — — | — — | ᴗ — — · |
fa'lun fa'ūlun fa'lun fa'ūlān. Mutaqārib.

18. — — — | — ᴗ — | ᴗ — — — |
maf'ūlun fā'ilun mafā'īlun. Hazaj.

19. — — — | — ᴗ — | ᴗ — — — · |
maf'ūlun fā'ilun mafā'īlān. Hazaj.

Nine Syllables

1. ◡ ◡ — | ◡ ◡ — | ◡ ◡ — |
fă‘ilun fă‘ilun fă‘ilun. Mutadārik.

2. ◡ — — | ◡ — — | ◡ — — |
fa‘ūlun fa‘ūlun fa‘ūlun. Mutaqārib.

3. — — ◡ — | — — ◡ ◡ | — |
mustaf‘ilun mustaf‘ilu fā‘. Sarī‘.

4. — ◡ — | — ◡ — | — ◡ — |
fā‘ilun fā‘ilun fā‘ilun. Mutadārik.

5. — — | ◡ ◡ — | ◡ — | — — · |
fa‘lun fă‘ilun fa‘al fa‘lān. Mutadārik.

6. — — — | — ◡ — | ◡ — — |
maf‘ūlun fā‘ilun fa‘ūlun. Hazaj. 13 group

7. — — — | — ◡ — | ◡ — — · |
maf‘ūlun fā‘ilun mafā‘īl. Hazaj.
See 10.12, 13.

8. — — — | — — — | — ◡ —
maf‘ūlun maf‘ūlun fā‘ilun. Sarī‘.

9. — — — | — — — | — ◡ — · |
maf‘ūlun maf‘ūlun fā‘ilān. Sarī‘.

9.8, 9 are derived from 11.9, 10 by running short syllables together into one long syllable. They are interchangeable.

Eight Syllables

1. — ◡ ◡ — | — — — | — · |
mufta‘ilun maf‘ūlun fā‘. Sarī‘.

2 and 3. — — | — — | ◡ — | — — | or | — — ·
fa‘lun fa‘lun fa‘al fa‘lun or fa‘lān. Mutadārik.

4. — — | — — | — — | — — |
fa‘lun fa‘lun fa‘lun fa‘lun. Mutadārik. 4
Any or all of these feet may be | ◡ ◡ — | *fă‘ilun.*
See 12.1 and 24.2.

Six Syllables

1. ◡ — | ◡ — | ◡ — |
fa‘al fa‘al fa‘al. Mutadārik.

Second List : *rubā‘ī* metres

These metres have been given in a separate list because, firstly, they are not used for any kind of poetry other than *rubā‘īs*, and, secondly, in any book of Urdū verse *rubā‘īs* are marked as such, and a student will always know when he is reading that form of verse.

There are twenty-four *rubā'ī* metres. They are both easy and difficult to distinguish from one another; easy, because a *rubā'ī* line is always written in one of these twenty-four, and difficult, because any line of any *rubā'ī* may be in any one of them; *so that a rubā'i* poem consisting of six stanzas may have twenty-four metres.

It has been stated on p. 4 that new varieties of metre are often produced from an old metre by running two short syllables into a single long one. This specially applies to *rubā'īs.* Indeed all the twenty-four metres are variations of two, which themselves are identical except for the fact that the second half of the second foot is a trochee in one and an iambus in the other.

The metres are here divided into two sections of twelve each and given in the order of short syllables, a short syllable getting preference over a long one. The first section begins with *maf'ūlu* and the second with *maf'ūlun,* this difference between them arising from making one long syllable of two short ones.

They are all derived from the *hazaj* metre which in its primitive form consists of four feet *mafā'īlun*—

⏑ — — — | ⏑ — — — | ⏑ — — — | ⏑ — — — |

From 1.5 below come fifteen others, making sixteen; from 1.1 come seven others making eight; twenty-four in all.

1.5 is — — ⏑ | ⏑ — — ⏑ | ⏑ — — ⏑ | ⏑ — |

maf'ūlu mafā'īlu mafā'īlu fa'al.

By changing the last syllable to — · we get 1.6.

— — ⏑ | ⏑ — — ⏑ | ⏑ — — ⏑ | ⏑ — · |

By joining the 11th and 12th syllables we get 1.7 and 8.

⏑ — — ⏑ | ⏑ — — ⏑ | ⏑ — — — | — or — · |

By joining the 7th and 8th syllables we get 1.9 and 10.

⏑ — — ⏑ | ⏑ — — — | — — ⏑ | ⏑ — or — · |

By joining the 3rd and 4th syllables we get 2.5 and 6.

— — — | — — ⏑ | ⏑ — — ⏑ | ⏑ — or — · |

By joining the 11th and 12th, and 7th and 8th we get 1.11 and 12.

— — ⏑ | ⏑ — — — | — — — | — or — · |

By joining the 11th and 12th, and 3rd and 4th we get 2.7 and 8.

— — — | — — ⏑ | ⏑ — — — | — or — · |

By joining the 7th and 8th, and 3rd and 4th we get 2.9 and 10.

— — — | — — — | — — ⏑ | ⏑ — or — · |

By joining the 11th and 12th, 7th and 8th, and 3rd and 4th we get 2.11 and 12.

— — — | — — — | — — — | — or — · |

In the same way from 1.1 we can obtain 1.2, and from these 1.3 and 4, and 2.1, 2, 3, 4.

It should be observed that all the metres in Section 2 are derived from those in Section 1 by combining the 3rd and 4th syllables into one long syllable.

Rubā‘ī Metres : all *hazaj*

Section 1 beginning with *maf‘ūlu.*

1. — — ⏑ | ⏑ — ⏑ — | ⏑ — — ⏑ | ⏑ — |
   maf‘ūlu mafā‘īlun mafā‘īlu fa‘al.
2. — — ⏑ | ⏑ — ⏑ — | ⏑ — — ⏑ | ⏑ — · |
   maf‘ūlu mafā‘īlun mafā‘īlu fa‘ūl.
3. — — ⏑ | ⏑ — ⏑ — | ⏑ — — — | — |
   maf‘ūlu mafā‘īlun mafā‘īlun fa‘.
4. — — ⏑ | ⏑ — ⏑ — | ⏑ — — — | ⏑ — · |
   maf‘ūlu mafā‘īlun mafā‘īlun fa‘ūl.
5. — — ⏑ | ⏑ — — ⏑ | ⏑ — — ⏑ | ⏑ — |
   maf‘ūlu mafā‘īlu mafā‘īlu fa‘al.
6. — — ⏑ | ⏑ — — ⏑ | ⏑ — — ⏑ | ⏑ — · |
   maf‘ūlu mafā‘īlu mafā‘īlu fa‘ūl.
7. — — ⏑ | ⏑ — — ⏑ | ⏑ — — — | — |
   maf‘ūlu mafā‘īlu mafā‘īlun fa‘.
8. — — ⏑ | ⏑ — — ⏑ | ⏑ — — — | — · |
   maf‘ūlu mafā‘īlu mafā‘īlun fā‘.
9. — — ⏑ | ⏑ — — — | — — ⏑ | ⏑ — |
   maf‘ūlu mafā‘īlun maf‘ūlu fa‘al.
10. — — ⏑ | ⏑ — — — | — — ⏑ | ⏑ — · |
    maf‘ūlu mafā‘īlun maf‘ūlu fa‘ūl.
11. — — ⏑ | ⏑ — — — | — — — | — |
    maf‘ūlu mafā‘īlun maf‘ūlun fa‘.
12. — — ⏑ | ⏑ — — — | — — — | — · |
    maf‘ūlu mafā‘īlun maf‘ūlun fā‘.

Section 2 beginning with *maf‘ūlun.*

These are derived, metre for metre, from Section 1 by combining the 3rd and 4th syllables into a single long syllable.

1. — — — | — ⏑ — | ⏑ — — ⏑ | ⏑ — |
   maf‘ūlun fā‘ilun mafā‘īlu fa‘al.
2. — — — | — ⏑ — | ⏑ — — ⏑ | ⏑ — · |
   maf‘ūlun fā‘ilun mafā‘īlu fa‘ūl.

3. — — — | — ⏑ — | ⏑ — — — | —
maf‘ūlun fā‘ilun mafā‘īlun fa‘.

4. — — — | — ⏑ — | ⏑ — — — | — · |
maf‘ūlun fā‘ilun mafā‘īlun fā‘.

5. — — — | — — ⏑ | ⏑ — — ⏑ | ⏑ — |
maf‘ūlun maf‘ūlu mafā‘īlu fa‘al.

6. — — — | — — ⏑ | ⏑ — — ⏑ | ⏑ — · |
maf‘ūlun maf‘ūlu mafā‘īlu fa‘ūl.

7. — — — | — — ⏑ | ⏑ — — — | — |
maf‘ūlun maf‘ūlu mafā‘īlun fa‘.

8. — — — | — — ⏑ | ⏑ — — — | — · |
maf‘ūlun maf‘ūlu mafā‘īlun fā‘.

9. — — — | — — — | — — ⏑ | ⏑ — |
maf‘ūlun maf‘ūlun maf‘ūlu fa‘al.

10. — — — | — — — | — — ⏑ | ⏑ — · |
maf‘ūlun maf‘ūlun maf‘ūlu fa‘ūl.

11. — — — | — — — | — — — | — |
maf‘ūlun maf‘ūlun maf‘ūlun fa‘.

12. — — — | — — — | — — — | — |
maf‘ūlun maf‘ūlun maf‘ūlun fā‘.

JUDGE COLEBROOKE'S SUPPOSED TRANSLATION OF THE GOSPELS INTO HINDI

(See *JRAS.*, July, 1936, pp. 491 to 499.)

While examining Hindi Gospels in connection with the article bearing the above title, I found the following entry in the card-index of the library of the Baptist Missionary Society :—

B. 9, 1. Indian Vernaculars—Bible. High Hindi.
The Gospels (tr. by Henry Thomas Colebrooke, 1765–1837 ?). (1806). No title page.
5360 Darlow-Moule.

If this were to be confirmed, it would mean that Judge Colebrooke did after all translate the Gospels into Hindi, though I was and am convinced that he did not.

The Librarian was good enough to let me loȯk at the volume, and I saw at once that these four Gospels were part of the first ed. of Carey's Hindi New Test., 1811. There was an added interest in the fact that the Baptist Mission in London were not known to possess a copy of the first ed. or any part of it. The earliest they were known to have was the second ed. of 1912.

I therefore asked them if they would allow me to take it to the library of the Bible Society, which contains two copies of the first ed., and they very kindly sent someone with me to bring it back.

There on comparing it with a known first ed. I found that the two were exactly alike except at the very end (John xxi), where there were one or two trifling differences of arrangement. In the Baptist Mission copy the page had evidently been reset, probably as a result of the fire in the Serampore College, March, 1812.

It was thus proved that the Baptist Mission did possess part, nearly half, of a Carey first ed., and there was still no evidence that Colebrooke's supposed translation had ever been made.

REVIEW OF PROFESSOR TURNER'S NEPĀLĪ DICTIONARY

DICTIONARY OF THE NEPĀLĪ LANGUAGE. Compiled by RALPH LILLEY TURNER. $12\frac{1}{4} \times 9\frac{1}{2}$, pp. xxiv + 935. London, 1931. £4 4*s.*

(Abbreviations: Ps., Pers. = Persian; Ar. = Arabic; N. = Nepālī; H. = Hindī; P., Pj. = Panjābī; K., Kś. = Kaśmīrī; lw. = loanword. Isolated numbers indicate pages.)

"Little streams of pure water sparkled among the grass, and trees laden with fruit grew here and there with spreading boughs."

I cannot think of better words than these to describe the remarkable work brought out this year by the Professor of Sanskrit in the University of London. No similar work, comparable in size, has been published before, though we had a forerunner on a smaller scale in the vocabulary (146 8vo pp.) of Jules Bloch's splendid monograph *La Langue Marathe.*

I do not profess to have studied every entry in the book, or read every page, but I have travelled extensively over the country to which it introduces us, wandered at will along the banks of its rivulets, and plucked luscious fruit off the overhanging branches, and this gives me a title to express the gratitude and admiration which I feel.

One does not know whether to admire most the author's industry or his learning or his intuition. It is hard to believe that one man has single-handed ransacked the dictionaries and vocabularies of forty or fifty languages in order to discover parallels to 26,000 entries, and has, in addition, sent innumerable letters and countless slips to scholars in the hope of obtaining information to make his dictionary complete. Yet this is what Professor Turner has done.

His original aim was to make a practical dictionary (a book, shall we say, of 100 pp., giving words and meanings), but he tells us with happy *meiosis* that the work has "somewhat outgrown" the first intention. It now weighs 9 lb. 3 oz., exactly the weight of the service rifle and bayonet carried by the Gurkha soldiers to whom he dedicates the result of his labour.

There is a valuable introduction of 7 pp., in which we see the principles which guided him in his etymologies, above all the principle which he, more than any other Indianist, has impressed upon us, that in tracing linguistic relationship we must take note of common innovations, not of common conservations. This truth, to the illustration of which he has devoted so much of his time, will render necessary the rewriting of many pages on Indian languages and the re-formulation of many theories about them.

Next to the etymologies, the most useful single feature of the dictionary is the series of indexes (correctly so called ; the incorrect form, indices, is not used). These indexes, which we owe to the labour of Mrs. Turner, give us, language by language, connected words from other tongues. Beginning with Indo-European and Indo-Aryan reconstructions, Mrs. Turner goes on to Sanskrit and its descendants, such as the ancient Pali and Prakrit, and the modern Romani, Ṣiṇā, Kaśmīrī, Hindī, Panjābī, Lahndī, Singhalese, etc. These occupy 271 pp. Other language-groups, such as Kāfirī, Muṇḍā, Dravidian, and European, take up five pp.

In these Professor Turner appears to have rejected mere loanwords. This limitation is useful for Sanskrit, because there is no clear boundary to possible words, but one would have been glad to see a list of loan-words from European languages, especially English and Portuguese. Such a list would serve a very useful purpose and it would be well worth while to make one even now and print it separately.

I would draw special attention to the astonishing collection on pp. 657–60 of over 400 words whose origin is in most cases unknown. Among them are a number of the commonest words in north India.

It is difficult to exaggerate the value of these indexes. Anyone possessing a knowledge of any of the better-known Indo-European languages, and desirous of ascertaining the comparative development of a word, can now look it up in the list containing the words of the language he knows. He is there referred to the Nep. word under which the forms in other languages are given. Without the index he would not know where to look.

Romani is referred to in three dialects. No such full use of Romani in connection with other Indian languages can be found anywhere except in Miklosich's *Mundarten*, which is over fifty years old. Professor Turner's monograph establishing Romani as a Central Indian language is in the mind of all scholars.

A work like this which aims at completeness and correctness must fall short in at least some details. This is inevitable in all human effort. There must be occasional words forgotten, meanings inaccurately given, analogies missed, etymologies mistaken or untraced, and errors of printing unnoticed. The marvel to my mind is that there are so few.

Feeling sure that Professor Turner is already at work on a supplement, with a list of errata, I venture to mention a few points which he may be good enough to consider.

Meanings.

The compiler usefully gives the fem. of occupational and caste terms; but what is the meaning of these fems.? Sometimes, as for *damini, guruṅini,* the meaning given is "woman of *damāi, guruṅ,* caste". This seems to me correct ("female" would be better still, so as to include little girls); but for other words, such as *khardārni, ojhi, dhobini, paṇḍitini, ghartini, kamini,* the words are said to mean "wife" of *khardār,* etc., and again for others, as *panerni, mālini,* "female water-carrier", etc. I think it would be better in all of them to give the meaning "female" of the caste. If, e.g., a *khardārni* were to be educated, and enter the House of Commons, she would remain a *khardārni,* whoever her husband might be.

One or two further points: "*thor bahut,* something, no matter how little"; does it not mean "a smallish amount of"?

kāpi, copy: add "notebook, copybook".

kānūn, military law: add "ordinary law, cf. *kānagoi*".

kāṛnu: six meanings given, but have not the essential meanings "take out, eject" been overlooked?

203 *chori mari ṭhulā ghar pari*: the meaning given strikes me as a mild libel on the cheery Gorkhāli. It is not difficult to get another.

Etymologies.

Dr. Turner is at his best in etymologies; examples of his research and remarkable power of seizing on the relevant facts may be seen on almost every page. I mention in particular *gachnu, jokhnu, khelnu, nibhāunu, celo, līṛ, hotro, choro, saṛnu, calnu, bhutte, dhasnu, sīṛi, kero.*

In a spirit of deep appreciation I make a few suggestions aiming at further perfection.

European words. These at present are given in different ways: (*a*) lw. H.; (*b*) lw. Eng.; (*c*) lw. H. fr. Eng. or Port.; (*d*) lw. H. fr. Pers. I think that the Eur. origin should always be referred to. Some said to be Eng. seem to me Port. The following changes suggest themselves.

"*mec,* lw. H. fr. Pers.": omit "fr. Pers.", add "cf. Pj. *mec,* Sh. *mec*; fr. Port. *mesa.*"

"*tamākhu* lw. H. fr. Pers.": omit "fr. Pers.", add "fr. Port. *tabaco*".

These two words are more likely to have gone to Persia from India, than come to India from Persia. In any case they are Port.

" *tauliyā*, lw. H." : add " fr. Port."

pistaul, *botal*, said to be Eng., are probably Port. *pistola*, *botelha* ; so perhaps *kārtus*, said to be Fr. (Port. *kartucho*).

Further, there are many entered simply as " lw. Eng." The question arises whether they should not be " lw. H. fr. Eng." In only a few cases does it appear likely that they came directly into N. from Eng.

For words at present left underived a few etyms. occur to me.

khawās, liberated slave ; lw. H. *khavāṣṣ*, servant ; fr. Pers.

khaĩjaṛī, tambourine, lw. H. *k͟hanjrī*, fr. Pers. id.

thāhā, information ; P. *thauh*, recollection (the Nep. also has this meaning).

juṅ juṅ, delay ; H. *jū̃ jū̃*, *jū̃ tū̃*.

jista, *dista*, quire of paper ; H. *dasta*, m. id. fr. Pers.

Corrections.

jimmā-, *-dār*, *-wār*, *-wāri*, are not fr. *ẓamān*, *ẓimn*, but lw. H. *ẓimma*, *-dār*, *-vār*, *-vārī*, fr. Pers. (*ẓimma* ult. fr. Ar.).

422 *barāmda*, verandah, is twice said to be Pers. It is not a Ps. word at all, but Urdu.

bāphre, *bāphrebāph*, not fr. *baburo*, but lw. H. *bāpre*, *bāprebāp*, id.

picche, per : omit H. and P. words given, and insert H. *pīche*, P. *picche*, id., as *bīghe pīche*, *vighe picche*, per acre (or half acre).

khatara, fraud ; not H. *k͟haṭra*, but H. *khacrā*, wicked ; P. *khacrā*, deceitful.

bāre mā, concerning ; not as stated, but lw. H. *bāre mẽ*, id.

bālwar : *bāl*, not conn. w. *bāl*, hair, which in Pj. would yield *vāḷbar*, whereas Pj. is *bālbar*. The *l* is mere change of *r* ; cf. N. *leṭar*, writer ; Pj. *bāliśṭar*, barrister ; *pippaḷmiṇṭ*, peppermint ; *fail*, fire ; *lūl*, rule ; *pāḷṭī*, party.

halkāro, messenger, is said to be a form of *ahalkār*. There is no connection between the two words, beyond similarity of meaning. *ahalkār* is correctly derived, p. 29, lw. H. *ahlkār* (Ps. *ahl.* and *kār*) *halkāro* is lw. H. *halkārā*, *harkārā* fr. Ps. *harkāra*, man who does all or any work (*har-kār*).

kuli, not fr. Ar. but from Turkish.

Minor Corrections.

113 H. *k͟haṭṭ*, not whiskers, beard, but incipient hair on face.

300 P. *thok*, not " heap ", but " thing ".

311 " P. *deh*, f. sun ", read " *dẽh*, m."

491 P. *maṇ*, mf.; omit f.

494 P. *marcā̃*, read *marc*; *marcā̃* is pl. of *marc*.

513 P. *muṇḍ*, m. not f.; for L. *mū̃ṇḍh*, f., head of canal, read *mū̃ḍh*, m.

520 P. *muṛnā*, not "twist", trans., but "turn", intr.

554 H.P. *lām*, not "line, brigade", but "war, expedition".

582 P. *saṛnā*, not "rot", but "be burnt".

309 *dābi*, H. *da'wī*. *da'wī*, a form given by Platts, has no existence. It should be *da'vā*.

Suggested additions to etymologies.

"*khasnu*, fall; Shina gur *khaźonŭ*": add "*ź* only in infin.; Imv. sing. has *s* (*khas*), otherwise *z*, (except past *-t-*)."

ṭako, money; add P. *ṭagā*, half anna.

jiraha, jirāha, H. *jarḥ*, fr. Ar. *jarḥ* is translated once "objection", and once "denial". The word is *jirah* in H., and means "cross-examination" or "surgical incision." In P. it is *jarhā*. The conn. of N. *jirāha* seems doubtful.

jyāsti, jesti, excessive; add lw. H. *jāstī* (fr. *ziyādatī*, Ps.).

thuṛnu, stumble; add P. *ṭhuḍḍā* (not *th-*), stumbling-block.

dāgnu, aim at; add H.P. *dagnā*, be fired (of *top*, cannon).

nā̃ghnu, jump over; add P. *nanghṇā*, pass by.

baṛiyā, very good; add P. *vadhīā*, with the note that *baṛhiyā*, *vadhīā*, and doubtless N. *baṛiyā*, have no fem. form.

phāltū, superfluous; add L. *phāltū*, coolie who waits for odd jobs.

phiṭṭe, separate; add H. *phaṭke*, separate; H.P. *phiṭṭe mūh*! your face be cursed! P. *phiṭṭ*, f., *phiṭak*, f., curse.

mutnu; add P. *mūtarnā*.

ranḍī; add P. *ranḍī*, widow.

karāi, cauldron; add P. *kaṛāhī*.

lāṛo; add P. *lauṛā*.

cilimci, basin, lw. H. fr. Ps.; add *cilam* fr. Ps., *-cī* fr. Turk.

chamchamnu, c.-garnu; add P. *chan chan*, jingling, tinkling.

Professor Turner derives *kāphar*, coward, fr. *kāfir*, but hesitates about *kābu*, cowed, fr. *qābū*, on account of "difference of meaning". The difference seems less in the latter case than in the former, and the derivation may surely be accepted.

katā-ho-katā, adv. expressing emphasis; add Cf. H. *kahī̃*, anywhere, much (more than); thus, to put the N. sentences into H.; *Silīguṛī se Dārjiling kahī̃ acchā hai* (much better than); *sārā shahr ghūmā, us ghaṛ kā kahī̃ patā nā lagā*. Professor Turner asks if this is derived from *katā*. No doubt it is. Might we not say that *katą* here means "anywhere", like *kahī̃*, and that *katā-ho-katā* is the emphatic form?

The following P. words are mere lws. fr. H. The forms which I add in parenthesis are the real ones: *khelnā* (*kheḍṇā*) *hillṇā* (*hallṇā*) shake, *phāṛnā* (*pāṛnā*) split, *jotṇā* (*joṇā*) yoke.

The accuracy of the proof-reading is extraordinary, and reflects the utmost credit on the compiler and his wife. Very little has escaped them. I have noticed the following errors. Some of them are probably quite correctly copied from the source consulted, and the proof-readers have no responsibility.

111 *kãghāṛṇā* and *-ūṛṇā*, read *kh-* and *-nā*.
111 *khãgālṇā*; better *hãgāḷṇā*.
125 *kullhṇā*, read *khullhṇā*.
137 *garmī*, read *garmī*.
209 *jam'āt*, read *jamā'at*.
246 P. *ṭekaṇ*, read *ṭekkaṇ*.
360 P. *paṭṭṇā*, better *puṭṭṇā*.
494 H. *marhaṭṭe*, read *marahṭe*, *marhaṭe*.
513 P. *munṇā*, read *munnṇā*.
555 *Lāhor*, read *Lāhaur*.
558 P. *lukṇā*, read *lukkṇā*.
645 *T. W. Bailey*, read *H. W. Bailey*.

Read *ṣ* for *s̱*, *s̤*, *s*, in the following H. words: 116 *khalāṣī*, 117 *khaṣm*, *khaṣī*, 272 *tafṣīl*, 539 *rukhṣat*, 609 *ṣirf*, 640 *hiṣṣa*, *hiṣṣadār*; and *ẓ* for *z̤* in 635 *ḥāẓirī*, 642 *haiẓa*; and *ḷ* for *l* in the Lahndī words 402 *phal*, 405 *phālā*, 436 *bālaṇ* (the verb; the noun would be *bāllaṇ*), 632 *hal*, pair of oxen.

We are told on p. xxiii that the Pj. words are taken from Mayā Singh's Dict. That useful, if somewhat loosely arranged, volume ignores the sound *ḷ*, and confuses *n* with *ṇ*. Consequently, many P. words containing *ḷ* appear in it with the south P. form in *l*, and infins. which have roots ending in *r* or *ṛ* are printed now with *n* and now with *ṇ*. This is a pity, for the distinction between *ḷ* and *l*, and between *ṇ* and *n* is well worth preserving. In the *Nep. Dict.* there was no choice but to print as the original source did. The best rule is to make all P. infins. end in *-ṇā*, except those with roots in *-r*, *-rh*, *-ṛ*, *-ṛh*, which should end in *-nā*. The difference between *ṛṇā* and *ṛnā* in rapid speech is negligible, but *rṇā* differs widely from *rnā*.

A few P. words taken at random which should have *ḷ* are *ubaḷṇā*, boil; *phaḷ*, fruit; *phaḷ*, blade; *paḷṇā*, be nourished; *miḷṇā*, meet.

A little point, illustrating the care which the compiler has everywhere exercised, is the use of *v* instead of the customary *w* in Pj. words. The amount of avoidable mispronunciation among Europeans which has been caused by the use of *w* for *v* in other books (including some of mine) is distressing to contemplate. *w* occurs in Pj. only as an alternative to *ŭ* in such words as *adw'āṇā*, water-melon; *dwāṇā*, cause to be given.

The *ṛ* dialect of Kś. This interesting village dialect is referred to twice (see *ghāro*, 157; *saṛnu*, 582). Under *moro*, 520, a village word *moṛ*^{u} is given for the town dialect along with the real town word *mor*^{u}. Under *laṛnu*, fight, K. *laḍun* is said to be "prob. lw. H.P."; I prefer to say "lw. vill. K. *laṛun*". In many other places I should recommend reference to the vill. dialect. Thus, to mention a few: *caro*, bird, K. *tsüṛ*^{u}; *caṛnu*, ascend, K. *tsaṛun*; *bhīṛ*, crowd, K. *bīṛ*; *birālo*, cat, K. *brôṛ*^{u}, *byôṛ*^{u}; *chaṛ*, basket, K. *tshaṛ*; *chaṛ*, bar, K. *chīṛ*^{u}; *chaṛnu*, sprinkle, K. *chiṛkāwun*; *choṛnu*, leave, K. *choṛun*; *jaṛnu*, set, K. *jaṛun*; *joṛ*, pair, K. *joṛā*; *joṛi*, pair, K. *jüṛ*^{i}; *guliyo*, sugar, K. *goṛ*; *laṛāi*, strife, add K. *laḍöy*^{i}, lw. vill. K. *laṛöy*^{i}; *paṛnu*, read, add K. *paḍun*, lw. vill. K. *paṛun*; *kāṛnu*, eject, add vill. K. *kaṛun*, lw. H. (for here the vill. form should be *kaḍun*). Such references would elucidate a matter of importance.

There is a large class of onomatopoetic words, and Dr. Turner often mentions that a word belongs to it. It might be too much to ask that he should always do this, yet sometimes it is not clear that a word is onomatopoetic (e.g. *khaṭākhaṭ*, without interruption; *kharkhar*, without stopping; *khuskhus*, whispering). One might not realize that these are merely imitative words or derived from such words, and it would be well to say it in each case.

-bāj, 431. Through an oversight it is stated simply that *-bāj* is a suffix in *naśebāj*, nothing being said about other words, such as *botalbāj*, *dagābāj*, etc. In the case of *-dār* many examples are given.

Great praise must be given for the careful differentiation of causal verbs, which breaks new ground in dictionaries, for this is the first in which the distinction has been consistently made. I made it for Urdu and Pj. (*Bull. S.O.S.*, V, iii, 519, 1929). Here it is made for Nepali. It applies doubtless to other Indo-Aryan languages. The rule is briefly this: causals of intr. verbs mean to cause to do; of trans. verbs to cause to be done. Thus *jokhāunu*, cause to be weighed, have weighed; but *dugurāunu*, cause to run.

Another feature of the dictionary is the occasional comparison of meanings (as distinct from forms). Thus for *lekh*, mountain-chain, we are referred to Eng. "line of mountains"; and for Pk. *thuṇṇa-*, proud, lit. stopped, to Eng. "stuck up", 298. There are only a few of these comparisons; it would be difficult to increase their number, for a systematic attempt to discuss comparative semantics would entail the compilation of a second dictionary.

And so we come to the end of this wonderful volume. I have mentioned above a few things for consideration in the forthcoming Supplement, but I feel almost as if I should be ashamed of myself for doing so. It is as if passing through undulating fields of the richest mellow corn, I had taken note of a half-ripe or over-ripe grain, here and there, among thousands of the best. Professor Turner's colleagues in the University of London, and his *alma mater*, the University of Cambridge, which has given him the degree of Litt.D. in recognition of his labours, will be proud to remember their association with one who has produced a work of such outstanding ability and learning.

I, too, bring my tribute of admiration, gratitude, and thanks.
